SOCIAL WELFARE

FIGHTING POVERTY AND HOMELESSNESS

For Reference

Not to be taken from this room

ISSN 1937-3295

SOCIAL WELFARE
FIGHTING POVERTY AND HOMELESSNESS

Melissa J. Doak

INFORMATION PLUS® REFERENCE SERIES
Formerly Published by Information Plus, Wylie, Texas

GALE
CENGAGE Learning™

Detroit • New York • San Francisco • New Haven, Conn • Waterville, Maine • London

Social Welfare: Fighting Poverty and Homelessness

Melissa J. Doak

Kepos Media, Inc., Paula Kepos and Janice Jorgensen, Series Editors

Project Editors: Kathleen J. Edgar, Elizabeth Manar, Kimberley A. McGrath

Rights Acquisition and Management: Sheila R. Spencer

Composition: Evi Abou-El-Seoud, Mary Beth Trimper

Manufacturing: Cynde Lentz

Cover photograph: Image copyright Sharon Day, 2009. Used under license from Shutterstock.com.

While every effort has been made to ensure the reliability of the information presented in this publication, Gale, a part of Cengage Learning, does not guarantee the accuracy of the data contained herein. Gale accepts no payment for listing; and inclusion in the publication of any organization, agency, institution, publication, service, or individual does not imply endorsement of the editors or publisher. Errors brought to the attention of the publisher and verified to the satisfaction of the publisher will be corrected in future editions.

Gale
27500 Drake Rd.
Farmington Hills, MI 48331-3535

ISBN-13: 978-0-7876-5103-9 (set)   ISBN-10: 0-7876-5103-6 (set)
ISBN-13: 978-1-4144-4867-1   ISBN-10: 1-4144-4867-8

ISSN 1937-3295

This title is also available as an e-book.
ISBN-13: 978-1-4144-7524-0 (set)
ISBN-10: 1-4144-7524-1 (set)
Contact your Gale sales representative for ordering information.

Printed in the United States of America
1 2 3 4 5 6 7 15 14 13 12 11

TABLE OF CONTENTS

PREFACE

Social Welfare: Fighting Poverty and Homelessness is part of the *Information Plus Reference Series*. The purpose of each volume of the series is to present the latest facts on a topic of pressing concern in modern American life. These topics include the most controversial and studied social issues of the 21st century: abortion, animal rights, capital punishment, care of senior citizens, crime, the environment, health care, immigration, minorities, national security, water, women, youth, and many more. Even though this series is written especially for high school and undergraduate students, it is an excellent resource for anyone in need of factual information on current affairs.

By presenting the facts, it is the intention of Gale, Cengage Learning to provide its readers with everything they need to reach an informed opinion on current issues. To that end, there is a particular emphasis in this series on the presentation of scientific studies, surveys, and statistics. These data are generally presented in the form of tables, charts, and other graphics placed within the text of each book. Every graphic is directly referred to and carefully explained in the text. The source of each graphic is presented within the graphic itself. The data used in these graphics are drawn from the most reputable and reliable sources, such as from the various branches of the U.S. government and from private organizations and associations. Every effort was made to secure the most recent information available. Readers should bear in mind that many major studies take years to conduct and that additional years often pass before the data from these studies are made available to the public. Therefore, in many cases the most recent information available in 2011 is dated from 2008 or 2009. Older statistics are sometimes presented as well, if they are landmark studies or of particular interest and no more-recent information exists.

Even though statistics are a major focus of the *Information Plus Reference Series*, they are by no means its only content. Each book also presents the widely held positions and important ideas that shape how the book's subject is discussed in the United States. These positions are explained in detail and, where possible, in the words of their proponents. Some of the other material to be found in these books includes historical background, descriptions of major events related to the subject, relevant laws and court cases, and examples of how these issues play out in American life. Some books also feature primary documents or have pro and con debate sections that provide the words and opinions of prominent Americans on both sides of a controversial topic. All material is presented in an evenhanded and unbiased manner; readers will never be encouraged to accept one view of an issue over another.

HOW TO USE THIS BOOK

Aid for the poor has long been a controversial topic in the United States. Most Americans agree that society should help those who have fallen on hard times, but there are many different opinions as to how this is best accomplished. The 1990s were a time of particularly heavy debate about this issue, and with the so-called Great Recession of 2007–09 and the passage of comprehensive health care reform in 2010, the second century of the 21st century may be another period of debate and change in means-tested assistance. This volume also describes those who make use of the welfare system, why they use it, and what they get out of it.

Social Welfare: Fighting Poverty and Homelessness consists of eight chapters and three appendixes. Each chapter is devoted to a particular aspect of social welfare. For a summary of the information covered in each chapter, please see the synopses provided in the Table of Contents. Chapters generally begin with an overview of the basic facts and background information on the chapter's topic, then proceed to examine subtopics of particular interest. For example,

Chapter 4, Who Receives Government Benefits?, begins with a general discussion of who gets government means-tested assistance. The chapter then looks at the demographic characteristics of people receiving Temporary Assistance for Needy Families, Supplemental Nutrition Assistance Program benefits, unemployment compensation, and Supplementary Security Insurance. Next, overlapping services are examined. The chapter concludes with a discussion of the duration of people's dependence on government assistance programs. Readers can find their way through a chapter by looking for the section and subsection headings, which are clearly set off from the text. They can also refer to the book's extensive index if they already know what they are looking for.

Statistical Information

The tables and figures featured throughout *Social Welfare: Fighting Poverty and Homelessness* will be of particular use to readers in learning about this topic. These tables and figures represent an extensive collection of the most recent and valuable statistics on social welfare, as well as related issues—for example, graphics cover the amount of money spent each year for various government welfare programs, the demographics of poverty, the role of child support payments in preventing poverty, and the number of people without health insurance in the United States. Gale, Cengage Learning believes that making this information available to readers is the most important way to fulfill the goal of this book: to help readers understand the issues and controversies surrounding social welfare and reach their own conclusions.

Each table or figure has a unique identifier appearing above it for ease of identification and reference. Titles for the tables and figures explain their purpose. At the end of each table or figure, the original source of the data is provided.

To help readers understand these often complicated statistics, all tables and figures are explained in the text. References in the text direct readers to the relevant statistics. Furthermore, the contents of all tables and figures are fully indexed. Please see the opening section of the index at the back of this volume for a description of how to find tables and figures within it.

Appendixes

Besides the main body text and images, *Social Welfare: Fighting Poverty and Homelessness* has three appendixes. The first is the Important Names and Addresses directory. Here, readers will find contact information for a number of government and private organizations that can provide further information on aspects of social welfare. The second appendix is the Resources section, which can also assist readers in conducting their own research. In this section the author and editors of *Social Welfare: Fighting Poverty and Homelessness* describe some of the sources that were most useful during the compilation of this book. The final appendix is the index. It has been greatly expanded from previous editions and should make it even easier to find specific topics in this book.

ADVISORY BOARD CONTRIBUTIONS

The staff of Information Plus would like to extend its heartfelt appreciation to the Information Plus Advisory Board. This dedicated group of media professionals provides feedback on the series on an ongoing basis. Their comments allow the editorial staff who work on the project to continually make the series better and more user-friendly. The staff's top priority is to produce the highest-quality and most useful books possible, and the Information Plus Advisory Board's contributions to this process are invaluable.

The members of the Information Plus Advisory Board are:

- Kathleen R. Bonn, Librarian, Newbury Park High School, Newbury Park, California

- Madelyn Garner, Librarian, San Jacinto College, North Campus, Houston, Texas

- Anne Oxenrider, Media Specialist, Dundee High School, Dundee, Michigan

- Charles R. Rodgers, Director of Libraries, Pasco-Hernando Community College, Dade City, Florida

- James N. Zitzelsberger, Library Media Department Chairman, Oshkosh West High School, Oshkosh, Wisconsin

COMMENTS AND SUGGESTIONS

The editors of the *Information Plus Reference Series* welcome your feedback on *Social Welfare: Fighting Poverty and Homelessness*. Please direct all correspondence to:

Editors
Information Plus Reference Series
27500 Drake Rd.
Farmington Hills, MI 48331-3535

CHAPTER 1
POVERTY IN THE UNITED STATES

THE FEDERAL DEFINITION OF POVERTY

The federal government began measuring poverty in 1959. During the 1960s President Lyndon B. Johnson (1908–1973) declared a national War on Poverty. Researchers realized that few statistical tools were available to measure the number of Americans who continued to live in poverty in one of the most affluent nations in the world. To fight this "war," it had to be determined who was poor and why.

During the early 1960s Mollie Orshansky (1915–2006) of the Social Security Administration suggested that the poverty income level be defined as the income sufficient to purchase a minimally adequate amount of goods and services. The necessary data for defining and pricing a full market basket of goods were not available then, nor are they available now. However, Orshansky noted that in 1955 the U.S. Department of Agriculture (USDA) had published the Household Food Consumption Survey, which showed that an average family of three or more people spent approximately one-third of its after-tax income on food. She multiplied the USDA's 1961 economy food plan (a no-frills food basket meeting the then-recommended dietary allowances) by three.

Basically, this defined a poor family as any family or person whose after-tax income was not sufficient to purchase a minimally adequate diet if one-third of the income was spent on food. Differences were allowed for size of family, gender of the head of the household, and whether it was a farm or nonfarm family. The threshold (the level at which poverty begins) for a farm family was set at 70% of a nonfarm household. (The difference between farm and non-farm households was eliminated in 1982.)

The poverty thresholds set by the U.S. Census Bureau are still based on the theoretical food budget. These thresholds are updated each year to reflect inflation. People with incomes below the applicable threshold are classified as living below the poverty level.

The poverty guidelines vary by family size and composition. In 2011 a family of four living in the 48 contiguous states and the District of Columbia earning $22,350 or less annually was considered impoverished. (See Table 1.1.) A person living alone who earned less than $10,890 was considered poor, as was a family of eight members making less than $37,630. The poverty level is considerably higher in Alaska and Hawaii, where the cost of living is higher than in the 48 contiguous states and the District of Columbia.

The poverty guidelines that are set by the U.S. Department of Health and Human Services are important because various government agencies use them as the basis for eligibility to key assistance programs. The Department of Health and Human Services uses the poverty guidelines to determine Community Services Block Grants, Low-Income Home Energy Assistance Block Grants, and Head Start allotments. The guidelines are also the basis for funding the USDA's Supplemental Nutrition Assistance Program (formerly the Food Stamp Program), the National School Lunch Program, and the Special Supplemental Food Program for Women, Infants, and Children. The U.S. Department of Labor uses the guidelines to determine funding for the Job Corps and other employment and training programs under the Workforce Investment Act of 1998. Some state and local governments choose to use the federal poverty guidelines for some of their own programs, such as state health insurance programs and financial guidelines for child support enforcement.

THE HISTORICAL EFFORT TO REDUCE POVERTY

Since the late 1950s Americans have seen some successes and some failures in the battle against poverty. For the total population in 1959, 22.4%, or 39.5 million people, lived below the poverty level. (See Table 1.2.) After an initial decline through the 1960s and 1970s, the

TABLE 1.1

Poverty guidelines for the 48 contiguous states and the District of Columbia, 2011

Persons in family	Poverty guideline
1	$10,890
2	14,710
3	18,530
4	22,350
5	26,170
6	29,990
7	33,810
8	37,630

Note: For families with more than 8 persons, add $3,820 for each additional person.

SOURCE: "2011 Poverty Guidelines for the 48 Contiguous States and the District of Columbia," in "Annual Update of the HHS Poverty Guidelines," *Federal Register*, vol. 76, no. 13, January 20, 2011, http://aspe.hhs.gov/poverty/11fedreg.pdf (accessed February 17, 2011)

poverty rate began to increase during the early 1980s, coinciding with a downturn in household and family incomes for all Americans. The poverty rate rose steadily until it reached a 17-year high of 15.2% in 1983, a year during which the country was climbing out of a serious economic recession.

The percentage of Americans living in poverty then began dropping, falling to 12.8% in 1989. (See Table 1.2.) After that, however, the percentage increased again, reaching 15.1% in 1993. It then dropped to 11.3% in 2000; however, because the nation's economy slowed, the poverty rate rose again to 14.3% in 2009. Wayne Vroman of the Urban Institute explains in "The Great Recession, Unemployment Insurance, and Poverty" (April 2010, http://www.urban.org/uploadedpdf/412072_great_recession.pdf) that during what some analysts are calling the "Great Recession," which began in December 2007 and ended in June 2009, rising unemployment rates led to rising poverty rates. Figure 1.1 provides a graphic representation of the number of poor people and the poverty rates between 1959 and 2009.

Analysts believe the overall decline in poverty between 1959 and 2009 was due to both the growth in the economy and the success of some of the antipoverty programs that were instituted during the late 1960s; yet not all demographic subcategories experienced the same level of change. For example, in *Income, Poverty, and Health Insurance Coverage in the United States: 2009* (September 2010, http://www.census.gov/prod/2010pubs/p60-238.pdf), Carmen DeNavas-Walt, Bernadette D. Proctor, and Jessica C. Smith of the Census Bureau note that the poverty rate of those aged 65 years and older had improved dramatically from 24.6% in 1970 to 8.9% in 2009. (See Figure 1.2.) For children under 18 years of age, however, the poverty rate actually increased during this period.

RATIO OF INCOME TO POVERTY LEVELS

For purposes of analysis, the Census Bureau uses income-to-poverty ratios that are calculated by dividing income by the respective poverty threshold for each family size. The resulting number is then tabulated on a scale that includes three categories: poor, near-poor, and nonpoor. Poor people have a poverty ratio below 1.00. People above the poverty level are divided into two groups: the near-poor and the nonpoor. The near-poor have a poverty ratio between 1.00 and 1.24 (100% to 124% of the poverty level) and the nonpoor have an income-to-poverty ratio of 1.25 (125% of the poverty level) and above.

In 2009, 14.3% of the total U.S. population, or 43.6 million people, had income-to-poverty ratios under 1.00. (See Table 1.3.) Fully 18.7% of the population, or 56.8 million people, were either poor or near-poor. Children were disproportionately poor. They were the most likely to be poor (20.7%), and over one out of four (26.3%) children were poor or near-poor. Young adults aged 18 to 24 years were also the most likely to be poor (20.7%), and 25.7% were poor or near-poor. Nearly one out of four (23.8%) families with children under six years of age had income-to-poverty ratios below 1.00; nearly three out of 10 (29.6%) of these families had income-to-poverty ratios below 1.25.

HOW ACCURATE IS THE POVERTY LEVEL?

Almost every year since the Census Bureau first defined the poverty level observers have been concerned about its accuracy. Since the early 1960s, when Orshansky defined the estimated poverty level based on an average family's food budget, living patterns have changed and food costs have become a smaller percentage of family spending. For example, the U.S. Bureau of Labor Statistics (BLS) reports in the news release "Consumer Expenditures—2009" (October 5, 2010, http://www.bls.gov/news.release/pdf/cesan.pdf) that the average family spent $6,372 (13%) of its total expenditures on food. By contrast, housing accounted for $16,895 (34.4%) of family spending. Based on these changes in buying patterns, should the amount spent on food be multiplied by a factor of eight instead of three? Or should the poverty level be based on housing or other factors? What about geographical differences in the cost of living?

The proportion of family income spent on food is not the only change in family budgets since the 1950s. In families headed by two parents, both parents are far more likely to be working than they were a generation ago. There is also a much greater likelihood that a single parent, usually the mother, will be heading the family. Child care costs, which were of little concern during the 1950s, have become a major issue for working parents in the 21st century.

TABLE 1.2

Poverty status of people by family relationship, 1959–2009

	All people				All families			People in families — Families with female householder, no husband present				Unrelated individuals		
		Below poverty level				Below poverty level				Below poverty level				Below poverty level	
Year	Total	Number	Percent	Total	Number	Percent	Total	Number	Percent	Total	Number	Percent			
2009	303,820	43,569	14.3	249,384	31,197	12.5	45,315	14,746	32.5	53,079	11,678	22.0
2008	301,041	39,829	13.2	248,301	28,564	11.5	44,027	13,812	31.4	51,534	10,710	20.8
2007	298,699	37,276	12.5	245,443	26,509	10.8	43,961	13,478	30.7	51,740	10,189	19.7
2006	296,450	36,460	12.3	245,199	25,915	10.6	43,223	13,199	30.5	49,884	9,977	20.0
2005	293,135	36,950	12.6	242,389	26,068	10.8	42,244	13,153	31.1	49,526	10,425	21.1
2004	290,617	37,040	12.7	240,754	26,544	11.0	42,053	12,832	30.5	48,609	9,926	20.4
2003	287,699	35,861	12.5	238,903	25,684	10.8	41,311	12,413	30.0	47,594	9,713	20.4
2002	285,317	34,570	12.1	236,921	24,534	10.4	40,529	11,657	28.8	47,156	9,618	20.4
2001	281,475	32,907	11.7	233,911	23,215	9.9	39,261	11,223	28.6	46,392	9,226	19.9
2000	278,944	31,581	11.3	231,909	22,347	9.6	38,375	10,926	28.5	45,624	8,653	19.0
1999	276,208	32,791	11.9	230,789	23,830	10.3	38,580	11,764	30.5	43,977	8,400	19.1
1998	271,059	34,476	12.7	227,229	25,370	11.2	39,000	12,907	33.1	42,539	8,478	19.9
1997	268,480	35,574	13.3	225,369	26,217	11.6	38,412	13,494	35.1	41,672	8,687	20.8
1996	266,218	36,529	13.7	223,955	27,376	12.2	38,584	13,796	35.8	40,727	8,452	20.8
1995	263,733	36,425	13.8	222,792	27,501	12.3	38,908	14,205	36.5	39,484	8,247	20.9
1994	261,616	38,059	14.5	221,430	28,985	13.1	37,253	14,380	38.6	38,538	8,287	21.5
1993	259,278	39,265	15.1	219,489	29,927	13.6	37,861	14,636	38.7	38,038	8,388	22.1
1992	256,549	38,014	14.8	217,936	28,961	13.3	36,446	14,205	39.0	36,842	8,075	21.9
1991	251,192	35,708	14.2	212,723	27,143	12.8	34,795	13,824	39.7	36,845	7,773	21.1
1990	248,644	33,585	13.5	210,967	25,232	12.0	33,795	12,578	37.2	36,056	7,446	20.7
1989	245,992	31,528	12.8	209,515	24,066	11.5	32,525	11,668	35.9	35,185	6,760	19.2
1988	243,530	31,745	13.0	208,056	24,048	11.6	32,164	11,972	37.2	34,340	7,070	20.6
1987	240,982	32,221	13.4	206,877	24,725	12.0	31,893	12,148	38.1	32,992	6,857	20.8
1986	238,554	32,370	13.6	205,459	24,754	12.0	31,152	11,944	38.3	31,679	6,846	21.6
1985	236,594	33,064	14.0	203,963	25,729	12.6	30,878	11,600	37.6	31,351	6,725	21.5
1984	233,816	33,700	14.4	202,288	26,458	13.1	30,844	11,831	38.4	30,268	6,609	21.8
1983	231,700	35,303	15.2	201,338	27,933	13.9	30,049	12,072	40.2	29,158	6,740	23.1
1982	229,412	34,398	15.0	200,385	27,349	13.6	28,834	11,701	40.6	27,908	6,458	23.1
1981	227,157	31,822	14.0	198,541	24,850	12.5	28,587	11,051	38.7	27,714	6,490	23.4
1980	225,027	29,272	13.0	196,963	22,601	11.5	27,565	10,120	36.7	27,133	6,227	22.9
1979	222,903	26,072	11.7	195,860	19,964	10.2	26,927	9,400	34.9	26,170	5,743	21.9
1978	215,656	24,497	11.4	191,071	19,062	10.0	26,032	9,269	35.6	24,585	5,435	22.1
1977	213,867	24,720	11.6	190,757	19,505	10.2	25,404	9,205	36.2	23,110	5,216	22.6
1976	212,303	24,975	11.8	190,844	19,632	10.3	24,204	9,029	37.3	21,459	5,344	24.9
1975	210,864	25,877	12.3	190,630	20,789	10.9	23,580	8,846	37.5	20,234	5,088	25.1
1974	209,362	23,370	11.2	190,436	18,817	9.9	23,165	8,462	36.5	18,926	4,553	24.1
1973	207,621	22,973	11.1	189,361	18,299	9.7	21,823	8,178	37.5	18,260	4,674	25.6
1972	206,004	24,460	11.9	189,193	19,577	10.3	21,264	8,114	38.2	16,811	4,883	29.0
1971	204,554	25,559	12.5	188,242	20,405	10.8	20,153	7,797	38.7	16,311	5,154	31.6
1970	202,183	25,420	12.6	186,692	20,330	10.9	19,673	7,503	38.1	15,491	5,090	32.9
1969	199,517	24,147	12.1	184,891	19,175	10.4	17,995	6,879	38.2	14,626	4,972	34.0
1968	197,628	25,389	12.8	183,825	20,695	11.3	18,048	6,990	38.7	13,803	4,694	34.0
1967	195,672	27,769	14.2	182,558	22,771	12.5	17,788	6,898	38.8	13,114	4,998	38.1
1966	193,388	28,510	14.7	181,117	23,809	13.1	17,240	6,861	39.8	12,271	4,701	38.3
1965	191,413	33,185	17.3	179,281	28,358	15.8	16,371	7,524	46.0	12,132	4,827	39.8
1964	189,710	36,055	19.0	177,653	30,912	17.4	(NA)	7,297	44.4	12,057	5,143	42.7
1963	187,258	36,436	19.5	176,076	31,498	17.9	(NA)	7,646	47.7	11,182	4,938	44.2
1962	184,276	38,625	21.0	173,263	33,623	19.4	(NA)	7,781	50.3	11,013	5,002	45.4
1961	181,277	39,628	21.9	170,131	34,509	20.3	(NA)	7,252	48.1	11,146	5,119	45.9
1960	179,503	39,851	22.2	168,615	34,925	20.7	(NA)	7,247	48.9	10,888	4,926	45.2
1959	176,557	39,490	22.4	165,858	34,562	20.8	(NA)	7,014	49.4	10,699	4,928	46.1

Note: Numbers in thousands. People as of March of the following year.
NA = Not available.

SOURCE: Adapted from "Table 2. Poverty Status of People by Family Relationship, Race, and Hispanic Origin: 1959 to 2009," in *Historical Poverty Tables—People*, U.S. Census Bureau, September 16, 2010, http://www.census.gov/hhes/www/poverty/data/historical/people.html (accessed February 17, 2011)

Critics of the current poverty calculations tend to believe that the poverty levels are set too low, because they are based on a 50-year-old concept of American life that does not reflect the economic and social realities of the 21st century. Food has become a shrinking proportion of the household budget as costs for things such as housing, health care, and transportation have skyrocketed. Others are concerned because the poverty threshold is different for elderly and nonelderly Americans. When the poverty threshold was first established, it was thought that older people did not need as much food. Therefore, the value of their basic food needs was lower.

FIGURE 1.1

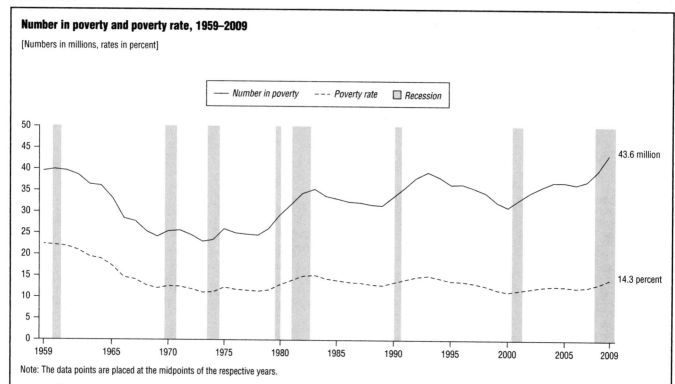

Number in poverty and poverty rate, 1959–2009

[Numbers in millions, rates in percent]

Note: The data points are placed at the midpoints of the respective years.

SOURCE: Carmen DeNavas-Walt, Bernadette D. Proctor, and Jessica C. Smith, "Figure 4. Number in Poverty and Poverty Rate: 1959 to 2009," in *Income, Poverty, and Health Insurance Coverage in the United States: 2009*, Current Population Reports, U.S. Census Bureau, September 2010, http://www.census .gov/prod/2010pubs/p60-238.pdf (accessed February 17, 2011)

FIGURE 1.2

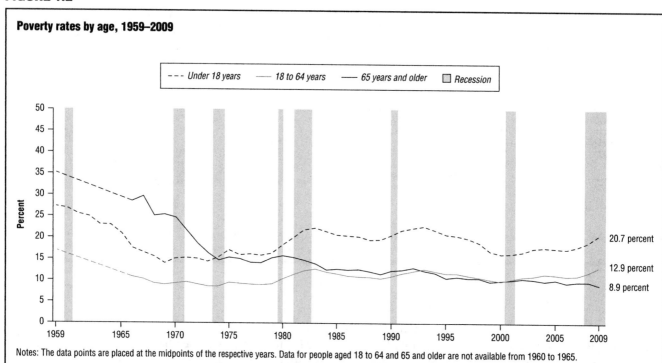

Poverty rates by age, 1959–2009

Notes: The data points are placed at the midpoints of the respective years. Data for people aged 18 to 64 and 65 and older are not available from 1960 to 1965.

SOURCE: Carmen DeNavas-Walt, Bernadette D. Proctor, and Jessica C. Smith, "Figure 5. Poverty Rates by Age: 1959 to 2009," in *Income, Poverty, and Health Insurance Coverage in the United States: 2009*, Current Population Reports, U.S. Census Bureau, September 2010, http://www.census.gov/prod/ 2010pubs/p60-238.pdf (accessed February 17, 2011)

TABLE 1.3

People with income below specified ratios of their poverty thresholds, by selected characteristics, 2009

[Numbers in thousands]

| Characteristic | Total | Income-to-poverty ratio | | | | | |
| | | Under 0.50 | | Under 1.00 | | Under 1.25 | |
		Number	Percent	Number	Percent	Number	Percent
All people	303,820	19,028	6.3	43,569	14.3	56,840	18.7
Age							
Under 18 years	74,579	6,914	9.3	15,451	20.7	19,588	26.3
18 to 24 years	29,313	3,039	10.4	6,071	20.7	7,523	25.7
25 to 34 years	41,085	2,845	6.9	6,123	14.9	7,884	19.2
35 to 44 years	40,447	1,967	4.9	4,756	11.8	6,197	15.3
45 to 54 years	44,387	1,961	4.4	4,421	10.0	5,718	12.9
55 to 59 years	19,172	719	3.8	1,792	9.3	2,349	12.3
60 to 64 years	16,223	587	3.6	1,520	9.4	2,074	12.8
65 years and older	38,613	994	2.6	3,433	8.9	5,507	14.3
Race* and Hispanic origin							
White	242,047	12,620	5.2	29,830	12.3	39,509	16.3
White, not Hispanic	197,164	8,009	4.1	18,530	9.4	24,853	12.6
Black	38,556	4,607	11.9	9,944	25.8	12,483	32.4
Asian	14,005	866	6.2	1,746	12.5	2,232	15.9
Hispanic (any race)	48,811	5,081	10.4	12,350	25.3	15,980	32.7
Family status							
In families	249,384	12,559	5.0	31,197	12.5	41,144	16.5
Householder	78,867	3,625	4.6	8,792	11.1	11,620	14.7
Related children under 18	73,410	6,418	8.7	14,774	20.1	18,857	25.7
Related children under 6	25,104	2,751	11.0	5,983	23.8	7,437	29.6
In unrelated subfamilies	1,357	451	33.2	693	51.1	771	56.8
Unrelated individuals	53,079	6,019	11.3	11,678	22.0	14,924	28.1
Male	26,269	2,900	11.0	5,255	20.0	6,598	25.1
Female	26,811	3,119	11.6	6,424	24.0	8,326	31.1

*Federal surveys now give respondents the option of reporting more than one race. Therefore, two basic ways of defining a race group are possible. A group such as Asian may be defined as those who reported Asian and no other race (the race-alone or single-race concept) or as those who reported Asian regardless of whether they also reported another race (the race-alone-or-in-combination concept). This table shows data using the first approach (race alone). The use of the single-race population does not imply that it is the preferred method of presenting or analyzing data. The Census Bureau uses a variety of approaches. About 2.6 percent of people reported more than one race in Census 2000. Data for American Indians and Alaska Natives, Native Hawaiians and other Pacific Islanders, and those reporting two or more races are not shown separately.
Note: Details may not sum to totals because of rounding.

SOURCE: Carmen DeNavas-Walt, Bernadette D. Proctor, and Jessica C. Smith, "Table 6. People with Income below Specified Ratios of Their Poverty Thresholds by Selected Characteristics: 2009," in *Income, Poverty, and Health Insurance Coverage in the United States: 2009*, Current Population Reports, U.S. Census Bureau, September 2010, http://www.census.gov/prod/2010pubs/p60-238.pdf (accessed February 17, 2011)

Consequently, when this figure was multiplied by three to get the poverty rate, it was naturally lower than the rate for nonelderly people. (The U.S. government, however, uses the poverty rate for nonelderly Americans when determining the eligibility for welfare services for all people, including the elderly.) Critics point out that even though the elderly might eat less than younger people, they have greater needs in other areas, which are not considered when their food needs are simply multiplied by three. Probably the most notable difference between the needs of the elderly and nonelderly is in the area of health care. The BLS (October 2010, http://www.bls.gov/cex/2009/Standard/age.pdf) finds that even though the total population interviewed spent $3,126 (6.4%) of its annual expenditure on health care, those over 65 years of age spent $4,846 (12.9%).

In June 2004 the Committee on National Statistics met to research alternative methods for measuring poverty, as recommended by the National Research Council's Panel on Poverty and Family Assistance in *Measuring Poverty:*

A New Approach (1995). The committee recommended adopting a new poverty measure, taking into account the current dollar value of food, clothing, shelter, and utilities, as well as taxes, the value of food stamps and other near-cash benefits, and child support payments. In addition, the committee recommended adjusting the new poverty measure based not only on inflation but also on data on yearly consumer expenditures. John Iceland, the rapporteur for the committee, notes in "The CNSTAT Workshop on Experimental Poverty Measures, June 2004" (*Focus*, vol. 23, no. 3, spring 2005), "The reasoning here is that [consumer expenditure] based calculations will allow the thresholds to retain their social significance for longer periods of time than absolute thresholds."

Testifying in 2008 before the Subcommittee on Income Security and Family Support of the U.S. House of Representatives' Committee on Ways and Means, Rebecca M. Blank (July 17, 2008, http://www.brookings.edu/~/media/Files/rc/testimonies/2008/0717_poverty_blank/0717_poverty_blank.pdf) of the Brookings Institution addressed the inadequacy of the current poverty measures by arguing that the measures "are numbers without any valid conceptual basis." She indicated that food constituted a smaller percentage of American household budgets in 2008 than it did when the poverty measure was developed and that threshold numbers should not be based on the cost of a single commodity. In addition, noncash assistance is not counted in the poverty measure, and therefore, "a cash income-based definition of family resources is highly insensitive to many of our nation's most effective anti-poverty programs." Blank suggested that the definition of the poverty threshold should be updated to reflect modern realities facing low-income families.

In 2011 the Census Bureau and the BLS received federal funding to develop a new Supplemental Poverty Measure. The new measure would not replace the official poverty thresholds, but it would provide additional data about economic conditions across the nation. According to David Johnson of the Census Bureau, in "Progress toward Improving the U.S. Poverty Measure: Developing the New Supplemental Poverty Measure" (*Focus*, vol. 27, no. 2, winter 2010), the new measure will be based on data from the Consumer Expenditure Survey. It will include expenditures on food, clothing, and shelter, plus 20% to cover all other expenses. The poverty threshold will be 33% of the average of these consumer expenditures over the past five years. The threshold will be further adjusted by family type; whether the home is rented, owned with a mortgage, or owned outright; geographic area; and additional family resources, such as cash assistance program participation, and near-cash benefits, such as housing subsidies or Supplemental Nutrition Assistance Program assistance. The first Supplemental Poverty Measure was expected to be released the same day as the official poverty measure in September 2011.

INCOME AND POVERTY
How Should Income Be Defined?

The Panel on Poverty and Family Assistance also recommended in 1995 that family resources be redefined to reflect the net amount available to buy goods and services in that budget for basic needs. Some critics point out that the definition of income used to set the poverty figure is not accurate because it does not include the value of all welfare services as income. If the value of these services were counted as income, they believe the proportion of Americans considered to be living in poverty would be lower.

During the 1990s the Census Bureau developed several experimental methods of estimating income for evaluating poverty levels, but the bureau has had considerable difficulty determining the value of many of these subsidies. For example, it first tried to consider Medicare and Medicaid at full market value (this meant taking the total

amount of money that the government spent on medical care for a particular group and then dividing it by the number of people in that group). The value was often greater than the actual earnings of the low-income family, which meant that even though the family's total earnings may not have been enough to cover food and housing, adding the market value of Medicare or Medicaid to its earnings put the family above the poverty threshold.

This did not make much sense, so the Census Bureau began trying a fungible value (giving equivalent value to units) for Medicare and Medicaid. When the bureau measures a household's income, Medicare and Medicaid are given no value if the earners cannot cover the cost of housing and food. However, if the family can cover the cost of food and shelter, the bureau calculates the difference between the household income and the amount that is needed to meet basic housing and food costs. It then values the health services at this difference (up to the amount of the market value of the medical benefits). Even though this is complicated, the formula is believed to give a fair value to these services. Similar problems have developed in trying to determine the value of housing subsidies, school lunches, and other benefits.

Still other observers point out that most income definitions do not include assets and liabilities. Perhaps the poor household has some assets, such as a home or a car, that could be converted into income. One experimental definition of income includes capital gains on earnings, although it seems to make little difference because approximately 90% of all capital gains are earned by those in the upper fifth of the earnings scale. Michael Sherraden of Washington University in St. Louis, Missouri, indicates in "Building Assets to Fight Poverty" (*Shelterforce Online*, no. 110, March–April 2000) that including assets generally means little, because the overwhelming majority of poor families have few financial assets.

Another major issue is the question of income before and after income taxes. Even though the Tax Reform Act of 1986 removed most poor households from the federal income tax rolls, many poor households still pay state and local taxes. Naturally, some critics claim, the taxes paid to local and state governments are funds that are no longer available for feeding and housing the family and, therefore, should not be counted as income.

Table 1.4 shows the difference between the official poverty thresholds and several alternative thresholds based on recommendations by the National Academy of Sciences. One definition bases the thresholds on out-of-pocket food, clothing, shelter, and utilities expenditures; another bases the thresholds on all these expenditures as well as on out-of-pocket medical expenditures. Some definitions exclude mortgage expenditures. Basing the thresholds on any of these alternative definitions substantially raises the poverty level for a two-adult, two-child

TABLE 1.4

Poverty thresholds for two-adult-two-child family following National Academy of Sciences recommendations, 1999–2009

	Official	FCSU-CE[a]	FCSUM-CE[a]	FCSU[b]	FCSUM[b]
1999	16,895	17,036	18,671	18,196	19,648
2000	17,463	17,884	19,549	19,097	20,731
2001	17,960	18,709	20,366	19,935	21,640
2002	18,244	19,329	21,088	20,757	22,600
2003	18,660	19,778	21,635	21,218	23,109
2004	19,157	19,984	22,034	21,895	23,738
2005	19,806	20,708	22,841	22,769	24,784
2006	20,444	21,818	23,935	24,026	25,834
2007	21,027	23,465	25,849	25,680	27,744
2008	21,834	24,755	27,601	27,043	29,654
2009	21,756	24,522	27,709	26,778	29,602

FCSU(M) represents the groups of items deemed as necessary expenditures by the NAS report; food, clothing, shelter, utilities and medical expenditures. CE = Consumer Expenditures.
[a]Based on out-of-pocket expenditures (based on CE definition of spending and omits repayment of mortgage principal for owned housing); food, clothing, shelter plus utilities, and medical-out-of-pocket expenses (FCSUM).
[b]Based on out-of-pocket expenditures (including repayment of mortgage principal for owned housing).
Notes: Thresholds for 2007 forward reflect implementation of questionnaire improvements about expenditures on food away from home and type of mortgage in the Consumer Expenditures Interview Survey beginning in Quarter 2 of 2007. These results were produced by Thesia I. Garner, Research Economist, Division of Price and Index Number Research, Bureau of Labor Statistics, for research purposes only using the Consumer Expenditures Interview Survey. These results are released to inform interested parties of ongoing research and to encourage discussion of work in progress.

SOURCE: "Poverty Thresholds for Two-Adult-Two-Child Family Following NAS Recommendations: 1999–2009," in *Tables of NAS-Based Poverty Estimates: 2009*, U.S. Census Bureau, October 2010, http://www.census.gov/hhes/povmeas/data/nas/tables/2009/index.html (accessed February 17, 2011)

family. Table 1.5 shows that in 2009 all alternative measurements of poverty would result in a poverty rate as much as three percentage points higher than the official measure of 14.3%.

Growing Income Inequality

The Census Bureau has released a number of studies that show a change in the distribution of wealth and earnings in the United States. This change has resulted in an increase in the gap between the rich and the poor. Unlike many short-term economic changes that are often the product of normal economic cycles of growth and recession, these changes seem to indicate fundamental changes in American society.

Arloc Sherman and Chad Stone of the Center on Budget and Policy Priorities explain in "Income Gaps between Very Rich and Everyone Else More Than Tripled in Last Three Decades, New Data Show" (June 25, 2010, http://www.cbpp.org/files/6-25-10inc.pdf) that the gaps between the richest 1% of Americans and the middle and poorest fifths of Americans more than tripled between 1979 and 2007. During this period average after-tax incomes for the top 1% rose by 281%, whereas the middle fifth of households saw their incomes increase by only 25% and the lowest fifth of households saw their incomes increase by only 16%. In 2007, 17.1% of all after-tax income was earned by the wealthiest 1% of Americans. Sherman and Stone also note that the recession of 2007 to 2009 was not likely to greatly effect this disparity, writing, "While the recession that began in December 2007 likely reduced the income of the wealthiest Americans substantially and may thereby shrink the income gap between rich and poor households, a similar development that occurred around

the bursting of the dot.com bubble and the 2001 recession turned out to be just a speed bump."

Census data on income and earnings provide additional information for 2008 and 2009. Census data show that in 2009 the income differences between income quintiles had shrunk slightly since 2007. However, before the recession only the top fifth had increased its percentage of the nation's income since the 1980s. (See Table 1.6.) In 2009 the quintile of households with the highest incomes received 50.3% of the national income, about the same as that received by the other 80% of the population combined. The lowest quintile received only 3.4% of the national income in 2009.

Why Is the Income Gap Growing?

Many reasons exist to explain the growing inequality, although observers disagree about which are more important. One reason is that the proportion of the elderly population, which is likely to earn less, is growing. According to the Census Bureau, 25.3 million of 117.5 million households, or 21.5%, were headed by a householder 65 years of age or older in 2009. (See Table 1.7; a household may consist of a single individual or a group of related or unrelated people living together, whereas a family consists of related individuals.) The median (the middle value—half are higher and half are lower) household income of households headed by a person aged 65 years or older was $31,354, compared with a median household income of $55,821 for households headed by someone under the age of 65 years.

In addition, more people than in previous years were living in nonfamily situations (either alone or with

TABLE 1.5

Alternative poverty estimates based on National Academy of Sciences recommendations, by selected characteristics, 2009

[Poverty rate estimates in percentages]

		NGA (No geographic adjustment of poverty thresholds)		GA (geographic adjustment of poverty thresholds)	
Characteristic	Official poverty measure	MSI-NGA (Medical out-of-pocket expenses (MOOP) subtracted from income)	MIT-NGA (MOOP included in the thresholds)	MSI-GA	MIT-GA
All people	**14.3**	**15.7**	**17.3**	**15.7**	**17.3**
People in families	12.5	13.3	14.9	13.3	15.1
People in married-couple families	7.2	8.1	9.3	8.3	9.6
People in families with a female householder, no husband present	32.5	31.6	34.3	31.0	34.0
People in families with a male householder, no wife present	17.8	22.5	24.5	22.3	25.3
Age					
Under 18 years	20.7	17.4	19.5	17.5	19.8
18 to 64 years	12.9	14.8	16.5	14.8	16.6
65 years and over	8.9	17.2	17.1	16.8	16.4
Race[a] and Hispanic origin					
White alone[b]	12.3	14.1	15.5	14.0	15.5
Non-Hispanic white alone	9.4	11.4	12.4	10.6	11.6
Black alone[c]	25.8	25.0	27.8	24.1	26.8
Non-Hispanic black alone	25.6	24.9	27.7	23.8	26.5
Asian alone[d]	12.5	14.6	16.5	17.3	19.3
Hispanic (of any race)	25.3	25.9	28.9	28.9	32.6
Region					
Northeast	12.2	12.5	13.6	15.1	16.7
Midwest	13.3	14.7	16.0	12.1	13.3
South	15.7	17.6	19.3	15.6	17.3
West	14.8	16.3	18.1	19.6	21.6

Note: While the alternative measures differ among one another in their computation of medical expenses and geographic variations in costs, they are similar in their scaling of thresholds by family size, their inflation adjustment method (based on the Consumer Expenditure Survey), and their treatment of noncash benefits and child care and work-related expenses.
[a]Data for American Indians and Alaska Natives, and Native Hawaiians and other Pacific Islanders, are not shown separately.
[b]The 2009 and 2010 Current Population Survey asked respondents to choose one or more races. White alone refers to people who reported "white" and did not report any other race category. The use of this single-race population does not imply that it is the preferred method of presenting or analyzing data. The Census Bureau uses a variety of approaches. About 2.6 percent of people reported more than one race in Census 2000.
[c]Black alone refers to people who reported "black" and did not report any other race category.
[d]Asian alone refers to people who reported Asian and did not report any other race category.

SOURCE: "Table 2. Alternative Poverty Estimates Based on National Academy of Sciences Recommendations, by Selected Demographic Characteristics and by Region: 2009," in *Tables of NAS-Based Poverty Estimates: 2009*, U.S. Census Bureau, October 2010, http://www.census.gov/hhes/povmeas/data/nas/tables/2009/index.html (accessed February 17, 2011)

nonrelatives). In 2009, 38.7 million of 117.5 million households, or 32.9%, were nonfamily households. (See Table 1.7.) These nonfamily households earned a median income of $30,444, compared with the $61,265 median income of family households.

The increase in the number of households headed by females and the increased labor force participation of women have also contributed to growing income inequality in the United States. In 2009, 14.8 million of 78.8 million family households, or 18.8%, were headed by women, and 20.4 million of 38.7 million nonfamily households, or 52.8%, were headed by women. (See Table 1.7.) Female-headed households typically earn significantly less than other types of households. The earnings of female-headed family households in 2009 were only 67.8% of the earnings of male-headed family households ($32,597 and $48,084, respectively) and female nonfamily householders earned only 69% of male nonfamily householders ($25,269 and $36,611, respectively). On average, female full-time workers earned only 77% of what male full-time workers earned in 2009. (See Figure 1.3.) Robert J. Gordon and Ian Dew-Becker of the National Bureau of Economic Research argue in "Controversies about the Rise of American Inequality: A Survey" (May 2008, http://papers.nber.org/papers/w13982) that the declining real value of the minimum wage has contributed to income inequality, particularly for female workers, who are more likely than males to work for minimum wages; among men, the decline of unions has contributed to growing income inequality.

HOMELESSNESS

Homelessness is a complex social problem. According to the National Coalition for the Homeless, in the fact sheet "How Many People Experience Homelessness?"

TABLE 1.6

Household income dispersion, selected years, 1967–2009

[Income in 2009 CPI-U-RS adjusted dollars.]

Measures of income dispersion	2009[a]	2008	2007	2002	1997	1992[b]	1987[c]	1982	1977	1972[d]	1967[e]
Measure											
Household income at selected percentiles											
10th percentile limit	12,120	12,115	12,581	12,662	12,279	11,234	11,265	10,801	11,291	10,816	9,152
20th percentile limit	20,453	20,633	20,991	21,361	20,520	18,873	19,507	17,927	18,487	18,570	16,845
50th (median)	49,777	50,112	51,965	50,563	49,309	45,888	47,071	43,048	43,758	44,462	40,108
80th percentile limit	100,000	99,860	103,448	100,170	95,273	86,886	87,353	77,683	77,380	75,655	66,481
90th percentile limit	137,632	137,775	140,690	136,053	130,133	116,159	115,242	102,445	98,691	97,205	84,449
95th percentile limit	180,001	179,317	183,103	178,844	168,626	148,318	146,172	128,232	122,518	121,759	106,684
Household income ratios of selected percentiles											
90th/10th	11.36	11.37	11.18	10.75	10.60	10.34	10.23	9.49	8.74	8.99	9.23
95th/20th	8.80	8.69	8.72	8.37	8.22	7.86	7.49	7.15	6.63	6.56	6.33
95th/50th	3.62	3.58	3.52	3.54	3.42	3.23	3.11	2.98	2.80	2.74	2.66
80th/50th	2.01	1.99	1.99	1.98	1.93	1.89	1.86	1.80	1.77	1.70	1.66
80th/20th	4.89	4.84	4.93	4.69	4.64	4.60	4.48	4.33	4.19	4.07	3.95
20th/50th	0.41	0.41	0.40	0.42	0.42	0.41	0.41	0.42	0.42	0.42	0.42
Mean household income of quintiles											
Lowest quintile	11,552	11,612	11,949	11,911	11,778	10,868	11,076	10,223	10,753	10,468	8,984
Second quintile	29,257	29,405	30,457	30,284	29,445	27,233	28,148	25,868	26,467	27,039	24,891
Third quintile	49,534	49,942	51,691	51,032	49,538	45,881	47,060	42,820	43,781	44,128	39,737
Fourth quintile	78,694	79,457	81,839	80,271	76,727	70,431	71,133	63,683	64,148	63,353	55,599
Highest quintile	170,844	170,408	173,763	171,382	163,581	136,470	135,278	116,800	114,393	113,735	100,059
Shares of household income of quintiles											
Lowest quintile	3.4	3.4	3.4	3.5	3.6	3.8	3.8	4.0	4.2	4.1	4.0
Second quintile	8.6	8.6	8.7	8.8	8.9	9.4	9.6	10.0	10.2	10.4	10.8
Third quintile	14.6	14.7	14.8	14.8	15.0	15.8	16.1	16.5	16.9	17.0	17.3
Fourth quintile	23.2	23.3	23.4	23.3	23.2	24.2	24.3	24.5	24.7	24.5	24.2
Highest quintile	50.3	50.0	49.7	49.7	49.4	46.9	46.2	45.0	44.0	43.9	43.6
Summary measures											
Gini index of income inequality	0.468	0.466	0.463	0.462	0.459	0.433	0.426	0.412	0.402	0.401	0.397
Mean logarithmic deviation of income	0.550	0.541	0.532	0.514	0.484	0.416	0.414	0.401	0.364	0.370	0.380
Theil	0.403	0.398	0.391	0.398	0.396	0.323	0.311	0.287	0.276	0.279	0.287
Atkinson:											
e = 0.25	0.097	0.096	0.095	0.095	0.094	0.080	0.077	0.072	0.069	0.070	0.071
e = 0.50	0.190	0.188	0.185	0.186	0.183	0.160	0.155	0.146	0.139	0.140	0.143
e = 0.75	0.288	0.285	0.281	0.279	0.272	0.242	0.238	0.226	0.213	0.216	0.220

[a]Medians are calculated using $2,500 income intervals. Beginning with 2009 income data, the Census Bureau expanded the upper income intervals used to calculate medians to $250,000 or more. Medians falling in the upper open-ended interval are plugged with "$250,000." Before 2009, the upper open-ended interval was $100,000 and a plug of "$100,000" was used.
[b]Implementation of 1990 census population controls.
[c]Implementation of a new CPS ASEC processing system.
[d]Full implementation of 1970 census-based sample design.
[e]Implementation of a new CPS ASEC processing system.
Notes: CPI-U-RS = Consumer Price Index Research Series. CPS ASEC = Current Population Survey Annual Social and Economic Supplement.

SOURCE: Adapted from Carmen DeNavas-Walt, Bernadette D. Proctor, and Jessica C. Smith, "Table A-2. Selected Measures of Household Income Dispersion: 1967 to 2009," in *Income, Poverty, and Health Insurance Coverage in the United States: 2009*, Current Population Reports, U.S. Census Bureau, September 2010, http://www.census.gov/prod/2010pubs/p60-238.pdf (accessed February 17, 2011)

(July 2009, http://www.nationalhomeless.org/factsheets/ How_Many.pdf), approximately 3.5 million people, 1.4 million of them children, lack a place to sleep at some time during the year. Social researchers (educators, sociologists, economists, and political scientists), who have studied homelessness for decades, have determined that homelessness is caused by a combination of poverty, misfortune, illness, and behavior.

What Does It Mean to Be Homeless?

During a period of growing concern about homelessness in the mid-1980s, the first major piece of federal legislation aimed specifically at helping the homeless was adopted: the Stewart B. McKinney Homeless Assistance Act of 1987 (also known as the McKinney-Vento Homeless Assistance Act). Part of the act officially defined a homeless person as:

TABLE 1.7

Income and earnings summary measures by selected characteristics, 2008 and 2009

[Income in 2009 dollars]

| Characteristic | 2008 | | 2009[a] | | Percentage change in real median income |
	Number (thousands)	Median income (dollars) Estimate	Number (thousands)	Median income (dollars) Estimate	Estimate
Households					
All households	**117,181**	**50,112**	**117,538**	**49,777**	**−0.7**
Type of household					
Family households	78,850	62,383	78,833	61,265	−1.8
Married-couple	59,118	72,733	58,410	71,830	−1.2
Female householder, no husband present	14,480	32,947	14,843	32,597	−1.1
Male householder, no wife present	5,252	48,999	5,580	48,084	−1.9
Nonfamily households	38,331	29,964	38,705	30,444	1.6
Female householder	20,637	24,919	20,442	25,269	1.4
Male householder	17,694	35,869	18,263	36,611	2.1
Race[b] and Hispanic origin of householder					
White	95,297	52,113	95,489	51,861	−0.5
White, not Hispanic	82,884	55,319	83,158	54,461	−1.6
Black	14,595	34,088	14,730	32,584	−4.4
Asian	4,573	65,388	4,687	65,469	0.1
Hispanic (any race)	13,425	37,769	13,298	38,039	0.7
Age of householder					
Under 65 years	92,346	56,575	92,268	55,821	−1.3
15 to 24 years	6,357	32,148	6,233	30,733	−4.4
25 to 34 years	19,302	51,205	19,257	50,199	−2.0
35 to 44 years	22,171	62,715	21,519	61,083	−2.6
45 to 54 years	24,633	64,105	24,871	64,235	0.2
55 to 64 years	19,883	57,048	20,387	56,973	−0.1
65 years and older	24,834	29,631	25,270	31,354	5.8
Nativity of householder					
Native born	101,585	50,862	102,039	50,503	−0.7
Foreign born	15,596	43,328	15,499	43,923	1.4
Naturalized citizen	7,668	51,328	7,834	51,975	1.3
Not a citizen	7,928	37,807	7,666	36,089	−4.5
Earnings of full-time, year-round workers					
Men with earnings	59,861	46,191	56,053	47,127	2.0
Women with earnings	44,156	35,609	43,217	36,278	1.9
Per capita income[c]					
Total[b]	**301,483**	**26,862**	**304,280**	**26,530**	**−1.2**
White	240,852	28,394	242,403	28,034	−1.3
White, not Hispanic	197,159	31,194	197,436	30,941	−0.8
Black	38,076	18,336	38,624	18,135	−1.1
Asian	13,315	30,177	14,011	30,653	1.6
Hispanic (any race)	47,485	15,615	48,901	15,063	−3.5

[a]Medians are calculated using $2,500 income intervals. Beginning with 2009 income data, the Census Bureau expanded the upper income intervals used to calculate medians to $250,000 or more. Medians falling in the upper open-ended interval are plugged with "$250,000." Before 2009, the upper open-ended interval was $100,000 and a plug of "$100,000" was used.

[b]Federal surveys now give respondents the option of reporting more than one race. Therefore, two basic ways of defining a race group are possible. A group such as Asian may be defined as those who reported Asian and no other race (the race-alone or single-race concept) or as those who reported Asian regardless of whether they also reported another race (the race-alone-or-in-combination concept). This table shows data using the first approach (race alone). The use of the single-race population does not imply that it is the preferred method of presenting or analyzing data. The Census Bureau uses a variety of approaches. Information on people who reported more than one race, such as white and American Indian and Alaska Native or Asian and black or African American, is available from Census 2000 through American FactFinder. About 2.6 percent of people reported more than one race in Census 2000. Data for American Indians and Alaska Natives, Native Hawaiians and other Pacific Islanders, and those reporting two or more races are not shown separately in this table.

[c]The data shown in this section are per capita incomes. Per capita income is the mean income computed for every man, woman, and child in a particular group. It is derived by dividing the total income of a particular group by the total population in that group (excluding patients or inmates in institutional quarters).

SOURCE: Adapted from Carmen DeNavas-Walt, Bernadette D. Proctor, and Jessica C. Smith, "Table 1. Income and Earnings Summary Measures by Selected Characteristics: 2008 and 2009," in *Income, Poverty, and Health Insurance Coverage in the United States: 2009*, Current Population Reports, U.S. Census Bureau, September 2010, http://www.census.gov/prod/2010pubs/p60-238.pdf (accessed February 17, 2011)

1. An individual who lacks a fixed, regular, and adequate nighttime residence; and

2. An individual who has a primary nighttime residence that is:

A. A supervised publicly or privately operated shelter designed to provide temporary living accommodations (including welfare hotels, congregate shelters, and transitional housing for the mentally ill);

FIGURE 1.3

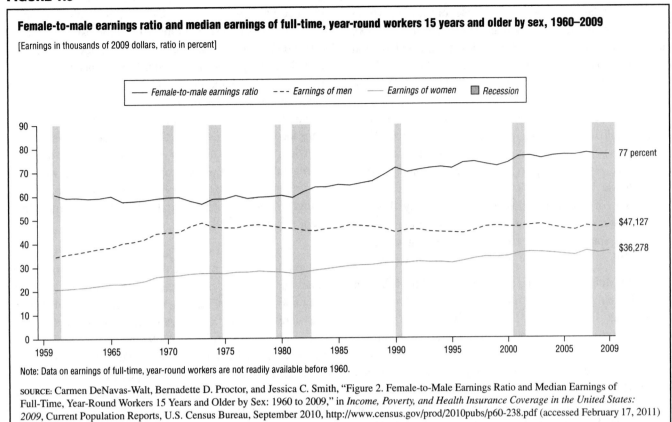

Female-to-male earnings ratio and median earnings of full-time, year-round workers 15 years and older by sex, 1960–2009

[Earnings in thousands of 2009 dollars, ratio in percent]

Legend: —— Female-to-male earnings ratio - - - Earnings of men —— Earnings of women ▨ Recession

Note: Data on earnings of full-time, year-round workers are not readily available before 1960.

SOURCE: Carmen DeNavas-Walt, Bernadette D. Proctor, and Jessica C. Smith, "Figure 2. Female-to-Male Earnings Ratio and Median Earnings of Full-Time, Year-Round Workers 15 Years and Older by Sex: 1960 to 2009," in *Income, Poverty, and Health Insurance Coverage in the United States: 2009*, Current Population Reports, U.S. Census Bureau, September 2010, http://www.census.gov/prod/2010pubs/p60-238.pdf (accessed February 17, 2011)

B. An institution that provides a temporary residence for individuals intended to be institutionalized; or

C. A public or private place not designed for, or ordinarily used as, a regular sleeping accommodation for human beings.

The government's definition of a homeless person focuses on whether a person is housed. Broader definitions of homelessness take into account whether a person has a home. For example, Martha Burt et al. report in *Helping America's Homeless: Emergency Shelter or Affordable Housing?* (2001) that as late as 1980 the Census Bureau identified people who lived alone and did not have a "usual home elsewhere"—in other words, a larger family—as homeless. In this sense the term *home* describes living within a family, rather than having a roof over one's head.

Burt et al. also state that homeless people themselves, when interviewed during the 1980s and 1990s, drew a distinction between having a house and having a home. Even when homeless people had spent significant periods of time in a traditional shelter, such as an apartment or rented room, if they felt those houses were transitional or insecure, they identified themselves as having been homeless while living there. According to Burt et al., these answers "reflect how long they have been without significant attachments to people."

Burt et al. and other homeless advocates disagree with the narrow government definition of a homeless person,

which focuses on a person's sleeping arrangements. They assert that the definition should be broadened to include groups of people who, while they may have somewhere to live, do not really have a home in the conventional sense. Considerable debate has resulted over expanding the classification to include people in situations such as the following:

- People engaging in prostitution who spend each night in a different hotel room, paid for by clients

- Children in foster or relative care

- People living in stable but inadequate housing (e.g., having no plumbing or heating)

- People doubled up in conventional dwellings for the short term

- People in hotels paid for by vouchers to the needy

- Elderly people living with family members because they cannot afford to live elsewhere

Official definitions are important because total counts of the homeless influence the levels of funding that Congress authorizes for homeless programs. With the availability of federal funds since the passage of the McKinney-Vento Homeless Assistance Act, institutional constituencies have formed that advocate for additional funding, an effort in which more expansive definitions are helpful.

Causes of Homelessness

In 2010 the U.S. Conference of Mayors, a nonpartisan organization of cities with populations higher than 30,000, surveyed the mayors of major cities on the extent and causes of urban homelessness and published the results in *Hunger and Homelessness Survey: A Status Report on Hunger and Homelessness in America's Cities, a 27-City Survey* (December 2010, http://www.usmayors.org/press releases/uploads/2010HungerHomelessnessReportfinalDec 212010.pdf). Three-quarters (76%) of the mayors cited unemployment as a major cause of family homelessness, 72% cited lack of affordable housing, and 56% cited poverty. Lack of affordable housing was cited by 31% of mayors as a major cause of homelessness among single adults and unaccompanied youth, while 19% cited mental illness, 19% cited substance abuse, and 15% cited poverty.

Jesse McKinley reports in "Cities Deal with a Surge in Shantytowns" (*New York Times*, March 25, 2009) that as a result of the foreclosure crisis, which began in 2007, tent cities sprang up in major cities around the nation. Public attention shifted to these modern-day "Hoovervilles" (shantytowns that arose during the Great Depression [1929–1939]) after the *Oprah Winfrey Show* focused on a tent city in Sacramento, California, in March 2009. In "'American Dream' Withers as Tent Cities Mushroom in Promised Land" (*International Business Times*, November 21, 2010), Jijo Jacob notes that tent cities continued to be erected after the recession officially ended. Jacob explains that continued high unemployment and surging foreclosures were feeding a mushrooming homelessness rate. Jacob suggests that the crisis had not reached its peak; Moody's had reported earlier in 2010 that 15 million Americans owed more to the bank than their homes were worth. Jennifer Jiggetts notes in "Virginia Beach Tent Cities for Homeless Keep Popping Up" (*Virginian-Pilot* [Hampton Roads, VA], April 10, 2011) that despite the improving economy in 2011, the homeless problem was still persistent.

COUNTING THE HOMELESS

Methodology

An accurate count of the U.S. homeless population has proved to be challenging for statisticians. The most formidable obstacle is the nature of homelessness itself. Typically, researchers contact people in their homes using in-person or telephone surveys to obtain information regarding income, education levels, household size, ethnicity, and other demographic data. Because homeless people cannot be counted at home, researchers have been forced to develop new methods for collecting data on these transient groups.

Counting each and every person without a home would be the most accurate way to establish the number of homeless people. However, such a count is almost impossible. In *Homeless Count Methodologies: An Annotated Bibliography* (February 1999), Anita Drever discusses other methods. One way to estimate the number of homeless people is to search records at homeless service provider locations. Alternatively, a sampling of those records combined with projections, called probability-based methods, can be used to count the number of homeless. Another method is to count the number of homeless at one particular time in one particular place. This snapshot method estimates the number of homeless at any one time. Longitudinal studies are a way to estimate the proportion of people in a population who may become homeless at some point in their life. These studies follow individuals over a period of time to determine if they become homeless.

Different types of counts and different methodologies will produce different results even if the intention is the same—namely to accurately enumerate the homeless population. For example, Table 1.8 shows the results of surveys that were conducted by the Association of Gospel Rescue Missions (AGRM) in 2008, 2009, and 2010 of people who use its services. The data presented in the table are based on the snapshot method (counts of a population at a point in time). The AGRM counted all people receiving homeless services during one specific night in each year at its rescue missions around the country. The 2010 results are based on data from 85 rescue missions, approximately one-third the number of missions that are operated by the AGRM in North America.

By contrast, Martha Burt et al. conducted a study in 1996 that sampled 76 geographical areas selected by the Urban Institute as being representative of all service providers in the United States and published their findings in *Homelessness: Programs and the People They Serve—Findings of the National Survey of Homeless Assistance Providers and Clients* (December 1999, http://www.hudu ser.org/publications/homeless/homeless_tech.html). The researchers then compared their results by demographic characteristics to the total population as enumerated by the U.S. census. The male-to-female ratios in the AGRM study are quite different from Burt et al.'s study, with the AGRM finding that males made up approximately three-quarters (75% in 2010) of the homeless population (see Table 1.8), whereas Burt et al.'s study shows that males were just over two-thirds (68% in 1996) of the homeless population. All studies, however, show that males greatly outnumber females among the homeless, although the proportion of females appears to be rising. This may be in part because, as the AGRM notes in "Women with Children Hit Hardest by Slow Economy" (November 7, 2008, http://www .agrm.org/i4a/pages/index.cfm?pageid=3387), as a result of the economic slowdown that began in 2007, the numbers of homeless women with children jumped by 11 percentage points between 2007 and 2008, from 55% to 66%.

TABLE 1.8

Demographic overview of the homeless population, 2008–10

	2010	2009	2008
Gender (of total mission population)			
Male	75%	75%	74%
Female	25%	25%	26%
Age groups (of total mission population)			
Under 18	9%	9%	12%
18–25	9%	8%	9%
26–35	15%	17%	18%
36–45	22%	25%	26%
46–65	40%	38%	31%
65+	4%	3%	4%
Race/ethic groups (of total mission population)			
Caucasian	47%	49%	48%
African-American	36%	36%	35%
Hispanic	11%	9%	11%
Asian	1%	1%	2%
Native American	2%	5%	5%
Women/children/families (of family united identified)			
Couples	12%	13%	15%
Women with children	57%	60%	66%
Men with children	9%	9%	5%
Intact families	22%	18%	14%
Other information			
Of total mission population:			
Veterans (male)	16%	19%	18%
Veterans (female)	4%	4%	3%
Of veterans identified:			
Served in Korea	3%	6%	4%
Served in Vietnam	26%	28%	33%
Served in Persian Gulf	16%	18%	15%
No conflict/none identified	55%	48%	48%
Of total mission population:			
Never before homeless	37%	37%	33%
Homeless once previously	25%	25%	24%
Homeless twice previously	16%	16%	18%
Homeless three-plus times previously	22%	22%	25%
Of total mission population:			
Homeless less than one year	59%	60%	60%
Resident of mission's city more than 6 months	71%	70%	73%
Victim of physical violence in last 12 months	15%	17%	18%
Lost government benefits in last 12 months	20%	22%	15%
Prefer spiritual emphasis in services	82%	83%	76%
Comes daily to the mission	84%	80%	77%

SOURCE: "Snapshot Survey Homeless Statistical Comparison," in *Many American Families Are Living on the Edge*, Association of Gospel Rescue Missions, November 2010, http://www.agrm.org/i4a/pages/index.cfm?pageID=3609 (accessed February 17, 2011).

Counting the Homeless for the U.S. Census

The official U.S. census, which takes place at 10-year intervals, is intended to count everyone in the United States. The results of the census are critical in determining how much federal money goes into different programs and to various regions of the country. Representation of the population in Congress is also based on the census. Because the Census Bureau counts people in their homes, counting the homeless presents special challenges.

In "The 1990 Census Shelter and Street Night Enumeration" (March 1992, http://www.amstat.org/sections/srms/proceedings/papers/1992_029.pdf), Diane F. Barrett, Irwin Anolik, and Florence H. Abramson of the Census Bureau indicate that in March 1990 census officials, on what was known as Shelter and Street Night (S-Night), counted homeless people found in shelters, emergency shelters, shelters for abused women, shelters for runaway and neglected youth, low-cost motels, Young Men's Christian Associations and Young Women's Christian Associations, and subsidized units at motels. Additionally, they counted people found in the early morning hours sleeping in abandoned buildings, bus and train stations, all-night restaurants, parks, and vacant lots. The results of this count were released the following year in the Census Bureau publication "Count of Persons in Selected Locations Where Homeless Persons Are Found." Homeless advocates criticized the methods and results as inadequate and charged that they provided a low estimate of homeless people in the United States. According to Annetta C. Smith and Denise I. Smith of the Census Bureau, in *Emergency and Transitional Shelter Population: 2000* (October 2001, http://www.census.gov/prod/2001pubs/censr01-2.pdf), the Census Bureau responded by emphasizing that S-Night "should not be used as a count of people experiencing homelessness." S-Night results were not a reflection of the prevalence of homelessness over a given year, but a count of homeless people identified during a single night, a snapshot, like the census itself.

The National Law Center on Homelessness and Poverty alleged that the methodology of the S-Night count was unconstitutional. In 1992 the law center, the Conference of Mayors, the cities of Baltimore, Maryland, and San Francisco, California, 15 local homeless organizations, and seven homeless people (the plaintiffs) filed suit in the federal district court in Washington, D.C. They charged the Census Bureau with excluding segments of the homeless population in the 1990 population count by not counting those in hidden areas and by not allocating adequate funds for S-Night.

In its suit, the law center cited an internal Census Bureau memorandum that stated, in part, "We know we will miss people by counting the 'open' rather than 'concealed' (two studies showed that about two-thirds of the street population sleep concealed)." Studies funded by the Census Bureau indicated that up to 70% of the homeless street population in Los Angeles, California, were missed, as were 32% in New Orleans, Louisiana, 47% in New York City, New York, and 69% in Phoenix, Arizona. Advocates were greatly concerned that this underrepresentation would negatively affect the funding of homeless initiatives.

In 1994 the district court dismissed the case, ruling that the plaintiffs' case was without merit. The court ruled that failure to count all the homeless was not a failure to perform a constitutional duty because the Constitution does not give individuals a right to be counted or a right to a perfectly accurate census. The court stated that the "methods used by the Bureau on S-Night were reasonably designed to count as nearly as practicable all those people residing in the United States and, therefore, easily pass constitutional muster." In *National Law Center on Homelessness and Poverty v. Michael Kantor* (No. 94-5312 [1996]), the U.S. Court of Appeals upheld the district court's finding.

For the 2000 census, the Census Bureau undertook a special operation, called Service-Based Enumeration (SBE). Between March 27 and March 29, 2000, census workers focused solely on counting the homeless population at the locations where they were the most likely to be found. On specific nights, counts of those staying in emergency and transitional shelters, of homeless people taking advantage of soup kitchens, and of those staying in outdoor locations were done.

The SBE methods were considered an improvement over the methods that were used in the 1990 census. Homeless citizens and advocates alike expected to see an increase in the number of homeless people reported by the Census Bureau in the 2000 census as compared with the 1990 census. Expectations that the higher population counts would translate into higher funding levels for services to the homeless were also raised.

In 2001 the Census Bureau reported that it would not be releasing a specific homeless count because of the liability issues raised after the 1990 census. The Census Bureau stated that it would have only one category showing the number of people tabulated at "emergency and transitional shelters." The people who were counted at domestic violence shelters, family crisis centers, soup kitchens, mobile food vans, and targeted nonsheltered outdoor locations (i.e., street people, car dwellers, and so on) during the March 2000 SBE night were to be included in the category of "other noninstitutional group quarters population." This category was overly inclusive; it included, for instance, students living in college dormitories. The homeless portion of the category could not be extracted.

As a result of this Census Bureau decision, Smith and Smith reported on people sleeping in shelters rather than on all homeless people. Census Bureau officials said the homeless people they did find during the exhaustive, three-day SBE count were included in total population figures for states, counties, and municipalities. Researchers voiced concern that the numbers teased from these data sets would be flawed, while people involved in the receipt or delivery of services to the homeless were worried that their programs would suffer from the lack of SBE night information.

The Census Bureau replicated the 2000 SBE count for the 2010 census. Enumerators counted the homeless residing in shelters on the night of May 29, interviewed people at soup kitchens and mobile food vans to determine their sheltered status on May 30, and counted people sleeping at preidentified outdoor locations on the night of May 31. As of April 2011, it was unclear how the Census Bureau would report the 2010 counts.

Only Estimates Are Available

The actual number of homeless people is unknown. Most organizations consider the Urban Institute study *America's Homeless II: Populations and Services* (February 1, 2000, http://www.urban.org/Presentations/Americas HomelessII/toc.htm) to be the most authoritative estimate. This study estimates that 3.5 million people were homeless at some point in 1996.

After the 2000 census Congress directed the U.S. Department of Housing and Urban Development (HUD) to conduct periodic surveys of representative communities to get a better idea of the extent of the homeless problem nationally. In June 2010 HUD published *The 2009 Annual Homeless Assessment Report to Congress* (http://www.hud hre.info/documents/5thHomelessAssessmentReport.pdf). This survey finds that on a single night in January 2009, 403,308 homeless people were in shelters and another 239,759 were unsheltered. (See Table 1.9.) The total number of homeless reported had fallen from 759,101 in 2006 to 643,067 in 2009, a 15.3% drop. (See Figure 1.4.) HUD reports that in 2009, 110,917 people, or 17.2% of the total homeless population, were chronically homeless (homeless for a year or more), which was a significant drop from the count of chronically homeless people in 2008.

TABLE 1.9

Total number of homeless persons on a single January night in 2009

Household type	Number	Percentage
Total people		
Sheltered	403,308	62.7%
Unsheltered	239,759	37.3%
Total	**643,067**	**100.0%**
Individuals		
Sheltered	215,995	53.3%
Unsheltered	188,962	46.7%
Total	**404,957**	**100.0%**
Persons in families		
Sheltered	187,313	78.7%
Unsheltered	50,797	21.3%
Total	**238,110**	**100.0%**
Total family households		
Sheltered	60,843	77.5%
Unsheltered	17,675	22.5%
Total	**78,518**	**100.0%**

SOURCE: "Exhibit 2-1. Homeless Persons and Households by Sheltered Status, Single Night in 2009," in *The 2009 Annual Homeless Assessment Report to Congress*, U.S. Department of Housing and Urban Development, Office of Community Planning and Development, June 2010, http://www .hudhre.info/documents/5thHomelessAssessmentReport.pdf (accessed February 17, 2011)

FIGURE 1.4

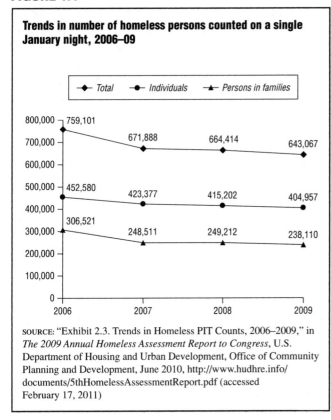

Trends in number of homeless persons counted on a single January night, 2006–09

◆ Total ● Individuals ▲ Persons in families

	2006	2007	2008	2009
Total	759,101	671,888	664,414	643,067
Individuals	452,580	423,377	415,202	404,957
Persons in families	306,521	248,511	249,212	238,110

SOURCE: "Exhibit 2.3. Trends in Homeless PIT Counts, 2006–2009," in *The 2009 Annual Homeless Assessment Report to Congress*, U.S. Department of Housing and Urban Development, Office of Community Planning and Development, June 2010, http://www.hudhre.info/documents/5thHomelessAssessmentReport.pdf (accessed February 17, 2011)

PUBLIC INTEREST IN HOMELESSNESS

Interest in and attitudes toward homelessness in the United States have changed over time. The mid- to late 1980s was a period of relatively high concern about homelessness. In 1986 the American public demonstrated concern over the plight of the homeless by initiating the Hands across America fund-raising effort. Some 6 million people locked hands across 4,152 miles (6,682 km) to form a human chain across the country, bringing an outpouring of national attention and concern to the issue. That same year the comedians Robin Williams (1951–), Whoopi Goldberg (1955–), and Billy Crystal (1948–) hosted the HBO comedy special *Comic Relief* to help raise money for the homeless. The show was a success and became an annual event. Magazines, art shows, books, and songs turned the nation's attention toward homelessness. Well-funded research studies came out by the dozens. The country was awash in statistical information regarding the homeless. All these activities pointed to the widely held belief that people became homeless because of circumstances outside their control.

By 2011, however, national concern about homelessness had faded. *Comic Relief* could only be seen in reruns. The annual fund-raiser ran out of steam in 1996 except for a revival show two years later. After that, there was no resurgence of public interest in the homeless problem, even though the problem worsened due to the foreclosure crisis beginning in 2007, and the Conference of Mayors reported in 2010 that the demand for services continued to increase.

In "The Real Face of Homelessness" (*Time*, January 13, 2003), Joel Stein explores a change in the national mood about homelessness. This change in national mood corresponded with efforts to criminalize homelessness. For example, a campaign was launched in Philadelphia, Pennsylvania, to discourage giving money to panhandlers. In Orlando, Florida, people could be jailed for sleeping on the sidewalk. In San Francisco, Proposition N ("Care Not Cash") reduced county housing support payments from $395 to $59 a month. In Dallas, Texas, the homeless complained that they were issued vagrancy tickets.

Moreover, as a result of the economic recession and the housing crisis that began in late 2007, localities across the country started to report a huge surge in homelessness, even among populations previously considered middle class. Wendy Koch reports in "Homelessness up as Families on the Edge Lose Hold" (*USA Today*, April 6, 2009) that homelessness was up sharply in 2009 and that the demand for homeless services such as shelter requests was up dramatically. She quotes Nancy Radner, the head of the Chicago Alliance to End Homelessness, who said, "We're getting requests from people earning more than $30,000 a year, even $65,000. That's unprecedented." Arthur Delaney notes in "Recession Increasing Interest in Homelessness" (*Huffington Post*, March 27, 2009) that some observers suggested in 2009 that the lengthening reach of homelessness was increasing public interest in the problem once again. For example, the National Center on Family Homelessness states in "Public Education and Policy" (2010, http://www.familyhomelessness.org/publiceducation.php?p=ts) that more than 3,000 media stories had reported on its findings on U.S. homeless children in 2009.

Treating the Homeless as Criminals

Matthew Philips explains in "OK, Sister, Drop That Sandwich!: Cities Fight Panhandling by Outlawing Food Giveaways in Parks" (*Newsweek*, November 6, 2006) that in Orlando, Florida, city lawmakers passed ordinances in 2006 that made it illegal to feed large groups of people in public parks—making not only homelessness but also helping the homeless illegal. According to Forrest Norman, in "Proposed Ordinance Targeting Shantytown Pulled" (*Daily Business Review*, January 9, 2007), an ordinance in Miami, Florida, that would make it illegal for homeless people to sleep on vacant city-owned lots missed emergency passage in December 2006 by only one vote and was pulled from the agenda in January 2007 because city commissioners "needed more time to consider the ordinance" due to community support of the targeted shantytown. In "Lacey to Revisit Homeless Ordinance" (*Olympian*, January 20, 2009), Christian Hill indicates that in 2009 the city council of Olympia, Washington, debated an ordinance that would require churches to house homeless people indoors, rather than in tents. Hill notes in "Lawmaker Pens Homeless Bill" (*Olympian*, February 5, 2009) that in response, the state representative Brendan Williams (1968–) introduced legislation in the Washington House of Representatives that would limit localities' ability to impose regulations on churches who shelter homeless people. In "Los Angeles Accused of Criminalizing Homelessness" (Reuters, July 14, 2009), Steve Gorman reports that even in the midst of the recession, Los Angeles maintained its "Safer City Initiative," a set of policies that, according to the initiative's critics, were designed to punish homelessness. For example, homeless people routinely receive tickets and are even arrested for small offenses such as jaywalking and loitering.

Addressing Homelessness Is a Low Priority

When asked, Americans in the 21st century state they continue to be troubled by the existence of homelessness. In *Americans' Worries About Economy, Budget Top Other Issues* (March 21, 2011, http://www.gallup.com/poll/1467 08/Americans-Worries-Economy-Budget-Top-Issues.aspx), Lydia Saad of the Gallup Organization indicates that in March 2011, 41% of Americans said they worry about hunger and homelessness a great deal and 34% said they worry about it a fair amount. Only 26% said they are worried only a little or not at all. Dennis Jacobe of the Gallup Organization explains in *Americans on Housing Aid: Unfair but Necessary* (February 25, 2009, http://www.gallup.com/poll/116101/Americans-Housing-Aid-Unfair-Necessary.aspx) that in 2009, 51% of Americans believed that providing government assistance to homeowners who cannot pay their mortgage is unfair, but 59% believed such aid is necessary nonetheless. When the question was phrased another way and Americans were asked about "giving aid to homeowners who are in danger of losing their homes to foreclosure," and thus potentially facing homelessness, nearly two-thirds (64%) of Americans said they are in favor of the plan.

Research studies, once so plentiful, were outdated by 2011, but some well-funded research centers and organizations continued to study the homeless population. Their studies are used throughout this book.

HOMELESS SERVICES

A substantial number of organizations provide services to homeless people across the country. Faith-based organizations have been providing assistance to the needy throughout history, including programs for the homeless. Many secular nonprofits (organizations with no religious affiliation) also provide such assistance. Since 1987, with the passage of the McKinney-Vento Homeless Assistance Act, federal funding targeted to help homeless people has been available.

According to HUD, in "Homelessness Prevention and Rapid Re-Housing Program" (2009, http://www.hudhre .info/HPRP/), the American Recovery and Reinvestment Act of 2009 created a Homelessness Prevention Fund of $1.5 billion that provides assistance to families who are facing or experiencing homelessness. The funds can be used for short- or medium-term rental assistance and housing relocation and stabilization services. In "FY 2012 Budget Rundown" (February 1, 2011, http://www.endho melessness.org/content/article/detail/3696), the National Alliance to End Homelessness notes that President Barack Obama's (1961–) proposed fiscal year (FY) 2012 budget would increase HUD's McKinney-Vento Homeless Assistance Grant funding to $2.4 billion, up by 27.2% from the FY 2010 budget of $1.9 billion; would provide $57 million for housing vouchers for homeless and at-risk families; would increase funding for U.S. Department of Veterans Affairs homeless programs by 51%; would hold tenant-based and section 8 housing funding steady while increasing project-based rental assistance to $9.4 billion; would cut the community development block grant by $300 million; and would cut public housing operating expenses by 17%.

HUD states in *2009 Annual Homeless Assessment Report to Congress* that it counted the number of beds for homeless people available in emergency and transitional assistance programs in 2009. There were 214,425 year-round beds available in emergency shelters—103,531 available for families and 110,894 for individuals. (See Table 1.10.) An additional 20,419 beds were available during certain months of the year (winter months in the North and summer months in the South), and 30,565 over-flow beds (beds made available during unanticipated emergencies) and voucher beds (beds provided in a motel or hotel) were available as well. In that same year, there were 110,064 family beds and 97,525 individual beds available in transitional housing. HUD notes that Permanent Supportive Housing contributed another 219,381 beds—87,718 for members of families and 131,663 for individuals. In 2009, 62.7% of all homeless people surveyed were sheltered and 37.3% were not sheltered. (See Table 1.9.)

HUD compares the demographics of the sheltered homeless population to the poor population of the United States in general. It finds that while males made up 40.5% of the poor population in 2008, they made up 63.7% of the sheltered homeless population in 2009. (See Table 1.11.) Non-Hispanic whites accounted for 46.2% of the entire poor population, but only 38.1% of the homeless population. African-Americans were over-represented among the homeless population; 22.1% of the poor population was African-American, whereas 38.7% of the sheltered homeless population was African-American. In addition, veterans and disabled adults were disproportionately homeless.

TABLE 1.10

Number of emergency and transitional beds in homeless assistance system nationwide, 2009

| | Year-round beds | | | | Other beds | |
	Total year-round beds	Family beds	Individual beds	Total year-round family units	Seasonal	Overflow or voucher
Emergency shelters						
Inventory	214,425	103,531	110,894	31,964	20,419	30,565
Transitional housing						
Inventory	207,589	110,064	97,525	35,119	0	0
Safe havens						
Inventory	2,028	0	2,028	0	0	0
Sub-total: beds for currently homeless persons						
Inventory	424,042	213,595	210,447	67,083	20,419	30,565
Permanent supportive housing (beds serving formerly homeless persons)						
Inventory	219,381	87,718	131,663	30,649	0	0

SOURCE: "Exhibit 5-2. Number of Beds and Units in Homeless Assistance System Nationwide, 2009," in *The 2009 Annual Homeless Assessment Report to Congress*, U.S. Department of Housing and Urban Development, Office of Community Planning and Development, June 2010, http://www.hudhre.info/documents/5thHomelessAssessmentReport.pdf (accessed February 17, 2011)

TABLE 1.11

Demographic characteristics of sheltered homeless persons in 2009 compared to the U.S. and poverty populations, 2008

Characteristic	Percentage of all sheltered homeless persons, 2009	Percentage of the 2008 U.S. poverty population	Percentage of the 2008 U.S. population
Gender of adults			
Male	63.7%	40.5%	48.7%
Female	36.3%	59.5%	51.3%
Ethnicity			
Non-Hispanic/non-Latino	80.5%	75.1%	84.6%
Hispanic/Latino	19.5%	24.9%	15.4%
Race			
White, Non-Hispanic	38.1%	46.2%	65.4%
White, Hispanic	11.6%	15.0%	9.6%
Black or African American	38.7%	22.1%	12.4%
Other single race	4.7%	13.8%	10.3%
Multiple races	7.0%	2.9%	2.3%
Age[a]			
Under age 18	22.2%	33.9%	24.3%
18 to 30	22.3%	23.8%	18.2%
31 to 50	38.3%	21.9%	28.2%
51 to 61	14.4%	9.2%	13.9%
62 and older	2.8%	11.3%	15.4%
Household size[b]			
1 person	64.1%	16.6%	13.0%
2 people	10.0%	18.4%	25.6%
3 people	10.2%	17.1%	18.9%
4 people	7.9%	18.5%	20.9%
5 or more people	7.9%	29.4%	21.6%
Special populations			
Veteran (adults only)[c]	11.1%	5.2%	9.7%
Disabled (adults only)[c]	37.8%	26.2%	15.5%

[a]Age is calculated based on a person's first time in shelter during the one-year reporting period.

[b]If a person is part of more than one household or the household size changed during the reporting period, the household size reflects the size of the first household in which the person presented during the one-year reporting period. For all population types, past reports counted each person in a multi-adult or multi-child household as an individual household composed of one person. In this report, persons in these households are counted as one household composed of multiple people. For example, a household composed of two adults with no children is counted as one household with a household size equal to two, rather than two households with each household size equal to 1.

[c]Veteran and disability status are recorded only for adults in Homeless Management Information Systems (HMIS). The percentage calculations shown indicate the percent of homeless adults with this characteristic. Some records were missing information on disability status (10.5 percent) and veteran status (5.3 percent) in 2009. The percentage calculations are for those whose disability and veteran status was known.

SOURCE: "Exhibit 3-1. Demographic Characteristics of Sheltered Homeless Persons in 2009 Compared to the 2008 U.S. and Poverty Populations," in *The 2009 Annual Homeless Assessment Report to Congress*, U.S. Department of Housing and Urban Development, Office of Community Planning and Development, June 2010, http://www.hudhre.info/documents/5thHomelessAssessmentReport.pdf (accessed February 17, 2011)

Special Populations

Many homeless assistance programs are open to anyone who wants to use them, but other programs are designed to serve only specific groups of people. The population served may be defined in several different ways: for example, men by themselves, women by themselves, households with children, youth by themselves, battered women, or veterans. In 2009, 12.5% of year-round emergency shelter and transitional housing beds were reserved for domestic violence victims, 2.9% were reserved for veterans, 1.7% were reserved for unaccompanied youth, and 1.4% were reserved for people with the human immunodeficiency virus (HIV) or the acquired immunodeficiency syndrome (AIDS). (See Figure 1.5.) Most beds (81.5%) in emergency shelters and transitional housing were for the general population.

FIGURE 1.5

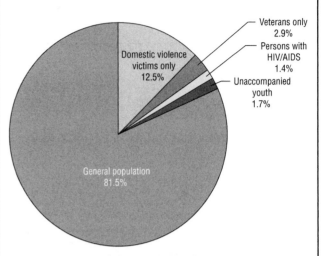

Year-round emergency shelter and transitional housing beds by homeless subpopulation, 2009

SOURCE: "Exhibit 5-3. Year-Round Emergency Shelter and Transitional Housing Beds by Homeless Subpopulation, 2009," in *The 2009 Annual Homeless Assessment Report to Congress*, U.S. Department of Housing and Urban Development, Office of Community Planning and Development, June 2010, http://www.hudhre.info/documents/5thHomelessAssessmentReport.pdf (accessed February 17, 2011)

CHAPTER 2

WHO ARE THE POOR?

CHARACTERISTICS OF THE POOR

Carmen DeNavas-Walt, Bernadette D. Proctor, and Jessica C. Smith of the U.S. Census Bureau indicate in *Income, Poverty, and Health Insurance Coverage in the United States: 2009* (September 2010, http://www.census.gov/prod/2010pubs/p60-238.pdf) that in 2009, 14.3% of the total U.S. population had income-to-poverty ratios under 1.00; in other words, 43.6 million people in the United States were poor. (See Table 1.3 in Chapter 1.) Another 4.4% had income-to-poverty ratios between 1.00 and 1.25, meaning that 18.7% of the U.S. population was poor or near-poor. Children under the age of 18 years and young adults aged 18 to 24 years were the most likely to be poor (20.7% in each case); another 5.6% of children and 5% of young adults were near-poor.

Young children suffer disproportionately from poverty and deprivation. In 2009 nearly one out of four (23.8%) children under the age of six years were poor, and three out of 10 (29.6%) children under the age of six years were poor or near-poor. (See Table 1.3 in Chapter 1.) More than one out of 10 (11%) children this age were desperately poor, living in families with income-to-poverty ratios of under 0.50.

Even though poverty rates were high throughout the first decade of the 21st century, individuals were not necessarily trapped in poverty for long periods of time. Robin J. Anderson of the Census Bureau finds in *Dynamics of Economic Well-Being: Poverty, 2004–2006* (March 2011, http://www.census.gov/hhes/www/poverty/publications/dynamics04/P70-123.pdf) that 28.9% of the U.S. population was in poverty for at least two months between January 2004 and December 2006, but that only 2.8% of the population was in poverty for the entire period. Of those who were in poverty between January and February 2004 at the start of the study period, about a quarter (23.1%) remained in poverty until the end of the study. However, more than half of people who exited poverty still had low incomes of less than 150% of the poverty threshold.

Race and Ethnicity

Historically, poverty rates have been consistently lower for whites than for minorities in the United States. According to DeNavas-Walt, Proctor, and Smith, in 1959, 18.1% (28.5 million) of all whites lived below the poverty level, whereas 55.1% (9.9 million) of African-Americans did. By 1970 the rate of poverty of white Americans had declined to 9.9% (17.5 million), where it remained for approximately the next 10 years. The poverty rate for African-Americans was more than three times that of whites in 1970, at 33.5% (7.5 million). By 2000, a year in which the U.S. economy was strong, only 9.5% of whites (21.6 million) lived in poverty, whereas 22.5% (8 million) of all African-Americans did.

In 2009 African-Americans and Hispanics continued to be disproportionately affected by poverty. In that year, 9.4% of non-Hispanic whites were poor, compared with 25.8% of African-Americans and 25.3% of Hispanics. (See Table 2.1.) The poverty rates for all racial and ethnic groups had risen since 2008 as a result of the so-called Great Recession (which lasted from late 2007 to mid-2009) and unemployment, although they rose faster for minority groups. The poverty rate rose 0.8% among non-Hispanic whites, 1.1% among African-Americans, and 2.1% among Hispanics.

Even more African-American and Hispanic children suffered from poverty. In 2008 one-third (34.7%) of African-Americans under the age of 18 years and 30.6% of Hispanics under the age of 18 years were poor, compared with only 10.6% of non-Hispanic white children in the same age group. (See Table 2.2.) Only 4.5% of non-Hispanic white children were desperately poor, compared with 12.5% of Hispanic children and 17.6% of African-American children.

TABLE 2.1

People and families in poverty, by selected characteristics, 2008 and 2009

[Numbers in thousands]

Characteristic	Total	2008 Below poverty Number	2008 Below poverty Percent	Total	2009 Below poverty Number	2009 Below poverty Percent	Change in poverty[a] Number	Change in poverty[a] Percent
People								
Total	301,041	39,829	13.2	303,820	43,569	14.3	3,740	1.1
Family status								
In families	248,301	28,564	11.5	249,384	31,197	12.5	2,634	1.0
Householder	78,874	8,147	10.3	78,867	8,792	11.1	644	0.8
Related children under 18	72,980	13,507	18.5	73,410	14,774	20.1	1,267	1.6
Related children under 6	24,884	5,295	21.3	25,104	5,983	23.8	688	2.6
In unrelated subfamilies	1,207	555	46.0	1,357	693	51.1	138	5.1
Reference person	452	207	45.7	521	253	48.7	47	2.9
Children under 18	712	341	47.8	747	423	56.6	82	8.7
Unrelated individuals	51,534	10,710	20.8	53,079	11,678	22.0	968	1.2
Male	25,240	4,759	18.9	26,269	5,255	20.0	496	1.1
Female	26,293	5,951	22.6	26,811	6,424	24.0	473	1.3
Race[b] and Hispanic origin								
White	240,548	26,990	11.2	242,047	29,830	12.3	2,841	1.1
White, not Hispanic	196,940	17,024	8.6	197,164	18,530	9.4	1,506	0.8
Black	37,966	9,379	24.7	38,556	9,944	25.8	565	1.1
Asian	13,310	1,576	11.8	14,005	1,746	12.5	169	0.6
Hispanic (any race)	47,398	10,987	23.2	48,811	12,350	25.3	1,363	2.1
Age								
Under 18 years	74,068	14,068	19.0	74,579	15,451	20.7	1,383	1.7
18 to 64 years	189,185	22,105	11.7	190,627	24,684	12.9	2,579	1.3
65 years and older	37,788	3,656	9.7	38,613	3,433	8.9	−223	−0.8
Nativity								
Native born	264,314	33,293	12.6	266,223	36,407	13.7	3,114	1.1
Foreign born	36,727	6,536	17.8	37,597	7,162	19.0	626	1.3
Naturalized citizen	15,470	1,577	10.2	16,024	1,736	10.8	160	0.6
Not a citizen	21,257	4,959	23.3	21,573	5,425	25.1	466	1.8
Region								
Northeast	54,123	6,295	11.6	54,571	6,650	12.2	355	0.6
Midwest	65,589	8,120	12.4	65,980	8,768	13.3	648	0.9
South	110,666	15,862	14.3	112,165	17,609	15.7	1,747	1.4
West	70,663	9,552	13.5	71,103	10,542	14.8	990	1.3
Residence								
Inside metropolitan statistical areas	253,048	32,570	12.9	256,028	35,655	13.9	3,085	1.1
Inside principal cities	97,217	17,222	17.7	97,725	18,261	18.7	1,039	1.0
Outside principal cities	155,831	15,348	9.8	158,302	17,394	11.0	2,046	1.1
Outside metropolitan statistical areas[c]	47,993	7,259	15.1	47,792	7,914	16.6	656	1.4
Work experience								
Total, 16 years and older	236,024	27,216	11.5	238,095	29,625	12.4	2,409	0.9
All workers	158,317	10,085	6.4	154,772	10,680	6.9	595	0.5
Worked full-time, year-round	104,023	2,754	2.6	99,306	2,641	2.7	−113	—
Less than full-time, year-round	54,294	7,331	13.5	55,466	8,039	14.5	708	1.0
Did not work at least 1 week	77,707	17,131	22.0	83,323	18,944	22.7	1,814	0.7

DeNavas-Walt, Proctor, and Smith indicate that the overall Asian-American poverty rate in 2009 was 12.5% (or 1.7 million people). (See Table 2.1.) The rate was substantially lower than it was in 1987, the first year that the Census Bureau kept statistics on Asian-Americans, when 16.1% lived below the poverty level. Even though the Asian-American poverty rate was higher than the non-Hispanic white rate (9.4%), it had risen just 0.6% since 2008, a smaller rise than what was experienced by other racial and ethnic groups.

The median (the middle value—half are higher and half are lower) household income reflects the disparity in poverty levels between different groups. In 2009 Asian-Americans and non-Hispanic whites had the highest median incomes, at $68,780 and $54,671, respectively. (See Table 2.3.) African-Americans ($33,463), Native Americans and Alaskan Natives ($35,381), and Hispanics ($39,923) had the lowest median household incomes.

Age

CHILD POVERTY. DeNavas-Walt, Proctor, and Smith note that young adults and children under the age of 18 years were the most likely to be poor in 2009. The child poverty rate, at 20.1%, was significantly higher than the

TABLE 2.1

People and families in poverty, by selected characteristics, 2008 and 2009 [CONTINUED]

[Numbers in thousands]

Characteristic	2008			2009			Change in poverty[a]	
	Total	Below poverty		Total	Below poverty		Number	Percent
		Number	Percent		Number	Percent		
Families								
Total	78,874	8,147	10.3	78,867	8,792	11.1	644	0.8
Type of family								
Married-couple	59,137	3,261	5.5	58,428	3,409	5.8	147	0.3
Female householder, no husband present	14,482	4,163	28.7	14,857	4,441	29.9	278	1.1
Male householder, no wife present	5,255	723	13.8	5,582	942	16.9	219	3.1

—Represents or rounds to zero.

[a]Details may not sum to totals because of rounding.

[b]Federal surveys now give respondents the option of reporting more than one race. Therefore, two basic ways of defining a race group are possible. A group such as Asian may be defined as those who reported Asian and no other race (the race-alone or single-race concept) or as those who reported Asian regardless of whether they also reported another race (the race-alone-or-in-combination concept). This table shows data using the first approach (race alone). The use of the single-race population does not imply that it is the preferred method of presenting or analyzing data. The Census Bureau uses a variety of approaches. Information on people who reported more than one race, such as white and American Indian and Alaska Native or Asian and black or African American, is available from Census 2000 through American FactFinder. About 2.6 percent of people reported more than one race in Census 2000. Data for American Indians and Alaska Natives, Native Hawaiians and other Pacific Islanders, and those reporting two or more races are not shown separately.

[c]The "Outside metropolitan statistical areas" category includes both micropolitan statistical areas and territory outside of metropolitan and micropolitan statistical areas.

SOURCE: Carmen DeNavas-Walt, Bernadette D. Proctor, and Jessica C. Smith, "Table 4. People and Families in Poverty by Selected Characteristics: 2008 and 2009," in *Income, Poverty, and Health Insurance Coverage in the United States: 2009*, Current Population Reports, U.S. Census Bureau, September 2010, http://www.census.gov/prod/2010pubs/p60-238.pdf (accessed February 17, 2011)

poverty rate for adults aged 18 to 64 years (12.9%) and adults aged 65 years and older (8.9%) in 2009. Very young children were at the greatest risk of being poor. According to Sylvia A. Allegretto, in "Child Poverty: U.S. Leads Industrialized Nations with Appallingly High Rates" (July 28, 2006, http://www.peoplesworld.org/child-poverty-u-s-leads-industrialized-nations-with-appallingly-high-rates/), the United States has the highest rate of child poverty among the eight richest nations in the world—and its public assistance policies do little to reduce child poverty. Wen-Hao Chen and Miles Corak find in "Child Poverty and Changes in Child Poverty in Rich Countries since 1990" (January 2005, http://www.unicef.org/socialpolicy/files/Child_poverty_and_changes_in_child_poverty_since_90.pdf) that the child poverty rate fell in the United States between 1990 and 2005 because of the structural changes in social assistance that linked social benefits with recipients' work status. For example, the Temporary Assistance for Needy Families program, which was introduced in 1997, requires recipients to work within two years. These changes occurred during a time of robust economic growth, so even though the average benefit levels fell, the average income rose. This analysis highlights the reasons why child poverty rose during the Great Recession: social benefits that were designed to shield children from poverty were tied to parents' labor market participation, so during the period of high unemployment these programs became much less effective.

In 2008 children living with a female householder were particularly likely to live in poverty. Over four out of 10 (43.5%) of these children lived in poverty, compared with 9.9% of children living with married parents. (See Table 2.2.) Younger children living with single mothers were even more likely to be poor. Over half (53.3%) of children aged five years and younger with female-householder parents were poor, compared with 38.7% of children aged six to 17 years. Half (51.9% each) of both African-American and Hispanic children living in female-householder families were poor, compared with 31.7% of non-Hispanic white children living in female-householder families.

Not only are children overrepresented among the poor but also they arguably suffer more from the deprivations of poverty than do adults. Childhood poverty is a matter of great concern because strong evidence suggests that food insecurity and lack of good medical care caused by poverty can limit a child's physical and cognitive development. In addition, poverty is the largest predictor of child abuse and neglect. In fact, the Children's Defense Fund argues in *America's Cradle to Prison Pipeline* (October 2007, http://www.childrensdefense.org/child-research-data-publications/data/cradle-prison-pipeline-report-2007-full-lowres.pdf) that poverty is the driving force behind what it calls the "Cradle to Prison Pipeline," a life cycle in which "so many poor and minority youths are and will remain trapped in a trajectory that leads to marginalized lives, imprisonment and premature death." Moreover, in "Poverty during Early Childhood May Last a Lifetime" (*Discovery News*, February 22, 2010), Jessica Marshall reports on several studies that show that early childhood poverty actually causes changes in the brain that lead to problems in adulthood, including lower adult income.

TABLE 2.2

Percentage of all children and related children living below selected poverty levels by selected characteristics, selected years 1980–2008

Characteristic	1980	1985	1990	1995	2000	2001	2002	2003	2004	2005	2006	2007	2008
Below 100% poverty													
All children[b]	**18.3**	**20.7**	**20.6**	**20.8**	**16.2**	**16.3**	**16.7**	**17.6**	**17.8**	**17.6**	**17.4**	**18.0**	**19.0**
Gender													
Male	18.1	20.3	20.5	20.4	16.0	16.2	16.8	17.7	17.8	17.4	17.2	17.9	18.8
Female	18.6	21.1	20.8	21.2	16.3	16.4	16.6	17.6	17.8	17.8	17.6	18.1	19.2
Age													
Ages 0–5	20.7	23.0	23.6	24.1	18.3	18.4	18.8	20.1	20.3	20.2	20.3	21.1	21.7
Ages 6–17	17.3	19.5	19.0	19.1	15.2	15.3	15.7	16.4	16.6	16.3	16.0	16.5	17.6
Race and Hispanic origin[c]													
White, non-Hispanic	11.8	12.8	12.3	11.2	9.1	9.5	—	—	—	—	—	—	—
White-alone, non-Hispanic	—	—	—	—	—	—	9.4	9.8	10.5	10.0	10.0	10.1	10.6
Black	42.3	43.6	44.8	41.9	31.2	30.2	—	—	—	—	—	—	—
Black-alone	—	—	—	—	—	—	32.3	34.1	33.7	34.5	33.4	34.5	34.7
Hispanic[d]	33.2	40.3	38.4	40.0	28.4	28.0	28.6	29.7	28.9	28.3	26.9	28.6	30.6
Region[e]													
Northeast	16.3	18.5	18.4	19.0	14.5	14.7	15.1	15.3	15.7	15.5	15.7	16.1	16.6
South	22.5	22.8	23.8	23.5	18.4	18.9	19.3	20.3	19.6	19.7	19.4	20.8	20.5
Midwest	16.3	20.7	18.8	16.9	13.1	13.3	13.4	14.9	16.8	15.9	16.3	16.6	18.7
West	16.1	19.3	19.8	22.1	16.9	16.0	17.1	17.8	17.5	17.5	16.6	16.3	18.6
Related children[a]													
Children in all families, total	17.9	20.1	19.9	20.2	15.6	15.8	16.3	17.2	17.3	17.1	16.9	17.6	18.5
Related children ages 0–5	20.3	22.6	23.0	23.7	17.8	18.2	18.5	19.8	20.0	20.0	20.0	20.8	21.3
Related children ages 6–17	16.8	18.8	18.2	18.3	14.5	14.6	15.2	15.9	16.0	15.7	15.4	16.0	17.1
White, non-Hispanic	11.3	12.3	11.6	10.6	8.5	8.9	—	—	—	—	—	—	—
White-alone, non-Hispanic	—	—	—	—	—	—	8.9	9.3	9.9	9.5	9.5	9.7	10.0
Black	42.1	43.1	44.2	41.5	30.9	30.0	—	—	—	—	—	—	—
Black-alone	—	—	—	—	—	—	32.1	33.6	33.4	34.2	33.0	34.3	34.4
Hispanic[d]	33.0	39.6	37.7	39.3	27.6	27.4	28.2	29.5	28.6	27.7	26.6	28.3	30.3
Children in married-couple families, total	—	—	10.2	10.0	8.0	8.0	8.5	8.6	9.0	8.5	8.1	8.5	9.9
Related children ages 0–5	—	—	11.6	11.1	8.7	9.2	9.7	9.6	10.1	9.9	9.4	9.5	11.0
Related children ages 6–17	—	—	9.5	9.4	7.6	7.4	7.8	8.1	8.4	7.7	7.5	8.0	9.2
White, non-Hispanic	—	—	6.8	5.9	4.7	4.7	—	—	—	—	—	—	—
White-alone, non-Hispanic	—	—	—	—	—	—	4.9	4.8	5.2	4.5	4.3	4.7	5.3
Black	—	—	18.1	12.8	8.8	10.1	—	—	—	—	—	—	—
Black-alone	—	—	—	—	—	—	11.5	11.2	12.6	12.5	12.0	11.0	11.0
Hispanic[d]	—	—	26.5	28.4	20.7	19.5	21.2	21.4	20.6	20.1	18.5	19.2	22.1
Children in female-householder families, no husband present, total	50.8	53.6	53.4	50.3	40.1	39.3	39.6	41.8	41.9	42.8	42.1	43.0	43.5
Related children ages 0–5	65.2	65.8	65.5	61.8	50.3	48.9	48.6	52.9	52.5	52.9	52.7	54.0	53.3
Related children ages 6–17	45.5	48.3	47.3	44.6	35.7	35.3	35.9	37.1	37.3	38.3	37.4	37.8	38.7
White, non-Hispanic	—	—	39.6	33.5	28.0	29.0	—	—	—	—	—	—	—
White-alone, non-Hispanic	—	—	—	—	—	—	29.2	30.7	31.5	33.1	32.9	32.4	31.7
Black	64.8	66.9	64.7	61.6	49.3	46.6	—	—	—	—	—	—	—
Black-alone	—	—	—	—	—	—	47.5	49.7	49.2	50.2	49.7	50.4	51.9
Hispanic[d]	65.0	72.4	68.4	65.7	49.8	49.3	47.9	50.6	51.9	50.2	47.2	51.6	51.9
Below 50% poverty													
All children[b]	**6.9**	**8.6**	**8.8**	**8.5**	**6.7**	**7.1**	**6.9**	**7.7**	**7.6**	**7.7**	**7.5**	**7.8**	**8.5**
Gender													
Male	6.9	8.6	8.8	8.4	6.6	6.9	7.1	7.8	7.6	7.3	7.5	7.8	8.4
Female	6.9	8.6	8.8	8.5	6.8	7.2	6.8	7.7	7.7	8.1	7.5	7.8	8.6
Age													
Ages 0–5	8.3	10.0	10.7	10.8	8.1	8.2	8.4	9.7	9.3	9.1	9.4	9.8	10.4
Ages 6–17	6.2	7.8	7.8	7.2	6.0	6.5	6.2	6.7	6.8	7.0	6.5	6.8	7.5
Race and Hispanic origin[c]													
White, non-Hispanic	—	—	5.0	3.9	3.7	3.9	—	—	—	—	—	—	—
White-alone, non-Hispanic	—	—	—	—	—	—	3.6	4.1	4.5	4.1	4.3	4.3	4.5
Black	—	—	22.8	20.6	15.2	16.1	—	—	—	—	—	—	—
Black-alone	—	—	—	—	—	—	15.4	17.9	17.1	17.3	16.0	17.3	17.6
Hispanic[d]	—	—	14.2	16.3	10.2	10.8	11.2	10.9	10.3	11.5	10.3	11.0	12.5

POVERTY AMONG THE ELDERLY. In contrast with children, senior citizens are underrepresented among the poor. DeNavas-Walt, Proctor, and Smith find that in 2009, 8.9% of adults aged 65 years and older were poor, down from 9.7% the year before. Between 1959 and 2009 the number of people aged 65 years and older living in

TABLE 2.2

Percentage of all children and related children living below selected poverty levels by selected characteristics, selected years 1980–2008 [CONTINUED]

Characteristic	1980	1985	1990	1995	2000	2001	2002	2003	2004	2005	2006	2007	2008
Region[e]													
Northeast	4.7	6.5	7.6	8.6	6.4	6.9	6.4	6.9	7.7	7.5	6.4	7.4	7.7
South	9.7	10.9	11.3	10.1	7.9	8.3	8.3	8.6	8.6	9.0	8.5	8.9	9.8
Midwest	6.3	9.5	8.9	6.6	5.5	6.1	6.1	7.0	7.0	6.5	7.3	7.4	8.4
West	5.1	5.6	6.1	7.8	6.2	6.3	6.1	7.5	6.8	7.0	6.8	6.7	7.1
Related children[a]													
Children in all families, total	—	—	8.3	7.9	6.3	6.6	6.6	7.3	7.2	7.2	7.1	7.4	8.1
Related children ages 0–5	—	—	10.3	10.4	7.9	8.1	8.2	9.5	9.1	8.9	9.2	9.6	10.1
Related children ages 6–17	—	—	7.2	6.6	5.5	5.9	5.8	6.2	6.3	6.4	6.0	6.3	7.0
White, non-Hispanic	—	—	4.4	3.4	3.3	3.4	—	—	—	—	—	—	—
White-alone, non-Hispanic	—	—	—	—	—	—	3.3	3.7	4.0	3.6	3.9	3.9	4.1
Black	—	—	22.3	20.1	14.8	15.9	—	—	—	—	—	—	—
Black-alone	—	—	—	—	—	—	15.1	17.4	16.8	16.9	15.7	17.1	17.1
Hispanic[d]	—	—	13.5	15.6	9.4	10.2	10.7	10.6	9.9	10.8	10.0	10.5	12.3
Children in married-couple families, total	—	—	2.7	2.6	2.2	2.3	2.3	2.4	2.5	2.4	2.2	2.6	3.2
Related children ages 0–5	—	—	3.1	2.9	2.2	2.6	2.7	2.8	2.8	2.8	2.8	2.8	3.7
Related children ages 6–17	—	—	2.4	2.5	2.2	2.1	2.1	2.2	2.3	2.1	1.9	2.5	2.9
White, non-Hispanic	—	—	1.9	1.4	1.5	1.5	—	—	—	—	—	—	—
White-alone, non-Hispanic	—	—	—	—	—	—	1.5	1.4	1.8	1.2	1.2	1.4	1.8
Black	—	—	3.9	2.9	3.1	3.3	—	—	—	—	—	—	—
Black-alone	—	—	—	—	—	—	2.8	4.0	3.6	4.5	2.9	4.4	4.4
Hispanic[d]	—	—	6.7	8.6	4.4	4.8	5.2	5.3	3.8	5.2	4.7	5.4	6.3
Children in female-householder families, no husband present, total	—	—	27.7	23.8	18.9	20.4	19.6	21.5	21.7	21.8	21.1	21.2	22.3
Related children ages 0–5	—	—	37.0	33.7	27.9	27.9	27.7	31.4	30.6	29.1	29.5	30.2	30.7
Related children ages 6–17	—	—	23.0	18.9	15.2	17.2	16.2	17.3	17.9	18.5	17.4	17.0	18.3
White, non-Hispanic	—	—	19.1	13.1	12.0	13.3	—	—	—	—	—	—	—
White-alone, non-Hispanic	—	—	—	—	—	—	12.2	14.6	14.6	15.2	16.1	15.9	14.6
Black	—	—	36.8	32.2	24.2	26.6	—	—	—	—	—	—	—
Black-alone	—	—	—	—	—	—	24.9	27.1	27.2	26.1	26.0	25.9	26.8
Hispanic[d]	—	—	31.9	32.5	24.8	25.8	26.3	25.3	27.7	27.7	22.9	24.4	28.5
Below 150% poverty													
All children[b]	**29.9**	**32.3**	**31.4**	**32.2**	**26.7**	**27.5**	**27.9**	**28.6**	**28.2**	**28.2**	**28.6**	**29.3**	**30.5**
Gender													
Male	29.6	32.2	31.3	31.7	26.6	27.3	27.8	28.5	28.1	28.0	28.4	29.2	30.4
Female	30.3	32.3	31.6	32.7	26.8	27.6	28.0	28.8	28.4	28.3	28.8	29.5	30.6
Age													
Ages 0–5	33.2	35.6	34.6	35.5	29.3	30.4	30.8	31.6	31.6	31.5	32.2	33.2	34.0
Ages 6–17	28.4	30.5	29.7	30.5	25.4	26.1	26.6	27.2	26.6	26.5	26.8	27.4	28.8
Race and Hispanic origin[c]													
White, non-Hispanic	—	—	21.4	20.1	16.4	17.4	—	—	—	—	—	—	—
White-alone, non-Hispanic	—	—	—	—	—	—	17.3	17.6	17.5	17.2	17.7	17.8	19.0
Black	—	—	57.9	56.8	45.7	45.8	—	—	—	—	—	—	—
Black-alone	—	—	—	—	—	—	48.0	48.5	48.0	48.8	48.1	49.0	50.5
Hispanic[d]	—	—	56.0	59.4	47.3	46.6	47.3	48.4	47.0	45.9	45.9	47.8	47.7
Region[e]													
Northeast	27.0	28.1	26.7	28.8	23.4	24.5	25.2	24.5	23.4	24.9	24.6	26.0	26.0
South	35.8	36.7	36.0	35.8	29.5	31.0	31.1	32.3	31.3	31.2	31.6	32.8	33.6
Midwest	26.0	31.0	28.7	26.8	21.8	22.8	23.0	24.5	25.6	25.0	26.5	26.3	28.7
West	27.9	30.4	31.4	35.0	29.3	28.4	29.8	29.8	29.5	28.8	28.7	29.0	30.5
Related children[a]													
Children in all families, total	—	—	30.6	31.5	26.1	26.9	27.4	28.1	27.7	27.6	28.1	28.8	29.9
Related children ages 0–5	—	—	33.9	35.1	28.9	30.1	30.5	31.3	31.3	31.2	31.7	32.9	33.5
Related children ages 6–17	—	—	28.8	29.6	24.7	25.4	26.0	26.5	26.0	25.8	26.2	26.8	28.1
White, non-Hispanic	—	—	20.5	19.3	15.8	16.8	—	—	—	—	—	—	—
White-alone, non-Hispanic	—	—	—	—	—	—	16.8	17.0	16.8	16.5	17.1	17.3	18.3
Black	—	—	57.4	56.3	45.4	45.6	—	—	—	—	—	—	—
Black-alone	—	—	—	—	—	—	47.8	48.1	47.7	48.5	47.8	48.9	50.0
Hispanic[d]	—	—	55.4	59.0	46.6	46.1	46.8	48.0	46.8	45.5	45.6	47.4	47.3

poverty dropped significantly, from about 35% to 8.9%. (See Figure 1.2 in Chapter 1.) Most observers credit Social Security for the sharp decline in poverty among the elderly. In contrast to children, senior citizens are now underrepresented among the poor.

Urban Areas

People living in inner cities are the most likely to suffer from poverty. In 2009, 18.7% of people living in inner cities lived below the poverty line. (See Table 2.1.) Only 11% of people who lived in suburban areas (inside

TABLE 2.2

Percentage of all children and related children living below selected poverty levels by selected characteristics, selected years 1980–2008 [CONTINUED]

Characteristic	1980	1985	1990	1995	2000	2001	2002	2003	2004	2005	2006	2007	2008
Children in married-couple families, total	—	—	19.9	19.9	16.2	16.8	17.5	17.6	17.3	17.0	17.1	17.4	18.8
Related children ages 0–5	—	—	22.1	21.3	17.8	19.2	20.0	19.9	20.0	19.7	19.6	19.5	21.2
Related children ages 6–17	—	—	18.7	19.1	15.4	15.6	16.3	16.5	16.0	15.6	15.8	16.3	17.6
White, non-Hispanic	—	—	14.6	13.4	10.0	10.6	—	—	—	—	—	—	—
White-alone, non-Hispanic	—	—	—	—	—	—	10.9	10.9	10.4	10.0	10.2	10.3	11.7
Black	—	—	31.7	26.2	20.7	21.3	—	—	—	—	—	—	—
Black-alone	—	—	—	—	—	—	25.0	22.0	22.7	23.3	23.1	21.2	23.0
Hispanic[d]	—	—	46.5	49.8	39.4	38.7	39.8	40.9	39.6	38.5	37.4	38.7	38.4
Children in female-householder families, no husband present, total	—	—	66.9	65.2	57.2	57.3	56.7	58.0	57.6	58.6	59.4	60.5	61.1
Related children ages 0–5	—	—	76.7	75.1	66.8	66.4	65.2	68.1	67.9	68.6	69.2	71.3	70.4
Related children ages 6–17	—	—	62.0	60.3	53.2	53.5	53.1	53.7	53.3	54.3	55.0	55.4	56.6
White, non-Hispanic	—	—	54.4	48.6	44.1	46.1	—	—	—	—	—	—	—
White-alone, non-Hispanic	—	—	—	—	—	—	45.0	45.6	46.0	46.8	48.3	49.1	48.7
Black	—	—	77.1	76.2	66.2	65.9	—	—	—	—	—	—	—
Black-alone	—	—	—	—	—	—	64.9	66.8	66.4	67.1	67.6	68.0	69.7
Hispanic[d]	—	—	80.3	81.6	70.1	65.9	66.0	68.2	68.0	66.9	67.1	69.7	70.1
Below 200% poverty													
All children[b]	**42.3**	**43.5**	**42.4**	**43.3**	**37.5**	**38.2**	**38.3**	**39.1**	**39.3**	**38.9**	**39.0**	**39.2**	**40.6**
Gender													
Male	42.3	43.2	42.5	43.1	37.5	38.1	38.3	38.8	39.0	38.6	38.8	39.1	40.4
Female	42.4	43.7	42.3	43.5	37.6	38.2	38.2	39.5	39.6	39.3	39.2	39.3	40.8
Age													
Ages 0–5	46.8	47.1	46.0	46.7	41.0	41.7	41.5	42.2	42.6	42.4	42.9	42.9	44.0
Ages 6–17	40.3	41.6	40.5	41.5	35.9	36.5	36.7	37.6	37.6	37.3	37.1	37.3	38.8
Race and Hispanic origin[c]													
White, non-Hispanic	—	—	32.3	30.5	25.5	26.7	—	—	—	—	—	—	—
White-alone, non-Hispanic	—	—	—	—	—	—	26.0	26.4	26.8	26.2	26.3	26.2	27.3
Black	—	—	68.3	68.1	59.2	57.3	—	—	—	—	—	—	—
Black-alone	—	—	—	—	—	—	59.5	61.3	60.6	61.3	60.2	60.6	60.9
Hispanic[d]	—	—	69.5	72.9	62.6	61.5	62.0	62.6	62.2	60.7	61.0	60.8	62.0
Region[e]													
Northeast	39.1	37.5	36.3	38.2	33.0	33.6	33.8	34.3	32.6	33.9	34.1	35.1	34.3
South	47.8	48.6	47.7	48.4	41.6	42.4	42.3	43.5	42.7	42.5	42.4	42.6	44.3
Midwest	39.1	42.5	39.6	36.9	31.2	32.5	33.4	34.2	36.3	35.3	35.9	36.4	38.4
West	40.5	41.7	42.7	46.1	40.5	40.0	40.2	40.6	41.6	40.5	40.1	39.4	41.1
Related children[a]													
Children in all families, total	—	—	41.7	42.6	36.9	37.6	37.8	38.6	38.7	38.4	38.5	38.7	40.0
Related children ages 0–5	—	—	45.4	46.3	40.5	41.4	41.2	42.0	42.3	42.1	42.5	42.6	43.6
Related children ages 6–17	—	—	39.6	40.7	35.2	35.8	36.1	37.0	36.9	36.6	36.5	36.7	38.2
White, non-Hispanic	—	—	31.4	29.8	24.8	26.0	—	—	—	—	—	—	—
White-alone, non-Hispanic	—	—	—	—	—	—	25.4	25.9	26.1	25.6	25.6	25.5	26.6
Black	—	—	67.9	67.8	58.9	57.2	—	—	—	—	—	—	—
Black-alone	—	—	—	—	—	—	59.3	60.9	60.3	61.1	60.0	60.5	60.5
Hispanic[d]	—	—	69.1	72.5	62.1	61.1	61.7	62.3	62.1	60.3	60.7	60.4	61.6
Children in married-couple families, total	—	—	31.2	31.0	26.4	26.7	26.9	27.2	27.4	27.0	26.6	26.3	28.3
Related children ages 0–5	—	—	34.3	33.2	29.1	30.0	30.3	30.3	30.5	30.1	30.1	28.9	31.2
Related children ages 6–17	—	—	29.5	29.9	25.1	25.0	25.1	25.7	25.8	25.4	24.8	24.9	26.8
White, non-Hispanic	—	—	25.2	23.3	18.2	18.8	—	—	—	—	—	—	—
White-alone, non-Hispanic	—	—	—	—	—	—	18.5	18.6	18.4	18.1	17.7	17.4	19.0
Black	—	—	44.6	39.1	35.9	32.9	—	—	—	—	—	—	—
Black-alone	—	—	—	—	—	—	35.8	35.9	35.6	35.7	34.9	33.2	34.0
Hispanic[d]	—	—	62.0	65.9	55.4	54.0	55.6	55.7	55.6	54.1	53.3	52.1	54.3

metropolitan statistical areas but outside principal cities) lived below the poverty line. In rural areas the poverty rate was also high, at 16.6%.

Family Status

In 2009 people living in families (12.5%) were much less likely than people living in unrelated subfamilies (51.1%) or in households with unrelated individuals (22%) to suffer from poverty. (See Table 2.1.) However, there was a major variation in the poverty rate between different family structures. Whereas 12.5% of families in the United States were living in poverty in 2009, families headed by married couples had the lowest poverty rate (5.8%). Three out of 10 (29.9%) families with a female householder (no husband present) were living in poverty. Male households were also more likely than married-couple families to be in poverty (16.9%), but they were much less likely than female householders to

TABLE 2.2

Percentage of all children and related children living below selected poverty levels by selected characteristics, selected years 1980–2008 [CONTINUED]

Characteristic	1980	1985	1990	1995	2000	2001	2002	2003	2004	2005	2006	2007	2008
Children in female-householder families, no husband present, total	—	—	77.0	76.0	69.4	69.9	68.9	70.2	70.5	71.0	71.6	72.1	71.9
Related children ages 0–5	—	—	85.1	84.1	78.3	78.5	76.1	78.4	78.8	79.9	79.9	80.7	79.0
Related children ages 6–17	—	—	72.9	72.0	65.6	66.3	65.9	66.8	67.0	67.1	67.8	68.1	68.6
White, non-Hispanic	—	—	66.5	61.3	56.0	59.3	—	—	—	—	—	—	—
White-alone, non-Hispanic	—	—	—	—	—	—	58.2	58.8	59.6	59.3	60.8	61.0	60.1
Black	—	—	85.6	86.8	78.6	77.0	—	—	—	—	—	—	—
Black-alone	—	—	—	—	—	—	76.1	78.4	78.9	78.8	79.0	79.5	79.5
Hispanic[d]	—	—	88.9	88.3	82.4	79.9	78.5	80.3	80.1	80.3	79.7	81.0	80.2

— Not available.

[a]Related children are persons ages 0–17 who are related to the householder (or subfamily reference person) by birth, marriage, or adoption, but are not themselves householders, spouses, or reference persons.

[b]Includes children not related to the householder.

[c]For race and Hispanic-origin data in this table: From 1980 to 2002, following the 1977 Office of Management and Budget (OMB) standards for collecting and presenting data on race, the Current Population Survey (CPS) asked respondents to choose one race from the following: White, black, American Indian or Alaskan Native, or Asian or Pacific Islander. The Census Bureau also offered an "Other" category. Beginning in 2003, following the 1997 OMB standards for collecting and presenting data on race, the CPS asked respondents to choose one or more races from the following: White, black, or African American, Asian, American Indian or Alaska Native, or Native Hawaiian or other Pacific Islander. All race groups discussed in this table from 2002 onward refer to people who indicated only one racial identity within the racial categories presented. People who responded to the question on race by indicating only one race are referred to as the race-alone population. The use of the race-alone population in this table does not imply that it is the preferred method of presenting or analyzing data. Data from 2002 onward are not directly comparable with data from earlier years. Data on race and Hispanic origin are collected separately.

[d]Persons of Hispanic origin may be of any race.

[e]Regions: Northeast includes CT, MA, ME, NH, NJ, NY, PA, RI, and VT. South includes AL, AR, DC, DE, FL, GA, KY, LA, MD, MS, NC, OK, SC, TN, TX, VA, and WV. Midwest includes IA, IL, IN, KS, MI, MN, MO, ND, NE, OH, SD, and WI. West includes AK, AZ, CA, CO, HI, ID, MT, NM, NV, OR, UT, WA, and WY.

Note: The 2004 data have been revised to reflect a correction to the weights in the 2005 Annual Social and Economic Supplement (ASEC). Data for 1999, 2000, and 2001 use Census 2000 population controls. Data for 2000 onward are from the expanded Current Population Survey (CPS) sample. The poverty level is based on money income and does not include non-cash benefits, such as food stamps. Poverty thresholds reflect family size and composition and are adjusted each year using the annual average Consumer Price Index level. The average poverty threshold for a family of four was $22,025 in 2008. The levels shown here are derived from the ratio of the family's income to the family's poverty threshold.

SOURCE: Adapted from "Table ECON1.A. Child Poverty: Percentage of All Children and Related Children Ages 0–17 Living below Selected Poverty Levels by Selected Characteristics, 1980–2008," in *America's Children in Brief: Key National Indicators of Well-Being, 2010*, Federal Interagency Forum on Child and Family Statistics, July 2010, http://www.childstats.gov/americaschildren/tables.asp (accessed February 18, 2011).

TABLE 2.3

Median household income in the past 12 months by race and Hispanic origin, 2009

[Household income by race and Hispanic or Latino origin of householder]

Subject	Total	Median income (dollars)
Households	**113,616,229**	**50,221**
One race—		
White	78.6%	53,131
Black or African American	11.9%	33,463
American Indian and Alaska Native	0.7%	35,381
Asian	3.8%	68,780
Native Hawaiian and Other Pacific Islander	0.1%	53,455
Some other race	3.4%	39,122
Two or more races	1.5%	44,014
Hispanic or Latino origin (of any race)	11.2%	39,923
White alone, not Hispanic or Latino	71.4%	54,671

SOURCE: Adapted from "S1903. Median Income in the Past 12 Months (in 2009 Inflation-Adjusted Dollars)," in *2009 American Community Survey*, U.S. Census Bureau, 2010, http://factfinder.census.gov/servlet/STTable?_bm=y&-qr_name=ACS_2009_1YR_G00_S1903&-geo_id=01000US&-ds_name=ACS_2009_1YR_G00_&-_lang=en&-format=&-CONTEXT=st (accessed February 18, 2011).

SINGLE-PARENT FAMILIES. An increasing number of children are being raised by one parent, usually the mother. The proportion of single-parent families steadily increased between 1970 and the early 1990s, whereas the proportion of married-couple families continued to decline. Since then, the structure of U.S. households and families has remained relatively stable. According to the Census Bureau, in *America's Families and Living Arrangements: 2010* (November 2010, http://www.census.gov/population/www/socdemo/hh-fam.html), in 1970 single-parent families with children under the age of 18 years made up 6.4% of the total number of families, whereas married-couple families accounted for 49.6%. By 1990 the proportion of single-parent families had increased to 11.7%, and married-couple families had decreased to 37.1%. In 2010 single-parent families had risen slightly to 13.5%, whereas married-couple families had dropped to 31.2%. Table 2.4 shows that in 2010 there were two and a half times as many single female-headed families (14.8 million) as there were single male-headed families (5.6 million).

One factor in the rise of single-parent families is the rise in the divorce rate. Jason Fields of the Census Bureau indicates in *America's Families and Living Arrangements: 2003* (November 2004, http://www.census.gov/prod/2004pubs/p20-553.pdf) that in 1970 only 3.5% of

have incomes below the poverty line. Single parents were much more likely to have household incomes below the poverty line if they did not work full time. (See Figure 2.1.)

FIGURE 2.1

Employment status of custodial parents, by poverty status, selected years 1993–2007

[Percent]

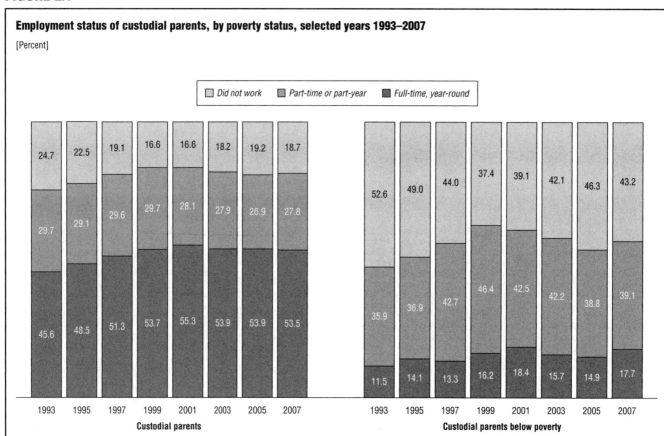

SOURCE: Timothy S. Grall, "Figure 2. Employment Status of Custodial Parents by Poverty Status: 1993 to 2007," in *Custodial Mothers and Fathers and Their Child Support: 2007,* Current Population Reports, U.S. Census Bureau, November 2009, http://www.census.gov/prod/2009pubs/p60-237.pdf (accessed February 18, 2011)

men and 5.7% of women were separated or divorced. By 2009, 9.9% of men and 13.3% of women were divorced and had not remarried. (See Table 2.5.) The percentage of divorced women is consistently higher than the percentage of divorced men because divorced men are more likely to remarry, whereas divorced women are more likely to raise the children from the first marriage. As Table 2.6 shows, in 2007 there were 11.4 million female custodial parents and only 2.4 million male custodial parents; in other words, 82.6% of custodial parents were mothers.

Another reason for the rise in single-parent families is the rise in people who never marry yet still have children. In *Families and Living Arrangements*, the Census Bureau indicates that the percentage of males aged 15 years and older who had never married rose from 28.1% in 1970 to 34.2% in 2010, whereas the percentage of females aged 15 years and older who had never married rose from 22.1% in 1970 to 27.4% in 2010. The proportion of those who have never married has increased as young adults delay the age at which they marry. The Census Bureau reports that between 1970 and 2010 the median age at first marriage rose from 20.8 years to 26.1 years for women, and from

23.2 years to 28.2 years for men. In addition, the proportion of all households that were unmarried-partner heterosexual households steadily rose between 1996 and 2010, from 2.9% to 6.4% of all households. Well over one-third (37.8%) of these households had children in 2010. (See Table 2.7.)

Single-parent women were more likely than single-parent men to have never been married. In 2010, 44.8% of single mothers and 29.5% of single fathers had never been married. (See Table 2.8.)

African-American children are far more likely to live with a single parent than are non-Hispanic white or Hispanic children. In 2010, 3.9 million of a total 11.3 million African-American children lived with married parents, 5.6 million lived with their mother only, and 405,000 lived with their father only. (See Table 2.9.) Therefore, 53.1% of African-American children lived with one parent. In contrast, 10.3 million of a total 16.9 million Hispanic children lived with married parents, 4.5 million lived with their mother only, and 462,000 lived with their father only. Therefore, 29.4% of Hispanic children lived with one parent. An even smaller proportion of non-Hispanic white

TABLE 2.4

Households by type and selected characteristics, 2010

[Numbers in thousands]

		Family households				Nonfamily households		
	Total	**Total**	**Married couple**	**Male householder**	**Female householder**	**Total**	**Male householder**	**Female householder**
All households	117,538	78,833	58,410	5,580	14,843	38,705	18,263	20,442
Size of household								
One member	31,399	—	—	—	—	31,399	13,971	17,428
Two members	39,487	33,592	25,299	2,295	5,998	5,895	3,283	2,612
Three members	18,638	17,770	11,627	1,646	4,497	868	611	258
Four members	16,122	15,764	12,394	891	2,479	357	260	98
Five members	7,367	7,246	5,731	443	1,071	121	96	25
Six members	2,784	2,746	2,113	173	459	38	30	9
Seven or more members	1,740	1,715	1,245	132	338	24	12	12
Number of nonrelatives in household								
No nonrelatives	105,695	74,296	57,577	4,066	12,653	31,399	13,971	17,428
One nonrelative	9,747	3,851	651	1,240	1,961	5,895	3,283	2,612
Two nonrelatives	1,323	455	112	173	169	868	611	258
Three or more nonrelatives	773	231	70	100	61	542	397	144
Race of householder								
White alone	95,489	64,120	50,163	4,194	9,762	31,369	14,902	16,467
Black alone	14,730	9,358	4,274	939	4,145	5,372	2,374	2,998
Asian alone	4,687	3,592	2,888	257	447	1,095	564	531
All remaining single races and all race combinations	2,632	1,763	1,084	190	489	869	423	446
Hispanic origin of householder								
Hispanic[a]	13,298	10,412	6,589	1,079	2,745	2,885	1,625	1,260
White alone, non-Hispanic	83,158	54,445	43,954	3,200	7,291	28,712	13,396	15,317
Other non-Hispanic	21,083	13,975	7,867	1,300	4,808	7,107	3,242	3,866
White alone or combination householder								
White alone or in combination with one or more other races	96,823	64,987	50,718	4,270	9,999	31,836	15,123	16,713
Other	20,715	13,846	7,692	1,310	4,844	6,869	3,140	3,729
Black alone or combination householder								
Black alone or in combination with one or more other races	15,212	9,652	4,427	968	4,257	5,560	2,457	3,103
Other	102,326	69,181	53,983	4,612	10,586	33,145	15,805	17,340
Asian alone or combination householder								
Asian alone or in combination with one or more other races	4,940	3,742	2,987	273	481	1,198	617	581
Other	112,598	75,091	55,423	5,307	14,362	37,507	17,646	19,861
Marital status of householder								
Married, spouse present	58,410	58,410	58,410	—	—	—	—	—
Married, spouse absent[b]	1,844	830	—	238	592	1,014	583	431
Widowed	11,823	2,936	—	572	2,364	8,887	1,871	7,016
Divorced	17,594	6,537	—	1,686	4,851	11,057	5,412	5,646
Separated[c]	3,625	1,936	—	386	1,550	1,689	998	691
Never married	24,242	8,185	—	2,698	5,486	16,058	9,399	6,658
Tenure								
Own/buying	78,779	58,373	47,964	3,175	7,234	20,407	8,945	11,462
Rent	37,080	19,616	9,900	2,324	7,391	17,464	8,877	8,587
No cash rent	1,679	845	545	82	218	834	441	394

—Rounds to zero.
[a]Hispanics may be of any race.
[b]In past reports: married spouse absent—other (excluding separated).
[c]In past reports: married spouse absent—separated.

SOURCE: "Table H1. Households by Type and Tenure of Householder for Selected Characteristics: 2010," in *America's Families and Living Arrangements: 2010*, U.S. Census Bureau, November 2010, http://www.census.gov/population/www/socdemo/hh-fam/cps2010.html (accessed February 18, 2011)

children lived with a single parent. In 2010, 30.8 million of a total 41.1 million non-Hispanic white children lived with married parents, 6.4 million lived with their mother only, and 1.6 million lived with their father only. Therefore, only 19.5% lived with one parent in 2010.

Moreover, in 2010 a higher percentage of African-American children than non-Hispanic white children or Hispanic children lived with neither parent. In that year, 843,000 (7.5%) African-American children, 677,000 (4%) Hispanic children, and 1.3 million (3.1%) non-Hispanic

TABLE 2.5

Marital status of the population 18 years old and over by sex, race, and Hispanic origin, selected years 1990–2009

[In millions, except percent (181.8 represents 181,800,000)]

Marital status, race and Hispanic origin	Total				Male				Female			
	1990	2000	2005	2009	1990	2000	2005	2009	1990	2000	2005	2009
Total[a]	181.8	201.8	217.2	226.9	86.9	96.9	104.8	110.0	95.0	104.9	112.3	116.9
Never married	40.4	48.2	53.9	59.1	22.4	26.1	29.6	32.4	17.9	22.1	24.3	26.7
Married[b]	112.6	120.1	127.4	130.3	55.8	59.6	63.3	64.8	56.7	60.4	64.0	65.5
Widowed	13.8	13.7	13.8	14.2	2.3	2.6	2.7	2.8	11.5	11.1	11.1	11.4
Divorced	15.1	19.8	22.1	23.2	6.3	8.5	9.2	9.9	8.8	11.3	12.9	13.3
Percent of total	100.0	100.0	100.0	100.0	100.0	100.0	100.0	100.0	100.0	100.0	100.0	100.0
Never married	22.2	23.9	24.8	26.1	25.8	27.0	28.2	29.5	18.9	21.1	21.6	22.8
Married[b]	61.9	59.5	58.6	57.4	64.3	61.5	60.4	58.9	59.7	57.6	56.9	56.0
Widowed	7.6	6.8	6.4	6.3	2.7	2.7	2.6	2.6	12.1	10.5	9.9	9.8
Divorced	8.3	9.8	10.2	10.2	7.2	8.8	8.8	9.0	9.3	10.8	11.5	11.4
White, total[c]	155.5	168.1	177.5	184.3	74.8	81.6	86.6	90.4	80.6	86.6	90.9	93.9
Never married	31.6	36.0	39.7	43.5	18.0	20.3	22.6	24.8	13.6	15.7	17.0	18.7
Married[b]	99.5	104.1	108.3	110.0	49.5	51.8	54.0	55.0	49.9	52.2	54.2	55.0
Widowed	11.7	11.5	11.5	11.8	1.9	2.2	2.3	2.4	9.8	9.3	9.2	9.4
Divorced	12.6	16.5	18.1	19.1	5.4	7.2	7.6	8.3	7.3	9.3	10.4	10.7
Percent of total	100.0	100.0	100.0	100.0	100.0	100.0	100.0	100.0	100.0	100.0	100.0	100.0
Never married	20.3	21.4	22.3	23.6	24.1	24.9	26.1	27.4	16.9	18.1	18.7	19.9
Married[b]	64.0	62.0	61.0	59.7	66.2	63.5	62.4	60.8	61.9	60.3	59.7	58.6
Widowed	7.5	6.8	6.5	6.4	2.6	2.7	2.6	2.6	12.2	10.8	10.2	10.0
Divorced	8.1	9.8	10.2	10.3	7.2	8.8	8.8	9.2	9.0	10.7	11.5	11.4
Black, total[c]	20.3	24.0	25.2	26.8	9.1	10.7	11.2	12.0	11.2	13.3	13.9	14.7
Never married	7.1	9.5	10.2	11.2	3.5	4.3	4.7	5.2	3.6	5.1	5.5	6.0
Married[b]	9.3	10.1	10.3	10.8	4.5	5.0	5.0	5.3	4.8	5.1	5.2	5.5
Widowed	1.7	1.7	1.7	1.7	0.3	0.3	0.3	0.3	1.4	1.4	1.4	1.4
Divorced	2.1	2.8	2.9	3.1	0.8	1.1	1.1	1.2	1.3	1.7	1.8	1.9
Percent of total	100.0	100.0	100.0	100.0	100.0	100.0	100.0	100.0	100.0	100.0	100.0	100.0
Never married	35.1	39.4	40.6	41.9	38.4	40.2	42.0	43.3	32.5	38.3	39.5	40.7
Married[b]	45.8	42.1	41.0	40.2	49.2	46.7	45.5	44.0	43.0	38.3	37.4	37.2
Widowed	8.5	7.0	6.6	6.5	3.7	2.8	2.7	2.7	12.4	10.5	10.0	9.5
Divorced	10.6	11.5	11.7	11.4	8.8	10.3	9.8	10.0	12.0	12.8	13.3	12.6
Asian, total[c]	(NA)	(NA)	9.4	10.2	(NA)	(NA)	4.5	4.8	(NA)	(NA)	4.9	5.4
Never married	(NA)	(NA)	2.3	2.4	(NA)	(NA)	1.3	1.4	(NA)	(NA)	1.0	1.1
Married[b]	(NA)	(NA)	6.2	6.9	(NA)	(NA)	2.9	3.2	(NA)	(NA)	3.3	3.7
Widowed	(NA)	(NA)	0.4	0.5	(NA)	(NA)	0.1	0.1	(NA)	(NA)	0.3	0.4
Divorced	(NA)	(NA)	0.5	0.5	(NA)	(NA)	0.2	0.2	(NA)	(NA)	0.3	0.3
Percent of total	100.0	100.0	100.0	100.0	100.0	100.0	100.0	100.0	100.0	100.0	100.0	100.0
Never married	(NA)	(NA)	24.8	23.7	(NA)	(NA)	29.7	28.4	(NA)	(NA)	20.3	19.4
Married[b]	(NA)	(NA)	65.6	67.1	(NA)	(NA)	64.7	66.6	(NA)	(NA)	66.5	67.6
Widowed	(NA)	(NA)	4.3	4.8	(NA)	(NA)	1.3	1.6	(NA)	(NA)	6.7	7.6
Divorced	(NA)	(NA)	5.3	4.4	(NA)	(NA)	4.1	3.4	(NA)	(NA)	6.4	5.4
Hispanic, total[d]	13.6	21.1	27.5	31.0	6.7	10.4	14.1	16.0	6.8	10.7	13.4	15.0
Never married	3.7	5.9	8.6	10.1	2.2	3.4	5.2	6.0	1.5	2.5	3.4	4.1
Married[b]	8.4	12.7	15.6	17.4	4.1	6.2	7.8	8.7	4.3	6.5	7.8	8.7
Widowed	0.5	0.9	1.0	1.1	0.1	0.2	0.2	0.2	0.4	0.7	0.8	0.9
Divorced	1.0	1.6	2.2	2.5	0.4	0.7	0.9	1.1	0.6	1.0	1.3	1.4
Percent of total	100.0	100.0	100.0	100.0	100.0	100.0	100.0	100.0	100.0	100.0	100.0	100.0
Never married	27.2	28.0	31.3	32.4	32.1	32.3	36.7	37.5	22.5	23.4	25.6	27.1
Married[b]	61.7	60.2	57.0	56.1	60.9	59.7	55.6	54.5	62.4	60.7	58.7	57.9
Widowed	4.0	4.2	3.7	3.4	1.5	1.6	1.5	1.3	6.5	6.5	6.1	5.7
Divorced	7.0	7.6	7.9	8.0	5.5	6.4	6.3	6.8	8.5	9.3	9.7	9.4

white children lived with neither parent. (See Table 2.9.) In part, this is because African-American children are more likely than children from other racial groups to live with grandparents without the presence of either parent; African-American children are also more likely than other children to live in foster care.

CHILD SUPPORT. Child support is becoming an increasingly important source of income for single mothers because of the time limits now in place for receiving cash assistance. In 2007, 56.9% of custodial mothers and 40.4% of custodial fathers had child support awards. (See Table 2.6.) However, less than half of all custodial parents received all child support payments due them (45% of custodial fathers and 47.1% of custodial mothers). Almost a quarter (23.4%) of all custodial mothers and over a quarter (25.8%) of all custodial fathers due child support payments received none at all.

TABLE 2.5

Marital status of the population 18 years old and over by sex, race, and Hispanic origin, selected years 1990–2009 [CONTINUED]

[In millions, except percent (181.8 represents 181,800,000)]

Marital status, race and Hispanic origin	Total				Male				Female			
	1990	2000	2005	2009	1990	2000	2005	2009	1990	2000	2005	2009
Non-Hispanic white, total[c, d]	**(NA)**	**(NA)**	**151.9**	**155.6**	**(NA)**	**(NA)**	**73.4**	**75.5**	**(NA)**	**(NA)**	**78.5**	**80.0**
Never married	(NA)	(NA)	31.8	34.3	(NA)	(NA)	17.8	19.3	(NA)	(NA)	13.9	15.0
Married[b]	(NA)	(NA)	93.5	93.7	(NA)	(NA)	46.6	46.8	(NA)	(NA)	47.0	46.9
Widowed	(NA)	(NA)	10.6	10.8	(NA)	(NA)	2.1	2.2	(NA)	(NA)	8.5	8.6
Divorced	(NA)	(NA)	16.0	16.8	(NA)	(NA)	6.8	7.3	(NA)	(NA)	9.2	9.5
Percent of total	**100.0**	**100.0**	**100.0**	**100.0**	**100.0**	**100.0**	**100.0**	**100.0**	**100.0**	**100.0**	**100.0**	**100.0**
Never married	(NA)	(NA)	20.9	22.1	(NA)	(NA)	24.3	25.5	(NA)	(NA)	17.7	18.8
Married[b]	(NA)	(NA)	61.5	60.2	(NA)	(NA)	63.5	62.0	(NA)	(NA)	59.7	58.6
Widowed	(NA)	(NA)	6.9	6.9	(NA)	(NA)	2.8	2.9	(NA)	(NA)	10.8	10.8
Divorced	(NA)	(NA)	10.6	10.8	(NA)	(NA)	9.3	9.7	(NA)	(NA)	11.7	11.8

NA = Not available.
[a]Includes persons of other races not shown separately.
[b]Includes persons who are married with spouse present, married with spouse absent, and separated.
[c]Beginning 2005, data represent persons who selected this race group only and exclude persons reporting more than one race. The Current Population Survey in 1990 and 2000 only allowed respondents to report one race group.
[d]Hispanic persons may be any race.
Notes: Excludes members of Armed Forces except those living off post or with their families on post. Beginning 2005, population controls based on Census 2000 and an expanded sample of households. Based on Current Population Survey.

SOURCE: "Table 56. Marital Status of the Population by Sex, Race, and Hispanic Origin: 1990 to 2009," in *Statistical Abstract of the United States: 2011*, 130th ed., U.S. Census Bureau, 2010, http://www.census.gov/compendia/statab/2011/tables/11s0056.pdf (accessed February 18, 2011)

Child support is often not enough to keep custodial mothers and their children out of poverty. According to the Census Bureau, between 1993 and 2001 the percent of custodial parents and their children living below the poverty level declined from 33.3% to 23.4%, and then remained statistically unchanged between 2001 and 2007. (See Figure 2.2.) However, the poverty rate among custodial mothers (27%) remained significantly higher than the poverty rate among custodial fathers (12.9%) in 2007.

The Census Bureau further breaks down whether custodial parents received their child support payments based on if their families were below the poverty level in 2007. A lower proportion of custodial parents with incomes below the poverty level (53.7%) received child support payments in 2007 than did all custodial parents (62.7%). (See Table 2.6.) In addition, a lower proportion of the poor custodial parents (40.2%) than all custodial parents (46.8%) received the full amount of child support due them.

The average amount of child support due to custodial mothers in 2007 was $5,366; they actually received an average of $3,355. (See Table 2.6.) The average amount of child support due to custodial fathers in 2007 was $5,239; they actually received an average of $3,343. According to the Census Bureau (January 2011, http://www.census.gov/compendia/statab/2011/tables/11s0566.pdf), the mean (average) total income of custodial parents who received no child support payments in 2007 was $29,261; among those who received at least some of the support due them it was $28,983, and among those with no support agreements it was $28,515.

By Race

The poverty rate differs among racial and ethnic groups. DeNavas-Walt, Proctor, and Smith find that in 2009 non-Hispanic whites had the lowest rate, at 9.4%, followed by Asian-Americans, at 12.5%. (See Table 2.1.) In contrast, more than a quarter of Hispanics (25.3%) and African-Americans (25.8%) lived in poverty. In addition, African-Americans and Hispanics were much more likely to be desperately poor or have incomes below 0.50 of the poverty level. Over one out of 10 African-Americans (11.9%) and Hispanics (10.4%) were desperately poor in 2009. (See Table 1.3 in Chapter 1.) Non-Hispanic whites (4.1%) and Asian-Americans (6.2%) had much lower rates of desperate poverty.

Work Experience

The probability of a family living in poverty is influenced by three primary factors: the size of the family, the number of workers, and the characteristics of the wage earners. As the number of wage earners in a family increases, the probability of poverty declines. The likelihood of a second wage earner is greatest in families that are headed by married couples.

In 2008 most Americans aged 16 years and older worked at some point during the year (160.7 million of 235.1 million, or 68.3%). (See Table 2.10.) Seven percent of all Americans who worked at some point during the year lived in poverty, compared with 21.4% of those who did not work that year. The rate of poverty was higher for those who worked only 26 weeks or less (18.4%) than for those who worked 27 weeks or more (6%). However, the

TABLE 2.6

Demographic characteristics of custodial parents by award status and payments received, 2007

[Numbers in thousands]

Characteristic	Total	With child support agreements or awards									
		Total	Percent	Due child support payments in 2007							
				Total	Average due (in dollars)	Average received (in dollars)	Percent received	Received all payments		Did not receive payments	
								Total	Percent	Total	Percent
Total	13,743	7,428	54.0	6,375	5,350	3,354	62.7	2,986	46.8	1,511	23.7
Sex											
Male	2,387	965	40.4	825	5,239	3,343	63.8	371	45.0	213	25.8
Female	11,356	6,463	56.9	5,551	5,366	3,355	62.5	2,615	47.1	1,298	23.4
Age											
Under 30 years	3,214	1,422	44.2	1,248	3,837	1,940	50.6	399	32.0	378	30.3
30 to 39 years	4,767	2,775	58.2	2,472	4,978	3,086	62.0	1,137	46.0	481	19.5
40 years and over	5,762	3,231	56.1	2,655	6,407	4,267	66.6	1,450	54.6	652	24.6
Race and ethnicity[a]											
White alone	9,519	5,471	57.5	4,780	5,650	3,710	65.7	2,323	48.6	1,081	22.6
White alone, not Hispanic	7,409	4,493	60.6	3,924	5,807	3,815	65.7	1,936	49.3	850	21.7
Black alone	3,431	1,563	45.6	1,276	3,980	2,185	54.9	532	41.7	362	28.4
Hispanic (any race)	2,334	1,052	45.1	911	5,430	3,267	60.2	408	44.8	248	27.2
Current marital status[b]											
Married	2,643	1,603	60.7	1,417	5,506	3,877	70.4	695	49.0	288	20.3
Divorced	4,790	3,010	62.8	2,640	5,823	3,756	64.5	1,352	51.2	643	24.4
Separated	1,712	798	46.6	633	6,116	3,419	55.9	270	42.7	132	20.9
Never married	4,380	1,904	43.5	1,587	4,163	2,207	53.0	629	39.6	420	26.5
Educational attainment											
Less than high school diploma	2,104	898	42.7	716	4,621	2,047	44.3	260	36.3	215	30.0
High school graduate	4,776	2,479	51.9	2,080	4,872	2,868	58.9	854	41.1	492	23.7
Less than 4 years of college	4,585	2,657	57.9	2,326	5,278	3,371	63.9	1,107	47.6	555	23.9
Bachelor's degree or more	2,279	1,394	61.2	1,253	6,691	4,874	72.8	766	61.1	248	19.8
Selected characteristics											
Family income below 2007 poverty level	3,375	1,580	46.8	1,278	4,380	2,352	53.7	514	40.2	392	30.7
Worked full-time, year-round	7,368	4,156	56.4	3,638	5,353	3,537	66.1	1,793	49.3	849	23.3
Public assistance program participation[c]	4,323	2,057	47.6	1,732	4,294	2,203	51.3	597	34.5	499	28.8
With one child	7,784	3,808	48.9	3,235	4,994	3,138	62.8	1,569	48.5	760	23.5
With two or more children	5,960	3,620	60.7	3,140	5,716	3,576	62.6	1,417	45.1	751	23.9
Child had contact with other parent in 2007	8,883	5,148	58.0	4,483	5,591	3,804	68.0	2,300	51.3	876	19.5

[a]Includes those reporting one race alone and not in combination with any other race.
[b]Excludes 218,000 with marital status of widowed.
[c]Received either Medicaid, food stamps, public housing or rent subsidy, Temporary Assistance for Needy Families (TANF), or general assistance.
Note: Parents living with own children under 21 years of age whose other parent is not living in the home.

SOURCE: Timothy S. Grall, "Table 2. Demographic Characteristics of Custodial Parents by Award Status and Payments Received: 2007," in *Custodial Mothers and Fathers and Their Child Support: 2007*, Current Population Reports, U.S. Census Bureau, November 2009, http://www.census.gov/prod/2009pubs/p60-237.pdf (accessed February 18, 2011)

poverty rate among individuals who worked 27 weeks or more was up significantly from 2007, when it was 5.1%. (See Table 2.11.)

Most poor children live in families in which one or more adults work. However, millions of working parents are not able to earn enough to lift their families out of poverty—even those who work full time all year.

Education

Not surprisingly, poverty rates drop sharply as years of schooling rise. The U.S. Bureau of Labor Statistics reports in *Highlights of Women's Earnings in 2009* (June 2010, http://www.bls.gov/cps/cpswom2009.pdf) that in 2009 the median weekly earnings for men aged 25 years and older who had not completed high school was $500; for women it was only $382, 76.4% of what their male peers earned. Male high school graduates earned median weekly wages of $716, whereas females earned $542, 75.7% of what males earned. Men with a four-year college degree earned a median of $1,327 per week, whereas women earned $970, 73.1% of what males earned. Ayana Douglas-Hall and Michelle Chau of the National Center for Children in Poverty report in "Parents' Low Education Leads to Low Income, Despite Full-Time Employment" (November 2007, http://nccp.org/publications/pub_786.html) that most children who live in low-income or poor families have parents without any college

TABLE 2.7

Opposite-sex unmarried couples, by age, earnings, education, race and Hispanic origin of both partners, and presence of biological children, 2010

[Numbers in thousands]

| All opposite sex unmarried couples | Total | | Presence of biological children | | | |
| | | | No biological children | | At least one biological child under 18, of either partner | |
	N	%	N	%	N	%
Total	7,529	100.0	4,686	100.0	2,843	100.0
Age of male partner						
15–24 years	1,128	15.0	686	14.6	442	15.6
25–29 years	1,621	21.5	969	20.7	651	22.9
30–34 years	1,099	14.6	541	11.6	557	19.6
35–39 years	827	11.0	382	8.2	445	15.7
40–44 years	740	9.8	392	8.4	348	12.3
45–49 years	614	8.2	397	8.5	217	7.6
50–54 years	591	7.9	481	10.3	110	3.9
55–64 years	572	7.6	508	10.8	64	2.3
65+ years	336	4.5	330	7.0	6	0.2
Age of female partner						
15–24 years	1,815	24.1	1,114	23.8	700	24.6
25–29 years	1,603	21.3	904	19.3	699	24.6
30–34 years	901	12.0	391	8.3	511	18.0
35–39 years	723	9.6	297	6.3	426	15.0
40–44 years	664	8.8	382	8.1	282	9.9
45–49 years	564	7.5	414	8.8	150	5.3
50–54 years	550	7.3	496	10.6	55	1.9
55–64 years	470	6.2	454	9.7	16	0.5
65+ years	239	3.2	234	5.0	5	0.2
Age difference						
Male 10+ years older than female	861	11.4	532	11.4	329	11.6
Male 6–9 years older than female	988	13.1	598	12.8	390	13.7
Male 4–5 years older than female	827	11.0	497	10.6	330	11.6
Male 2–3 years older than female	1,243	16.5	729	15.6	514	18.1
Male and female within 1 year	2,044	27.2	1,291	27.6	753	26.5
Female 2–3 years older than male	544	7.2	350	7.5	195	6.9
Female 4–5 years older than male	389	5.2	240	5.1	149	5.2
Female 6–9 years older than male	342	4.5	239	5.1	103	3.6
Female 10+ years older than male	288	3.8	209	4.5	80	2.8
Race of male partner						
White alone—Non-Hispanic	4,896	65.0	3,430	73.2	1,466	51.6
Black alone—Non-Hispanic	1,011	13.4	514	11.0	497	17.5
Hispanic[a]	1,297	17.2	554	11.8	743	26.2
All remaining single races and all race combinations, non-Hispanic	324	4.3	188	4.0	136	4.8
Race of female partner						
White alone—Non-Hispanic	5,042	67.0	3,444	73.5	1,598	56.2
Black alone—Non-Hispanic	835	11.1	445	9.5	389	13.7
Hispanic[a]	1,242	16.5	514	11.0	728	25.6
All remaining single races and all race combinations, non-Hispanic	410	5.4	283	6.0	127	4.5
Race difference[b]						
Both white alone—non-Hispanic	4,451	59.1	3,113	66.4	1,338	47.1
Both black alone—non-Hispanic	750	10.0	397	8.5	352	12.4
Both other alone or any combination—non-Hispanic	169	2.2	91	1.9	79	2.8
Both Hispanic	947	12.6	345	7.4	602	21.2
Neither Hispanic	567	7.5	363	7.7	204	7.2
One Hispanic, other non-Hispanic	644	8.6	377	8.0	267	9.4
Race of male partner						
White alone	6,085	80.8	3,936	84.0	2,149	75.6
Black alone	1,064	14.1	533	11.4	531	18.7
Asian alone	121	1.6	77	1.7	43	1.5
All remaining single races and all race combinations	259	3.4	140	3.0	119	4.2

TABLE 2.7

Opposite-sex unmarried couples, by age, earnings, education, race and Hispanic origin of both partners, and presence of biological children, 2010 [CONTINUED]

[Numbers in thousands]

	Total		No biological children		At least one biological child under 18, of either partner	
All opposite sex unmarried couples	N	%	N	%	N	%
Race of female partner						
White alone	6,163	81.9	3,912	83.5	2,251	79.2
Black alone	906	12.0	473	10.1	432	15.2
Asian alone	175	2.3	125	2.7	50	1.8
All remaining single races and all race combinations	285	3.8	176	3.8	109	3.8
Race difference						
Both white alone	5,809	77.2	3,727	79.5	2,082	73.2
Both black alone	828	11.0	426	9.1	402	14.1
Both Asian alone	87	1.2	53	1.1	35	1.2
Both other alone or any combination	124	1.7	54	1.2	70	2.5
Partners identify as different races	680	9.0	426	9.1	254	8.9
Origin of male partner						
Hispanic	1,297	17.2	554	11.8	743	26.2
Non-Hispanic	6,231	82.8	4,132	88.2	2,099	73.8
Origin of female partner						
Hispanic	1,242	16.5	514	11.0	728	25.6
Non-Hispanic	6,287	83.5	4,172	89.0	2,114	74.4
Origin difference						
Neither Hispanic	5,937	78.9	3,964	84.6	1,973	69.4
Both Hispanic	947	12.6	345	7.4	602	21.2
Male Hispanic, female not	350	4.6	209	4.5	141	5.0
Female Hispanic, male not	295	3.9	169	3.6	126	4.4
Labor force status of male partner						
Not in labor force	1,119	14.9	786	16.8	334	11.7
In labor force	6,409	85.1	3,900	83.2	2,509	88.3
Labor force status of female partner						
Not in labor force	1,972	26.2	1,053	22.5	919	32.3
In labor force	5,556	73.8	3,633	77.5	1,923	67.7
Labor force difference						
Both in labor force	5,014	66.6	3,275	69.9	1,738	61.2
Only male in labor force	1,396	18.5	625	13.3	770	27.1
Only female in labor force	543	7.2	358	7.6	185	6.5
Neither in labor force	577	7.7	428	9.1	149	5.2
Employment of male partner						
Not employed	2,221	29.5	1,336	28.5	885	31.1
Employed	5,308	70.5	3,350	71.5	1,958	68.9
Employment of female partner						
Not employed	2,680	35.6	1,470	31.4	1,210	42.6
Employed	4,848	64.4	3,215	68.6	1,633	57.4
Employment difference						
Both in labor force—both employed	3,706	49.2	2,542	54.2	1,164	40.9
Both in labor force—only male employed	446	5.9	283	6.0	163	5.7
Both in labor force—only female employed	659	8.8	354	7.6	305	10.7
Both in labor force—both unemployed	202	2.7	96	2.0	106	3.7
Male in labor force—male employed	1,155	15.3	525	11.2	631	22.2
Male in labor force—male unemployed	240	3.2	100	2.1	140	4.9
Female in labor force—female employed	483	6.4	319	6.8	164	5.8
Female in labor force—female unemployed	60	0.8	38	0.8	21	0.8
Not in labor force—note employed	577	7.7	428	9.1	149	5.2
Male education						
Not high school graduate	1,192	15.8	570	12.2	621	21.9
High school graduate	3,018	40.1	1,731	36.9	1,287	45.3
Some college	2,070	27.5	1,370	29.2	701	24.6
Bachelor's degree or higher	1,248	16.6	1,015	21.7	234	8.2

TABLE 2.7

Opposite-sex unmarried couples, by age, earnings, education, race and Hispanic origin of both partners, and presence of biological children, 2010 [CONTINUED]

[Numbers in thousands]

	Total		No biological children		At least one biological child under 18, of either partner	
All opposite sex unmarried couples	N	%	N	%	N	%
Female education						
Not high school graduate	1,102	14.6	514	11.0	589	20.7
High school graduate	2,445	32.5	1,407	30.0	1,037	36.5
Some college	2,435	32.3	1,539	32.8	896	31.5
Bachelor's degree or higher	1,546	20.5	1,226	26.2	320	11.3
Education difference						
Neither has bachelor's degree	5,518	73.3	3,115	66.5	2,404	84.6
One has bachelor's degree, other has less	1,226	16.3	902	19.2	324	11.4
Both have bachelor's degree or more	785	10.4	670	14.3	115	4.0
Personal earnings of male partner						
Under $5,000 or loss	415	5.5	241	5.2	174	6.1
Without income	1,366	18.1	887	18.9	479	16.9
$5,000 to $9,999	454	6.0	289	6.2	166	5.8
$10,000 to $14,999	573	7.6	319	6.8	254	8.9
$15,000 to $19,999	555	7.4	286	6.1	269	9.5
$20,000 to $24,999	586	7.8	354	7.6	232	8.1
$25,000 to $29,999	569	7.6	329	7.0	240	8.5
$30,000 to $39,999	926	12.3	541	11.5	385	13.5
$40,000 to $49,999	730	9.7	492	10.5	237	8.4
$50,000 to $74,999	849	11.3	586	12.5	263	9.3
$75,000 to $99,999	252	3.3	179	3.8	72	2.6
$100,000 and over	254	3.4	183	3.9	71	2.5
Personal earnings of female partner						
Under $5,000 or loss	503	6.7	277	5.9	226	8.0
Without income	2,043	27.1	1,142	24.4	901	31.7
$5,000 to $9,999	520	6.9	291	6.2	229	8.0
$10,000 to $14,999	679	9.0	409	8.7	270	9.5
$15,000 to $19,999	566	7.5	354	7.5	213	7.5
$20,000 to $24,999	668	8.9	432	9.2	236	8.3
$25,000 to $29,999	531	7.0	340	7.3	191	6.7
$30,000 to $39,999	765	10.2	540	11.5	225	7.9
$40,000 to $49,999	445	5.9	315	6.7	130	4.6
$50,000 to $74,999	538	7.1	391	8.3	147	5.2
$75,000 to $99,999	158	2.1	114	2.4	44	1.6
$100,000 and over	112	1.5	82	1.7	31	1.1
Personal earnings difference						
Male earns $50,000+ more	530	7.0	350	7.5	180	6.3
Male earns $30,000–$49,999 more	785	10.4	481	10.3	304	10.7
Male earns $10,000–$29,999 more	1,774	23.6	980	20.9	795	28.0
Male earns $5,000–$9,999 more	629	8.4	381	8.1	248	8.7
Male earns within $4,999 of female	1,897	25.2	1,257	26.8	640	22.5
Female earns $5,000–$9,999 more	386	5.1	234	5.0	152	5.3
Female earns $10,000–$29,999 more	967	12.8	601	12.8	366	12.9
Female earns $30,000–$49,999 more	326	4.3	237	5.1	89	3.1
Female earns $50,000+ more	235	3.1	165	3.5	69	2.4

Note: Biological children excludes ever-married children under 18 years.
[a]Hispanics may be of any race.
[b]"White" refers to Non-Hispanic white alone, "black" to Non-Hispanic black alone, and "other" to Non-Hispanic other alone or in combination.

SOURCE: "Table UC3. Opposite Sex Unmarried Couples by Presence of Biological Children under 18, and Age, Earnings, Education, and Race and Hispanic Origin of Both Partners: 2010," in *America's Families and Living Arrangements: 2010*, U.S. Census Bureau, November 2010, http://www.census.gov/population/www/socdemo/hh-fam/cps2010.html (accessed February 18, 2011)

education and that full-time employment does not protect families from low earnings.

GOVERNMENT ASSISTANCE

The demand for welfare assistance increased sharply during the 1990s. However, because of decreased funding and welfare reform measures that gave states more flexibility in dispersing benefits, a smaller proportion of eligible families actually received benefits. In the fact sheet "A Decade of Welfare Reform: Facts and Figures—Assessing the New Federalism" (June 2006, http://www.urban.org/UploadedPDF/900980_welfarereform.pdf), the Urban Institute explains that the number of eligible families enrolled in welfare programs decreased

TABLE 2.8

Single-parent family groups with own children under 18, by marital status and demographic characteristics, 2010

[Numbers in thousands]

	All one-parent unmarried family groups		Maintained by father										Maintained by mother										
			Total		Never married		Divorced		Separated*		Widowed		Total		Never married		Divorced		Separated*		Widowed	
	N	%	N	%	N	%	N	%	N	%	N	%	N	%	N	%	N	%	N	%	N	%
All family groups	11,686	100.0	1,762	15.1	520	29.5	807	45.8	326	18.5	109	6.2	9,924	84.9	4,448	44.8	3,134	31.6	1,950	19.6	392	4.0
Region																						
Northeast	2,012	17.2	308	15.3	107	34.8	124	40.2	62	20.1	15	4.9	1,704	84.7	812	47.6	494	29.0	327	19.2	71	4.2
Midwest	2,519	21.6	416	16.5	130	31.3	197	47.3	67	16.1	22	5.3	2,102	83.4	994	47.3	729	34.7	299	14.2	80	3.8
South	4,676	40.0	617	13.2	167	27.1	291	47.2	110	17.8	49	7.9	4,059	86.8	1,794	44.2	1,241	30.6	862	21.2	162	4.0
West	2,479	21.2	422	17.0	116	27.5	195	46.2	88	20.9	23	5.4	2,057	83.0	848	41.2	669	32.5	461	22.4	79	3.8
Size of family group																						
Two members	5,184	44.4	997	19.2	381	38.2	421	42.2	147	14.7	48	4.8	4,187	80.8	2,209	52.8	1,224	29.2	607	14.5	147	3.5
Three members	3,808	32.6	500	13.1	91	18.2	269	53.8	102	20.3	38	7.7	3,306	86.8	1,294	39.1	1,213	36.7	674	20.4	125	3.8
Four members	1,647	14.1	162	9.8	22	13.3	76	46.8	50	31.1	14	8.7	1,485	90.2	542	36.5	468	31.5	392	26.4	83	5.6
Five members	622	5.3	72	11.6	16	21.9	29	40.4	22	30.6	5	7.1	548	88.1	223	40.7	150	27.4	159	29.0	16	2.9
Six or more members	425	3.6	30	7.1	11	35.4	11	37.9	5	16.7	3	10.1	395	92.9	179	45.2	78	19.8	117	29.6	21	5.4
Age of reference person																						
Under 20 years	241	2.1	8	3.3	8	100.0	—	—	—	—	—	—	233	96.7	221	94.8	1	0.4	11	4.8	—	—
20–24 years	1,251	10.7	64	5.1	60	93.4	1	2.0	3	4.5	—	—	1,185	94.7	996	84.0	56	4.7	124	10.5	9	0.8
25–29 years	1,824	15.6	201	11.0	138	68.7	35	17.6	22	10.8	6	2.9	1,624	89.0	1,032	63.6	234	14.4	342	21.1	16	1.0
30–34 years	1,943	16.6	242	12.5	107	44.4	82	33.8	47	19.5	6	2.3	1,701	87.5	838	49.3	469	27.6	372	21.9	22	1.3
35–39 years	2,086	17.9	303	14.5	69	22.8	160	52.8	64	21.1	10	3.3	1,783	85.5	633	35.5	708	39.7	392	22.0	50	2.8
40–44 years	1,780	15.2	321	18.0	61	19.1	164	51.0	79	24.5	17	5.4	1,458	81.9	365	25.1	708	48.6	304	20.8	81	5.6
45–54 years	2,174	18.6	491	22.6	71	14.5	285	58.1	95	19.3	40	8.2	1,683	77.4	316	18.8	859	51.1	360	21.4	148	8.8
55+ years	388	3.3	130	33.5	5	3.9	79	60.5	17	13.1	29	22.4	256	66.0	47	18.5	99	38.5	44	17.3	66	25.7
Family income																						
Family income under $10,000	1,921	16.4	157	8.2	63	40.1	53	33.8	26	16.5	15	9.6	1,764	91.8	1,002	56.8	352	19.9	371	21.1	39	2.2
$10,000 to $14,999	1,053	9.0	117	11.1	40	34.4	42	35.9	29	24.7	6	4.9	936	88.9	503	53.7	203	21.7	196	20.9	34	3.6
$15,000 to $19,999	1,101	9.4	139	12.6	42	30.1	58	41.6	32	23.0	7	5.3	961	87.3	481	50.0	257	26.8	190	19.8	33	3.4
$20,000 to $24,999	1,009	8.6	131	13.0	49	37.1	50	37.9	30	23.2	2	1.8	877	86.9	397	45.3	270	30.8	175	20.0	35	3.9
$25,000 to $29,999	851	7.3	93	10.9	39	42.0	33	35.3	14	15.5	7	7.3	758	89.1	322	42.5	268	35.3	135	17.9	33	4.3
$30,000 to $39,999	1,504	12.9	232	15.4	64	27.4	126	54.2	27	11.8	15	6.6	1,271	84.5	502	39.5	461	36.3	257	20.2	51	4.0
$40,000 to $49,999	1,046	9.0	204	19.5	58	28.5	96	47.1	34	16.8	16	7.6	841	80.4	303	36.1	342	40.7	160	19.0	36	4.2
$50,000 to $74,999	1,710	14.6	351	20.5	95	27.2	166	47.3	73	20.7	17	4.8	1,359	79.5	486	35.7	532	39.2	261	19.2	80	5.9
$75,000 to $99,999	712	6.1	150	21.1	28	18.8	90	60.2	25	16.6	7	4.4	563	79.1	213	37.8	227	40.4	90	15.9	33	5.9
$100,000 and over	780	6.7	189	24.2	43	22.6	93	49.5	36	18.9	17	9.0	592	75.9	239	40.3	221	37.3	113	19.1	19	3.3
Poverty status																						
Below poverty level	3,938	33.7	340	8.6	120	35.5	115	33.8	80	23.4	25	7.2	3,598	91.4	1,961	54.5	755	21.0	784	21.8	98	2.7
At or above poverty level	7,748	66.3	1,423	18.4	400	28.1	692	48.6	247	17.3	84	5.9	6,325	81.6	2,487	39.3	2,379	37.6	1,165	18.4	294	4.6
Number of own children under 18																						
One own child under 18	6,510	55.7	1,198	18.4	423	35.3	521	43.5	186	15.5	68	5.6	5,313	81.6	2,570	48.4	1,665	31.3	837	15.8	241	4.5
Two own children under 18	3,445	29.5	406	11.8	72	17.8	208	51.3	98	24.1	28	6.8	3,038	88.2	1,228	40.4	1,053	34.7	657	21.6	100	3.3
Three own children under 18	1,241	10.6	117	9.4	17	14.9	62	53.0	26	22.1	12	10.0	1,124	90.6	446	39.7	318	28.3	317	28.2	43	3.9
Four or more own children under 18	490	4.2	43	8.8	8	18.3	16	37.0	17	40.6	2	4.1	447	91.2	204	45.5	98	21.9	138	30.9	7	1.7

TABLE 2.8

Single-parent family groups with own children under 18, by marital status and demographic characteristics, 2010 [CONTINUED]

[Numbers in thousands]

	All one-parent unmarried family groups		Maintained by father										Maintained by mother									
			Total		Never married		Divorced		Separated*		Widowed		Total		Never Married		Divorced		Separated*		Widowed	
	N	%	N	%	N	%	N	%	N	%	N	%	N	%	N	%	N	%	N	%	N	%
Own children 6–17 years																						
Without own children 6–17	2,819	24.1	348	12.3	225	64.6	69	19.9	50	14.5	4	1.0	2,470	87.6	1,783	72.2	281	11.4	380	15.4	26	1.0
One own child 6–17	5,503	47.1	992	18.0	246	24.9	499	50.3	177	17.8	70	7.0	4,512	82.0	1,723	38.2	1,708	37.8	831	18.4	250	5.5
Two own children 6–17	2,424	20.7	315	13.0	34	10.9	180	57.1	77	24.4	24	7.7	2,108	87.0	648	30.7	882	41.8	502	23.8	76	3.6
Three own children 6–17	713	6.1	85	11.9	10	11.3	49	57.6	17	20.1	9	10.9	628	88.1	207	32.9	213	34.0	173	27.6	35	5.5
Four or more own children 6–17	226	1.9	21	9.3	5	22.5	9	44.2	5	24.8	2	8.4	205	90.7	87	42.2	50	24.4	62	30.3	6	3.1
Own children 12–17 years																						
Without own children 12–17	6,355	54.4	879	13.8	380	43.2	312	35.5	159	18.1	28	3.2	5,476	86.2	3,146	57.5	1,222	22.3	999	18.2	109	2.0
One own child 12–17	4,068	34.8	708	17.4	130	18.4	399	56.4	122	17.2	57	8.0	3,360	82.6	974	29.0	1,480	44.1	695	20.7	211	6.3
Two own children 12–17	1,082	9.3	152	14.0	9	5.7	82	53.9	41	26.9	20	13.5	931	86.0	269	28.9	383	41.1	217	23.3	62	6.7
Three or more own children 12–17	180	1.5	24	13.3	2	8.4	14	58.3	5	19.8	3	13.5	156	86.7	59	37.9	49	31.2	38	24.7	10	6.2
Own children 6–11 years																						
Without own children 6–11	6,579	56.3	1,058	16.1	337	31.9	465	44.0	184	17.4	72	6.8	5,521	83.9	2,650	48.0	1,648	29.9	971	17.6	252	4.6
One own child 6–11	3,820	32.7	546	14.3	159	29.1	252	46.2	108	19.8	27	4.9	3,273	85.7	1,392	42.5	1,117	34.1	649	19.8	115	3.5
Two own children 6–11	1,055	9.0	136	12.9	21	15.1	82	60.0	25	18.6	8	6.2	921	87.3	308	33.5	308	33.4	281	30.5	24	2.6
Three or more own children 6–11	231	2.0	22	9.5	4	16.6	7	34.3	9	41.1	2	8.0	210	90.9	99	47.0	61	29.2	49	23.2	1	0.6
Own children under 6 years																						
Without own children under 6	7,110	60.8	1,277	18.0	264	20.7	686	53.7	229	17.9	98	7.6	5,833	82.0	1,904	32.6	2,461	42.2	1,135	19.5	333	5.7
One own child under 6	3,531	30.2	409	11.6	227	55.5	98	23.9	74	18.1	10	2.5	3,123	88.4	1,949	62.4	548	17.5	578	18.5	48	1.5
Two own children under 6	887	7.6	68	7.7	25	37.1	23	33.8	19	28.2	1	0.9	819	92.3	495	60.4	107	13.1	208	25.3	9	1.2
Three or more own children under 6	158	1.4	10	6.3	5	48.0	0	1.6	5	50.4	—	—	149	94.3	100	67.2	18	11.9	30	19.9	1	0.9
Own children under 3 years																						
Without own children under 3	9,245	79.1	1,555	16.8	387	24.9	773	49.7	290	18.6	105	6.7	7,689	83.2	2,896	37.7	2,874	37.4	1,552	20.2	367	4.8
One own child under 3	2,187	18.7	198	9.1	130	65.7	31	15.8	33	16.7	4	1.8	1,990	91.0	1,361	68.4	247	12.4	357	17.9	25	1.3
Two or more own children under 3	254	2.2	10	3.9	4	40.6	2	21.4	4	38.0	—	—	244	96.1	191	78.1	13	5.4	40	16.4	—	—
Age of own children																						
With own children under 18 years	11,686	100.0	1,762	15.1	520	29.5	807	45.8	326	18.5	109	6.2	9,924	84.9	4,448	44.8	3,134	31.6	1,950	19.6	392	4.0
Without own children under 12 years	3,484	29.8	693	19.9	111	16.1	390	56.2	128	18.5	64	9.3	2,791	80.1	750	26.9	1,295	46.4	534	19.1	212	7.6
With own children under 12 years	8,201	70.2	1,068	13.0	409	38.3	417	39.0	198	18.6	44	4.1	7,132	87.0	3,698	51.8	1,839	25.8	1,415	19.8	180	2.5
Without own children under 6 years	7,110	60.8	1,277	18.0	264	20.7	686	53.7	229	17.9	98	7.6	5,833	82.0	1,904	32.6	2,461	42.2	1,135	19.5	333	5.7
With own children under 6 years	4,576	39.2	485	10.6	256	52.8	121	24.9	97	20.1	11	2.3	4,091	89.4	2,544	62.2	673	16.5	815	19.9	59	1.4
Without own children under 5 years	7,773	66.5	1,361	17.5	300	22.0	710	52.2	250	18.4	101	7.4	6,413	82.5	2,170	33.8	2,619	40.8	1,276	19.9	348	5.4

TABLE 2.8

Single-parent family groups with own children under 18, by marital status and demographic characteristics, 2010 [CONTINUED]

[Numbers in thousands]

	All one-parent unmarried family groups		Maintained by father										Maintained by mother									
			Total		Never married		Divorced		Separated*		Widowed		Total		Never Married		Divorced		Separated*		Widowed	
	N	%	N	%	N	%	N	%	N	%	N	%	N	%	N	%	N	%	N	%	N	%
With own children under 5 years	3,913	33.5	401	10.2	220	54.9	97	24.2	76	18.9	8	2.0	3,512	89.8	2,278	64.9	515	14.7	674	19.2	45	1.3
Without own children under 3 years	9,245	79.1	1,555	16.8	387	24.9	773	49.7	290	18.6	105	6.7	7,689	83.2	2,896	37.7	2,874	37.4	1,552	20.2	367	4.8
With own children under 3 years	2,441	20.9	207	8.5	133	64.5	33	16.1	37	17.7	4	1.8	2,234	91.5	1,552	69.5	260	11.6	397	17.8	25	1.1
Without own children under 1 year	10,901	93.3	1,706	15.6	482	28.3	799	46.8	318	18.6	107	6.3	9,193	84.3	3,870	42.1	3,076	33.5	1,862	20.3	385	4.2
With own children under 1 year	785	6.7	55	7.0	38	69.1	8	13.8	8	14.6	1	2.5	729	92.9	577	79.1	58	8.0	87	12.0	7	1.0
Without own children 3–5 years	8,932	76.4	1,440	16.1	380	26.4	706	49.1	253	17.5	101	7.0	7,491	83.9	3,115	41.6	2,648	35.3	1,377	18.4	351	4.7
With own children 3–5 years	2,754	23.6	322	11.7	140	43.5	100	31.2	74	22.9	8	2.5	2,431	88.3	1,332	54.8	486	20.0	572	23.5	41	1.7
Without own children 6–11 years	6,579	56.3	1,058	16.1	337	31.9	465	44.0	184	17.4	72	6.8	5,521	83.9	2,650	48.0	1,648	29.9	971	17.6	252	4.6
With own children 6–11 years	5,107	43.7	704	13.8	183	26.0	341	48.5	143	20.2	37	5.3	4,403	86.2	1,798	40.8	1,486	33.7	979	22.2	140	3.2
Without own children 12–17 years	6,355	54.4	879	13.8	380	43.2	312	35.5	159	18.1	28	3.2	5,476	86.2	3,146	57.5	1,222	22.3	999	18.2	109	2.0
With own children 12–17 years	5,330	45.6	884	16.6	141	15.9	495	56.0	167	18.9	81	9.1	4,447	83.4	1,301	29.3	1,912	43.0	951	21.4	283	6.4
Without own children 6–17 years	2,819	24.1	348	12.3	225	64.6	69	19.9	50	14.5	4	1.0	2,470	87.6	1,783	72.2	281	11.4	380	15.4	26	1.0
With own children 6–17 years	8,867	75.9	1,413	15.9	295	20.9	737	52.2	276	19.5	105	7.4	7,453	84.1	2,665	35.8	2,853	38.3	1,569	21.1	366	4.9
Own children in specified age groups																						
Children in two or more age groups	4,448	38.1	470	10.6	83	17.7	229	48.7	116	24.7	42	8.9	3,979	89.5	1,498	37.6	1,292	32.5	1013	25.4	176	4.4
Families with children 12–17 only	2,677	22.9	565	21.1	98	17.4	321	56.8	101	17.9	45	7.9	2,113	78.9	627	29.7	969	45.9	376	17.8	141	6.7
Families with children 6–11 only	2,168	18.5	408	18.8	129	31.6	196	48.0	64	15.7	19	4.7	1,760	81.2	782	44.4	646	36.7	275	15.7	57	3.2
Families with children 3–5 only	1,081	9.3	178	16.5	100	56.1	48	27.1	27	15.3	3	1.5	903	83.5	608	67.3	142	15.8	138	15.3	15	1.6
Families with children under 3 only	1,311	11.2	143	10.9	111	77.2	14	9.8	18	12.9	0	0.1	1,169	89.2	933	79.8	84	7.2	148	12.7	4	0.3
Under 6 only	2,819	24.1	348	12.3	225	64.6	69	19.9	50	14.5	4	1.0	2,470	87.6	1,783	72.2	281	11.4	380	15.4	26	1.0
Some under 6, some 6–17	1,757	15.0	136	7.7	31	22.5	51	37.5	47	34.5	7	5.4	1,621	92.3	761	47.0	392	24.2	435	26.8	33	2.0
6–17 only	7,110	60.8	1,277	18.0	264	20.7	686	53.7	229	17.9	98	7.6	5,833	82.0	1,904	32.6	2,461	42.2	1,135	19.5	333	5.7

Notes: "Own children" excludes ever-married children under 18 years. ("—") represents or rounds to zero.
*Includes "Married spouse absent."

SOURCE: "Table FG6. One-Parent Unmarried Family Groups with Own Children under 18, by Marital Status of the Reference Person: 2010," in *America's Families and Living Arrangements: 2010*, U.S. Census Bureau, November 2010, http://www.census.gov/population/www/socdemo/hh-fam/cps2010.html (accessed February 18, 2011)

TABLE 2.9

Living arrangements of children and marital status of parents, by age, sex, race, Hispanic origin, and selected characteristics, 2010

[Numbers in thousands]

	Total	Living with both parents		Living with mother only					Living with father only					Living with neither parent
		Married to each other	Not married to each other	Married spouse absent	Widowed	Divorced	Separated	Never married	Married spouse absent	Widowed	Divorced	Separated	Never married	No parent present
All children	74,718	49,106	2,717	1,073	624	5,316	2,727	7,543	157	163	1,221	371	660	3,041
Male	38,194	25,116	1,408	542	314	2,727	1,354	3,733	92	85	689	214	372	1,548
Female	36,524	23,989	1,309	531	310	2,589	1,373	3,810	65	79	532	157	288	1,493
Both sexes														
Total	74,718	49,106	2,717	1,073	624	5,316	2,727	7,543	157	163	1,221	371	660	3,041
Age of child														
Under 1 year	4,199	2,718	508	41	7	63	61	647	—	2	9	9	39	95
1–2 years	8,627	5,628	660	118	20	232	262	1,246	23	2	33	16	101	287
3–5 years	12,690	8,497	562	215	46	570	460	1,542	17	7	123	70	156	427
6–8 years	12,502	8,272	380	181	73	898	549	1,285	28	23	207	60	112	434
9–11 years	12,109	8,037	262	153	98	1,057	472	1,068	18	21	223	77	90	532
12–14 years	11,956	7,874	162	163	158	1,211	416	913	23	54	292	60	97	534
15–17 years	12,635	8,080	183	203	221	1,285	507	844	49	53	333	78	66	733
Race														
White alone	56,416	40,327	1,916	635	450	3,902	1,889	3,440	118	124	975	327	419	1,895
Black alone	11,272	3,911	513	303	135	966	649	3,548	22	31	142	31	179	843
Asian alone	3,300	2,777	45	72	19	125	51	68	10	1	41	5	16	70
All remaining single races and all race combinations	3,730	2,092	243	64	20	323	137	488	7	7	63	8	46	232
Race														
Hispanic*	16,941	10,325	1,020	418	116	984	952	1,987	83	20	127	93	139	677
White alone, non-Hispanic	41,089	30,835	1,024	282	345	3,067	974	1,715	45	103	865	234	307	1,293
All remaining single races and all race combinations, non-Hispanic	16,688	7,945	673	373	164	1,265	801	3,842	29	40	228	43	213	1,071
Race														
White alone or in combination with one or more other races	58,948	41,811	2,057	677	461	4,105	1,974	3,822	125	126	1,012	329	448	2,002
Other	15,770	7,295	660	396	163	1,211	753	3,721	32	38	209	42	211	1,039
Race														
Black alone or in combination with one or more other races	12,653	4,541	622	316	139	1,099	703	3,876	23	38	147	32	200	919
Other	62,065	44,565	2,095	757	485	4,217	2,024	3,667	135	126	1,073	339	460	2,122
Race														
Asian alone or in combination with one or more other races	3,984	3,314	58	83	23	165	65	105	10	6	55	6	17	77
Other	70,734	45,792	2,659	990	600	5,151	2,662	7,438	147	157	1,166	364	643	2,964

TABLE 2.9

Living arrangements of children and marital status of parents, by age, sex, race, Hispanic origin, and selected characteristics, 2010 [CONTINUED]

[Numbers in thousands]

	Total	Living with both parents		Living with mother only					Living with father only					Living with neither parent
		Married to each other	Not married to each other	Married spouse absent	Widowed	Divorced	Separated	Never married	Married spouse absent	Widowed	Divorced	Separated	Never married	No parent present
Presence of siblings														
None	15,704	7,501	852	170	135	1,226	440	2,355	30	47	428	108	363	2,049
One sibling	28,909	20,137	963	378	253	2,301	903	2,516	57	61	466	139	163	572
Two siblings	18,326	13,199	535	307	172	1,172	790	1,487	36	38	211	70	87	223
Three siblings	7,469	5,188	246	148	42	446	380	687	32	7	103	47	34	110
Four siblings	2,831	1,999	89	62	14	139	138	321	3	—	1	7	2	56
Five or more siblings	1,479	1,082	32	8	8	32	75	178	—	11	11	—	11	31
Presence of parent's unmarried partner														
Child's parent does not have opposite sex partner	70,104	49,106	218	1,026	582	4,654	2,566	6,800	154	140	1,013	340	467	3,038
Child's parent has opposite sex partner	4,614	—	2,499	48	42	662	160	743	3	23	208	30	193	3
Partner is also other parent	2,499	—	2,499	—	—	—	—	—	—	—	—	—	—	—
Partner is not other parent	2,115	—	—	48	42	662	160	743	3	23	208	30	193	3
Highest education of either parent														
Less than 9th grade	2,495	1,569	78	95	42	149	198	266	22	18	15	22	21	—
9th to 12th grade, no diploma	5,483	2,355	304	157	55	407	419	1,532	14	25	63	41	108	2
High school graduate	16,537	8,899	986	310	198	1,420	895	2,832	65	54	446	145	287	1
Some college or a degree	21,111	13,461	991	344	202	2,120	871	2,332	16	42	422	126	183	—
Bachelor's degree	15,474	13,176	250	96	84	855	256	444	27	11	210	23	42	—
Prof or graduate degree	10,581	9,645	108	73	42	365	87	137	14	12	65	13	19	—
No parents present	3,038	—	—	—	—	—	—	—	—	—	—	—	—	3,038
Poverty status														
Below 100% of poverty	15,798	5,352	1,246	498	181	1,528	1,272	3,873	60	46	180	89	179	1,293
100% to 199% of poverty	15,970	9,120	696	277	199	1,568	761	1,949	17	25	330	116	203	709
200% of poverty and above	42,950	34,634	775	298	244	2,220	693	1,721	80	92	711	166	278	1,039
100 percent of poverty														
Below 100% of poverty	15,798	5,352	1,246	498	181	1,528	1,272	3,873	60	46	180	89	179	1,293
100% of poverty and above	58,920	43,754	1,471	575	443	3,788	1,455	3,670	97	117	1,041	282	481	1,748
125 percent of poverty														
Below 125% of poverty	19,916	7,367	1,445	609	252	2,016	1,478	4,502	67	51	272	123	239	1,494
125% of poverty and above	54,802	41,739	1,272	464	371	3,300	1,248	3,041	90	112	949	248	421	1,547

—Rounds to zero.

Note: Excludes children in group quarters, and those who are a family reference person or spouse.

*Hispanics may be of any race.

SOURCE: Adapted from "Table C3. Living Arrangements of Children under 18 Years and Marital Status of Parents, by Age, Sex, Race, and Hispanic Origin and Selected Characteristics of the Child for All Children: 2010," in *America's Families and Living Arrangements: 2010*, U.S. Census Bureau, November 2010, http://www.census.gov/population/www/socdemo/hh-fam/cps2010.html (accessed February 18, 2011)

FIGURE 2.2

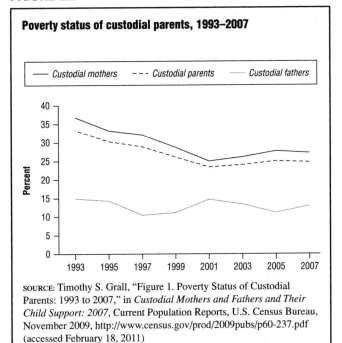

Poverty status of custodial parents, 1993–2007

— Custodial mothers - - - Custodial parents — Custodial fathers

SOURCE: Timothy S. Grall, "Figure 1. Poverty Status of Custodial Parents: 1993 to 2007," in *Custodial Mothers and Fathers and Their Child Support: 2007*, Current Population Reports, U.S. Census Bureau, November 2009, http://www.census.gov/prod/2009pubs/p60-237.pdf (accessed February 18, 2011)

from 80% in 1996 to 48% in 2002. Some were ineligible because they had assets such as a car or a savings account that brought them above permitted limits. Others did not know they were eligible for benefits, and some knew they were eligible but chose not to accept benefits or thought the effort was not worth the amount of benefits they would receive.

The economic recession that began in late 2007 increased the number of people receiving means-tested benefits. The American Recovery and Reinvestment Act, which was signed by President Barack Obama (1961–) in February 2009, contained provisions for a $5 billion contingency fund for Temporary Assistance to Needy Families programs under which states could receive up to 80% of the cost of spending increases in fiscal years 2009 and 2010. The act also allocated an additional $500 million to support participation in the Supplemental Nutrition Assistance Program (SNAP). The act authorized an increase in SNAP benefits to families of up to 113.6% of the value of the Thrifty Food Plan (a plan that serves as the basis for maximum food stamp allotments).

TABLE 2.10

Poverty status and work experience of people in families and unrelated individuals, 2008

[Numbers in thousands]

| Poverty status and work experience | Total persons | In married-couple families | | | | In families maintained by women | | | In families maintained by men | | | Unrelated individuals |
		Husbands	Wives	Related children under 18	Other relatives	Householder	Related children under 18	Other relatives	Householder	Related children under 18	Other relatives	
Total												
All people[a]	235,079	58,404	59,088	5,823	19,522	14,457	2,245	12,073	5,236	591	5,644	51,994
With labor force activity	160,652	45,889	38,512	1,729	12,969	10,383	508	7,516	4,157	136	3,883	34,969
1 to 26 weeks	12,814	1,406	2,965	1,009	2,626	704	296	999	211	85	330	2,184
27 weeks or more	147,838	44,483	35,546	720	10,343	9,679	213	6,516	3,947	52	3,553	32,785
With no labor force activity	74,427	12,515	20,577	4,095	6,552	4,074	1,737	4,557	1,078	455	1,761	17,025
At or above poverty level												
All people[a]	207,945	55,189	55,827	5,366	18,495	10,307	1,554	10,015	4,516	489	5,091	41,097
With labor force activity	149,416	44,103	37,579	1,666	12,575	8,126	402	6,733	3,764	119	3,663	30,685
1 to 26 weeks	10,461	1,261	2,725	965	2,497	299	227	813	153	71	275	1,175
27 weeks or more	138,955	42,842	34,854	701	10,078	7,828	175	5,921	3,611	48	3,388	29,511
With no labor force activity	58,529	11,086	18,248	3,700	5,920	2,180	1,152	3,282	752	370	1,427	10,412
Below poverty level												
All people[a]	27,134	3,216	3,261	457	1,027	4,151	691	2,058	720	102	553	10,897
With labor force activity	11,236	1,787	933	63	394	2,257	106	783	394	17	219	4,284
1 to 26 weeks	2,353	145	241	43	129	406	68	187	57	13	55	1,009
27 weeks or more	8,883	1,641	692	20	265	1,851	38	596	336	—	165	3,275
With no labor force activity	15,898	1,429	2,329	394	632	1,894	585	1,276	326	85	334	6,613
Rate[b]												
All people[a]	11.5	5.5	5.5	7.9	5.3	28.7	30.8	17.0	13.7	17.3	9.8	21.0
With labor force activity	7.0	3.9	2.4	3.6	3.0	21.7	20.8	10.4	9.5	12.4	5.7	12.3
1 to 26 weeks	18.4	10.3	8.1	4.3	4.9	57.6	23.0	18.7	27.2	15.9	16.6	46.2
27 weeks or more	6.0	3.7	1.9	2.7	2.6	19.1	17.8	9.1	8.5	(c)	4.6	10.0
With no labor force activity	21.4	11.4	11.3	9.6	9.7	46.5	33.7	28.0	30.3	18.7	19.0	38.8

Note: Dash represents or rounds to zero.
[a]Data on families include people in primary families and unrelated subfamilies.
[b]Number below the poverty level as a percent of the total.
[c]Data not shown where base is less than 80,000.

SOURCE: "Table 6. People in Families and Unrelated Individuals: Poverty Status and Work Experience, 2008," in *A Profile of the Working Poor, 2008*, U.S. Department of Labor, Bureau of Labor Statistics, March 2010, http://www.bls.gov/cps/cpswp2008.pdf (accessed February 17, 2011)

TABLE 2.11

Poverty status of persons and primary families in the labor force for 27 or more weeks, 2005–08

[Numbers in thousands]

Characteristic	2005	2006	2007	2008
Total persons[a]	142,824	145,229	146,567	147,838
In poverty	7,744	7,427	7,521	8,883
Poverty rate	5.4	5.1	5.1	6.0
Unrelated individuals	31,422	31,887	33,226	32,785
In poverty	2,846	2,741	2,558	3,275
Poverty rate	9.1	8.6	7.7	10.0
Primary families[b]	64,360	65,388	65,158	65,907
In poverty	4,094	3,960	4,169	4,538
Poverty rate	6.4	6.1	6.4	6.9

[a]Includes persons in families, not shown separately.
[b]Primary families with at least one member in the labor force for more than half the year.
Note: Updated population controls are introduced annually with the release of January data.

SOURCE: "Table A. Poverty Status of Persons and Primary Families in the Labor Force for 27 or More Weeks, 2005–08," in *A Profile of the Working Poor, 2008*, U.S. Department of Labor, Bureau of Labor Statistics, March 2010, http://www.bls.gov/cps/cpswp2008.pdf (accessed February 17, 2011)

Who Receives Benefits?

The Census Bureau reports that in 2009, 92 million people, or 30.3% of the total U.S. population, lived in households that received some form of means-tested assistance (assistance based on earning below a certain amount). (See Table 2.12.) This number was up substantially from 2006, before the recession began, when 77.1 million people (26% of the total U.S. population) lived in households that received these benefits. In 2009 approximately 43.6 million people were living below the poverty level, up substantially from 36.5 million in 2006. (See Table 2.13.) Of those living in poverty in 2009, 31.6 million (72.5%) were receiving some form of means-tested aid.

Certain types of households were more likely than others to receive means-tested assistance in 2009. Almost nine out of 10 (89.2%) poor families with children under the age of 18 years received government assistance. (See Table 2.13.) Poor families with children under the age of 18 years headed by a single mother were the most likely to receive government assistance; 92.5% of these families received some form of government assistance. In fact, nearly three-quarters (73%) of all families (not just those in poverty) with children under the age of 18 years headed by a single mother received some form of means-tested assistance in 2009. (See Table 2.12.) In comparison, 58% of families with children under the age of 18 years headed by a single father received means-tested assistance in that year.

In 2009 a slightly higher proportion of females (31.6%) than males (28.9%) lived in a household that received means-tested assistance or welfare benefits of any kind. (See Table 2.12.) About 48.8 million females

received program assistance in 2009, compared with 43.2 million males. Among those living below the poverty level, 17.8 million women, or 73.8% of females living below the poverty line, received benefits during some part of the year, compared with 13.8 million males, or 70.8% of males living below the poverty line. (See Table 2.13.)

One reason for the larger percentage of females receiving assistance is that women are more likely to live in a family without a spouse present. DeNavas-Walt, Proctor, and Smith indicate that another reason is that women, on average, earned only 77% of what men earned in 2009. Age may also play a role in the higher number of women in poverty; there are far more elderly women than men. Another reason is that fewer single mothers participate in the workforce permanently and full time than do single fathers. In *Custodial Mothers and Fathers and Their Child Support: 2007* (November 2009, http://www.census.gov/prod/2009pubs/p60-237.pdf), Timothy S. Grall of the Census Bureau reports that even though 79.5% of custodial mothers worked in 2007, only 49.8% of them worked full-time year-round, whereas 71.7% of custodial fathers held full-time, full-year jobs. Grall suggests one reason that might be part of the cause of this disparity: Custodial mothers were more likely than custodial fathers to have two or more children living with them (45.7% and 32.3%, respectively).

African-Americans and Hispanics were more likely than Asian-Americans and non-Hispanic whites to receive some form of means-tested assistance in 2009. The Census Bureau reports in "Program Participation Status of Household-Poverty Status of People" (2010, http://www.census.gov/hhes/www/cpstables/032010/pov/new26_000.htm) that 53.3% of Hispanics, 50.9% of African-Americans, 27.9% of Asian-Americans, and 20.5% of non-Hispanic whites lived in households that received some form of means-tested assistance. Among those with incomes below the poverty line, 84.1% of African-Americans, 82.5% of Hispanics, 61.4% of Asian-Americans, and 60.1% of non-Hispanic whites received benefits. The lower proportion of Asian-Americans and non-Hispanic whites living below the poverty line who receive means-tested benefits may be due to the fact that a lower proportion of these groups live in desperate poverty than do others.

Nearly half (44.7%) of children under the age of 18 years lived in households that received means-tested assistance in 2009. (See Table 2.12.) Approximately one out of six (18.6%) people aged 65 years and older received assistance.

Only 23.8% of those living in families headed by married couples received assistance in 2009. (See Table 2.12.) Six out of 10 (61.1%) individuals in female-headed families with no spouse present received benefits. In contrast, only 43.2% of those living in families headed by a single male

TABLE 2.12

Program participation status of household for all income levels, 2009

[Numbers in thousands]

	Total	In household that received means-tested assistance		In household that received means-tested assistance excluding school lunch		In household that received means-tested cash assistance		In household that received food stamps		In household in which one or more persons were covered by Medicaid		Lived in public or authorized housing	
		Number	Percent	Number	Percent	Number	Percent	Number	Percent	Number	Percent	Number	Percent
All races													
All income levels													
Both sexes													
Total[a]	**303,820**	**92,005**	**30.3**	**84,107**	**27.7**	**19,608**	**6.5**	**34,377**	**11.3**	**74,457**	**24.5**	**11,098**	**3.7**
Under 18 years	74,579	33,565	45.0	29,791	39.9	5,666	7.6	13,917	18.7	27,748	37.2	3,989	5.3
18 to 24 years	29,313	9,886	33.7	9,224	31.5	1,985	6.8	3,786	12.9	8,119	27.7	1,251	4.3
25 to 34 years	41,085	13,081	31.8	12,137	29.5	2,337	5.7	5,230	12.7	10,839	26.4	1,366	3.3
35 to 44 years	40,447	11,519	28.5	10,137	25.1	2,131	5.3	3,836	9.5	9,035	22.3	1,027	2.5
45 to 54 years	44,387	10,174	22.9	9,352	21.1	2,754	6.2	3,450	7.8	8,051	18.1	1,070	2.4
55 to 59 years	19,172	3,693	19.3	3,573	18.6	1,425	7.4	1,227	6.4	2,949	15.4	475	2.5
60 to 64 years	16,223	2,921	18.0	2,843	17.5	1,120	6.9	941	5.8	2,302	14.2	427	2.6
65 years and over	38,613	7,167	18.6	7,050	18.3	2,190	5.7	1,990	5.2	5,414	14.0	1,493	3.9
65 to 74 years	20,956	3,901	18.6	3,811	18.2	1,229	5.9	1,127	5.4	3,046	14.5	727	3.5
75 years and over	17,657	3,266	18.5	3,239	18.3	962	5.4	862	4.9	2,367	13.4	766	4.3
Male													
Total	**149,237**	**43,163**	**28.9**	**39,369**	**26.4**	**9,087**	**6.1**	**15,242**	**10.2**	**34,954**	**23.4**	**4,388**	**2.9**
Under 18 years	38,076	17,094	44.9	15,128	39.7	2,904	7.6	6,953	18.3	14,123	37.1	1,948	5.1
18 to 24 years	14,837	4,511	30.4	4,166	28.1	911	6.1	1,568	10.6	3,630	24.5	465	3.1
25 to 34 years	20,689	5,910	28.6	5,544	26.8	1,093	5.3	2,113	10.2	4,898	23.7	447	2.2
35 to 44 years	20,074	5,174	25.8	4,609	23.0	949	4.7	1,585	7.9	4,125	20.5	362	1.8
45 to 54 years	21,784	4,719	21.7	4,309	19.8	1,189	5.5	1,486	6.8	3,701	17.0	379	1.7
55 to 59 years	9,318	1,724	18.5	1,661	17.8	654	7.0	527	5.7	1,360	14.6	157	1.7
60 to 64 years	7,667	1,321	17.2	1,288	16.8	535	7.0	354	4.6	1,034	13.5	145	1.9
65 years and over	16,793	2,711	16.1	2,664	15.9	852	5.1	657	3.9	2,083	12.4	485	2.9
65 to 74 years	9,735	1,615	16.6	1,578	16.2	481	4.9	415	4.3	1,282	13.2	250	2.6
75 years and over	7,058	1,097	15.5	1,086	15.4	371	5.3	242	3.4	801	11.4	235	3.3
Female													
Total	**154,582**	**48,842**	**31.6**	**44,738**	**28.9**	**10,521**	**6.8**	**19,135**	**12.4**	**39,503**	**25.6**	**6,710**	**4.3**
Under 18 years	36,504	16,470	45.1	14,663	40.2	2,761	7.6	6,964	19.1	13,625	37.3	2,041	5.6
18 to 24 years	14,476	5,375	37.1	5,059	34.9	1,074	7.4	2,218	15.3	4,488	31.0	786	5.4
25 to 34 years	20,396	7,171	35.2	6,593	32.3	1,245	6.1	3,117	15.3	5,941	29.1	919	4.5
35 to 44 years	20,373	6,345	31.1	5,528	27.1	1,182	5.8	2,251	11.0	4,911	24.1	664	3.3
45 to 54 years	22,604	5,456	24.1	5,043	22.3	1,564	6.9	1,965	8.7	4,351	19.2	692	3.1
55 to 59 years	9,854	1,969	20.0	1,912	19.4	771	7.8	700	7.1	1,589	16.1	318	3.2
60 to 64 years	8,556	1,601	18.7	1,555	18.2	585	6.8	587	6.9	1,268	14.8	282	3.3
65 years and over	21,820	4,455	20.4	4,386	20.1	1,338	6.1	1,333	6.1	3,331	15.3	1,008	4.6
65 to 74 years	11,221	2,286	20.4	2,232	19.9	748	6.7	713	6.4	1,764	15.7	477	4.3
75 years and over	10,599	2,169	20.5	2,153	20.3	590	5.6	620	5.9	1,566	14.8	531	5.0

TABLE 2.12

Program participation status of household for all income levels, 2009 [CONTINUED]

[Numbers in thousands]

Household relationship	Total	In household that received means-tested assistance		In household that received means-tested assistance excluding school lunch		In household that received means-tested cash assistance		In household that received food stamps		In household in which one or more persons were covered by Medicaid		Lived in public or authorized housing	
		Number	Percent	Number	Percent	Number	Percent	Number	Percent	Number	Percent	Number	Percent
Total[a]	**303,820**	**92,005**	**30.3**	**84,107**	**27.7**	**19,608**	**6.5**	**34,377**	**11.3**	**74,457**	**24.5**	**11,098**	**3.7**
65 years and over	38,613	7,167	18.6	7,050	18.3	2,190	5.7	1,990	5.2	5,414	14.0	1,493	3.9
In families[b]	249,384	79,395	31.8	71,772	28.8	16,157	6.5	28,932	11.6	65,223	26.2	8,172	3.3
Householder	78,867	21,434	27.2	19,496	24.7	4,627	5.9	7,935	10.1	17,361	22.0	2,477	3.1
Under 65 years	65,461	19,144	29.2	17,262	26.4	3,855	5.9	7,314	11.2	15,469	23.6	2,269	3.5
65 years and over	13,405	2,290	17.1	2,234	16.7	772	5.8	621	4.6	1,892	14.1	208	1.5
Related children under 18 years[e]	73,410	32,807	44.7	29,091	39.6	5,524	7.5	13,572	18.5	27,091	36.9	3,942	5.4
Under 6 years	25,104	11,906	47.4	11,228	44.7	1,959	7.8	5,475	21.8	10,541	42.0	1,552	6.2
6 to 17 years	48,306	20,901	43.3	17,863	37.0	3,565	7.4	8,097	16.8	16,550	34.3	2,390	4.9
Own children 18 years and over[g]	25,296	8,337	33.0	7,686	30.4	2,433	9.6	2,614	10.3	6,902	27.3	698	2.8
In married-couple families[f]	188,001	44,750	23.8	40,024	21.3	7,544	4.0	12,001	6.4	36,766	19.6	2,509	1.3
Husbands[f]	58,428	10,814	18.5	9,786	16.7	1,970	3.4	2,807	4.8	8,758	15.0	667	1.1
Under 65 years	46,692	9,395	20.1	8,396	18.0	1,516	3.2	2,531	5.4	7,595	16.3	525	1.1
65 years and over	11,737	1,419	12.1	1,390	11.8	454	3.9	276	2.3	1,163	9.9	142	1.2
Wives[f]	58,428	10,814	18.5	9,786	16.7	1,970	3.4	2,807	4.8	8,758	15.0	667	1.1
Under 65 years	49,421	9,848	19.9	8,836	17.9	1,658	3.4	2,627	5.3	7,980	16.1	565	1.1
65 years and over	9,007	966	10.7	950	10.6	311	3.5	180	2.0	778	8.6	102	1.1
Related children under 8 years[e]	50,964	17,104	33.6	14,904	29.2	2,081	4.1	5,172	10.1	14,050	27.6	997	2.0
Under 6 years	17,705	6,346	35.8	5,883	33.2	715	4.0	2,200	12.4	5,574	31.5	441	2.5
6 to 17 years	33,259	10,758	32.3	9,021	27.1	1,366	4.1	2,972	8.9	8,477	25.5	556	1.7
Own children 18 years and over[g]	16,057	4,170	26.0	3,780	23.5	1,057	6.6	775	4.8	3,556	22.1	140	0.9
In families with male householder, no spouse present	16,067	6,944	43.2	6,395	39.8	1,409	8.8	2,468	15.4	5,607	34.9	488	3.0
Householder	5,582	2,235	40.0	2,047	36.7	473	8.5	805	14.4	1,766	31.6	176	3.2
Under 65 years	5,086	2,044	40.2	1,863	36.6	397	7.8	752	14.8	1,604	31.5	168	3.3
65 years and over	496	191	38.6	184	37.1	76	15.2	53	10.7	162	32.7	8	1.6
Related children under 18 years[e]	4,539	2,634	58.0	2,362	52.0	393	8.7	996	21.9	2,167	47.7	182	4.0
Under 6 years	1,617	1,032	63.8	1,008	62.4	146	9.0	452	28.0	937	58.0	65	4.0
6 to 17 years	2,923	1,602	54.8	1,354	46.3	247	8.4	544	18.6	1,229	42.1	117	4.0
Own children 18 years and over[g]	1,766	597	33.8	562	31.8	167	9.4	187	10.6	465	26.3	19	1.1
In families with female householder, no spouse present	45,315	27,701	61.1	25,353	55.9	7,204	15.9	14,463	31.9	22,850	50.4	5,175	11.4
Householder	14,857	8,385	56.4	7,663	51.6	2,184	14.7	4,324	29.1	6,837	46.0	1,633	11.0
Under 65 years	12,838	7,560	58.9	6,861	53.4	1,902	14.8	4,010	31.2	6,146	47.9	1,565	12.2
65 years and over	2,019	825	40.9	802	39.7	282	14.0	314	15.6	691	34.2	68	3.4
Related children under 18 years[e]	17,907	13,069	73.0	11,825	66.0	3,050	17.0	7,405	41.4	10,874	60.7	2,763	15.4
Under 6 years	5,782	4,528	78.3	4,337	75.0	1,098	19.0	2,824	48.8	4,030	69.7	1,046	18.1
6 to 17 years	12,125	8,541	70.4	7,488	61.8	1,952	16.1	4,582	37.8	6,844	56.4	1,717	14.2
Own children 18 years and over[g]	7,473	3,570	47.8	3,344	44.8	1,209	16.2	1,652	22.1	2,882	38.6	539	7.2
In unrelated subfamilies[c]	1,357	904	66.6	843	62.1	187	13.8	442	32.5	807	59.5	42	3.1
Under 18 years	747	521	69.7	486	65.1	113	15.2	265	35.4	464	62.1	24	3.2
Under 6 years	267	213	79.8	203	76.1	51	19.1	125	46.9	194	72.5	20	7.4
6 to 17 years	480	308	64.1	283	59.0	62	13.0	140	29.1	270	56.2	4	0.8
18 years and over	610	383	62.8	357	58.6	74	12.1	177	29.0	343	56.3	19	3.1

TABLE 2.12

Program participation status of household for all income levels, 2009 [CONTINUED]

[Numbers in thousands]

	Total	In household that received means-tested assistance		In household that received means-tested assistance excluding school lunch		In household that received means-tested cash assistance		In household that received food stamps		In household in which one or more persons were covered by Medicaid		Lived in public or authorized housing	
		Number	Percent	Number	Percent	Number	Percent	Number	Percent	Number	Percent	Number	Percent
Unrelated individuals[d]	53,079	11,707	22.1	11,492	21.6	3,263	6.1	5,003	9.4	8,427	15.9	2,884	5.4
Male	26,269	5,590	21.3	5,455	20.8	1,561	5.9	2,311	8.8	4,117	15.7	1,055	4.0
Under 65 years	22,502	4,785	21.3	4,650	20.7	1,352	6.0	2,084	9.3	3,606	16.0	734	3.3
Living alone	10,779	1,439	13.4	1,439	13.3	550	5.1	654	6.1	909	8.4	494	4.6
65 years and over	3,766	805	21.4	805	21.4	210	5.6	226	6.0	511	13.6	321	8.5
Living alone	3,199	623	19.5	623	19.5	151	4.7	155	4.8	347	10.8	302	9.4
Female	26,811	6,117	22.8	6,037	22.5	1,702	6.3	2,693	10.0	4,310	16.1	1,829	6.8
Under 65 years	18,125	4,275	23.6	4,195	23.1	1,238	6.8	2,078	11.5	3,130	17.3	1,021	5.6
Living alone	9,322	1,872	20.1	1,870	20.1	680	7.3	1,053	11.3	1,210	13.0	838	9.0
65 years and over	8,686	1,842	21.2	1,842	21.2	465	5.3	615	7.1	1,180	13.6	809	9.3
Living alone	8,137	1,693	20.8	1,693	20.8	418	5.1	573	7.0	1,050	12.9	788	9.7

Note: People who lived with someone (a nonrelative or a relative) who received aid. Not every person tallied here received the aid themselves.

[a]Universe: All people except unrelated individuals under age 15 (such as foster children). Since the Current Population Survey asks income questions only to people age 15 and over, if a child under age 15 is not part of a family by birth, marriage, or adoption, we do not know their income and cannot determine whether or not they are poor. Those people are excluded from the totals so as not to affect the percentages.

[b]People in families: People who are related to the householder by birth, marriage, or adoption. People who are related to each other but not to the householder are counted elsewhere (usually as unrelated subfamilies).

[c]People in unrelated subfamilies: People who are not related to the householder, but who are related to each other, either as a married couple or as a parent-child relationship with an unmarried child under 18.

[d]Unrelated individuals: People who are not in primary families (the householder's family) or unrelated subfamilies.

[e]People in families with related children: People living in a family where at least one member is a related child—a person under 18 who is related to the householder but is not the householder or spouse.

[f]In married-couple families the householder may be either the husband or the wife.

[g]Own children: Sons and daughters, including stepchildren and adopted children, of the householder.

SOURCE: "Pov26. Program Participation Status of Household—Poverty Status of People: 2009, All Races—All Income Levels," in *Current Population Survey (CPS), 2010 Annual Social and Economic Supplement (ASEC)*, U.S. Census Bureau, 2010, http://www.census.gov/hhes/www/cpstables/032010/pov/new26_001_01.htm (accessed February 18, 2011).

TABLE 2.13

Program participation status of household for persons below poverty level, 2009

[Numbers in thousands]

	Total	In household that received means-tested assistance		In household that received means-tested assistance excluding school lunch		In household that received means-tested cash assistance		In household that received food stamps		In household in which one or more persons were covered by Medicaid		Lived in public or authorized housing	
		Number	Percent	Number	Percent	Number	Percent	Number	Percent	Number	Percent	Number	Percent
All races													
Below poverty level													
Both sexes													
Total[a]	**43,569**	**31,567**	**72.5**	**29,724**	**68.2**	**8,130**	**18.7**	**19,970**	**45.8**	**26,225**	**60.2**	**6,459**	**14.8**
Under 18 years	15,451	13,787	89.2	12,857	83.3	3,203	20.7	9,181	59.4	11,937	77.3	2,857	18.5
18 to 24 years	6,071	3,592	59.2	3,420	56.3	840	13.8	2,205	36.3	2,964	48.8	724	11.9
25 to 34 years	6,123	4,416	72.1	4,171	68.1	950	15.5	2,811	45.9	3,650	59.6	830	13.6
35 to 44 years	4,756	3,549	74.6	3,282	69.0	821	17.3	2,130	44.8	2,865	60.2	535	11.2
45 to 54 years	4,421	2,924	66.1	2,765	62.5	1,051	23.8	1,847	41.8	2,268	51.3	579	13.1
55 to 59 years	1,792	976	54.5	943	52.6	417	23.3	574	32.0	768	42.8	218	12.2
60 to 64 years	1,520	739	48.6	719	47.3	288	18.9	453	29.8	569	37.4	202	13.3
65 years and over	3,433	1,583	46.1	1,568	45.7	560	16.3	769	22.4	1,204	35.1	514	15.0
65 to 74 years	1,675	861	51.4	852	50.9	340	20.3	427	25.5	687	41.0	278	16.6
75 years and over	1,758	722	41.1	716	40.7	220	12.5	341	19.4	517	29.4	236	13.4
Male													
Total	**19,475**	**13,796**	**70.8**	**12,904**	**66.3**	**3,398**	**17.4**	**8,407**	**43.2**	**11,371**	**58.4**	**2,455**	**12.6**
Under 18 years	7,770	6,966	89.7	6,468	83.2	1,628	21.0	4,543	58.5	6,019	77.5	1,389	17.9
18 to 24 years	2,578	1,341	52.0	1,257	48.8	309	12.0	768	29.8	1,056	41.0	232	9.0
25 to 34 years	2,534	1,652	65.2	1,559	61.5	310	12.2	961	37.9	1,309	51.7	212	8.4
35 to 44 years	2,025	1,404	69.4	1,304	64.4	318	15.7	786	38.8	1,146	56.6	145	7.2
45 to 54 years	1,989	1,250	62.8	1,169	58.8	399	20.1	744	37.4	922	46.4	195	9.8
55 to 59 years	825	415	50.2	396	48.0	177	21.4	223	27.0	326	39.5	65	7.9
60 to 64 years	650	302	46.5	292	44.9	104	16.0	161	24.8	230	35.4	62	9.5
65 years and over	1,104	466	42.1	459	41.5	153	13.8	222	20.1	363	32.9	153	13.9
65 to 74 years	583	270	46.3	265	45.5	79	13.6	126	21.7	209	35.9	90	15.5
75 years and over	522	195	37.5	193	37.1	73	14.1	96	18.3	154	29.5	63	12.1
Female													
Total	**24,094**	**17,772**	**73.8**	**16,820**	**69.8**	**4,732**	**19.6**	**11,562**	**48.0**	**14,854**	**61.7**	**4,004**	**16.6**
Under 18 years	7,682	6,821	88.8	6,390	83.2	1,575	20.5	4,639	60.4	5,918	77.0	1,468	19.1
18 to 24 years	3,493	2,251	64.4	2,162	61.9	531	15.2	1,437	41.1	1,908	54.6	492	14.1
25 to 34 years	3,590	2,764	77.0	2,612	72.8	640	17.8	1,851	51.6	2,341	65.2	618	17.2
35 to 44 years	2,731	2,144	78.5	1,978	72.4	502	18.4	1,344	49.2	1,720	63.0	390	14.3
45 to 54 years	2,433	1,674	68.8	1,595	65.6	652	26.8	1,103	45.3	1,346	55.3	383	15.8
55 to 59 years	967	562	58.1	547	56.6	240	24.8	351	36.3	441	45.7	153	15.8
60 to 64 years	871	437	50.2	428	49.1	184	21.1	292	33.5	339	38.9	141	16.1
65 years and over	2,329	1,117	48.0	1,109	47.6	407	17.5	547	23.5	840	36.1	361	15.5
65 to 74 years	1,093	591	54.1	587	53.7	261	23.9	301	27.5	478	43.7	188	17.2
75 years and over	1,236	526	42.6	522	42.2	147	11.9	246	19.9	363	29.3	172	13.9

TABLE 2.13

Program participation status of household for persons below poverty level, 2009 [CONTINUED]

[Numbers in thousands]

Household relationship	Total	In household that received means-tested assistance		In household that received means-tested assistance excluding school lunch		In household that received means-tested cash assistance		In household that received food stamps		In household in which one or more persons were covered by Medicaid		Lived in public or authorized housing	
		Number	Percent	Number	Percent	Number	Percent	Number	Percent	Number	Percent	Number	Percent
Total[a]	**43,569**	**31,567**	**72.5**	**29,724**	**68.2**	**8,130**	**18.7**	**19,970**	**45.8**	**26,225**	**60.2**	**6,459**	**14.8**
65 years and over	3,433	1,583	46.1	1,568	45.7	560	16.3	769	22.4	1,204	35.1	514	15.0
In families[b]	31,197	25,410	81.4	23,721	76.0	6,129	19.6	16,567	53.1	21,538	69.0	4,974	15.9
Householder	8,792	6,760	76.9	6,348	72.2	1,711	19.5	4,443	50.5	5,683	64.6	1,431	16.3
Under 65 years	8,035	6,415	79.8	6,011	74.8	1,580	19.7	4,271	53.2	5,390	67.1	1,380	17.2
65 years and over	757	345	45.6	337	44.6	131	17.3	172	22.8	293	38.8	52	6.8
Related children under 18 years[e]	14,774	13,229	89.5	12,341	83.5	3,095	21.0	8,891	60.2	11,449	77.5	2,823	19.1
Under 6 years	5,983	5,358	89.6	5,166	86.3	1,218	20.4	3,686	61.6	4,843	80.9	1,199	20.0
6 to 17 years	8,791	7,871	89.5	7,175	81.6	1,877	21.4	5,205	59.2	6,607	75.2	1,624	18.5
Own children 18 years and over[g]	2,383	1,795	75.3	1,663	69.8	570	23.9	1,148	48.2	1,441	60.5	290	12.2
In married-couple families[f]	13,594	10,210	75.1	9,316	68.5	1,676	12.3	5,798	42.7	8,505	62.6	1,215	8.9
Husbands[f]	3,409	2,228	65.4	2,050	60.1	373	10.9	1,256	36.8	1,821	53.4	270	7.9
Under 65 years	2,914	2,069	71.0	1,897	65.1	321	11.0	1,184	40.6	1,690	58.0	239	8.2
65 years and over	494	159	32.2	153	30.9	53	10.6	71	14.4	131	26.4	31	6.4
Wives[f]	3,409	2,228	65.4	2,050	60.1	373	10.9	1,256	36.8	1,821	53.4	270	7.9
Under 65 years	3,059	2,130	69.6	1,955	63.9	342	11.2	1,219	39.9	1,748	57.1	256	8.4
65 years and over	349	99	28.3	95	27.2	31	8.9	36	10.3	73	20.8	15	4.2
Related children under 18 years[e]	5,624	4,877	86.7	4,433	78.8	733	13.0	2,838	50.5	4,153	73.8	616	11.0
Under 6 years	2,368	2,049	86.5	1,927	81.3	303	12.8	1,229	51.9	1,823	77.0	286	12.1
6 to 17 years	3,256	2,828	86.9	2,506	77.0	430	13.2	1,610	49.4	2,331	71.6	329	10.1
Own children 18 years and over[g]	806	593	73.6	513	63.7	143	17.8	291	36.1	472	58.5	42	5.2
In families with male householder, no spouse present	2,857	2,138	74.8	1,980	69.3	530	18.6	1,211	42.4	1,716	60.1	234	8.2
Householder	942	680	72.2	627	66.6	159	16.9	390	41.4	534	56.7	85	9.0
Under 65 years	907	659	72.7	607	66.9	152	16.7	386	42.6	514	56.6	85	9.3
65 years and over	35	21	59.5	20	59.1	7	21.2	4	12.0	20	59.1	0	1.0
Related children under 18 years[e]	1,208	1,009	83.5	923	76.5	231	19.1	579	48.0	841	69.6	116	9.6
Under 6 years	474	406	85.7	399	84.1	92	19.5	263	55.4	365	76.9	48	10.2
6 to 17 years	733	602	82.1	524	71.5	138	18.9	317	43.2	476	64.9	67	9.2
Own children 18 years and over[g]	158	98	61.9	91	57.9	26	16.4	55	34.9	67	42.8	7	4.4
In families with female householder, no spouse present	14,746	13,062	88.6	12,424	84.3	3,923	26.6	9,557	64.8	11,317	76.7	3,526	23.9
Householder	4,441	3,852	86.7	3,670	82.6	1,179	26.5	2,797	63.0	3,329	75.0	1,076	24.2
Under 65 years	4,156	3,665	88.2	3,484	83.8	1,102	26.5	2,688	64.7	3,169	76.2	1,050	25.3
65 years and over	285	187	65.5	186	65.2	77	27.0	110	38.5	160	56.2	26	9.1
Related children under 18 years[e]	7,942	7,343	92.5	6,985	87.9	2,131	26.8	5,474	68.9	6,455	81.3	2,091	26.3
Under 6 years	3,140	2,902	92.4	2,840	90.5	822	26.2	2,195	69.9	2,655	84.6	864	27.5
6 to 17 years	4,802	4,441	92.5	4,144	86.3	1,309	27.3	3,279	68.3	3,800	79.1	1,227	25.5
Own children 18 years and over[g]	1,419	1,104	77.8	1,058	74.6	401	28.3	802	56.5	902	63.5	241	17.0

TABLE 2.13

Program participation status of household for persons below poverty level, 2009 [CONTINUED]

[Numbers in thousands]

	Total	In household that received means-tested assistance		In household that received means-tested assistance excluding school lunch		In household that received means-tested cash assistance		In household that received food stamps		In household in which one or more persons were covered by Medicaid		Lived in public or authorized housing	
		Number	Percent	Number	Percent	Number	Percent	Number	Percent	Number	Percent	Number	Percent
In unrelated subfamilies[c]	693	626	90.3	584	84.3	137	19.8	366	52.8	561	81.0	31	4.5
Under 18 years	423	387	91.5	361	85.4	85	20.2	226	53.4	346	81.8	18	4.2
Under 6 years	177	167	94.7	161	91.1	39	21.9	109	61.6	153	86.4	15	8.5
6 to 17 years	246	220	89.2	200	81.3	47	18.9	117	47.5	193	78.6	3	1.1
18 years and over	270	239	88.6	223	82.6	52	19.3	140	51.9	215	79.6	13	5.0
Unrelated individuals[d]	11,678	5,531	47.4	5,419	46.4	1,864	16.0	3,037	26.0	4,127	35.3	1,454	12.4
Male	5,255	2,392	45.5	2,330	44.3	767	14.6	1,299	24.7	1,763	33.5	512	9.7
Under 65 years	4,749	2,150	45.3	2,088	44.0	688	14.5	1,182	24.9	1,589	33.5	395	8.3
Living alone	1,709	735	43.0	734	43.0	304	17.8	442	25.8	495	29.0	254	14.9
65 years and over	505	242	47.9	242	47.9	79	15.5	117	23.2	174	34.4	117	23.1
Living alone	391	186	47.5	186	47.5	54	13.9	90	23.1	122	31.3	110	28.1
Female	6,424	3,139	48.9	3,089	48.1	1,097	17.1	1,738	27.0	2,364	36.8	942	14.7
Under 65 years	4,910	2,433	49.6	2,384	48.5	822	16.7	1,405	28.6	1,848	37.6	631	12.9
Living alone	1,921	1,067	55.6	1,065	55.4	468	24.4	730	38.0	743	38.7	526	27.4
65 years and over	1,514	706	46.6	706	46.6	275	18.2	332	21.9	516	34.1	310	20.5
Living alone	1,380	660	47.8	660	47.8	252	18.3	320	23.2	472	34.2	302	21.9

Notes: People who lived with someone (a nonrelative or a relative) who received aid. Not every person tallied here received the aid themselves.

ᵃUniverse: All people except unrelated individuals under age 15 (such as foster children). Since the Current Population Survey asks income questions only to people age 15 and over, if a child under age 15 is not part of a family by birth, marriage, or adoption, we do not know their income and cannot determine whether or not they are poor. Those people are excluded from the totals so as not to affect the percentages.

ᵇPeople in families: People who are related to the householder by birth, marriage, or adoption. People who are related to each other but not to the householder are counted elsewhere (usually as unrelated subfamilies).

ᶜPeople in unrelated subfamilies: People who are not related to the householder, but who are related to each other, either as a married couple or as a parent-child relationship with an unmarried child under 18.

ᵈUnrelated individuals: People who are not in primary families (the householder's family) or unrelated subfamilies.

ᵉPeople in families with related children: People living in a family where at least one member is a related child—a person under 18 who is related to the householder but is not the householder or spouse.

ᶠIn married-couple families the householder may be either the husband or the wife.

ᵍOwn children: Sons and daughters, including stepchildren and adopted children, of the householder.

SOURCE: "Pov26. Program Participation Status of Household—Poverty Status of People: 2009, All Races—Below Poverty Level," in *Current Population Survey (CPS), 2010 Annual Social and Economic Supplement (ASEC)*, U.S. Census Bureau, 2010, http://www.census.gov/hhes/www/cpstables/032010/pov/new26_002_01.htm (accessed February 18, 2011)

received means-tested benefits. The highest rate of assistance was provided to families headed by women with children under the age of six years (78.3%).

LENGTH OF TIME IN POVERTY
Entering and Exiting Poverty

For most poor Americans poverty is not a static condition. Some people near the poverty level improve their economic status within two years or less, whereas others at near-poverty levels become poor through economic catastrophes, such as an illness or job loss. Most data collected by the Census Bureau reflect a single point in time—in other words, show how many people are in poverty or participating in a means-tested government program in a certain month. These surveys, however, do not reflect the dynamic nature of poverty for individual people and families.

The Census Bureau collects longitudinal information (measurements over time for specific individuals or families) about poverty and government program participation rates in its Survey of Income and Program Participation (SIPP). This makes it possible to measure the movement of individuals and families into and out of poverty (entry and exit rates), the duration of poverty spells (the number of months in poverty for those who were not poor during the first interview month, but who became poor at some point during the study), and the length of time individuals and families use government programs.

In *Dynamics of Economic Well-Being, Poverty 2004-2006* (March 2011, http://www.census.gov/hhes/www/poverty/publications/dynamics04/P70-123.pdf), Robin J. Anderson of the Census Bureau uses data from the 2004 SIPP panel to examine poverty in the period from January 2004 to December 2006. Anderson focuses on monthly measures of poverty and distinguishes between short- and long-term poverty. As shown in Figure 2.3, the episodic (monthly) poverty rate is significantly higher than the annual poverty rate. In 2006 the episodic poverty rate hovered around 20%, whereas the annual poverty rate was about half that. Other highlights of the survey include:

- Nearly three out of 10 (28.9%) people were poor for at least two months in the three years between 2004 and 2006. (See Figure 2.3.)

- Approximately 2.8% of the population was chronically poor. That is, the population was poor during all 36 months from January 2004 to December 2006.

- About 23.1% of people in poverty in January and February 2004 remained in poverty for the entire study period.

- Nonelderly adults were more likely to exit poverty than children and the elderly.

- Children had the highest entry rates into poverty and, along with retirement-age adults, had a low exit rate.

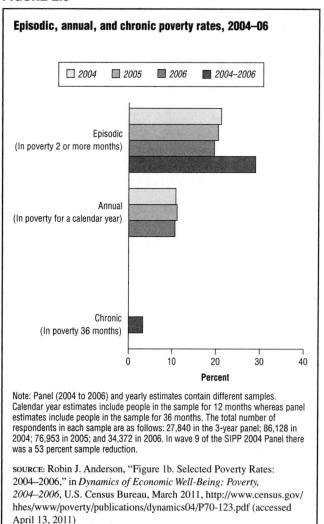

FIGURE 2.3

Episodic, annual, and chronic poverty rates, 2004–06

Note: Panel (2004 to 2006) and yearly estimates contain different samples. Calendar year estimates include people in the sample for 12 months whereas panel estimates include people in the sample for 36 months. The total number of respondents in each sample are as follows: 27,840 in the 3-year panel; 86,128 in 2004; 76,953 in 2005; and 34,372 in 2006. In wave 9 of the SIPP 2004 Panel there was a 53 percent sample reduction.

SOURCE: Robin J. Anderson, "Figure 1b. Selected Poverty Rates: 2004–2006," in *Dynamics of Economic Well-Being: Poverty, 2004–2006*, U.S. Census Bureau, March 2011, http://www.census.gov/hhes/www/poverty/publications/dynamics04/P70-123.pdf (accessed April 13, 2011)

- About half (47.7%) of all poverty spells lasted two to four months, whereas 12.4% lasted more than two years.

RACE. Anderson notes that of the poor in 2004, non-Hispanic whites (49.6%) were more likely to have left poverty by 2006 than either African-Americans (29.5%) or Hispanics (42.1%). (See Figure 2.4.) Also, non-Hispanic whites who were not poor at the beginning of the study period were less likely to have entered poverty by 2006 than African-Americans or Hispanics. (See Figure 2.5.)

Figure 2.6 shows the proportion of the entire population, the episodically poor population, and the chronically poor population made up of white, African-American, and other racial groups. Even though whites made up 80.7% of the total population, they made up only 72.5% of the episodically poor population and only 54.5% of the chronically poor population. In contrast, African-Americans made up 12.5% of the total population, but 19.6% of the episodically poor population and 37.6% of the chronically poor population. Therefore, African-Americans are disproportionally represented among the poor, especially among the chronically poor.

FIGURE 2.4

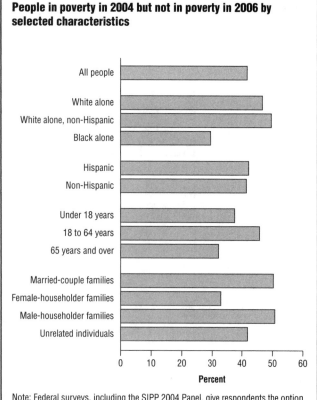

People in poverty in 2004 but not in poverty in 2006 by selected characteristics

Note: Federal surveys, including the SIPP 2004 Panel, give respondents the option of reporting more than one race. These data can be shown in two ways (1) as mutually exclusive from other race groups, which may be denoted by "alone" or (2) not mutually exclusive with other race groups, denoted by "alone or in combination with other race groups." This figure shows race using the first method. Because Hispanics may be of any race, data for Hispanics are not mutually exclusive with race. Female householders have no husband present and male householders have no wife present.

SOURCE: Robin J. Anderson, "Figure 4. Poverty Exit Rates: People in Poverty in 2004 but Not in Poverty in 2006 by Selected Characteristics," in *Dynamics of Economic Well-Being: Poverty, 2004–2006*, U.S. Census Bureau, March 2011, http://www.census.gov/ hhes/www/poverty/publications/dynamics04/P70-123.pdf (accessed April 13, 2011)

FIGURE 2.5

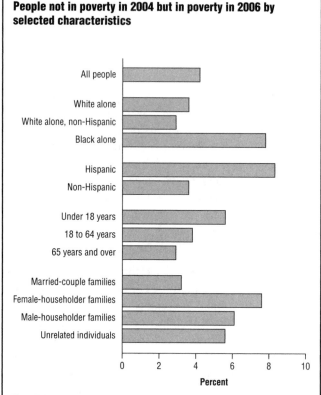

People not in poverty in 2004 but in poverty in 2006 by selected characteristics

Note: Federal surveys, including the SIPP 2004 Panel, give respondents the option of reporting more than one race. These data can be shown in two ways (1) as mutually exclusive from other race groups, which may be denoted by "alone" or (2) not mutually exclusive with other race groups, denoted by "alone or in combination with other race groups." This figure shows race using the first method. Because Hispanics may be of any race, data for Hispanics are not mutually exclusive with race. Female householders have no husband present and male householders have no wife present.

SOURCE: Robin J. Anderson, "Figure 3. Poverty Entry Rates: People Not in Poverty in 2004 but in Poverty in 2006 by Selected Characteristics," in *Dynamics of Economic Well-Being: Poverty, 2004–2006*, U.S. Census Bureau, March 2011, http://www.census.gov/hhes/www/ poverty/publications/dynamics04/P70-123.pdf (accessed April 13, 2011)

AGE. The elderly and children are less likely to exit poverty than are people of other ages. About 32.2% of the elderly and 37.6% of children under the age of 18 years who were poor in 2004 were able to escape poverty by 2006. (See Figure 2.4.) In contrast, adults aged 18 to 64 years were the most likely to escape poverty—45.8% moved out of poverty. However, children under the age of 18 years were much more likely to enter poverty at some point during the study period than were adults of any age. (See Figure 2.5.)

Figure 2.6 shows the proportion of the entire population, the episodically poor population, and the chronically poor population made up of different age groups. Children are disproportionally represented among the poor. Even though they made up 26.1% of the population as a whole, they represent 32.8% of the episodically poor population and 44.9% of the chronically poor population.

Adults aged 18 to 64 years were underrepresented among the poor, especially among the chronically poor, whereas senior citizens, who often live on fixed incomes, were underrepresented among the episodically poor.

FAMILY STATUS. According to Anderson, poor families headed by married couples were much more likely than other poor family types to have left poverty by 2006, underscoring how having two potential wage earners in a family helps protect a family from poverty. Of the poor families headed by married couples in 2004, 50.3% were able to escape poverty by 2006. (See Figure 2.4.) Only 33% of the poor families headed by women recovered from poverty by 2006. Families headed by married couples were also significantly less likely to have entered poverty by 2006. (See Figure 2.5.) With at least two adults in the household, these families are more likely to have at least one person working than a family headed by a single person.

FIGURE 2.6

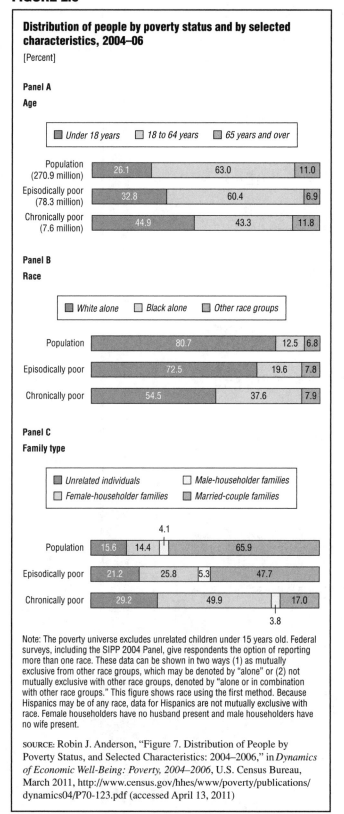

Distribution of people by poverty status and by selected characteristics, 2004–06

[Percent]

Panel A
Age

Legend: Under 18 years | 18 to 64 years | 65 years and over

Population (270.9 million): 26.1 | 63.0 | 11.0
Episodically poor (78.3 million): 32.8 | 60.4 | 6.9
Chronically poor (7.6 million): 44.9 | 43.3 | 11.8

Panel B
Race

Legend: White alone | Black alone | Other race groups

Population: 80.7 | 12.5 | 6.8
Episodically poor: 72.5 | 19.6 | 7.8
Chronically poor: 54.5 | 37.6 | 7.9

Panel C
Family type

Legend: Unrelated individuals | Male-householder families | Female-householder families | Married-couple families

Population: 15.6 | 14.4 | 4.1 | 65.9
Episodically poor: 21.2 | 25.8 | 5.3 | 47.7
Chronically poor: 29.2 | 49.9 | 3.8 | 17.0

Note: The poverty universe excludes unrelated children under 15 years old. Federal surveys, including the SIPP 2004 Panel, give respondents the option of reporting more than one race. These data can be shown in two ways (1) as mutually exclusive from other race groups, which may be denoted by "alone" or (2) not mutually exclusive with other race groups, denoted by "alone or in combination with other race groups." This figure shows race using the first method. Because Hispanics may be of any race, data for Hispanics are not mutually exclusive with race. Female householders have no husband present and male householders have no wife present.

SOURCE: Robin J. Anderson, "Figure 7. Distribution of People by Poverty Status, and Selected Characteristics: 2004–2006," in *Dynamics of Economic Well-Being: Poverty, 2004–2006*, U.S. Census Bureau, March 2011, http://www.census.gov/hhes/www/poverty/publications/dynamics04/P70-123.pdf (accessed April 13, 2011)

up 14.4% of households in 2006, were overrepresented among the poor; they made up 25.8% of the episodically poor households and 49.9% of the chronically poor households. In contrast, married-couple families made up 65.9% of all households, but only 47.7% of the episodically poor households and only 17% of the chronically poor households.

Having a Job Does Not Guarantee Escape from Poverty

The working poor are those people who participated in the labor force for at least 27 weeks (either working or looking for work) and who lived in families with incomes below the official poverty level. Nearly 8.9 million workers in 2008 (6% of individuals aged 16 years and older in the labor force) found that their jobs did not provide enough income to keep them out of poverty. (See Table 2.14.)

In 2008, 4.5 million working women and 4.4 million working men had incomes below the poverty level. (See Table 2.14.) Therefore, working women had a higher poverty rate (6.5%) than working men (5.6%). Even though 71.2% of the working poor were white (6.3 million of 8.9 million workers), African-American and Hispanic workers continued to experience poverty while employed at more than twice the rates of whites. African-Americans (11%) and Hispanics (12.4%) with at least 27 weeks in the labor force had a far higher poverty rate than whites (5.2%) or Asian-Americans (5.1%). Younger workers were more likely to be in poverty than older workers. Much of the reason for this is that many younger workers are still in school and work at part-time or entry-level jobs that often do not pay well.

In general, the lower the educational level, the higher the risk of poverty among workers. Among workers in the labor force for at least 27 weeks in 2008, those with less than a high school diploma had well over twice the poverty rate (18.3%) of high school graduates (7.2%). (See Table 2.15.) Far lower poverty rates were reported for workers with an associate's degree (3.5%) or a four-year college degree (1.7%). African-American and Hispanic workers, regardless of education levels, had higher poverty rates than white workers. Women had a higher poverty rate than men at all educational levels and among all race and ethnic groups. The highest poverty rate (32.5%) was for African-American women workers without a high school diploma.

In 2008 working families headed by married couples without children were less likely than other family types to be poor (1.7%). (See Table 2.16.) The presence of children under the age of 18 years increased the married-couple poverty rate to 6.2%, reflecting the added monetary burdens of raising children and the decreased likelihood that a family will have two adults working full time. Single women with children were the most likely to be living in poverty (24.8%), although a significant portion of single men with children were among the working poor (12.1%).

Figure 2.6 shows the proportion of the entire population, the episodically poor population, and the chronically poor population made up of unrelated individuals, female-householder families, male-householder families, and married-couple families. Female-householder families, which make

TABLE 2.14

Poverty status of people in the labor force for 27 weeks or more, by age, sex, race, and Hispanic origin, 2008

[Numbers in thousands]

Age and sex	Total	White	Black or African American	Asian	Hispanic or Latino ethnicity	Below poverty level Total	White	Black or African American	Asian	Hispanic or Latino ethnicity	Rate[a] Total	White	Black or African American	Asian	Hispanic or Latino ethnicity
Total, 16 years and older	**147,838**	**120,660**	**16,817**	**6,772**	**21,005**	**8,883**	**6,321**	**1,844**	**349**	**2,604**	**6.0**	**5.2**	**11.0**	**5.1**	**12.4**
16 to 19 years	4,079	3,357	494	73	654	518	365	110	16	117	12.7	10.9	22.3	21.4	17.9
20 to 24 years	13,311	10,688	1,680	453	2,415	1,525	1,094	303	38	368	11.5	10.2	18.1	8.4	15.2
25 to 34 years	32,349	25,626	4,121	1,627	6,172	2,555	1,753	614	72	858	7.9	6.8	14.9	4.4	13.9
35 to 44 years	33,689	26,892	4,120	1,852	5,539	1,953	1,389	398	99	716	5.8	5.2	9.7	5.4	12.9
45 to 54 years	35,633	29,385	3,906	1,654	3,941	1,462	1,053	291	75	366	4.1	3.6	7.5	4.5	9.3
55 to 64 years	22,349	19,088	2,000	891	1,849	738	558	111	45	156	3.3	2.9	5.5	5.1	8.5
65 years and older	6,428	5,624	495	221	434	132	109	16	3	22	2.0	1.9	3.2	1.3	5.1
Men, 16 years and older	**79,280**	**65,908**	**7,817**	**3,621**	**12,593**	**4,418**	**3,331**	**698**	**195**	**1,585**	**5.6**	**5.1**	**8.9**	**5.4**	**12.6**
16 to 19 years	2,066	1,701	235	46	353	232	164	46	9	59	11.2	9.6	19.7	b	16.7
20 to 24 years	7,042	5,720	813	238	1,419	694	510	118	15	221	9.8	8.9	14.5	6.3	15.6
25 to 34 years	17,854	14,522	1,935	859	3,947	1,229	941	192	39	539	6.9	6.5	9.9	4.6	13.7
35 to 44 years	18,403	15,014	1,922	1,021	3,363	1,053	807	152	63	458	5.7	5.4	7.9	6.2	13.6
45 to 54 years	18,618	15,622	1,777	853	2,210	750	557	128	40	196	4.0	3.6	7.2	4.7	8.9
55 to 64 years	11,705	10,147	901	467	1,053	398	302	57	25	95	3.4	3.0	6.3	5.4	9.0
65 years and older	3,593	3,182	234	137	248	61	50	5	3	16	1.7	1.6	1.9	2.0	6.5
Women, 16 years and older	**68,558**	**54,752**	**9,000**	**3,151**	**8,412**	**4,464**	**2,990**	**1,146**	**154**	**1,020**	**6.5**	**5.5**	**12.7**	**4.9**	**12.1**
16 to 19 years	2,013	1,655	260	27	301	286	201	64	7	59	14.2	12.1	24.8	b	19.4
20 to 24 years	6,269	4,968	868	216	996	831	584	185	23	147	13.3	11.7	21.4	10.8	14.7
25 to 34 years	14,495	11,104	2,186	768	2,225	1,326	813	422	33	319	9.1	7.3	19.3	4.3	14.3
35 to 44 years	15,286	11,877	2,198	831	2,176	899	583	246	36	258	5.9	4.9	11.2	4.3	11.9
45 to 54 years	17,015	13,763	2,129	801	1,731	712	496	163	35	170	4.2	3.6	7.7	4.3	9.8
55 to 64 years	10,644	8,942	1,099	424	797	340	256	54	20	61	3.2	2.9	4.9	4.8	7.7
65 years and older	2,836	2,441	261	84	186	70	59	11	—	6	2.5	2.4	4.3	0.2	3.2

[a]Number below the poverty level as a percent of the total in the labor force for 27 weeks or more.

[b]Data not shown where base is less than 80,000.

Notes: Estimates for the above race groups (white, black or African American, and Asian) do not sum to totals because data are not presented for all races. Persons whose ethnicity is identified as Hispanic or Latino may be of any race. Dash represents or rounds to zero.

SOURCE: "Table 2. People in the Labor Force for 27 Weeks or More: Poverty Status by Age, Sex, Race, and Hispanic or Latino Ethnicity, 2008," in *A Profile of the Working Poor, 2008*, U.S. Department of Labor, Bureau of Labor Statistics, March 2010, http://www.bls.gov/cps/cpswp2008.pdf (accessed February 17, 2011).

TABLE 2.15

Poverty status by educational attainment, race and Hispanic origin, and sex, 2008

[Numbers in thousands]

Educational attainment, race, and Hispanic or Latino ethnicity	Total	Men	Women	Below poverty level Total	Below poverty level Men	Below poverty level Women	Rate[a] Total	Rate[a] Men	Rate[a] Women
Total, 16 years and older	**147,838**	**79,280**	**68,558**	**8,883**	**4,418**	**4,464**	**6.0**	**5.6**	**6.5**
Less than a high school diploma	15,097	9,580	5,517	2,769	1,628	1,141	18.3	17.0	20.7
Less than 1 year of high school	4,733	3,210	1,522	942	633	309	19.9	19.7	20.3
1–3 years of high school	8,616	5,282	3,334	1,554	832	722	18.0	15.7	21.7
4 years of high school, no diploma	1,749	1,087	661	273	164	109	15.6	15.1	16.5
High school graduates, no college[b]	43,085	24,404	18,681	3,113	1,508	1,605	7.2	6.2	8.6
Some college or associate degree	43,132	21,272	21,860	2,201	907	1,294	5.1	4.3	5.9
Some college, no degree	28,650	14,677	13,974	1,696	736	960	5.9	5.0	6.9
Associate degree	14,482	6,596	7,886	505	171	334	3.5	2.6	4.2
Bachelor's degree and higher[c]	46,524	24,024	22,500	800	375	425	1.7	1.6	1.9
White, 16 years and older	**120,660**	**65,908**	**54,752**	**6,321**	**3,331**	**2,990**	**5.2**	**5.1**	**5.5**
Less than a high school diploma	12,319	8,117	4,202	2,076	1,309	767	16.9	16.1	18.2
Less than 1 year of high school	4,110	2,877	1,233	804	556	247	19.6	19.3	20.0
1–3 years of high school	6,913	4,399	2,513	1,109	650	459	16.0	14.8	18.3
4 years of high school, no diploma	1,297	842	456	163	103	60	12.6	12.2	13.3
High school graduates, no college[b]	35,023	20,162	14,861	2,178	1,110	1,068	6.2	5.5	7.2
Some college or associate degree	34,913	17,544	17,369	1,491	661	830	4.3	3.8	4.8
Some college, no degree	22,928	12,019	10,909	1,152	538	614	5.0	4.5	5.6
Associate degree	11,985	5,525	6,460	339	123	217	2.8	2.2	3.4
Bachelor's degree and higher[c]	38,404	20,084	18,320	576	251	325	1.5	1.2	1.8
Black or African American, 16 years and older	**16,817**	**7,817**	**9,000**	**1,844**	**698**	**1,146**	**11.0**	**8.9**	**12.7**
Less than a high school diploma	1,715	849	866	474	193	282	27.7	22.7	32.5
Less than 1 year of high school	229	116	113	67	33	34	29.1	28.2	29.9
1–3 years of high school	1,174	566	608	324	115	209	27.6	20.3	34.4
4 years of high school, no diploma	312	166	146	84	45	39	26.8	26.9	26.5
High school graduates, no college[b]	5,888	3,083	2,804	735	284	451	12.5	9.2	16.1
Some college or associate degree	5,619	2,362	3,257	539	175	365	9.6	7.4	11.2
Some college, no degree	3,990	1,734	2,256	413	144	269	10.3	8.3	11.9
Associate degree	1,629	628	1,001	127	31	96	7.8	4.9	9.5
Bachelor's degree and higher[c]	3,595	1,523	2,072	95	47	48	2.6	3.1	2.3
Asian, 16 years and older	**6,772**	**3,621**	**3,151**	**349**	**195**	**154**	**5.1**	**5.4**	**4.9**
Less than a high school diploma	520	274	245	84	48	36	16.2	17.5	14.9
Less than 1 year of high school	230	106	124	39	23	16	16.9	21.7	12.8
1–3 years of high school	211	125	86	33	17	16	15.7	13.6	18.6
4 years of high school, no diploma	79	43	35	13	8	5	d	d	d
High school graduates, no college[b]	1,156	576	580	85	50	34	7.3	8.7	5.9
Some college or associate degree	1,334	704	631	73	28	45	5.5	4.0	7.1
Some college, no degree	844	463	382	60	24	36	7.1	5.1	9.4
Associate degree	490	241	249	13	4	9	2.7	1.8	3.6
Bachelor's degree and higher[c]	3,762	2,067	1,695	107	68	38	2.8	3.3	2.3
Hispanic or Latino ethnicity, 16 years and older	**21,005**	**12,593**	**8,412**	**2,604**	**1,585**	**1,020**	**12.4**	**12.6**	**12.1**
Less than a high school diploma	6,764	4,673	2,091	1,438	953	484	21.3	20.4	23.2
Less than 1 year of high school	3,474	2,447	1,027	730	504	226	21.0	20.6	22.0
1–3 years of high school	2,731	1,820	912	615	377	238	22.5	20.7	26.1
4 years of high school, no diploma	559	406	153	93	73	21	16.7	17.9	13.5
High school graduates, no college[b]	6,502	3,939	2,563	712	418	294	10.9	10.6	11.5
Some college or associate degree	4,844	2,496	2,348	362	175	187	7.5	7.0	8.0
Some college, no degree	3,466	1,843	1,623	266	137	128	7.7	7.5	7.9
Associate degree	1,379	653	725	96	37	59	7.0	5.7	8.1
Bachelor's degree and higher[c]	2,894	1,485	1,410	93	39	54	3.2	2.6	3.8

[a]Number below the poverty level as a percent of the total in the labor force for 27 weeks or more.
[b]Includes people with a high school diploma or equivalent.
[c]Includes people with bachelor's, master's, professional, and doctoral degrees.
[d]Data not shown where base is less than 80,000.
Notes: Estimates for the above race groups (white, black or African American, and Asian) do not sum to totals because data are not presented for all races. Persons whose ethnicity is identified as Hispanic or Latino may be of any race.

SOURCE: "Table 3. People in the Labor Force for 27 Weeks or More: Poverty Status by Educational Attainment, Race, Hispanic or Latino Ethnicity, and Sex, 2008," in *A Profile of the Working Poor, 2008*, U.S. Department of Labor, Bureau of Labor Statistics, March 2010, http://www.bls.gov/cps/cpswp2008.pdf (accessed February 17, 2011)

TABLE 2.16

Poverty status of families, by presence of related children and work experience of family members, 2008

[Numbers in thousands]

Characteristic	Total families	At or above poverty level	Below poverty level	Rate*
Total primary families	**65,907**	**61,369**	**4,538**	**6.9**
With related children under 18 years	35,700	31,928	3,772	10.6
Without children	30,207	29,441	765	2.5
With one member in the labor force	27,612	23,850	3,762	13.6
With two or more members in the labor force	38,295	37,519	776	2.0
With two members	32,115	31,433	682	2.1
With three or more members	6,180	6,086	94	1.5
Married-couple families	**49,906**	**47,915**	**1,992**	**4.0**
With related children under 18 years	25,646	24,060	1,586	6.2
Without children	24,261	23,855	406	1.7
With one member in the labor force	16,659	15,186	1,473	8.8
Husband	11,959	10,812	1,147	9.6
Wife	4,004	3,734	269	6.7
Relative	696	639	56	8.1
With two or more members in the labor force	33,247	32,729	519	1.6
With two members	28,145	27,683	462	1.6
With three or more members	5,102	5,046	56	1.1
Families maintained by women	**11,419**	**9,281**	**2,138**	**18.7**
With related children under 18 years	7,661	5,764	1,897	24.8
Without children	3,759	3,518	241	6.4
With one member in the labor force	8,213	6,267	1,946	23.7
Householder	6,774	5,082	1,692	25.0
Relative	1,439	1,185	255	17.7
With two or more members in the labor force	3,206	3,014	192	6.0
Families maintained by men	**4,581**	**4,173**	**408**	**8.9**
With related children under 18 years	2,394	2,105	289	12.1
Without children	2,187	2,069	119	5.4
With one member in the labor force	2,740	2,398	343	12.5
Householder	2,284	1,994	291	12.7
Relative	456	404	52	11.4
With two or more members in the labor force	1,841	1,776	65	3.5

*Number below the poverty level as a percent of the total in the labor force for 27 weeks or more.
Note: Data relate to primary families with at least one member in the labor force for 27 weeks or more.

SOURCE: "Table 5. Primary Families: Poverty Status, Presence of Related Children, and Work Experience of Family Members in the Labor Force for 27 Weeks or More, 2008," in *A Profile of the Working Poor, 2008*, U.S. Department of Labor, Bureau of Labor Statistics, March 2010, http://www.bls.gov/cps/cpswp2008 .pdf (accessed February 17, 2011)

In a family headed by a married couple, a greater likelihood exists that two members of the family are working than exists in a single-parent family. Two-income families are rarely poor. Only 1.6% of families headed by married couples with two or more wage earners were poor in 2008. (See Table 2.16.) In *A Profile of the Working Poor, 2008* (March 2010, http://www.bls.gov/cps/cpswp2008.pdf), the Bureau of Labor Statistics states that of the 4.5 million working-poor families, 2.1 million (47.1%) were families maintained by women. Working women who were the sole supporters of their families had the highest poverty rate, at 25%.

Several factors affect the poverty status of working families: the size of the family, the number of workers in the family, the characteristics of the workers, and various labor market problems. The addition of a child puts a financial strain on the family and increases the chances that a parent might have to stay home to care for the child. Even though a child in a single-parent family may

work, children are usually employed for low pay and at part-time jobs. In addition, the more education a person has, the more his or her job is likely to pay. Single mothers are more likely to have less education than married women with children.

Finally, the labor market plays a major role in whether a working family lives in poverty. Three major labor market problems contributed to poverty among workers in 2008: unemployment, low earnings, and involuntary part-time employment. Only 0.6% of workers who did not suffer from any of these problems were poor in 2008. (See Table 2.17.) By contrast, 21.5% of low-paid workers were in poverty. Unemployment accounted for the poverty of 5.8% of workers, and involuntary part-time work for 2.5%. However, it was the combination of two or more factors that had the most devastating effect on families. Among workers who experienced unemployment, low earnings, and involuntary part-time employment, 46.7% were in poverty.

TABLE 2.17

Poverty status and labor market problems of full-time wage and salary workers, 2008

[Numbers in thousands]

Labor market problems	Total	At or above poverty level	Below poverty level	Rate[a]
Total, full-time wage and salary workers	**114,029**	**109,980**	**4,050**	**3.6**
No unemployment, involuntary part-time employment, or low earnings[b]	90,912	90,336	576	0.6
Unemployment only	7,788	7,334	454	5.8
Involuntary part-time employment only	2,975	2,900	75	2.5
Low earnings only	7,488	5,880	1,607	21.5
Unemployment and involuntary part-time employment	1,594	1,472	122	7.7
Unemployment and low earnings	1,786	1,107	679	38.0
Involuntary part-time employment and low earnings	906	641	265	29.3
Unemployment, involuntary part-time employment, and low earnings	580	309	271	46.7
Unemployment (alone or with other problems)	11,749	10,223	1,526	13.0
Involuntary part-time employment (alone or with other problems)	6,056	5,322	734	12.1
Low earnings (alone or with other problems)	10,760	7,937	2,823	26.2

[a]Number below the poverty level as a percent of the total in the labor force for 27 weeks or more.
[b]The low-earnings threshold in 2008 was $316.89 per week.

SOURCE: "Table 8. People in the Labor Force for 27 Weeks or More: Poverty Status and Labor Market Problems of Full-Time Wage and Salary Workers, 2008," in *A Profile of the Working Poor, 2008*, U.S. Department of Labor, Bureau of Labor Statistics, March 2010, http://www.bls.gov/cps/cpswp2008.pdf (accessed February 17, 2011)

CHAPTER 3
PUBLIC PROGRAMS TO FIGHT POVERTY

The federal government and individual states use many methods to combat poverty. There are a variety of programs that provide assistance to those in or at risk of poverty. These are often referred to as welfare. Some of these programs, such as Temporary Aid for Needy Families (TANF), are designed to help people improve their situation so they will no longer be poor. The Supplemental Security Income program provides assistance to people who have conditions that make it difficult for them to earn a living. A number of programs, including the Supplemental Nutrition Assistance Program and Medicaid, are designed to help those in poverty meet their basic needs for food, shelter, and medical care (these programs are discussed in Chapter 8). Besides welfare programs, the government has established programs and policies such as the minimum wage and unemployment compensation that are intended to help people avoid poverty in the first place.

The most far-reaching welfare law is the Personal Responsibility and Work Opportunity Reconciliation Act (PRWORA). First enacted in 1996 and renewed since, the PRWORA replaced a welfare system that was based primarily on the Aid to Families with Dependent Children (AFDC) program with one centered on TANF. Critics of the AFDC felt that the system produced welfare dependency rather than temporary assistance to help recipients move into a job and off welfare. TANF was specifically designed to limit the amount of time individuals could receive benefits and to require them to work. The intention of the law was to reduce the number of people receiving welfare by bringing them into the workforce and out of poverty. The PRWORA also changed some other welfare programs to place greater emphasis on these priorities. In "Policy Basics: An Introduction to TANF" (March 19, 2009, http://www.cbpp.org/cms/index.cfm?fa=view&id=936), Liz Schott of the Center on Budget and Policy Priorities (CBPP) notes that additional work requirements for TANF recipients put in place by the Deficit Reduction Act of 2005 further reduced the TANF caseload.

According to the U.S. Department of Health and Human Services (HHS), the welfare caseload fell from a monthly average of 4.4 million families in fiscal year (FY) 1996 to an average of 1.9 million families in FY 2006, a drop of 57%. (See Table 3.1.) This represents the largest welfare caseload decline in history. Observers agreed that some of the decline was the result of a strong economy in which unemployment was around 4%, rather than welfare reform. For example, a study conducted by the City University of New York and cited by the HHS in *Temporary Assistance for Needy Families Program (TANF): Fourth Annual Report to Congress* (April 2002, http://www.acf.hhs.gov/programs/ofa/data-reports/ar2001/indexar.htm) attributes 60% of the reductions in caseloads to welfare reform and 20% to the effects of a robust economy.

Critics of the PRWORA question if the reduction in welfare caseloads is really a good thing. They are concerned that the current system causes former welfare recipients—without adequate health care, child care, and affordable housing—to slip through the cracks of the welfare system into destitution and homelessness. For example, in states in which living wage jobs are unavailable, the poor population may simply be moved from welfare into low-wage work and deeper into poverty. Figure 3.1 shows that the percent of the population with incomes that qualified for cash assistance and that actually received assistance declined from 84.3% in 1994 to 40.4% in 2005. Sharon Parrott and Arloc Sherman of the CBPP state in *TANF at 10: Program Results Are More Mixed Than Often Understood* (August 17, 2006, http://www.cbpp.org/files/8-17-06tanf.pdf) that "more than half—57%—of the caseload decline during the first decade of welfare reform reflects a decline in the extent to which TANF programs serve families that are poor enough to qualify, rather than to a reduction in the number of families who are poor enough to qualify for aid."

In addition, TANF's ability to respond to worsening economic conditions during the so-called Great Recession,

TABLE 3.1

Trends in the cash welfare caseload, fiscal years 1960–2006

Year	Cash welfare caseload (numbers in thousands)			Children in families receiving cash welfare as a percent of	
	Families	Recipients	Children	All children	Children in poverty
1960	791	3,012	2,330	3.4	12.1
1961	873	3,363	2,598	3.7	14.3
1962	939	3,704	2,844	4.0	15.7
1963	963	3,945	2,957	4.1	17.4
1964	1,010	4,195	3,145	4.3	18.6
1965	1,060	4,422	3,321	4.5	21.5
1966	1,096	4,546	3,434	4.7	26.5
1967	1,220	5,014	3,771	5.2	31.2
1968	1,410	5,702	4,274	5.9	37.8
1969	1,696	6,689	4,973	6.9	49.7
1970	2,207	8,462	6,212	8.6	57.7
1971	2,763	10,242	7,435	10.4	68.5
1972	3,048	10,944	7,905	11.1	74.9
1973	3,148	10,949	7,903	11.2	79.9
1974	3,219	10,847	7,805	11.2	75.0
1975	3,481	11,319	8,071	11.8	71.2
1976	3,565	11,284	7,982	11.8	76.2
1977	3,568	11,015	7,743	11.6	73.9
1978	3,517	10,551	7,363	11.2	72.8
1979	3,509	10,312	7,181	11.0	68.0
1980	3,712	10,774	7,419	11.5	63.2
1981	3,835	11,079	7,527	11.7	59.2
1982	3,542	10,358	6,903	10.8	49.6
1983	3,686	10,761	7,098	11.1	50.1
1984	3,714	10,831	7,144	11.2	52.3
1985	3,701	10,855	7,198	11.3	54.4
1986	3,763	11,038	7,334	11.5	56.0
1987	3,776	11,027	7,366	11.5	56.4
1988	3,749	10,915	7,329	11.4	57.8
1989	3,798	10,992	7,419	11.5	57.9
1990	4,057	11,695	7,911	12.1	57.9
1991	4,497	12,930	8,715	13.2	59.8
1992	4,829	13,773	9,303	13.9	59.9
1993	5,012	14,205	9,574	14.1	60.0
1994	5,033	14,161	9,568	13.9	61.7
1995	4,791	13,418	9,135	13.1	61.5
1996	4,434	12,321	8,600	12.3	58.7
1997	3,740	10,376	NA	NA	NA
1998	3,050	8,347	6,320	8.9	46.1
1999	2,578	6,924	5,109	7.2	40.9
2000	2,303	6,143	4,479	6.1	38.1
2001	2,192	5,717	4,195	5.7	35.3
2002	2,187	5,609	4,119	5.6	33.6
2003	2,180	5,490	4,063	5.5	31.3
2004	2,153	5,342	3,969	5.4	30.2
2005	2,061	5,028	3,756	5.1	28.9
2006	1,908	4,591	3,457	4.7	26.7

Note: For 2000 through 2006 the cash welfare caseload includes families receiving assistance under the Temporary Assistance for Needy Families (TANF) program and under "Separate State Programs (SSPs)" funded with TANF dollars. NA = not available.

SOURCE: Adapted from "Table 7-8. Trends in the Cash Welfare Caseload, Selected Years 1936 to 1960 and 1960–2006," in *Background Material and Data on the Programs within the Jurisdiction of the Committee on Ways and Means (Green Book)*, U.S. House of Representatives Committee on Ways and Means, 2008, http://democrats.waysandmeans.house.gov/media/pdf/110/tanf.pdf (accessed February 18, 2011)

which lasted from late 2007 to mid-2009, was limited. The administration of President Barack Obama (1961–) responded to the economic crisis by passing the American Recovery and Reinvestment Act (ARRA), which was signed into law in February 2009. The law provided additional TANF resources through an emergency contingency fund to states to help them assist poor families during the recession while leaving the basic principles of TANF in place. Nevertheless, LaDonna Pavetti, Danilo Trisi, and Liz Schott of the CBPP find in *TANF Responded Unevenly to Increase in Need during Downturn: Findings Suggest Needed Improvements When Program Reauthorized* (January 25, 2011, http://www.cbpp.org/files/1-25-11tanf.pdf) that even though the number of unemployed people doubled and the Supplemental Nutrition Assistance Program caseload rose by 45%, TANF caseloads increased by only 13%. Moreover, because states are provided block grants and are not obligated to increase caseloads, in 22 states TANF caseloads had small increases or declines. The following pages discuss the specific provisions of the PRWORA.

FIGURE 3.1

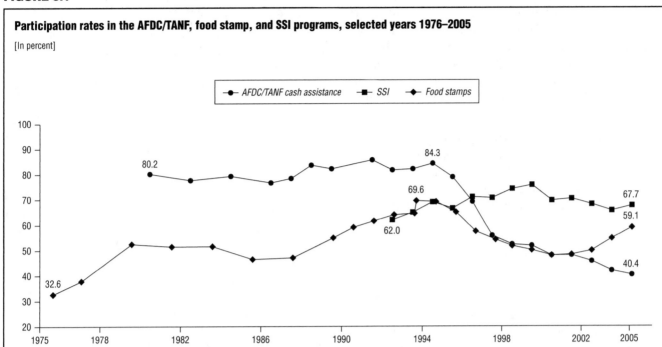

Participation rates in the AFDC/TANF, food stamp, and SSI programs, selected years 1976–2005

[In percent]

Note: AFDC/TANF and SSI participation rates are estimated by an Urban Institute model (TRIM3) that uses CPS data to simulate program eligibility and participation for an average month, by calendar year. There have been small changes in estimating methodology over time, due to model improvements and revisions to the CPS. Most notably, since 1994 the model has been revised to more accurately estimate SSI participation among children, and in 1997 and 1998 the model was adjusted to more accurately exclude ineligible immigrants. For TANF, in contrast to editions prior to 2004, this table includes families receiving assistance under Separate State Programs (SSPs). Note that families subject to full-family sanctions are counted as nonparticipating eligible families due to modeling limitations. Although the coverage rate estimates take into account the number of families who lost aid due to the time limit (and do not count such families in the denominator of the coverage rate estimate), they do not make any allowance for families staying off of TANF to conserve their time-limited assistance months. Also, the numbers of eligible and participating families include the territories and pregnant women without children, even though these two small groups are excluded from the TRIM model. The numbers shown here implicitly assume that participation rates for the territories and for pregnant women with no other children are the same as for all other eligibles. In 2004 the methods for identifying potential child-only units capture the fact that non-parent caretakers generally have a choice of whether or not to be included in the TANF unit. TRIM now excludes those caretakers whose income would make the unit ineligible, increasing the number of potential child-only units.

Food stamp eligible households are estimated from a Mathematica Policy Research, Inc. model that uses CPS data to simulate the Food Stamp Program. Food stamp caseload data are from USDA, FNS program operations caseload data. There have been small changes in the methodology over time, due to model improvements and revisions. Notably, the model was revised in 1994 to produce more accurate and lower estimates of eligible households. The estimates for previous years show higher estimates of eligibles and lower participation rates relative to the revised estimate for 1994 and estimates for subsequent years. The two estimates for 1999 are due to re-weighting of the March 2000–2003 CPS files to Census 2000 and revised methodologies for determining food stamp eligibility. The original estimate (September 1999) is consistent methodologically with estimates from September 1994–September 1998, while the revised estimate (fiscal year 1999) is consistent with the estimates for fiscal year 2000–fiscal year 2005.

Unlike the Food Stamp and SSI programs, TANF is a block grant program for which there is no individual entitlement. One of the main goals of TANF is to move people from cash assistance to self-sufficiency, which may be inconsistent with achieving a higher coverage rate.

AFDC = Aid to Families with Dependent Children. TANF = Temporary Assistance for Needy Families. SSI = Supplemental Security Income. TRIM = Transfer Income Model. CPS = Current Population Survey.

SOURCE: Gil Grouse, Susan Hauan, and Annette Waters Rogers, "Figure IND 4. Participation Rates in the AFDC/TANF, Food Stamp and SSI Programs: Selected Years," in *Indicators of Welfare Dependence: Annual Report to Congress, 2008*, U.S. Department of Health and Human Services, December 2008, http://aspe.hhs.gov/hsp/indicators08/ch2.pdf (accessed February 18, 2011)

THE PERSONAL RESPONSIBILITY AND WORK OPPORTUNITY RECONCILIATION ACT

Title I: Block Grants

Under the PRWORA, each state receives a single block grant (a lump sum of money). The amount of money available under TANF is actually decreasing. Federal funding for this TANF block grant was reduced from $16.4 billion per FY 1996 through June 30, 2004, to $16 billion per FYs 2006 to 2010. TANF was due to be reauthorized in 2010, but Congress extended the TANF block grant through September 30, 2011. Liz Schott and Ife Finch of the CBPP point out in *TANF Benefits Are Low and Have Not Kept Pace with Inflation: Benefits Are Not Enough to Meet Families' Basic Needs* (October 14, 2010, http://www.cbpp.org/files/10-14-10tanf.pdf) that TANF cash

assistance benefit levels in all states in 2010 were not high enough for a family to meet its basic needs. In fact, benefits were less than half of the federal poverty level and did much less to alleviate deep poverty in 2010 than benefits had done in 1996.

States have considerable control over how they implement the programs that are covered by the block grant, but the act requires that:

- Families on welfare for five cumulative years no longer receive further cash assistance. States can set shorter time limits and can exempt up to 20% of their caseload from the time limits.

- To count toward meeting the work requirement, a state must require individuals to participate in employment (public or private), on-the-job training, community service, work experience, vocational training (up to 12 months), or child care for other workers for at least 20 hours per week. State and local communities are responsible for the development of work, whether by creating community service jobs or by providing income subsidies or hiring incentives for potential employers.

- Unmarried parents under the age of 18 years must live with an adult or with adult supervision and must participate in educational or job training to receive benefits. In addition, the law encourages second-chance homes to provide teen parents with the skills and support they need. The law also provides $50 million per year in new funding for state abstinence education activities that are geared toward discouraging teen pregnancy through abstinence rather than through birth control.

None of the block grant funds can be used for adults who have been on welfare for over five years or who do not work after receiving benefits for two years. However, states are given some flexibility in how they spend their TANF funds.

Title II: Supplemental Security Income

The PRWORA redefined the term *disability* for children who receive Supplemental Security Income (SSI). A child is considered disabled if he or she has a medically determinable physical or mental impairment that results in marked and severe functional limitations that have lasted or can be expected to last at least 12 months or that can be expected to cause death. The PRWORA removed "maladaptive behavior" as a medical criterion from the listing of impairments used for evaluating mental disabilities in children.

Title III: Child Support

To be eligible for federal funds, each state must operate a Child Support Enforcement program that meets federal guidelines. The state must establish centralized registries of child support orders and centers for the collection and disbursement of child support payments, and parents must sign their child support rights over to the state to be eligible for TANF benefits. The state must also establish enforcement methods, such as revoking the driver's and professional licenses of delinquent parents. The Administration for Children and Families (ACF) notes in the fact sheet "Office of Child Support Enforcement (OCSE)" (January 2009, http://www.acf.hhs.gov/opa/fact_sheets/cse_factsheet.html) that in FY 2007 the program handled 15.8 million cases and collected $25 billion at a cost of $3.7 billion.

To receive full benefits, a mother must cooperate with state efforts to establish paternity. She may be denied assistance if she refuses to disclose the father.

Title IV: Restricting Welfare and Public Benefits for Noncitizens

The PRWORA originally severely limited or banned benefits to most legal immigrants who entered the country on or after August 22, 1996, when the bill became law. Ineligibility continued for a five-year period or until the legal immigrants attained citizenship. In addition, states had the option of withholding eligibility for Medicaid, TANF, and other social services from legal immigrants already residing in the United States.

Illegal immigrants no longer had any entitlement to benefit programs, such as TANF or Medicaid. They could receive emergency medical care, short-term disaster relief, immunizations, and treatment for communicable diseases (in the interest of public health). They could also use community services such as soup kitchens and shelters, some housing programs, and school lunches/breakfasts if their children were eligible for free public education. States have established programs to verify the legal residence of immigrants before paying benefits and may elect to deny Special Supplemental Food Program for Women, Infants, and Children benefits and other child nutrition programs to illegal aliens.

The Balanced Budget Act of 1997 and the Noncitizen Technical Amendment Act of 1998 invested $11.5 billion to restore disability and health benefits to 380,000 legal immigrants who were in the United States before the PRWORA became law in August 1996. The Balanced Budget Act also extended the SSI and Medicaid eligibility period for refugees and people seeking asylum from five years after entry to seven years to give these residents more time to naturalize.

Title V: Child Protection

The PRWORA gave states the authority to use current federal funds to pay for foster care for children in child care institutions. It extended the enhanced federal match for statewide automated child welfare information systems through 1997 and appropriated $6 million per year (FYs 1996 to 2002) for a national random sample study of abused and neglected children.

Title VI: Child Care

The law required that states maintain spending for child care for low-income families at the level of FY 1994 or FY 1995, whichever was greater, to be eligible for federally matched funds. Mandatory funding was set at $13.9 billion through June 30, 2004, with states receiving an estimated $1.2 billion per year before matching began. The remainder of the funds was available for state matching at the Medicaid rate. Total federal and state expenditures on child care totaled $3.2 billion in 2000, an increase of 60% over 1999 ($2 billion). In the press release "The Next Phase of Welfare Reform: Implementing the Deficit Reduction

Act of 2005" (December 2006, http://www.dhhs.gov/), the HHS explains that the Deficit Reduction Act of 2005, which reauthorized the PRWORA, provided for increased annual federal funding for child care by $1 billion by FY 2010. Hannah Matthews of the Center for Law and Social Policy reports in "TANF Child Care in 2009" (September 28, 2010, http://www.clasp.org/issues/in_focus?type=child _care_and_early_education&id=0271) that TANF funds used for child care in 2009 increased by 6% over 2008, from $3.3 billion to $3.5 billion.

As under previous laws, states must establish standards for the prevention and control of infectious diseases, such as immunization programs, and for building codes and physical safety in child care institutions. Child care workers must also receive minimal training in health and safety. However, many low-income people rely on informal sources of child care, including relatives and friends.

Pamela Holcomb et al. of the Urban Institute indicate in *Child Care Subsidies and TANF: A Synthesis of Three Studies on Systems, Policies, and Parents* (2006, http:// www.urban.org/UploadedPDF/311302_synthesis.pdf) that despite increased federal funding for child care, the need outweighs the resources that are available under the law. As a result of more parents working while still on welfare or leaving welfare to work, the critical need for child care has become more pronounced.

The U.S. Government Accountability Office (GAO) finds in *Child Care: Multiple Factors Could Have Contributed to the Recent Decline in the Number of Children Whose Families Receive Subsidies* (May 2010, http:// www.gao.gov/new.items/d10344.pdf) that between 2006 and 2008 the average number of children served by the Child Care and Development Block Grant had decreased by about 170,000, or 10%. The GAO also reports that the percentage of eligible children whose families received child care subsidies had declined. Only about a third or fewer eligible children received subsidies between 2004 and 2007. The GAO indicates that several reasons might account for this decline, including state policy allocating resources to other areas, decreased numbers of regulated child care providers, as well as a decreased demand for child care due to unemployment and reduced hours caused by the recession. The ARRA included an additional $2 billion to be distributed to the states to help fund the Child Care and Development Block Grant and provide access to subsidies to a larger number of families.

Title VII: Child Nutrition Programs

The PRWORA continued existing child nutrition programs, such as the National School Lunch Program and the School Breakfast Program. However, maximum reimbursement was reduced for the Summer Food Service Program and for some institutional food programs. States were allowed to decide whether to include or exclude legal immigrants from these programs. According to the U.S. Department of Agriculture (USDA), in *FY 2012 Budget Summary and Annual Performance Plan* (February 2011, http://www.obpa.usda.gov/budsum/FY12budsum.pdf), the budget for Child Nutrition Programs rose from $17.5 billion in FY 2011 to $19 billion in FY 2012.

Title VIII: Supplemental Nutrition Assistance Program

In 2008 the Food Stamp Program changed its name to the Supplemental Nutrition Assistance Program (SNAP). The PRWORA reduced maximum benefits to the level of the Thrifty Food Plan (a plan that serves as the basis for maximum food stamp allotments), the index set by the USDA that reflects the amount of money needed to purchase food to meet minimal nutrition requirements. Benefits were indexed to the rate of inflation so that they increase as inflation rises.

The law also restructured the way certain expenses and earnings were counted in establishing eligibility for food stamps. Under the PRWORA, when recipients' benefits are calculated, their countable monthly income is reduced by several deductions, including a standard deduction, a deduction for excessively high shelter expenses, a dependent care deduction, and medical expenses for the elderly and disabled. These deductions raised food stamp allotments. The Farm Bill of 2008 increased the minimum monthly benefit from $10 to $14 and excluded education and retirement accounts from countable resources.

In response to the severe economic recession that began in 2007, President Obama signed the ARRA in February 2009. According to the USDA, in the memo "Economic Stimulus—Adjustments to the Maximum Supplemental Nutrition Assistance Program (SNAP) Monthly Allotments" (February 18, 2009, http://www.fns.usda.gov/ snap/rules/Memo/2009/021809.pdf), the act increased SNAP benefits by 13.6% over the June value of the Thrifty Food Plan. Maximum monthly benefits for a family of four in the continental United States increased to $668; the maximum monthly allotment for a family of three increased to $526. As a result of the ARRA, these benefits remained unchanged in FY 2011.

By law, all SNAP recipients who are 18 to 50 years old and without children (known as able-bodied adults without dependents [ABAWD]) must work at least part time or be limited to three months of assistance in a 36-month period. Recipients who were in a workfare program (a welfare program that usually requires recipients to perform public-service duties) for 30 days but lost their placement may qualify for an additional three months of food assistance. (This provision was revised to allow states to exempt 15% of ABAWD recipients from this restriction.)

Reauthorization of the PRWORA

Since 1996 many changes have been made to the PRWORA. The PRWORA was reauthorized through 2010 when President George W. Bush (1946–) signed the Deficit Reduction Act in February 2006. The CBPP explains in *Implementing the TANF Changes in the Deficit Reduction Act: "Win-Win" Solutions for Families and States* (February 2007, http://www.cbpp.org/files/2-9-07tanf.pdf) that this bill did not increase funding for TANF programs; however, it did make the eligibility requirements more strict. The basic TANF block grant did not increase with inflation but remained capped at $16 billion. The reauthorization bill required 50% of TANF recipients to work in 2006, increasing by 5% each year to 70% in 2010. Funding for child care was set at $2 billion for each year between 2006 and 2010. Child support enforcement funding was reduced. Drug testing became required for every TANF applicant and recipient. Finally, the bill allowed TANF funds to be used to promote the value of marriage through public advertising and high school and adult classes and mentoring programs. In September 2010 Congress extended the PRWORA another year; it was scheduled to be reauthorized in September 2011.

ELIGIBILITY FOR TANF AND BENEFIT PAYMENTS

Under TANF, states decide how much to aid a needy family. No federal guidelines exist for determining eligibility, and no requirement mandates that states aid all needy families. TANF does not require states to have a need standard or a gross income limit, as the AFDC did, but many states base their TANF programs in part on their earlier practices.

The maximum benefit is the amount paid to a family with no countable income. (Federal law specifies what income counts toward figuring benefits and what income, such as child support, is to be disregarded by the state.) The maximum benefit is to be paid only to those families that comply with TANF's work requirements or other program requirements established by the state, such as parental and personal responsibility rules.

Even though most states vary benefits according to family size, some eliminate or restrict benefit increases due to the birth of a new child to a recipient already receiving benefits. Instead, benefits depend on family size at the time of enrollment in 16 states. Idaho pays a flat monthly grant that is the same regardless of family size. Wisconsin pays benefits based on work activity of the recipient and not on family size. Five states provide an increase in benefits to TANF families following the birth of an additional child.

Most states did not change their maximum benefits between July 1994 and January 2009, despite the major changes brought about by the PRWORA. When looking at

the maximum benefits as a percent of the poverty guidelines, benefits have actually declined in many states. Overall, the average maximum AFDC benefits in 1996 were $394 per month, or 34.9% of the poverty level for a family of three. (See Table 3.2.) By 2009 TANF benefits had risen to an average of $431 per month, providing an annual income of $5,172, only 27.9% of the poverty level for a family of three. (See Table 1.1 in Chapter 1.)

Many families receiving TANF benefits are also eligible for SNAP. A single benefit determination is made for both cash and food assistance. Even though the eligibility

TABLE 3.2

Maximum TANF benefit for a family of three with no income, by state, selected years 1996–2009

[July]

State	1996	2000	2004	2009
Alabama	$164	$164	$215	$215
Alaska	$923	$923	$923	$923
Arizona	$347	$347	$347	$278
Arkansas	$204	$204	$204	$204
California	$596	—	—	—
Nonexempt	—	$626	$723	$694
Exempt	—	$699	$808	$776
Colorado	$356	$356	$356	$462
Connecticut	$543	$543	$543	$560
Delaware	$338	$338	$338	$338
D.C.	$415	$379	$379	$428
Florida	$303	$303	$303	$303
Georgia	$280	$280	$280	$280
Hawaii	$712	$570[a]	$570[a]	$636[b]
Idaho	$317	$293	$309	$309
Illinois	$377	$377	$396	$432
Indiana	$288	$288	$288	$288
Iowa	$426	$426	$426	$426
Kansas	$429	$429	$429	$429
Kentucky	$262	$262	$262	$262
Louisiana	$190	$240	$240	$240
Maine	$418	$461	$485	$485
Maryland	$373	$417	$477	$574
Massachusetts				
Exempt	$579	$633	$633	$633
Nonexempt	$565	$618	$618	$618
Michigan	$459	$459[c]	$459[c]	$492
Minnesota	$532	$532	$532	$532
Mississippi	$120	$170	$170	$170
Missouri	$292	$292	$292	$292
Montana	$425	$477	$375	$504
Nebraska	$364	$364	$364	$364
Nevada	$348	$348	$348	$383
New Hampshire	$550	$600	$625	$675
New Jersey	$424	$424	$424	$424
New Mexico	$389	$439	$389	$447
New York	$577	$577	$691	$721
North Carolina	$272	$272	$272	$272
North Dakota	$431	$457	$477	$477
Ohio	$341	$373	$373	$434
Oklahoma	$307	$292	$292	$292
Oregon	$460	$503	$503	$514
Pennsylvania	$403	$403	$403	$403
Rhode Island	$554	$554	$554	$554
South Carolina	$200	$203	$205	$270
South Dakota	$430	$430	$501	$539
Tennessee	$185	$185[d]	$185[d]	$185[d]
Texas	$188	$201	$217	$249
Utah	$426	$451	$474	$498
Vermont	$597	$622	$640	$640
Virginia	$291	$320	$320	$320
Washington	$546	$546	$546	$562
West Virginia	$253	$353	$453	$340

TABLE 3.2

Maximum TANF benefit for a family of three with no income, by state, selected years 1996–2009 [CONTINUED]

[July]

State	1996	2000	2004	2009
Wisconsin	$518	—	—	—
W-2 transition	—	$628	$628	$628
Community service jobs	—	$673	$673	$673
Trial jobs/unsubsidized employment	—	—e	—e	—e
Wyoming	$360	$340	$340	$546
Meanf	**$394**	**$405**	**$413**	**$431**
Medianf	**$377**	**$379**	**$389**	**$429**

Note: Maximum benefits are calculated assuming that the unit contains one adult and two children who are not subject to a family cap, has no special needs, pays for shelter, and lives in the most populated area of the state.

TANF = Temporary Assistance for Needy Families.

SSI = Supplemental Security Income.

aApplies to units that have received assistance for two or more months in a lifetime. For units applying for their first or second months of benefits, the maximum monthly benefit for a family of three is $712.

bApplies to units that have received assistance for two or more months in a lifetime. For units applying for their first or second months of benefits, the maximum monthly benefit for a family of three is $795.

cApplies to units that have at least one employable adult. For units where all adults either receive SSI or are exempt from work requirements for reasons other than caring for a child under 3 months old, the maximum monthly benefit for a family of three is $477.

dFor units where the caretaker is over 60, disabled, caring full time for a disabled family member, or excluded from the assistance unit, the maximum monthly benefit for a family of three is $232.

eThe benefits in these components are based on the wages earned by individual recipients.

fThe calculations only include one value per state (the policy affecting the largest percent of the caseload).

SOURCE: Gretchen Rowe, Mary Murphy, and Ei Yin Mon, "Table L5. Maximum Monthly Benefit for a Family of Three with No Income, 1996–2009 (July)," in *Welfare Rules Databook: State TANF Policies as of July 2009*, The Urban Institute, August 2010, http://www.urban.org/UploadedPDF/412252-Welfare-Rules-Databook.pdf (accessed February 18, 2011)

and benefit amounts for TANF are determined by the states, SNAP eligibility and benefit amounts are determined by federal law and are consistent in all states.

SNAP benefits, which are administered by the USDA, are not counted in determining the TANF cash benefit. However, TANF benefits are considered part of a family's countable income in determining SNAP benefits, which are reduced $0.30 for each dollar of countable income. Therefore, SNAP benefits are higher in states with lower TANF benefits and vice versa. As of FY 2010, the average monthly SNAP benefits per household were lowest in Oregon ($237.97), Massachusetts ($238.54), and Washington ($243.41). (See Table 3.3.) Alaska ($436.40) and Hawaii ($430.04) had the highest average monthly SNAP benefits. (Poverty guidelines are higher in these two states because of higher costs of living.) Other states that paid the most in benefits included California ($341.04), Texas ($322.62), and South Dakota ($318.48).

THE WELFARE-TO-WORK CONCEPT

TANF recipients are expected to participate in work activities while receiving benefits. After 24 months of assistance, states must require recipients to work at least part time to continue to receive cash benefits. States are permitted to exempt certain groups of people from the work-activity requirements, including parents of very young children (up to one year) and disabled adults. TANF defines the work activities that count when determining a state's work participation rate.

As part of their plans, states must require parents to work after two years of receiving benefits. In 2000 states were required to have 40% of all parents and at least one adult in 90% of all two-parent families engaged in a work activity for a minimum of 20 hours per week for single parents and 35 hours per week for at least one adult in two-parent families. This work requirement is becoming stricter. The 2006 reauthorization of the PRWORA required 50% of all single-parent TANF recipients to work in 2006, increasing by 5% each year to 70% in 2010.

TANF recipients required to work must spend a minimum number of hours per week engaged in one of the following activities:

- An unsubsidized job (no government help)
- A subsidized private job
- A subsidized public job
- Work experience
- On-the-job training
- Job search and job readiness (a usual maximum of six weeks total)
- Community service
- Vocational educational training (a 12-month maximum)
- Job skills training
- Education related to employment
- High school or a general equivalency diploma completion
- Providing child care for a community service participant

Additional provisions apply to young parents who are under the age of 20 years and are either household heads or married and who lack a high school diploma. They are considered "engaged in work" if they either maintain satisfactory attendance in high school (no hours specified) or participate in education directly related to work (20 hours per week).

Education and Training

Reflecting a work-first philosophy, the 1996 welfare law limits the number of TANF recipients who may get work credit through participation in education and training. No more than 30% of TANF families who are counted as engaged in work may consist of people who are participating in vocational educational training. Vocational edu-

TABLE 3.3

Supplemental Nutrition Assistance Program (SNAP) average monthly benefit per household by state, fiscal years 2006–10

State/territory	Fiscal year 2006	Fiscal year 2007	Fiscal year 2008	Fiscal year 2009	Fiscal year 2010 *Preliminary*
Alabama	224.53	226.86	238.74	288.33	296.32
Alaska	338.42	336.51	357.45	430.24	436.40
Arizona	236.90	242.44	249.00	299.21	301.14
Arkansas	216.70	217.42	227.80	275.19	289.44
California	247.73	258.87	273.04	325.19	341.04
Colorado	249.45	242.12	247.63	302.70	325.09
Connecticut	177.96	186.32	196.86	249.36	263.07
Delaware	207.29	213.88	220.89	267.36	282.40
District of Columbia	190.89	191.95	196.15	234.88	247.22
Florida	208.47	185.80	198.73	246.94	268.56
Georgia	237.00	242.29	254.89	302.81	313.54
Guam	552.96	586.26	604.01	685.23	694.93
Hawaii	274.50	287.46	315.10	394.20	430.04
Idaho	225.85	222.27	237.89	307.48	318.49
Illinois	225.18	229.20	240.32	285.85	299.40
Indiana	216.47	222.29	240.50	296.39	309.35
Iowa	202.00	204.51	216.53	258.11	280.10
Kansas	192.26	193.90	205.23	252.06	272.91
Kentucky	208.77	210.70	217.92	264.36	279.87
Louisiana	257.86	233.68	262.96	307.50	303.14
Maine	172.98	173.85	189.17	245.01	259.83
Maryland	199.50	202.26	215.37	262.53	275.27
Massachusetts	154.57	163.99	183.47	229.53	238.54
Michigan	200.44	205.07	212.38	252.86	270.43
Minnesota	187.13	187.45	195.58	237.96	248.19
Mississippi	233.24	206.87	219.65	268.98	284.52
Missouri	206.05	207.37	216.14	263.06	277.56
Montana	212.55	214.61	221.22	274.02	287.64
Nebraska	202.00	203.26	225.21	259.78	280.66
Nevada	190.05	195.45	209.90	256.39	267.87
New Hampshire	176.17	180.46	190.45	251.24	255.39
New Jersey	195.71	202.72	210.62	257.53	282.65
New Mexico	221.09	225.17	234.23	286.76	299.42
New York	199.63	203.54	206.82	267.54	283.92
North Carolina	203.80	207.21	219.58	267.69	282.46
North Dakota	199.69	212.03	226.30	276.40	290.76
Ohio	219.56	218.59	236.44	288.95	303.22
Oklahoma	214.99	216.93	232.02	278.22	298.40
Oregon	173.18	175.71	185.74	228.81	237.97
Pennsylvania	198.32	197.80	206.79	250.80	262.61
Rhode Island	196.96	203.20	216.06	275.54	271.85
South Carolina	216.53	220.81	230.34	275.99	291.21
South Dakota	231.81	237.72	248.20	300.09	318.48
Tennessee	210.12	215.86	226.33	272.23	285.58
Texas	240.78	239.13	257.03	309.84	322.62
Utah	216.82	218.58	234.20	297.64	309.45
Vermont	176.16	178.08	187.42	233.56	244.13
Virginia	194.84	199.56	206.99	260.05	277.19
Virgin Islands	367.39	368.01	378.22	447.73	439.35
Washington	183.38	183.61	193.95	232.26	243.41
West Virginia	187.69	190.68	204.08	246.53	261.99
Wisconsin	186.90	186.85	198.22	241.25	263.00
Wyoming	216.34	221.83	229.95	276.22	297.54
Total	**214.41**	**214.72**	**226.60**	**275.51**	**289.61**

Notes: The following outlying areas received Nutrition Assistance Grants which provide benefits analogous to the Supplement Nutrition Assistance Program: Puerto Rico, American Samoa, and the Northern Marianas. Annual averages are total benefits divided by total annual household participation. All data are subject to revision.

SOURCE: "Supplemental Nutrition Assistance Program: Average Monthly Benefit per Household," in *Program Data: Supplemental Nutrition Assistance Program*, U.S. Department of Agriculture, Food and Nutrition Service, January 31, 2011, http://www.fns.usda.gov/pd/19SNAPavg$HH.htm (accessed February 18, 2011)

cational training is the only creditable work activity not explicitly confined to high school dropouts.

Finding and Creating Jobs for TANF Recipients

Job availability is one of the most difficult challenges that states face when moving recipients from welfare to work. Even though the national unemployment rate fell from a high of 7.5% in 1992 to 4% in 2000, it then began to rise again. The severe recession that began in 2007 further affected the unemployment rate. The U.S. Bureau of Labor Statistics (BLS) notes in the news release "Employment Situation Summary—March 2011" (April

1, 2011, http://www.bls.gov/news.release/pdf/empsit.pdf) that the rate was 8.8% in March 2011, down from 9.7% in March 2010. However, even when the national unemployment rate is low, unemployment in some areas of the country might be much higher, and the skill level of unemployed people may not match the skills that are required for available jobs. Welfare recipients often lack job skills and work experience. If suitable jobs cannot be found, states must create work-activity placements and may use TANF block grant funds to do so.

Welfare agencies have had to change their focus and train staff to function more as job developers and counselors than as caseworkers. They make an initial assessment of recipients' skills as required by TANF. They may then develop personal responsibility plans for recipients, identifying what is needed (e.g., training, job-placement services, and support services) to move them into the workforce.

States have developed a variety of approaches to finding and creating job opportunities. Even though most rely on existing unemployment offices, many states have tried other options to help recipients find work:

- Collaboration with the business community to develop strategies that provide recipients with the skills and training employers want

- Use of several types of subsidies for employers who hire welfare recipients directly (subsidizing wages, providing tax credits to employers, and subsidizing workers' compensation and unemployment compensation taxes)

- Targeting state jobs for welfare recipients

- Financial encouragement for entrepreneurship and self-employment

- Creation of community service positions, often within city departments, such as parks and libraries (recipients usually participate in this workfare as a condition of continuing to receive benefits rather than wages)

However, when the economy slows and the unemployment rate climbs, fewer jobs exist for former welfare recipients. In a testimony before the U.S. Senate's Committee on Finance, Gordon L. Berlin (September 21, 2010, http://www.mdrc.org/publications/566/testimony.html), the president of MDRC, a nonprofit social policy research organization, stated that "the Great Recession has been an unprecedented test of antipoverty programs like TANF, demonstrating the limits of a social safety net built predominantly around work when unemployment is high."

The ARRA provided an additional emergency contingency fund of $2 billion. Several states created jobs programs or expanded existing jobs programs with this additional funding. The CBPP (http://www.cbpp.org/) provides several examples, including:

- Ohio created a subsidized jobs program that provided work for 1,500 parents and 8,000 youth across the state

- A Pennsylvania program subsidized 12,000 private- and public-sector jobs to provide employment for parents and youth

- Illinois created Put Illinois to Work, a program that subsidizes jobs for unemployed parents and youth

All these programs, and others, were put in jeopardy when Congress failed to extend the TANF Emergency Fund by September 30, 2010.

Support Services Necessary for Moving Recipients to Work

The Urban Institute points out in "Jobs in an Uncertain Economy: A Research Focus of the Urban Institute" (2010, http://www.urban.org/toolkit/issues/jobs.cfm) that low-income adults and public assistance recipients face multiple barriers to working that need to be addressed, such as a lack of basic skills and access to quality jobs, child care, and transportation. This section addresses federal efforts to remove some of these barriers.

CHILD CARE. The offer of affordable child care is one critical element in encouraging low-income mothers to seek and keep jobs. Holcomb et al. note that "child care is a key work support that can help those leaving cash assistance for work keep their jobs and avoid returning to welfare." The National Association of Child Care Resource and Referral Agencies shows in *Parents and the High Cost of Child Care* (August 2010, http://www.naccrra.org/docs/Cost_Report_073010-final.pdf) that in 2009 the average yearly cost for child care in a child care center for a four-year-old ranged from $4,050 in Mississippi to $13,150 in Massachusetts. For an infant, annual costs ranged from $4,550 in Mississippi to $18,750 in Massachusetts.

The 1996 welfare reform law created a block grant to states for child care. The amount of the block grant was equivalent to what states received under the AFDC. However, states that maintain the amount that they spent for child care under the AFDC are eligible for additional matching funds. The block grant and the supplemental matching funds are referred to as the Child Care Development Fund (CCDF). In addition, states were given the option of transferring some of their TANF funds to the CCDF or spending them directly on child care services. In the fact sheet "Government Work Supports and Low-Income Families: Facts and Figures" (July 2006, http://www.urban.org/UploadedPDF/900981_worksupports.pdf), the Urban Institute reports that the amount allocated for child care through the CCDF and TANF drawn from both federal and state funds tripled from $4 billion in 1996 to $12 billion in 2002. The ACF indicates in "Child Care and Development Fund Fact Sheet" (September 2010, http://www.acf.hhs.gov/programs/ccb/ccdf/

factsheet.htm) that by FY 2010 the federal government provided $5 billion to fund CCDF programs in the states. Even though some states cut the amount of money in their child care programs in response to the Great Recession, the ARRA included an additional $2 billion to be distributed to the states specifically to fund the CCDF.

Because states can use TANF funds for child care, they have more flexibility to design child care programs, not only for welfare recipients but also for working-poor families who may need child care support to continue working and stay off welfare. States determine who is eligible for child care support, how much those parents will pay (often using a sliding fee scale), and the amount the state will reimburse providers of subsidized care. Children under the age of 13 years are eligible for child care subsidies; depending on the state, families with incomes up to 85% of the state's median income for a family of that size are eligible, although few states guarantee payments to all eligible families. For example, the Urban Institute notes that in 2005, 20 states either had waiting lists or had stopped taking applications for child care subsidies.

In *Child Care and Development Fund (CCDF) Report to Congress for FY 2006 and FY 2007* (October 2010, http://www.acf.hhs.gov/programs/ccb/ccdf/rtc/rtc2006/rtc _2006_2007.pdf), the ACF reports that in FY 2007 states provided child care subsidies to approximately 1.7 million low-income children in 991,500 families, down from 1.8 million children the year before. About 60% of the children were cared for in child care centers and 29% were cared for in licensed family child care homes. The remaining 11% of children were cared for in more informal settings, including arrangements with friends and relatives. Despite the dramatic increase in the provision of child care to low-income families, many eligible families were still not receiving assistance. About one out of five (18%) families received TANF assistance.

TRANSPORTATION AND ACCESS TO JOBS. According to the U.S. Department of Transportation (DOT), in "Use of TANF, WtW, and Job Access Funds for Transportation" (August 22, 2007, http://www.fta.dot.gov/printer_friendly/ grants_financing_3715.html), transportation is another critical factor facing welfare recipients moving into a job. Recipients without a car must depend on public transportation. Yet, two out of three new jobs are in suburban areas, often outside the range of public transportation, whereas three out of four welfare recipients live in rural areas or in central cities. Even when jobs are accessible to public transportation, many day care centers and schools are not. Some jobs require weekend or night shift work, when public transportation schedules are limited. Even for those recipients with cars, the expense of gas and repairs can deplete earnings.

To promote employment, TANF's vehicle asset limits are broader than they were under the AFDC. Each state has the flexibility to determine its own vehicle asset level, but all states have chosen to increase the limit for the value of the primary automobile in the family beyond that set under the AFDC. In addition, the U.S. House of Representatives' Committee on Ways and Means indicates in *The Green Book: Background Material and Data on the Programs within the Jurisdiction of the Committee on Ways and Means* (2008, http://democrats.waysand means.house.gov/media/pdf/110/tanf.pdf) that in 2008, 31 states and the District of Columbia disregarded the value of at least one vehicle in the family. The remaining states excluded from $1,500 to $15,000 of the car's value.

The DOT notes that states use a variety of approaches to provide transportation for TANF recipients moving into the workforce, such as:

- Reimbursing work-related transportation expenses (automobile expenses or public transportation)

- Providing financial assistance in the form of loans or grants to purchase or lease an automobile

- Filling transit service gaps, such as new routes or extended hours

- Providing transit alternatives, such as vanpools or shuttle services

- Offering entrepreneurial opportunities for recipients to become transportation providers

- Transferring TANF funds to the Social Services Block Grant to develop the transportation infrastructure for the working poor in rural areas and inner cities

OTHER PUBLIC PROGRAMS TO FIGHT POVERTY
Unemployment Compensation

To qualify for unemployment compensation benefits, an unemployed person usually must have worked recently for a covered employer for some period of time and for a certain amount of pay. Almost all wage and salary workers and most of the civilian labor force are covered by unemployment insurance. Many of those not covered are people who are self-employed, agricultural or domestic workers, certain alien farm workers, and railroad workers (who have their own unemployment program). Unemployed people can receive up to 26 weeks of benefits, but that period can be extended during periods of high unemployment.

The severe recession that began in 2007 led to the expansion of unemployment compensation. In June 2008 the Supplemental Appropriations Act extended unemployment benefits for an additional 13 weeks. In November 2008 the Unemployment Compensation Extension Act extended the period of time individuals could receive compensation to an additional 20 weeks. Furthermore, the ARRA extended the time during which individuals could file claims and be paid unemployment; workers in some areas of particularly high unemployment could collect benefits for up to 99 weeks. In April 2011 President Obama signed a tax package that reauthorized this extension of unemployment benefits through May 2012. Even though this action did not lengthen the number of weeks that unemployed workers could collect benefits, it did extend the time that unemployed workers would be able to collect those maximum benefits. If workers had already run out of unemployment benefits, they could not file another claim.

Federal Minimum Wage

The federal minimum wage dates back to the passage of the Fair Labor Standards Act of 1938, which established basic national standards for minimum wages, overtime pay, and the employment of child workers. (The minimum wage is a cash wage only and does not include any fringe benefits. Consequently, the total compensation for minimum-wage workers is even lower than the total compensation for higher-paid workers, who generally receive some kind of benefits besides wages. Most minimum-wage workers do not receive any benefits.) The provisions of the act have been extended to cover many other areas of employment since 1938.

The first minimum wage instituted in 1938 was $0.25 per hour. (See Table 3.4.) It gradually increased over the years, reaching $4.25 in 1991. In July 1996 Congress passed legislation that raised the minimum wage to $5.15 in 1997 by means of two $0.45 increases. In July 2007 the minimum wage was raised to $5.85, in July 2008 it was raised to $6.55, and in July 2009 it was raised to $7.25.

Despite the minimum wage increases, a person working 40 hours per week for 50 weeks per year at minimum wage ($7.25 per hour) would gross $290 per week, or $14,500 per year, well below the poverty level for a family of three ($18,530 in 2011). (See Table 1.1 in Chapter 1.) For adults, this means that day laborers (those without a permanent job who look for a job every day) and those employed in service jobs for minimum wages will not be able to earn enough to escape poverty.

WHO WORKS FOR MINIMUM WAGE? Even though workers must receive at least the minimum wage for most jobs, there are some exceptions in which a person may be paid less than the minimum wage. Full-time students working on a part-time basis in the service and retail industries or at the students' academic institution, certain disabled people, and workers who are "customarily and regularly" tipped may receive less than the minimum wage. According to the BLS, in *Characteristics of Minimum Wage Workers: 2009* (March 1, 2010, http://www.bls.gov/cps/minwage2009.pdf), 980,000 people earned exactly the federal minimum wage in 2009 and nearly 2.6 million earned below the minimum. These numbers were up substantially from the 2007 survey. In *Characteristics of*

TABLE 3.4

Federal minimum wage rates under the Fair Labor Standards Act, 1938–2011

Effective date	1938 Act[a]	1961 Amendments[b]	1966 & Subsequent amendments[c] Nonfarm	1966 & Subsequent amendments[c] Farm
Oct. 24, 1938	$0.25			
Oct. 24, 1939	$0.30			
Oct. 24, 1945	$0.40			
Jan. 25, 1950	$0.75			
Mar. 1, 1956	$1.00			
Sept. 3, 1961	$1.15	$1.00		
Sept. 3, 1963	$1.25			
Sept. 3, 1964		$1.15		
Sept. 3, 1965		$1.25		
Feb. 1, 1967	$1.40	$1.40	$1.00	$1.00
Feb. 1, 1968	$1.60	$1.60	$1.15	$1.15
Feb. 1, 1969			$1.30	$1.30
Feb. 1, 1970			$1.45	
Feb. 1, 1971			$1.60	
May 1, 1974	$2.00	$2.00	$1.90	$1.60
Jan. 1, 1975	$2.10	$2.10	$2.00	$1.80
Jan. 1, 1976	$2.30	$2.30	$2.20	$2.00
Jan. 1, 1977			$2.30	$2.20
Jan. 1, 1978	$2.65 for all covered, nonexempt workers			
Jan. 1, 1979	$2.90 for all covered, nonexempt workers			
Jan. 1, 1980	$3.10 for all covered, nonexempt workers			
Jan. 1, 1981	$3.35 for all covered, nonexempt workers			
Apr. 1, 1990[d]	$3.80 for all covered, nonexempt workers			
Apr. 1, 1991	$4.25 for all covered, nonexempt workers			
Oct. 1, 1996[e]	$4.75 for all covered, nonexempt workers			
Sept. 1, 1997	$5.15 for all covered, nonexempt workers			
Jul. 24, 2007	$5.85 for all covered, nonexempt workers			
Jul. 24, 2008	$6.55 for all covered, nonexempt workers			
Jul. 24, 2009	$7.25 for all covered, nonexempt workers			

[a]The 1938 Act was applicable generally to employees engaged in interstate commerce or in the production of goods for interstate commerce.
[b]The 1961 Amendments extended coverage primarily to employees in large retail and service enterprises as well as to local transit, construction, and gasoline service station employees.
[c]The 1966 Amendments extended coverage to state and local government employees of hospitals, nursing homes, and schools, and to laundries, dry cleaners, and large hotels, motels, restaurants, and farms. Subsequent amendments extended coverage to the remaining federal, state and local government employees who were not protected in 1966, to certain workers in retail and service trades previously exempted, and to certain domestic workers in private household employment.
[d]Grandfather Clause: Employees who do not meet the tests for individual coverage, and whose employers were covered by the FLSA, on March 31, 1990, and fail to meet the increased annual dollar volume (ADV) test for enterprise coverage, must continue to receive at least $3.35 an hour.
[e]A subminimum wage—$4.25 an hour—is established for employees under 20 years of age during their first 90 consecutive calendar days of employment with an employer.

SOURCE: "Federal Minimum Wage Rates under the Fair Labor Standards Act," U.S. Department for Labor, Wage and Hour Division, 2007, http://www.dol.gov/whd/minwage/chart.pdf (accessed February 17, 2011)

Minimum Wage Workers: 2007 (March 24, 2008, http://www.bls.gov/cps/minwage2007.pdf), the BLS reports that 267,000 people earned the prevailing minimum wage and 1.5 million made less than the minimum wage in 2007. This large increase was probably due to the minimum wage increases in 2007, 2008, and 2009.

The BLS also notes that in 2009, 2.3 million (63%) of the 3.6 million people who worked for the minimum wage or below were employed in the service sector. About 2.2 million (62%) women aged 16 years and older were minimum-wage workers in 2009, compared with 1.4 million

(38%) men aged 16 years and older. (See Table 3.5.) White workers predominated among minimum-wage workers; 2.9 million (80%) minimum-wage workers were white, 622,000 (17.4%) were Hispanic, 495,000 (13.9%) were African-American, and 117,000 (3.3%) were Asian-American.

Supplemental Security Income

SSI is a means-tested income assistance program authorized in 1972 by Title XVI of the Social Security Act. The SSI program replaced the combined federal-state programs of Old Age Assistance, Aid to the Blind, and Aid to the Permanently and Totally Disabled in the 50 states and the District of Columbia. However, these programs still exist in the U.S. territories of Guam, Puerto Rico, and the Virgin Islands. Since the first payments in 1974, SSI has provided monthly cash payments to needy aged, blind, and disabled individuals who meet the eligibility requirements. States may supplement the basic federal SSI payment.

TABLE 3.5

Workers paid hourly rates at or below minimum wage, by selected characteristics, 2009

| Characteristic | Number of workers (in thousands) | | | | Percent distribution | | | | Percent of workers paid hourly rates | | |
| | Total paid hourly rates | At or below minimum wage | | | Total paid hourly rates | At or below minimum wage | | | At or below minimum wage | | |
		Total	At minimum wage	Below minimum wage		Total	At minimum wage	Below minimum wage	Total	At minimum wage	Below minimum wage
Age and sex											
Total, 16 years and over	**72,611**	**3,572**	**980**	**2,592**	**100.0**	**100.0**	**100.0**	**100.0**	**4.9**	**1.3**	**3.6**
16 to 24 years	14,389	1,737	508	1,229	19.8	48.6	51.8	47.4	12.1	3.5	8.5
16 to 19 years	4,397	818	288	530	6.1	22.9	29.4	20.4	18.6	6.5	12.1
25 years and over	58,222	1,835	472	1,363	80.2	51.4	48.2	52.6	3.2	0.8	2.3
Men, 16 years and over	**35,185**	**1,358**	**368**	**990**	**48.5**	**38.0**	**37.6**	**38.2**	**3.9**	**1.0**	**2.8**
16 to 24 years	7,045	674	214	460	9.7	18.9	21.8	17.7	9.6	3.0	6.5
16 to 19 years	2,053	322	121	201	2.8	9.0	12.3	7.8	15.7	5.9	9.8
25 years and over	28,140	684	154	530	38.8	19.1	15.7	20.4	2.4	0.5	1.9
Women, 16 years and over	**37,426**	**2,215**	**612**	**1,603**	**51.5**	**62.0**	**62.4**	**61.8**	**5.9**	**1.6**	**4.3**
16 to 24 years	7,344	1,064	295	769	10.1	29.8	30.1	29.7	14.5	4.0	10.5
16 to 19 years	2,345	496	167	329	3.2	13.9	17.0	12.7	21.2	7.1	14.0
25 years and over	30,082	1,151	318	833	41.4	32.2	32.4	32.1	3.8	1.1	2.8
Race, sex, and Hispanic or Latino ethnicity											
White[a]	58,633	2,857	763	2,094	80.7	80.0	77.9	80.8	4.9	1.3	3.6
Men	28,873	1,074	300	774	39.8	30.1	30.6	29.9	3.7	1.0	2.7
Women	29,760	1,783	463	1,320	41.0	49.9	47.2	50.9	6.0	1.6	4.4
Black or African American[a]	9,269	495	168	327	12.8	13.9	17.1	12.6	5.3	1.8	3.5
Men	4,038	192	50	142	5.6	5.4	5.1	5.5	4.8	1.2	3.5
Women	5,231	302	117	185	7.2	8.5	11.9	7.1	5.8	2.2	3.5
Asian[a]	2,718	117	21	96	3.7	3.3	2.1	3.7	4.3	0.8	3.5
Men	1,258	47	6	41	1.7	1.3	0.6	1.6	3.7	0.5	3.3
Women	1,460	70	15	55	2.0	2.0	1.5	2.1	4.8	1.0	3.8
Hispanic or Latino[a]	12,740	622	183	439	17.5	17.4	18.7	16.9	4.9	1.4	3.4
Men	7,291	290	80	210	10.0	8.1	8.2	8.1	4.0	1.1	2.9
Women	5,449	331	102	229	7.5	9.3	10.4	8.8	6.1	1.9	4.2
Full- and part-time status and sex											
Full-time workers[b]	52,454	1,272	320	952	72.2	35.6	32.7	36.7	2.4	0.6	1.8
Men	28,388	579	137	442	39.1	16.2	14.0	17.1	2.0	0.5	1.6
Women	24,066	694	183	511	33.1	19.4	18.7	19.7	2.9	0.8	2.1
Part-time workers[b]	20,027	2,281	656	1,625	27.6	63.9	66.9	62.7	11.4	3.3	8.1
Men	6,721	769	229	540	9.3	21.5	23.4	20.8	11.4	3.4	8.0
Women	13,307	1,513	428	1,085	18.3	42.4	43.7	41.9	11.4	3.2	8.2

[a]Estimates for the above race groups (white, black or African American, and Asian) do not sum to totals because data are not presented for all races. Persons whose ethnicity is identified as Hispanic or Latino may be of any race.
[b]The distinction between full- and part-time workers is based on hours usually worked. These data will not sum to totals because full- or part-time status on the principal job is not identifiable for a small number of multiple jobholders.
Note: Data exclude all self-employed persons whether or not their businesses are incorporated.

SOURCE: "Table 1. Employed Wage and Salary Workers Paid Hourly Rates with Earnings at or below the Prevailing Federal Minimum Wage by Selected Characteristics, 2009 Annual Averages," in *Characteristics of Minimum Wage Workers: 2009*, U.S. Department of Labor, Bureau of Labor Statistics, March 2010, http://www.bls.gov/cps/minwage2009.pdf (accessed February 18, 2011)

A number of requirements must be met to receive financial benefits from SSI. First, a person must meet the program criteria for age, blindness, or disability. The aged, or elderly, are people 65 years and older. To be considered legally blind, a person must have vision of 20/200 or less in the better eye with the use of corrective lenses, have tunnel vision of 20 degrees or less (can only see a small area straight ahead), or have met state qualifications for the earlier Aid to the Blind program. A person is disabled if he or she cannot earn money at a job because of a physical or mental illness or injury that may cause his or her death, or if the condition lasts for 12 months or longer. Those who met earlier state Aid to the Permanently Disabled requirements may also qualify for assistance.

Unmarried children under the age of 18 (or age 22 if a full-time student) may qualify for SSI if they have a medically determinable physical or mental impairment that substantially reduces their ability to function independently or to engage in age-appropriate activities. This impairment must be expected to last for a continuous period of more than 12 months or to result in death.

Because SSI is a means-tested benefit, a person's income and property must be counted before he or she can receive benefits. In *Green Book*, the Committee on Ways and Means indicates that in 2008 individuals and couples receiving Social Security benefits could not earn more than $657 and $976 per month, respectively. In addition, a person could have no more than $2,000 worth of property, and a couple could have no more than $3,000 worth of property (mainly in savings accounts or in stocks and bonds). Not included in countable resources are the person's home, as well as household goods and personal effects worth less than $2,000. A car is not counted if a member of the household uses it to go to and from work or to medical treatments or if it has been adapted for a disabled person. Someone applying for SSI may have life insurance with a cash value of $1,500 or less and/or a burial policy up to the same value.

Tax Relief for the Poor

Both conservatives and liberals hailed the Tax Reform Act of 1986 as a major step toward relieving the tax burden of low-income families, one group of Americans whose wages and benefits have been eroding since 1979. The law enlarged and inflation-proofed the Earned Income Tax Credit (EITC), which provides a refundable tax credit that both offsets taxes and often operates as a wage supplement. Only those who work can qualify. The amount is determined, in part, by how much each qualified individual or family earns. It is also adjusted to the size of the family. To be eligible for the family EITC, workers must live with their children, who must be under 19 years old or full-time students under 24 years old.

The maximum credit for 2011 was $3,121 for taxpayers with one child, $5,160 for taxpayers with two children, $5,805 for taxpayers with three or more children, and $469 for people with no children. (See Figure 3.2.) Families received less if their income was low because they were also eligible for public assistance. A family of four received the maximum benefit if its earnings were slightly below the poverty line, but many families well above the poverty line received some credit. Single-parent families with one child were eligible for some credit up to an income of $36,372, and single-parent families with at least two children were eligible for some credit up to an income of $41,341. Benefits phased down gradually when income surpassed $16,840 for single-parent families or $21,970 for married-couple families.

The largest EITC benefits go to families that no longer need welfare. The gradual phaseout and availability of the EITC at above-poverty income levels help stabilize a parent's employment by providing additional money to cover expenses that are associated with working, such as child care and transportation. Research finds that the EITC has been an effective work incentive and has significantly increased work participation among single mothers. The Urban Institute states in "Government Work Supports and Low-Income Families" that eight out of 10 low-income working families are eligible to receive

FIGURE 3.2

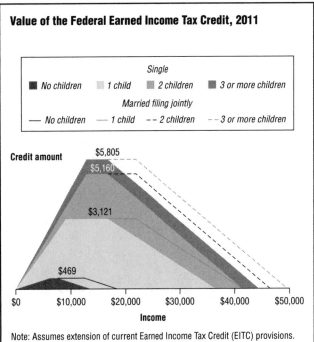

Value of the Federal Earned Income Tax Credit, 2011

Note: Assumes extension of current Earned Income Tax Credit (EITC) provisions.

SOURCE: Erica Williams, Nicholas Johnson, and Jon Shure, "Figure 2. Value of Federal Earned Income Tax Credit, 2011," in *State Earned Income Tax Credits: 2010 Legislative Update*, Center on Budget and Policy Priorities, December 2010, http://www.cbpp.org/files/11-10-09sfp.pdf (accessed February 17, 2011)

the tax credit and that the EITC is the support program with the highest participation rate.

Those who do not owe income tax, or who owe an amount smaller than the credit, receive a check directly from the Internal Revenue Service for the credit due them. Most recipients claim the credit when they file an income tax form.

Even though the Tax Reform Act of 1986 has helped ease the burden of federal taxes, most of the poor still pay a substantial share of their income in state and local taxes. Erica Williams, Nicholas Johnson, and Jon Shure of the CBPP note in *State Earned Income Tax Credits: 2010 Legislative Update* (December 9, 2010, http://www.cbpp.org/files/11-10-09sfp.pdf) that as of December 2010, 23 states and the District of Columbia had enacted a state EITC to supplement the federal credit. These state programs boost the income of families that move from welfare to work and prevent states from taxing poor families deeper into poverty.

CHAPTER 4
WHO RECEIVES GOVERNMENT BENEFITS?

A variety of government programs exist to assist low-income and impoverished families. These means-tested assistance programs (programs that are based on earning below a certain threshold) provide the most assistance to the most impoverished families. The public perception is that welfare is for people who refuse to or cannot work; however, it should be noted that these programs also provide assistance to working families. Figure 4.1 shows that even among families deep in poverty (less than 50% of the poverty line), 25.3% of the family income was provided by earnings in 2005. Among families under 100% of the poverty line, 46.6% of the family income was provided by earnings.

Certain groups receive a larger share of their total income from means-tested assistance programs. Preschool-aged children in the deepest poverty received approximately 65.5% of their family income from means-tested assistance programs in 2005, whereas adults received much lower proportions of their income from means-tested assistance programs. (See Table 4.1.) People living in female-headed families received a greater proportion of their income from means-tested assistance programs, regardless of their income, than did people in male-headed or married-couple families. The following pages describe some of the characteristics of those who receive assistance from different government programs.

WHO GETS TANF BENEFITS?

Gil Grouse, Susan Hauan, and Annette Waters Rogers of the U.S. Department of Health and Human Services note in *Indicators of Welfare Dependence: Annual Report to Congress, 2008* (December 2008, http://aspe.hhs.gov/hsp/indicators08/) that in 2006, the most recent year for which detailed data were available as of April 2011, 4.7 million people, or 1.6% of the general population, received Temporary Assistance for Needy Families (TANF) benefits. In 2005, 47.7% of TANF recipients lived in

households with no one in the labor force, 25.4% had at least one part-time worker in the labor force, and 26.9% had at least one full-time worker in the labor force. (See Figure 4.2.) Some groups in the population are more likely to receive these benefits than others. Fully 4.8% of children under the age of 18 years received TANF benefits in 2006, compared with only 0.5% of adults. However, as Figure 4.3 shows, rates of receipt of TANF benefits have declined sharply since 1992, especially among children.

Tracy A. Loveless and Jan Tin of the U.S. Census Bureau provide more detailed information about TANF recipients in *Dynamics of Economic Well-Being: Participation in Government Programs, 2001 through 2003: Who Gets Assistance?* (October 2006, http://www.census.gov/prod/2006pubs/p70-108.pdf). A higher proportion of African-Americans (3.7%) received TANF benefits each month in 2003 than any other racial or ethnic group. Among other groups, 2.7% of Hispanics, 1.5% of Asians or Pacific Islanders, and 0.5% of non-Hispanic whites received benefits each month. Single female-headed families were by far the most likely family group to receive TANF benefits in 2003. Fully 5.6% of these families received TANF benefits each month, compared with 1.3% of single male-headed families and 0.5% of married-couple families. Adults who had a high school education or less were much more likely than their better-educated peers to receive TANF in 2003, reflecting the difficulty of earning a living wage without some higher education. In that year 1.4% of adults who had not received a high school diploma received TANF benefits each month, compared with 0.5% of high school graduates and 0.2% of adults who had attended college.

Mothers

According to Jane Lawler Dye of the Census Bureau, in *Participation of Mothers in Government Assistance Programs: 2004* (May 2008, http://www.census.gov/

FIGURE 4.1

Percentage of total income from various sources by poverty status, 2005

[In percent]

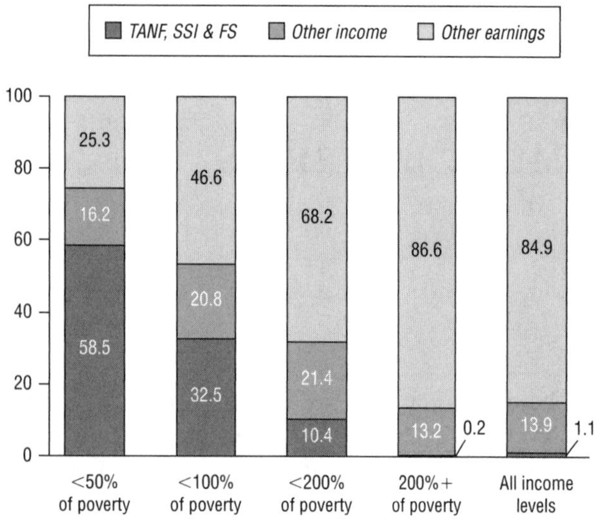

TANF = Temporary Assistance for Needy Families.
SSI = Supplemental Security Income.
FS = food stamps.
Note: Total income is total annual family income, including the value of food stamps. Other income is non-means-tested, non-earnings income such as child support, alimony, pensions, Social Security benefits, interest and dividends. Poverty status categories are not mutually exclusive.

SOURCE: Gil Grouse, Susan Hauan, and Annette Waters Rogers, "Figure IND 1b. Percentage of Total Income from Various Sources by Poverty Status: 2005," in *Indicators of Welfare Dependence: Annual Report to Congress, 2008*, U.S. Department of Health and Human Services, December 2008, http://aspe.hhs.gov/hsp/indicators08/ch2.pdf (accessed February 18, 2011)

was 17.5% and 35 to 44 years was 15%. By contrast, the participation rates for unmarried mothers remained well over 50% even in the oldest age group.

According to Dye, the participation rate varied by demographic characteristics. African-American mothers were the most likely to participate in public assistance programs in 2004. Nearly two-thirds (62.4%) of African-American women with a birth in the past year participated in a public assistance program, compared with 49.4% of Asian-Americans, 47.6% of Hispanics, and 23.9% of non-Hispanic whites. (See Table 4.2.)

Better-educated and more highly paid mothers were less likely than other mothers to participate in public assistance programs in 2004. Among mothers with a birth in the past year, those without a high school degree (58.3%) were the most likely to participate in public assistance programs, whereas those with even some college (19.7%) were the least likely. (See Table 4.2.) Dye finds that 72.4% of recent mothers whose monthly family income was less than $500 participated in public assistance programs, whereas only 8.4% of mothers whose monthly income was $4,000 or more did. Women in poverty were more likely to participate in public assistance programs than were other women. In sum, certain groups were more likely to receive government assistance in 2004 than others. The most likely candidates for this assistance were young, poorly educated, unmarried, and African-American mothers with a birth in the last year.

Figure 4.6 shows events that were associated with the entry of families headed by single mothers into TANF between 2001 and 2003. Half (50.3%) of the recipients stated that their earnings decreased and another 19.8% stated that other household members' earnings had decreased. One out of five (20.2%) single mothers entered TANF because a new child had entered the family. Nearly one out of five stated that there was a decrease in the number of adults in the household because of a divorce or separation (4.2%) or for another reason (15.3%). Other reasons included the onset of a work limitation (11.6%), the loss of Supplemental Security Income (SSI) benefits (4.5%) or other government benefits (6.1%), or a move across state lines (2.1%). Between 1993 and 2003 there was a decrease in the number of single-mother recipients who entered TANF because their earnings had decreased, because other household members' earnings had decreased, because of a divorce or separation, or because of a decrease in the number of adults. (See Table 4.3.) There was an increase in recipients who stated the spell began because they lost SSI benefits or because of the onset of a work limitation.

prod/2008pubs/p70-116.pdf), mothers who had a birth in the last year were more likely than other mothers to participate in public assistance programs in 2004—24.8% of new mothers received Medicaid, 18.8% received food stamps, 12.1% received benefits from the Special Supplemental Food Program for Women, Infants, and Children, 4.4% received housing assistance, and 3.3% received TANF. (See Figure 4.4.) Approximately one-third (34.2%) of recent mothers participated in any public assistance program in 2004, compared with 19.9% of other mothers. (See Figure 4.5.) Mothers who had a birth in the last year were also more likely than other mothers to participate in multiple programs.

Dye finds that in 2004 the rates of unmarried mothers who participated in public assistance programs were much higher than those of married mothers. Unmarried mothers had a participation rate of 64.2%, whereas married mothers had a participation rate of only 21.7%. Dye also notes that the participation rate of young married mothers aged 15 to 24 years was fairly high, at 44.8%, whereas the rate for older mothers aged 25 to 34 years

Figure 4.7 shows events that were associated with the exit of families headed by single mothers from TANF between 2001 and 2003. The most likely reason single mothers exited TANF was an increase in their own earnings

TABLE 4.1

Percentage of total income from various sources by poverty status and selected characteristics, 2005

	<50% poverty	<100% of poverty	<200% of poverty	200%+ of poverty	All persons
All persons					
TANF, SSI and food stamps	58.5	32.5	10.4	0.2	1.1
Earnings	25.3	46.6	68.2	86.6	84.9
Other income	16.2	20.8	21.4	13.2	13.9
Racial/ethnic categories					
Non-Hispanic white					
TANF, SSI and food stamps	53.1	29.9	8.0	0.1	0.6
Earnings	25.5	41.9	62.7	85.6	84.3
Other income	21.4	28.3	29.4	14.3	15.1
Non-Hispanic black					
TANF, SSI and food stamps	66.3	43.5	17.9	0.5	4.0
Earnings	18.9	35.3	60.6	88.1	82.5
Other income	14.7	21.2	21.6	11.5	13.5
Hispanic					
TANF, SSI and food stamps	55.6	26.5	9.4	0.5	2.7
Earnings	32.7	62.4	81.5	91.6	89.1
Other income	11.7	11.1	9.0	7.9	8.2
Age categories					
Children ages 0–5					
TANF, SSI and food stamps	65.5	37.2	13.5	0.2	2.3
Earnings	22.8	52.0	78.0	94.6	92.1
Other income	11.6	10.7	8.5	5.2	5.7
Children ages 6–10					
TANF, SSI and food stamps	65.1	35.5	12.0	0.2	1.9
Earnings	20.7	50.2	77.4	93.7	91.3
Other income	14.2	14.3	10.6	6.2	6.8
Children ages 11–15					
TANF, SSI and food stamps	61.8	36.1	12.5	0.1	1.7
Earnings	22.6	47.3	74.3	92.0	89.8
Other income	15.6	16.6	13.2	7.9	8.5
Women ages 16–64					
TANF, SSI and food stamps	55.6	33.3	11.2	0.2	1.1
Earnings	26.6	46.3	71.4	89.1	87.7
Other income	17.8	20.5	17.5	10.7	11.2
Men ages 16–64					
TANF, SSI and food stamps	48.0	27.4	8.0	0.2	0.7
Earnings	34.4	53.1	76.4	90.2	89.3
Other income	17.6	19.5	15.5	9.6	10.0
Adults ages 65 and over					
TANF, SSI and food stamps	37.2	21.4	6.5	0.3	1.0
Earnings	9.2	6.5	9.9	40.2	36.6
Other income	53.6	72.2	83.5	59.5	62.4
Family categories					
Persons in married-couple families					
TANF, SSI and food stamps	49.7	22.4	5.9	0.1	0.5
Earnings	35.0	62.0	77.0	87.6	86.9
Other income	15.3	15.6	17.1	12.3	12.6
Persons in female-headed families					
TANF, SSI and food stamps	66.9	45.2	21.7	1.0	6.9
Earnings	17.8	36.4	58.6	81.9	75.3
Other income	15.2	18.4	19.7	17.1	17.8
Persons in male-headed families					
TANF, SSI and food stamps	65.8	31.2	11.0	0.5	2.0
Earnings	21.0	50.7	72.1	87.3	85.2
Other income	13.2	18.0	16.9	12.2	12.8

TANF = Temporary Assistance for Needy Families.
SSI = Supplemental Security Income.
Note: Total income is total annual family income, including the value of food stamps. Other income is non-means-tested, non-earnings income such as child support, alimony, pensions, Social Security benefits, interest and dividends. Poverty status categories are not mutually exclusive. Spouses are not present in the female-headed and male-headed family categories. Persons of Hispanic ethnicity may be of any race. Beginning in 2002, estimates for whites and blacks are for persons reporting a single race only. Persons who reported more than one race are included in the total for all persons but are not shown under any race category. Due to small sample size, American Indians/Alaska Natives, Asians and Native Hawaiians/other Pacific Islanders are included in the total for all persons but are not shown separately.

SOURCE: Gil Grouse, Susan Hauan, and Annette Waters Rogers, "Table IND 1c. Percentage of Total Income from Various Sources by Poverty Status and Selected Characteristics: 2005," in *Indicators of Welfare Dependence: Annual Report to Congress, 2008*, U.S. Department of Health and Human Services, 2009, http://aspe.hhs.gov/hsp/indicators08/ch2.pdf (accessed February 18, 2011)

FIGURE 4.2

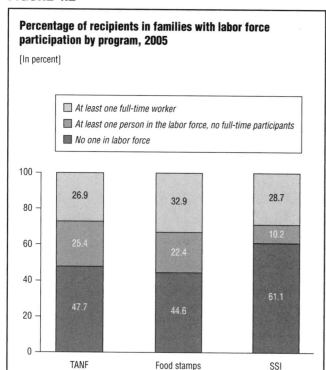

Percentage of recipients in families with labor force participation by program, 2005

[In percent]

- ☐ At least one full-time worker
- ☐ At least one person in the labor force, no full-time participants
- ■ No one in labor force

TANF = Temporary Assistance for Needy Families.
SSI = Supplemental Security Income.
Note: Recipients are limited to those individuals or family members directly receiving benefits in a month. Full-time workers are those who usually work 35 hours or more per week. Part-time labor force participation includes part-time workers and those who are unemployed, laid off and/or looking for work. This indicator measures, on an average monthly basis, the combination of individual benefit receipt and labor force participation by any family member in the same month.

SOURCE: Gil Grouse, Susan Hauan, and Annette Waters Rogers, "Figure IND 2. Percentage of Recipients in Families with Labor Force Participants by Program: 2005," in *Indicators of Welfare Dependence: Annual Report to Congress, 2008*, U.S. Department of Health and Human Services, December 2008, http://aspe.hhs.gov/hsp/indicators08/ch2.pdf (accessed February 18, 2011)

Katy Suellentrop notes in *The Costs and Consequences of Teen Childbearing* (August 17, 2010, http://www.cdc.gov/nchs/ppt/nchs2010/29_Suellentrop.pdf) that 34% of women who give birth as teenagers do not earn a high school diploma or a general education diploma (GED) before the age of 22, compared with 6% of women who do not give birth as teenagers. Suellentrop also indicates that 43% of women who give birth before the age of 18 do not attain a high school diploma or GED. As a result, teen mothers have less education and fewer job skills than women who delay childbearing until their 20s.

In "Teen Pregnancy and Overall Child Well-Being" (February 2007, http://www.thenationalcampaign.org/why-it-matters/pdf/child_well-being.pdf), the National Campaign to Prevent Teen Pregnancy indicates that teen mothers tend to have less education and less ability to support and care for their children. It also notes that compared with babies born to mothers who delay child-bearing until their 20s, babies born to teen mothers are:

- More likely to be born prematurely and to be of low birth weight, and therefore at a higher risk for infant death, deafness, chronic respiratory problems, blindness, developmental disabilities, cerebral palsy, and hyperactivity, among other problems

- Less likely to display readiness for school

- More likely to repeat a grade or drop out of high school

- More likely to suffer from mental health problems such as anxiety, low self-esteem, or sadness

- Twice as likely as children of older mothers to be neglected or abused

Furthermore, the National Campaign to Prevent Teen Pregnancy explains that male babies born to teen mothers are twice as likely as sons of older mothers to be imprisoned and that female babies born to teen mothers are three times as likely as daughters of older mothers to become teen mothers themselves.

TANF contains provisions to encourage two-parent families and reduce out-of-wedlock births. Several provisions deal specifically with the reduction of births among teen mothers. Nevertheless, Dye explains that teen mothers have a much higher participation rate in major means-tested government programs than do mothers in other age groups. In 2004, 68% of unmarried mothers aged 15 to 24 years who had a child in the last year received some form of government assistance, compared with 64.2% of all unmarried mothers who had a child in the last year.

To receive TANF benefits, states are required to submit plans that detail their efforts to reduce out-of-wedlock births, especially among teenagers. To be eligible for TANF benefits, unmarried minor parents are required to remain in high school or its equivalent as well as to live in an adult-supervised setting. One provision in the law allows

(34.1%). Other common reasons were an increase in other household members' earnings (12.1%), an increase in the number of adults in the household because of a marriage (2.2%) or for another reason (12.8%), and the ending of a work limitation (9%).

TEEN MOTHERS. In "Births: Preliminary Data for 2009" (*National Vital Statistics Reports*, vol. 59, no. 3, December 21, 2010), Brady E. Hamilton, Joyce A. Martin, and Stephanie J. Ventura of the Centers for Disease Control and Prevention indicate that the teen birth rate has declined significantly since the 1990s. In 2009 the teen birth rate was 39.1 births per 1,000 teenagers aged 15 to 19 years, down 6% from the year before. The birth rate among Hispanic teens was 70.1 births per 1,000 women; among non-Hispanic African-American teens, 59 births per 1,000 women; among Native American or Alaskan Native teens, 55.5 births per 1,000 women; among non-Hispanic white teens, 25.6 births per 1,000 women; and among Asian-American teens, 14.6 births per 1,000 women. (See Figure 4.8.)

FIGURE 4.3

Percentage of the total population receiving AFDC/TANF by age, 1970–2006

[In percent]

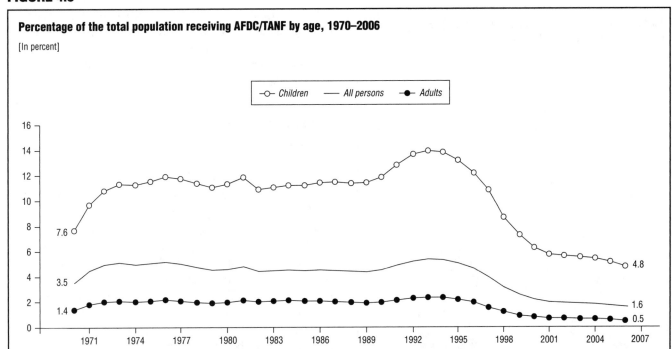

Notes: Recipients are expressed as the fiscal year average of monthly caseloads from administrative data, excluding recipients in the territories. Tribal TANF recipients are also excluded. Child recipients include a small number of dependents ages 18 and older who are students. The average number of adult and child recipients in 1998 and 1999 are estimated using data from the National Emergency TANF Data Files and thereafter using the National TANF Data Files. Beginning in 2000, the data include both TANF and SSP recipients who have comprised as much as 11 percent of total recipients.
AFDC = Aid to Families with Dependent Children. TANF = Temporary Assistance for Needy Families. SSP = Separate State Programs.

SOURCE: Gil Grouse, Susan Hauan, and Annette Waters Rogers, "Figure IND 3a. Percentage of the Total Population Receiving AFDC/TANF by Age: 1970–2006," in *Indicators of Welfare Dependence: Annual Report to Congress, 2008*, U.S. Department of Health and Human Services, December 2008, http://aspe.hhs.gov/hsp/indicators08/ch2.pdf (accessed February 18, 2011)

FIGURE 4.4

Mothers by participation in public assistance programs, by program and fertility status, 1996–2004

[Percent]

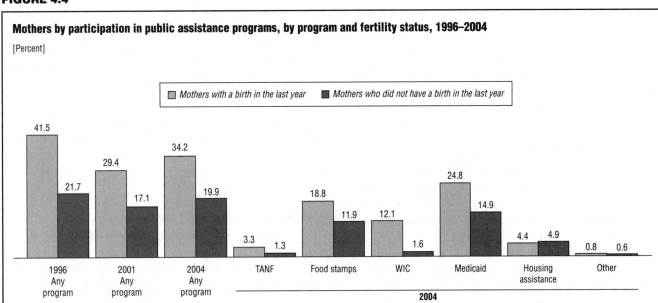

Note: TANF = Temporary Assistance for Needy Families. WIC = Women, Infants and Children.

SOURCE: Jane Lawler Dye, "Figure 1. Mothers by Participation in Public Assistance Programs by Program and Fertility Status: 1996–2004," in *Participation of Mothers in Government Assistance Programs: 2004*, Current Population Reports, U.S. Census Bureau, May 2008, http://www.census.gov/prod/2008pubs/p70-116.pdf (accessed February 17, 2011)

FIGURE 4.5

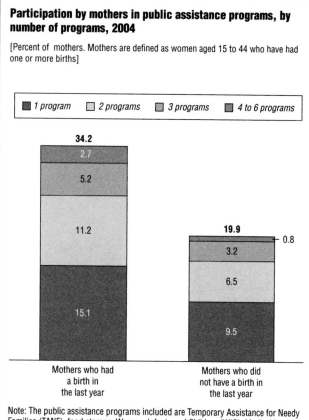

Participation by mothers in public assistance programs, by number of programs, 2004

[Percent of mothers. Mothers are defined as women aged 15 to 44 who have had one or more births]

Legend: ■ 1 program □ 2 programs ▨ 3 programs ▨ 4 to 6 programs

Note: The public assistance programs included are Temporary Assistance for Needy Families (TANF), food stamps, Women, Infants and Children (WIC), Medicaid, housing assistance, and other (which includes general assistance and other welfare).

SOURCE: Jane Lawler Dye, "Figure 2. Participation in Public Assistance Programs by Number of Programs: 2004," in *Participation of Mothers in Government Assistance Programs: 2004*, Current Population Reports, U.S. Census Bureau, May 2008, http://www.census.gov/prod/2008pubs/p70-116.pdf (accessed February 17, 2011)

for the creation of second-chance homes for teen parents and their children, a type of home that already existed in some states. These homes require that all residents either enroll in school or participate in a job-training program. They also provide parenting and life skills classes, counseling, and support services.

A performance bonus that is separate from the TANF block grant rewards states for reductions in births outside of marriage. The administration of George W. Bush (1946–) promoted abstinence-only education programs as the best way to prevent teen pregnancy and provided grant money for states to implement abstinence-only education programs that stressed that teens should not be sexually active outside of marriage. The welfare reform law directs the Department of Health and Human Services to provide a strategy to prevent unmarried teen pregnancies and to ensure that 25% of the communities in the United States implement a teen pregnancy prevention program. The 2006 reauthorization of the Personal Responsibility and Work Opportunity Reconciliation Act

(PRWORA) provided an additional $100 million per year between fiscal years 2006 and 2010 to fund "healthy marriage initiatives"—that is, a variety of activities designed to promote the value of marriage to the general population and teach interpersonal skills to help ensure the stability of marital relationships.

SUPPLEMENTAL NUTRITION ASSISTANCE PROGRAM

The Supplemental Nutrition Assistance Program (SNAP; previously called the Food Stamp Program) is administered by the U.S. Department of Agriculture (USDA) and is the largest food assistance program in the United States. According to the USDA's Food and Nutrition Service, in "Characteristics of Supplemental Nutrition Assistance Program Households: Fiscal Year 2009 Summary" (October 2010, http://www.fns.usda.gov/ora/MENU/Published/snap/FILES/Participation/2009Characteristics Summary.pdf), during an average month in 2009 approximately 33.7 million people in 15.2 million households received SNAP benefits. SNAP issues an electronic debit card that may only be used to buy food that is prepared at home. The value of the benefits is based on family size and household income.

The Food and Nutrition Service notes that in 2009, 48% of the participants were children and 8% were 60 years old and older. Three out of 10 (29%) SNAP recipients lived in a household with earnings as the primary source of income. In 2005, 44.6% of SNAP recipients lived in households with no one in the labor force, 22.4% had at least one part-time worker in the labor force, and 32.9% had at least one full-time worker in the labor force. (See Figure 4.2.) Most SNAP households did not receive cash welfare benefits—only 10% received TANF. Even though 29% of SNAP recipients' primary source of income was earnings, most SNAP households were poor; 86% of households lived in poverty and more than 41% had incomes at or below half the poverty line.

Figure 4.9 shows that after a drop during the mid-1990s, participation in SNAP began to rise in 2000. By 2006, 8.9% of all Americans were receiving SNAP benefits; 17.1% of all children were receiving benefits.

UNEMPLOYMENT COMPENSATION

Unemployment affects some groups of workers more than others. More specifically, the unemployment rate of African-American and Hispanic workers is higher than that of white and Asian-American workers. The U.S. Bureau of Labor Statistics indicates that in 2010 the unemployment rate for white male workers aged 16 years and older was 9.6% and for Asian-American male workers of the same age it was 7.8%, compared with 18.4% for African-American male workers and 12.7% for Hispanic male

TABLE 4.2

Mothers 15 to 44 years old, by participation status and selected characteristics, 2004

[Numbers in thousands]

	Mothers who had a child in the last year						Mothers who did not have a child in the last year					
	Total		Participants[a]		Nonparticipants[b]		Total		Participants[a]		Nonparticipants[b]	
Characteristic	Number	Participation rate[c]	Number	Percent	Number	Percent	Number	Participation rate[c]	Number	Percent	Number	Percent
Total	4,138	34.2	1,417	100.0	2,721	100.0	30,435	19.9	6,070	100.0	24,365	100.0
Race and Hispanic origin												
White	3,275	29.9	978	69.0	2,298	84.5	23,367	16.3	3,800	62.6	19,568	80.3
Non-Hispanic	2,388	23.9	570	40.2	1,818	66.8	18,355	13.5	2,486	41.0	15,869	65.1
Black	527	62.4	329	23.2	198	7.3	4,739	38.2	1,810	29.8	2,928	12.0
Asian	170	49.4	84	5.9	86	3.2	1,123	28.2	317	5.2	806	3.3
Hispanic (any race)	956	47.6	455	32.1	502	18.4	5,409	27.0	1,460	24.1	3,949	16.2
Nativity status												
Native[d]	3,557	33.7	1,198	84.5	2,359	86.7	27,138	19.8	5,360	88.3	21,777	89.4
Foreign born	581	37.7	219	15.5	362	13.3	3,297	21.5	710	11.7	2,587	10.6
Labor force status												
Had a job during last 4 months	2,303	23.7	545	38.5	1,758	64.6	22,094	15.1	3,338	55.0	18,757	77.0
No job last 4 months[e]	1,835	47.5	872	61.5	963	35.4	8,341	32.8	2,733	45.0	5,608	23.0
Unable to find work	57	(B)	49	3.5	7	0.3	451	57.6	260	4.3	191	0.8
Not able to work due to disability	35	(B)	28	2.0	7	0.3	851	76.3	649	10.7	202	0.8
Educational attainment												
Not a high school graduate	791	58.3	461	32.5	331	12.2	3,783	42.3	1,601	26.4	2,183	9.0
High school graduate	1,066	47.5	506	35.7	560	20.6	8,339	23.6	1,968	32.4	6,371	26.1
College, 1 or more years	2,281	19.7	450	31.8	1,831	67.3	18,312	13.7	2,501	41.2	15,811	64.9
Monthly family income[f]												
Less than $500	250	72.4	181	14.6	69	2.6	1,253	62.3	781	14.0	472	2.0
$500 to $1,499	612	67.0	410	33.2	202	7.6	3,650	57.2	2,087	37.5	1,563	6.6
$1,500 and over	3,016	21.4	645	52.2	2,370	89.7	24,520	11.0	2,695	48.4	21,825	91.5
$1,500 to $2,499	601	47.3	284	23.0	317	12.0	4,265	31.2	1,331	23.9	2,934	12.3
$2,500 to $3,999	724	30.2	219	17.7	505	19.1	5,569	13.6	758	13.6	4,811	20.2
$4,000 and over	1,691	8.4	142	11.5	1,548	58.6	14,686	4.1	605	10.9	14,081	59.0
Poverty level[f]												
Below poverty level	818	70.0	573	46.4	245	9.3	4,311	61.3	2,642	47.5	1,670	7.0
100 to 199 percent of poverty level	979	43.6	427	34.5	552	20.9	6,465	30.0	1,940	34.9	4,525	19.0
200 percent of poverty level or higher	2,080	11.3	236	19.1	1,844	69.8	18,647	5.3	981	17.6	17,665	74.0
Child support[g]												
Received payments	348	51.7	180	23.6	168	33.9	4,751	29.8	1,414	34.1	3,337	48.5
Did not receive payments	910	64.1	583	76.4	327	66.1	6,280	43.6	2,736	65.9	3,544	51.5
Type of residence												
Metropolitan	3,760	33.9	1,274	89.9	2,486	91.4	27,186	19.1	5,198	85.6	21,988	90.2
In central city	1,862	35.9	668	47.1	1,194	43.9	15,387	23.1	3,557	58.6	11,830	48.6
Not in central city	1,898	31.9	606	42.8	1,292	47.5	11,799	13.9	1,641	27.0	10,158	41.7
Nonmetropolitan	378	37.8	143	10.1	235	8.6	3,249	26.8	872	14.4	2,377	9.8

(B) Derived measure not shown when base is less than 75,000.
[a]Currently participating in or covered by one or more programs.
[b]Not currently participating in any program.
[c]Percent of mothers participating in or covered by one or more programs.
[d]Includes people born in U.S. outlying areas and abroad to parents who were U.S. citizens.
[e]Includes people not in the labor force.
[f]Percent distribution based only on families reporting income in the past 4 months. Average income for 4 months prior to the interview date.
[g]Data shown only for mothers whose children are under 21 years old and whose marital status is other than married, spouse present unless the spouse is a stepparent. Percent distribution based on this specified universe of mothers.

SOURCE: Jane Lawler Dye, "Table 4. Mothers 15 to 44 Years Old by Program Participation Status and Selected Characteristics: 2004," in *Participation of Mothers in Government Assistance Programs: 2004*, Current Population Reports, U.S. Census Bureau, May 2008, http://www.census.gov/prod/2008pubs/p70-116.pdf (accessed February 17, 2011)

workers. (See Table 4.4.) Single men and women have a higher unemployment rate than other workers. The unemployment rate for single women in 2010 was 12.8%, compared with 9.6% for widowed, divorced, or separated women and 5.9% for married women; the unemployment rate for single men in 2010 was 16.5%, compared with 12.8% for widowed, divorced, or separated men and 6.8% for married men.

FIGURE 4.6

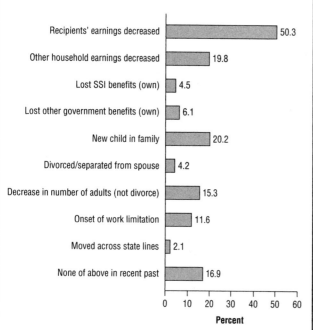

Events associated with single mother TANF entries during the 2001–03 period

Event	Percent
Recipients' earnings decreased	50.3
Other household earnings decreased	19.8
Lost SSI benefits (own)	4.5
Lost other government benefits (own)	6.1
New child in family	20.2
Divorced/separated from spouse	4.2
Decrease in number of adults (not divorce)	15.3
Onset of work limitation	11.6
Moved across state lines	2.1
None of above in recent past	16.9

TANF = Temporary Assistance for Needy Families.
SSI = Supplemental Security Income.
Note: Welfare entries are defined as moving from receipt to non-receipt between two successive Survey of Income and Program Participation (SIPP) interviews (conducted 4 months apart); an event was associated with a welfare transition if the event was observed within two interviews (i.e., 8 months) of the interview marking the welfare entry. In general, events are neither mutually exclusive nor exhaustive, and transition events may sum to more than 100 percent. Two exceptions are that "Other household earnings decreased" was limited to cases when there were decreases in household earnings without a decrease in recipient earnings, and "Decrease in number of adults (not divorce)" was limited to cases where the adult leaving the household was not married to the head of the household. While only affecting a small number of cases, General Assistance income is included within TANF income. Other government benefits include unemployment insurance, foster care, railroad retirement, veterans payments and workers compensation. An decrease in earnings must be a decrease of at least $50 per month. A work limitation is defined as a condition that limits the kind or amount of work. The category "None of above in recent past" represents the percentage of all spell beginnings during the period that were not associated with any of the events measured.
Spells of welfare receipt and associated events are measured using *monthly* data from the SIPP. In the 2003 *Indicators of Welfare Dependence* volume (and earlier volumes), events associated with the beginning and ending of program spells were measured using *annual* data from the Panel Study of Income Dynamics (PSID). Thus, the estimates shown above are not comparable to estimates reported in volumes prior to 2004.
Events sum to more than 100 percent because the same household could experience more than one event associated with a specific welfare entry or exit.

SOURCE: Gil Grouse, Susan Hauan, and Annette Waters Rogers, "Figure IND 10b. Events Associated with Single Mother TANF Entries during 2001–2003 Period," in *Indicators of Welfare Dependence: Annual the Report to Congress, 2008*, U.S. Department of Health and Human Services, December 2008, http://aspe.hhs.gov/hsp/indicators08/ch2.pdf (accessed February 18, 2011)

TABLE 4.3

Percentage of single mother AFDC/TANF spell entries associated with specific events, 1993–95, 1996–99, and 2001–03

	Spell began 1993–1995	Spell began 1996–1999	Spell began 2001–2003
Recipients' earnings decreased	57.1	52.6	50.3
Other household earnings decreased	24.0	21.0	19.8
Lost SSI benefits (own)	1.4	5.1	4.5
Lost other government benefits (own)	8.1	5.1	6.1
New child in family	22.0	17.1	20.2
Divorced/separated from spouse	8.7	6.7	4.2
Decrease in number of adults (not divorce)	19.2	17.6	15.3
Onset of work limitation	7.2	10.9	11.6
Moved across state lines	1.7	1.4	2.1
None of above in recent past	8.8	14.1	16.9

AFDC = Aid to Families with Dependent Children.
TANF = Temporary Assistance for Needy Families.
SSI = Supplemental Security Income.
Note: Welfare entries are defined as moving from receipt to non-receipt between two successive Survey of Income and Program Participation (SIPP) interviews (conducted 4 months apart); an event was associated with a welfare transition if the event was observed within two interviews (i.e., 8 months) of the interview marking the welfare entry. In general, events are neither mutually exclusive nor exhaustive, and transition events may sum to more than 100 percent. Two exceptions are that "Other household earnings decreased" was limited to cases when there were decreases in household earnings without a decrease in recipient earnings, and "Decrease in number of adults (not divorce)" was limited to cases where the adult leaving the household was not married to the head of the household. While only affecting a small number of cases, General Assistance income is included within AFDC/TANF income. Other government benefits include unemployment insurance, foster care, railroad retirement, veterans payments and workers compensation. An decrease in earnings must be a decrease of at least $50 per month. A work limitation is defined as a condition that limits the kind or amount of work. The category "None of above in recent past" represents the percentage of all spell beginnings during the period that were not associated with any of the events measured.
Spells of welfare receipt and associated events are measured using *monthly* data from the SIPP. In the 2003 *Indicators of Welfare Dependence* volume (and earlier volumes), events associated with the beginning and ending of program spells were measured using *annual* data from the Panel Study of Income Dynamics (PSID). Thus, the estimates shown above are not comparable to estimates reported in volumes prior to 2004.
Events sum to more than 100 percent because the same household could experience more than one event associated with a specific welfare entry or exit.

SOURCE: Gil Grouse, Susan Hauan, and Annette Waters Rogers, "Table IND 10b. Percentage of Single Mother AFDC/TANF Spell Entries Associated with Specific Events: Selected Periods," in *Indicators of Welfare Dependence: Annual Report to Congress, 2008*, U.S. Department of Health and Human Services, December 2008, http://aspe.hhs.gov/hsp/indicators08/ch2.pdf (accessed February 18, 2011)

Unemployment compensation varies widely by state. Table 4.5 shows the percentages of the unemployed receiving unemployment benefits in each state during the third quarter of 2010. Pennsylvania (4.6%), New Jersey (4.5%), California (4.3%), and Oregon (4.3%) had the highest rates of those receiving unemployment compensation, whereas South Dakota (0.8%), North Dakota (1%), and Virginia (1.7%) had the lowest rates.

The maximum a state may offer is 39 weeks of coverage (except for special programs, such as in response to the Great Recession, which lasted from late 2007 to mid-2009), but all states provide up to 26 weeks of benefits, except Massachusetts and Washington, which offer 30 weeks of benefits. Benefits vary dramatically from state to state. In 2008 the average weekly benefits in Hawaii ($413.07), Massachusetts ($390.69), New Jersey ($377.48), Rhode Island ($370.46), and Minnesota ($346.93) were significantly higher than those offered by Mississippi ($182.74), Alabama ($196.23), Alaska ($202.16), Louisiana ($209.12), and Arizona ($217.72). (See Table 4.6.)

SUPPLEMENTAL SECURITY INCOME

SSI is a means-tested income assistance program that was created in 1972 to provide monthly cash assistance to senior citizens, blind people, and disabled individuals. A

FIGURE 4.7

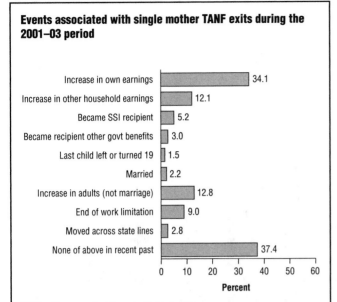

Events associated with single mother TANF exits during the 2001–03 period

Event	Percent
Increase in own earnings	34.1
Increase in other household earnings	12.1
Became SSI recipient	5.2
Became recipient other govt benefits	3.0
Last child left or turned 19	1.5
Married	2.2
Increase in adults (not marriage)	12.8
End of work limitation	9.0
Moved across state lines	2.8
None of above in recent past	37.4

TANF = Temporary Assistance for Needy Families.
SSI = Supplemental Security Income.
Note: Welfare exits are defined as moving from receipt to non-receipt between two successive Survey of Income and Program Participation (SIPP) interviews (conducted 4 months apart); an event was associated with a welfare transition if the event was observed within two interviews (i.e., 8 months) of the interview marking the welfare exit. In general, events are neither mutually exclusive nor exhaustive, and transition events may sum to more than 100 percent. Two exceptions are that "Increase in other household earnings" was limited to cases when there were increases in household earnings without an increase in recipient earnings, and "Increase in adults (not marriage)" was limited to cases where the adult joining the household was not marrying the head of the household. While only affecting a small number of cases, General Assistance income is included within TANF income. Other government benefits include unemployment insurance, foster care, railroad retirement, veterans payments and workers compensation. An increase in earnings must be an increase of at least $50 per month. A work limitation is defined as a condition that limits the kind or amount of work. The category "None of above in recent past" represents the percentage of all spell beginnings during the period that were not associated with any of the events measured.
Spells of welfare receipt and associated events are measured using *monthly* data from the SIPP. In the 2003 *Indicators of Welfare Dependence* volume (and earlier volumes), events associated with the beginning and ending of program spells were measured using *annual* data from the Panel Study of Income Dynamics (PSID). Thus, the estimates shown above are not comparable to estimates reported in volumes prior to 2004.
Events sum to more than 100 percent because the same household could experience more than one event associated with a specific welfare entry or exit.

SOURCE: Gil Grouse, Susan Hauan, and Annette Waters Rogers, "Figure IND 10a. Events Associated with Single Mother TANF Exits during the 2001–2003 Period," in *Indicators of Welfare Dependence: Annual Report to Congress, 2008*, U.S. Department of Health and Human Services, December 2008, http://aspe.hhs.gov/hsp/indicators08/ch2.pdf (accessed February 18, 2011).

number of requirements must be met to receive financial benefits from SSI. First, a person must meet the program criteria for age, blindness, or disability. In addition, because SSI is a means-tested program, only those who meet the income eligibility requirements receive payments. Total SSI payments to all recipients grew from $5.1 billion in 1974 to $43 billion in 2008, the highest sum in the program's history. Table 4.7 shows the annual amount of payments by source of payment and category between 1974 and 2008.

The Social Security Administration notes in *Fast Facts and Figures about Social Security, 2010* (August 2010, http://www.ssa.gov/policy/docs/chartbooks/fast_facts/2010/fast_facts10.pdf) that 7.7 million people received SSI payments in 2009. Of these, 84% were disabled, 15% were elderly, and 1% were blind. (See Figure 4.10.) In 2005, 61.1% of SSI recipients lived in a household with no one in the labor force, 10.2% lived in a household with at least one part-time worker, and 28.7% lived in a household with at least one full-time worker. (See Figure 4.2.) Most of those receiving SSI benefits were between the ages of 18 and 64 years (58%). About 47.4% of SSI recipients in 2008 were female and 52.6% were male. (See Table 4.8.)

As shown in Figure 4.11, the percentage of all people who received SSI benefits rose from 2% in 1975 to 2.4% in 2006. The percentage of senior citizens who received SSI benefits declined from 10.9% in 1975 to 5.3% in 2006, whereas the percentage of younger adults and children who received benefits rose from 0.2% to 1.5% during the same period.

OVERLAPPING SERVICES

Poor households that receive one form of social welfare assistance are likely to qualify for and receive others. In 2005, 11.3% of those who received means-tested assistance received both SSI and SNAP benefits and 14.5% received both TANF and SNAP benefits. (See Figure 4.12.) Table 4.9 shows that people in female-headed families were the most likely to receive both TANF and SNAP benefits in 2005; 7.4% of these individuals did so, compared with 1.9% of people in male-headed families and only 0.5% of people in married-couple families. Preschool-aged children were the most likely to receive both TANF and SNAP benefits (5.3%), followed by children aged six to 10 years (4.2%) and children aged 11 to 15 years (3.3%).

Data from 2004 also show substantial overlap in individuals participating in public assistance programs. In that year 15.1% of mothers who had a birth in the last year participated in one public assistance program, 11.2% participated in two programs, 5.2% participated in three programs, and 2.7% participated in four to six programs. (See Figure 4.5.) Mothers who did not have a birth in the last year had lower participation rates. Nearly one out of 10 (9.5%) participated in one government assistance program, 6.5% participated in two programs, 3.2% participated in three programs, and 0.8% participated in four to six programs.

In *Assessing the Evidence about Work Support Benefits and Low-Income Families: Rationale for a Demonstration and Evaluation* (February 2011, http://www.urban.org/uploadedpdf/412303-Work-Support-Benefits.pdf), Gregory Mills, Jessica F. Compton, and Olivia Golden of the Urban Institute point out how important the "package of supports" can be to working, low-income families. The package can include Medicaid, SNAP, and child care subsidies. However, most working families do not receive all

FIGURE 4.8

Birth rates for teenagers aged 15–19, by race and Hispanic origin, selected years 1991–2009

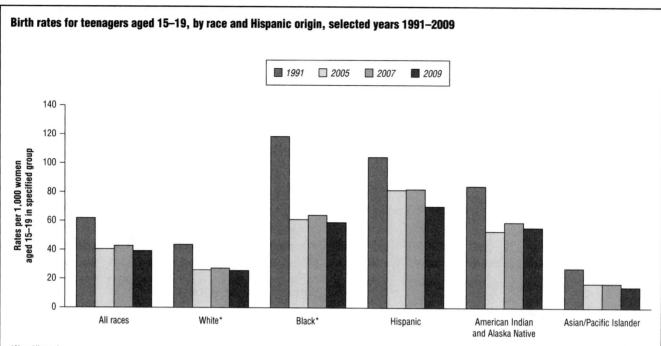

*Non-Hispanic

SOURCE: Brady E. Hamilton, Joyce A. Martin, and Stephanie J. Ventura, "Figure 2. Birth Rates for Teenagers 15–19 Years by Race and Hispanic Origin: United States, Final 1991, 2005, and 2007, and Preliminary 2009," in "Births: Preliminary Data for 2009," *National Vital Statistics Reports*, vol. 59, no. 3, December 21, 2010, http://www.cdc.gov/nchs/data/nvsr/nvsr59/nvsr59_03.pdf (accessed February 18, 2011)

FIGURE 4.9

Percentage of the total population receiving food stamps by age, 1975–2006

[In percent]

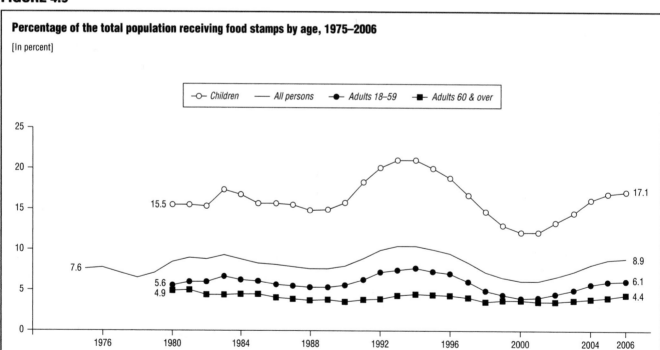

Note: Recipient totals exclude the territories and are the fiscal year averages of monthly caseloads from administrative data. From 1975 to 1983 the number of participants includes the Family Food Assistance Program (FFAP) that was largely replaced by the Food Stamp Program in 1975. From 1975 to 1983 the number of FFAP participants averaged only 88 thousand.

SOURCE: Gil Grouse, Susan Hauan, and Annette Waters Rogers, "Figure IND 3b. Percentage of the Total Population Receiving Food Stamps by Age: 1975–2006," in *Indicators of Welfare Dependence: Annual Report to Congress, 2008*, U.S. Department of Health and Human Services, December 2008, http://aspe.hhs.gov/hsp/indicators08/ch2.pdf (accessed February 18, 2011)

TABLE 4.4

Unemployed persons by marital status, race and Hispanic origin, age, and sex, 2009 and 2010

Marital status, race, Hispanic or Latino ethnicity, and age	Men				Women			
	Thousands of persons		Unemployment rates		Thousands of persons		Unemployment rates	
	2009	2010	2009	2010	2009	2010	2009	2010
Total, 16 years and over	8,453	8,626	10.3	10.5	5,811	6,199	8.1	8.6
Married, spouse present	3,115	3,138	6.6	6.8	2,057	2,160	5.5	5.9
Widowed, divorced, or separated	1,326	1,352	12.8	12.8	1,330	1,397	9.2	9.6
Single (never married)	4,011	4,135	16.3	16.5	2,424	2,642	12.0	12.8
White, 16 years and over	6,421	6,476	9.4	9.6	4,227	4,440	7.3	7.7
Married, spouse present	2,498	2,490	6.2	6.3	1,694	1,748	5.4	5.6
Widowed, divorced, or separated	1,058	1,056	12.4	12.2	993	1,059	8.8	9.3
Single (never married)	2,864	2,929	14.8	15.0	1,540	1,632	10.5	11.0
Black or African American, 16 years and over	1,448	1,550	17.5	18.4	1,159	1,302	12.4	13.8
Married, spouse present	367	408	10.3	11.6	193	226	6.6	7.9
Widowed, divorced, or separated	205	239	16.4	17.9	257	246	10.9	10.7
Single (never married)	876	903	25.3	25.5	709	830	17.3	19.3
Asian, 16 years and over	306	305	7.9	7.8	216	238	6.6	7.1
Married, spouse present	167	165	6.6	6.5	116	124	5.6	6.1
Widowed, divorced, or separated	26	20	8.2	6.6	30	40	6.2	8.7
Single (never married)	112	120	11.2	11.5	70	73	9.4	8.6
Hispanic or Latino ethnicity, 16 years and over	1,670	1,711	12.5	12.7	1,036	1,132	11.5	12.3
Married, spouse present	688	683	9.5	9.6	410	422	9.8	10.0
Widowed, divorced, or separated	223	213	13.3	12.3	218	239	11.1	11.8
Single (never married)	759	815	17.3	17.4	408	471	14.0	15.7
Total, 25 years and over	6,226	6,365	8.8	8.9	4,279	4,603	6.9	7.4
Married, spouse present	3,012	3,028	6.5	6.6	1,933	2,050	5.3	5.7
Widowed, divorced, or separated	1,262	1,305	12.5	12.6	1,263	1,334	8.9	9.4
Single (never married)	1,952	2,032	13.3	13.4	1,083	1,219	9.5	10.2
White, 25 years and over	4,777	4,833	8.1	8.2	3,157	3,341	6.4	6.8
Married, spouse present	2,413	2,407	6.1	6.2	1,589	1,657	5.2	5.5
Widowed, divorced, or separated	1,007	1,021	12.1	12.1	947	1,006	8.6	9.1
Single (never married)	1,358	1,404	12.0	12.0	621	677	8.0	8.4
Black or African American, 25 years and over	1,022	1,102	14.7	15.5	809	920	10.1	11.5
Married, spouse present	358	389	10.2	11.2	182	215	6.5	7.8
Widowed, divorced, or separated	197	228	16.2	17.5	239	239	10.4	10.6
Single (never married)	467	485	20.8	20.9	388	466	13.6	15.6
Asian, 25 years and over	253	249	7.2	7.0	176	197	5.9	6.5
Married, spouse present	163	162	6.5	6.4	113	120	5.6	6.0
Widowed, divorced, or separated	26	19	8.1	6.5	29	39	6.2	8.6
Single (never married)	65	67	9.2	9.2	34	38	6.7	6.6
Hispanic or Latino ethnicity, 25 years and over	1,218	1,226	10.9	10.8	737	816	9.9	10.7
Married, spouse present	655	648	9.4	9.5	374	390	9.5	9.8
Widowed, divorced, or separated	201	201	12.7	12.1	201	222	10.7	11.4
Single (never married)	362	377	13.8	13.3	161	204	9.9	12.0

Note: Estimates for the above race groups (white, black or African American, and Asian) do not sum to totals because data are not presented for all races. Persons whose ethnicity is identified as Hispanic or Latino may be of any race. Updated population controls are introduced annually with the release of January data.

SOURCE: "24. Unemployed Persons by Marital Status, Race, Hispanic or Latino Ethnicity, Age, and Sex," in *Current Population Survey (CPS) Tables: Household Data Annual Averages*, Bureau of Labor Statistics, 2011, http://www.bls.gov/cps/cpsaat24.pdf (accessed February 18, 2011)

the supports they could have. In fact, in 2001 only 5% of low-income families received a full work support package of health insurance, SNAP benefits, and child care subsidies. The researchers note that the positive results for families receiving the full package of benefits include fuller employment and higher earnings. Furthermore, Mills, Compton, and Golden note that the children and teens in these families experience several long-term positive results, such as better health and lower mortality rates, better school

attendance, improved reading scores, and stronger engagement in school and work activities.

DURATION OF PROGRAM SPELLS

In *Dynamics of Economic Well-Being*, Loveless and Tin examine the use of government programs between 2001 and 2003. Some of the highlights of Loveless and Tin's survey include:

TABLE 4.5

Unemployment compensation recipiency rates by state, third quarter 2010

State	Insured unemployment rate (%)	Total unemployment rate (%)	(In thousands)		
			Covered employment	Civilian labor force	Total unemployment
Alabama	2.6	9.2	1,736	2,121	195.5
Alaska	4.1	7.0	285	369	26.0
Arizona	3.2	9.9	2,304	3,192	315.8
Arkansas	3.5	7.6	1,099	1,353	102.7
California	4.3	12.5	13,966	18,329	2,283.7
Colorado	2.7	8.0	2,087	2,684	215.2
Connecticut	4.1	9.2	1,541	1,906	174.4
Delaware	3.1	8.4	380	424	35.5
District of Columbia	2.7	10.0	475	335	33.4
Florida	3.2	12.2	6,983	9,309	1,132.6
Georgia	3.0	10.1	3,608	4,682	474.7
Hawaii	3.1	6.6	548	636	41.9
Idaho	3.3	8.5	575	762	64.7
Illinois	3.7	10.0	5,292	6,684	669.0
Indiana	2.5	9.9	2,603	3,142	310.0
Iowa	2.3	6.4	1,383	1,683	108.5
Kansas	2.7	6.7	1,252	1,502	101.1
Kentucky	2.6	9.9	1,636	2,088	206.6
Louisiana	2.9	7.8	1,783	2,124	166.4
Maine	2.4	7.1	542	707	50.3
Maryland	2.7	7.4	2,255	2,983	222.1
Massachusetts	3.5	8.5	3,023	3,508	297.3
Michigan	3.5	13.0	3,608	4,873	635.9
Minnesota	2.4	6.8	2,456	2,982	203.6
Mississippi	3.2	10.0	1,033	1,307	131.0
Missouri	2.7	9.3	2,475	2,998	278.9
Montana	2.9	6.7	394	502	33.7
Nebraska	1.9	4.5	859	979	44.2
Nevada	4.1	14.4	1,079	1,355	194.6
New Hampshire	2.6	5.5	581	751	41.6
New Jersey	4.5	9.5	3,631	4,535	429.8
New Mexico	3.0	8.4	741	961	81.1
New York	3.5	8.2	8,069	9,747	799.1
North Carolina	3.4	9.6	3,658	4,512	434.1
North Dakota	1.0	3.3	334	374	12.5
Ohio	2.6	9.9	4,702	5,975	588.9
Oklahoma	2.1	6.7	1,414	1,763	118.4
Oregon	4.3	10.2	1,531	1,984	202.6
Pennsylvania	4.6	8.8	5,238	6,427	565.2
Puerto Rico	6.3	16.4	919	1,287	211.6
Rhode Island	3.7	11.5	425	576	66.2
South Carolina	3.4	11.1	1,693	2,170	241.8
South Dakota	0.8	4.2	364	449	18.9
Tennessee	2.4	9.4	2,469	3,067	289.8
Texas	2.1	8.2	9,822	12,187	1,005.3
Utah	2.0	7.4	1,093	1,361	101.1
Vermont	2.9	5.5	282	360	19.8
Virgin Islands	2.2		44		
Virginia	1.7	6.8	3,297	4,197	286.7
Washington	3.2	8.7	2,663	3,549	310.4
West Virginia	2.7	8.7	651	784	68.0
Wisconsin	3.8	7.5	2,527	3,059	229.8
Wyoming	2.0	6.3	253	295	18.5
United States	**3.2**	**9.5**	**123,661**	**154,601**	**14,679.0**

Note: Blank cells indicate that information is unavailable.

SOURCE: Adapted from "Labor Force Information by State (Levels in Thousands), for CYQ 2010.3," in *Unemployment Insurance Data Summary*, U.S. Department of Labor, Employment and Training Administration, 2010, http://workforcesecurity.doleta.gov/unemploy/content/data_stats/datasum10/DataSum_2010_3.pdf (accessed February 18, 2011)

- In 2003, 20% of people took part in one or more major aid programs (housing assistance, SSI, TANF, SNAP, or Medicaid) for at least one month.

- More individuals participated in Medicaid (16% for at least one month in 2003) than in any other single aid program.

- During an average month in 2003, 50.8% of people in poverty received benefits, compared with only 9.7% of people who were not poor.

- In 2003, 48% of all households headed by a single female participated in a major means-tested program for at least one month, compared with 25.7%

TABLE 4.6

Amount and duration of weekly benefits for total unemployment under regular state programs, 2008

State or area	Average weekly benefit for total employment		Average weekly insured unemployment	Average actual duration (weeks)	Benefits paid[c] (millions of dollars)
	Amount (dollars)[a]	Percent of average weekly wages[b]			
Total	297.09	34.4	3,306,433	14.9	42,719
Alabama	196.23	26.9	37,385	11.2	312
Alaska	202.16	23.5	10,955	14.6	107
Arizona	217.72	26.9	47,672	14.9	449
Arkansas	264.86	40.0	34,320	13.0	334
California	307.12	31.1	503,043	16.6	6,987
Colorado	340.72	38.4	30,130	12.8	416
Connecticut	321.97	28.7	47,487	15.8	736
Delaware	256.89	28.1	10,433	17.1	132
District of Columbia	291.43	21.4	5,130	22.1	112
Florida	238.41	30.9	177,559	15.2	1,844
Georgia	272.78	33.7	84,015	11.6	944
Hawaii	413.07	54.4	11,699	13.9	220
Idaho	272.18	42.3	19,139	11.9	218
Illinois	312.09	33.5	160,296	16.7	2,310
Indiana	297.73	40.6	74,029	12.8	995
Iowa	302.14	42.8	29,261	11.6	418
Kansas	316.03	43.4	22,008	13.9	319
Kentucky	299.68	42.1	39,876	14.1	562
Louisiana	209.12	27.2	26,567	13.7	222
Maine	264.78	38.6	12,634	14.1	144
Maryland	304.93	33.2	49,847	15.1	644
Massachusetts	390.69	35.9	96,030	17.4	1,584
Michigan	299.58	35.4	164,022	15.0	2,235
Minnesota	346.93	39.5	59,388	16.3	885
Mississippi	182.74	28.9	25,285	12.9	182
Missouri	244.10	31.7	58,853	13.9	595
Montana	255.19	40.8	9,651	14.1	101
Nebraska	241.25	35.0	10,765	11.5	109
Nevada	292.32	35.6	39,936	14.6	579
New Hampshire	272.03	31.7	10,173	13.1	124
New Jersey	377.48	35.6	133,888	17.8	2,339
New Mexico	278.07	39.2	14,027	15.9	172
New York	306.54	26.5	209,550	16.2	2,735
North Carolina	287.32	37.9	108,348	13.2	1,070
North Dakota	286.21	43.1	3,676	10.3	49
Ohio	302.69	38.9	127,314	14.9	1,493
Oklahoma	272.43	38.7	16,803	13.6	191
Oregon	301.69	39.1	61,904	13.9	822
Pennsylvania	335.40	39.6	194,274	16.1	2,753
Rhode Island	370.46	45.4	15,801	16.3	278
South Carolina	239.81	34.8	53,296	13.3	492
South Dakota	238.82	38.5	2,290	10.2	26
Tennessee	220.98	29.0	53,591	13.3	567
Texas	302.94	34.5	120,735	13.4	1,553
Utah	311.60	43.3	14,663	13.6	194
Vermont	293.62	40.3	7,945	14.4	112
Virginia	281.86	32.0	43,215	12.3	517
Washington	355.33	40.0	67,808	13.1	1,052
West Virginia	241.52	35.9	14,828	13.2	165
Wisconsin	273.11	36.5	87,695	13.2	1,035
Wyoming	307.52	38.9	2,470	13.2	52
Outlying areas					
Puerto Rico	112.28	23.4	43,981	18.4	222
U.S. Virgin Islands	328.43	47.0	741	16.7	13

Notes: Except where noted, excludes data for federal employees and for ex-servicemembers; includes data for state and local government empoyees where covered by state law after 1955. Totals do not necessarily equal the sum of rounded components.
[a]Includes dependents' allowances for states that provide such benefits.
[b]Based on average total weekly wage in current year.
[c]Percentages based on first payments for 12-month period.

SOURCE: Adapted from "Table 9.A2. Summary Data on State Programs, by State or Other Area, 2008," in *Annual Statistical Supplement to the Social Security Bulletin, 2009*, Social Security Administration, February 2010, http://www.ssa.gov/policy/docs/statcomps/supplement/2009/9a.pdf (accessed February 17, 2011)

TABLE 4.7

Total annual amount of Supplemental Security Income (SSI) payments by eligibility category, selected years 1974–2008

[In thousands of dollars]

Year	Total	Federal Supplemental Security Income	Federally administered state supplementation
All recipients			
1974	5,096,813	3,833,161	1,263,652
1975	5,716,072	4,313,538	1,402,534
1980	7,714,640	5,866,354	1,848,286
1985	10,749,938	8,777,341	1,972,597
1990	16,132,959	12,893,805	3,239,154
1995	27,037,280	23,919,430	3,117,850
2000	30,671,699	27,290,248	3,381,451
2001	32,165,856	28,705,503	3,460,353
2002	33,718,999	29,898,765	3,820,234
2003	34,693,278	30,688,029	4,005,249
2004	36,065,358	31,886,509	4,178,849
2005	37,235,843	33,058,056	4,177,787
2006	38,888,961	34,736,088	4,152,873
2007	41,204,645	36,884,066	4,320,579
2008	43,040,481	38,655,780	4,384,701
Aged			
1974	2,414,034	1,782,742	631,292
1975	2,516,515	1,842,980	673,535
1980	2,617,023	1,860,194	756,829
1985	2,896,671	2,202,557	694,114
1990	3,559,388	2,521,382	1,038,006
1995	4,239,222	3,374,772	864,450
2000	4,540,045	3,597,516	942,530
2001	4,664,076	3,708,527	955,549
2002	4,802,792	3,751,491	1,051,301
2003	4,856,875	3,758,070	1,098,805
2004	4,894,070	3,773,901	1,133,324
2005	4,964,627	3,836,625	1,128,002
2006	5,115,911	3,953,106	1,162,804
2007	5,301,277	4,113,424	1,187,853
2008	5,378,921	4,180,786	1,198,135
Blind			
1974	125,791	91,308	34,483
1975	127,240	92,427	34,813
1980	185,827	131,506	54,321
1985	259,840	195,183	64,657
1990	328,949	238,415	90,534
1995	367,441	298,238	69,203
2000	385,927	312,238	73,688
2001	398,624	323,895	74,729
2002	416,454	335,405	81,049
2003	409,293	325,878	83,415
2004	412,414	327,446	85,364
2005	414,147	330,591	83,556
2006	409,287	326,230	83,057
2007	418,835	336,789	82,046
2008	416,017	335,179	80,838

of single-male households and 13.7% of married-couple households.

- Adults who had not graduated from high school were more likely than high school graduates to participate in means-tested programs during an average month in 2003 (25.6% and 11.7%, respectively).

The length of time people received assistance, which is referred to as a spell, differed by program. As Figure 4.13 shows, 49.6% of the families receiving TANF benefits between 2001 and 2003 received benefits for less than four months and 23.7% received benefits from five to 12 months. Only about a quarter (26.8%) of recipients received TANF benefits for a longer period. The duration

of program spells followed the same pattern for SNAP and SSI, although 43.5% of SSI recipients collected benefits for 20 months or longer.

Loveless and Tin explore in more detail the characteristics of people by the length of time they participated in major means-tested programs between 2001 and 2003. Among racial and ethnic groups, non-Hispanic whites (7 months), Hispanics (7.2 months), and African-Americans (7.5 months) had similar median (the middle value—half are higher and half are lower) durations of participation in means-tested programs, whereas Asians or Pacific Islanders (3.9 months) had a significantly lower median duration of program participation. Adults who had not graduated from

TABLE 4.7

Total annual amount of Supplemental Security Income (SSI) payments by eligibility category, selected years 1974–2008 [CONTINUED]

[In thousands of dollars]

Year	Total	Federal Supplemental Security Income	Federally administered state supplementation
Disabled			
1974	2,556,988	1,959,112	597,876
1975	3,072,317	2,378,131	694,186
1980	4,911,792	3,874,655	1,037,137
1985	7,593,427	6,379,601	1,213,826
1990	12,244,622	10,134,007	2,110,615
1995	22,430,612	20,246,415	2,184,197
2000	25,745,710	23,380,477	2,365,233
2001	27,125,707	24,695,630	2,430,077
2002	28,499,771	25,811,887	2,687,884
2003	29,429,428	26,606,400	2,823,028
2004	30,745,406	27,785,246	2,960,160
2005	31,857,069	28,890,840	2,966,229
2006	33,363,762	30,456,751	2,907,011
2007	35,484,533	32,433,853	3,050,680
2008	37,245,543	34,139,815	3,105,728

Note: Totals do not necessarily equal the sum of rounded components.

SOURCE: "Table 7.A4. Total Federally Administered Payments, by Eligibility Category, Selected Years 1974–2008," in *Annual Statistical Supplement to the Social Security Bulletin, 2009*, Social Security Administration, February 2010, http://www.ssa.gov/policy/docs/statcomps/supplement/2009/7a.pdf (accessed February 17, 2011)

high school had a longer median duration of participation (7.4 months) than did high school graduates (5.6 months) or those with at least some college (3.9 months), reflecting the increased economic opportunities of those with higher educational attainments.

Most states have imposed a lifetime limit of 60 months for the receipt of TANF benefits for adults, although states are allowed to extend benefits for hardship cases or victims of domestic violence. Some states have set limits lower than 60 months. Families in which there is no adult head of household are exempt from time limits. The actual median amount of time recipients receive TANF benefits is much lower than the lifetime limit. According to Loveless and Tin, between 2001 and 2003 TANF recipients received benefits for a median of 4.9 months. Children under the age of 18 years tended to received TANF benefits for a longer period; they received benefits for a median of 6.3 months, compared with a median of 4 months for adults aged 18 to 64 years.

Figure 4.14 takes a closer look at the length of time recipients of Aid to Families with Dependent Children (AFDC)/TANF received benefits between 1995 and 2004. (The AFDC program was established by the Social Security Act of 1935; in 1996 the AFDC was replaced by TANF,

following passage of the PRWORA.) Two-thirds (65.3%) of recipients received AFDC/TANF benefits for one or two years. Another quarter (24.7%) received benefits for three to five years. Only 10% of recipients received benefits for a longer period. These short spells of benefits are consistent with the 1996 provisions of the PRWORA, which limited the amount of time individuals could receive TANF. Figure 4.3 shows the drop in benefits to both adults and children after 1996.

Loveless and Tin find that some groups tended to receive TANF benefits longer than other groups between 2001 and 2003. Asians or Pacific Islanders had a much higher median duration of participation in TANF than did other racial and ethnic groups. Asians or Pacific Islanders had a median duration of 11.4 months, compared with 6.5 months for African-Americans and 4 months each for Hispanics and non-Hispanic whites. People in families headed by a single female also had a higher median duration of participation in TANF than did other family types. Between 2001 and 2003 these families had a median duration of 5.8 months, compared with 3.9 months for married-couple families and 3.8 months for single male-headed families.

FIGURE 4.10

Supplemental Security Income (SSI) recipients, by basis of eligibility and age, December 2009

Basis for eligibility

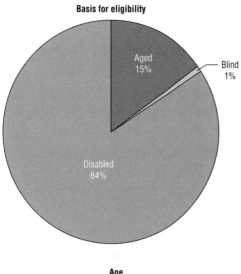

Age

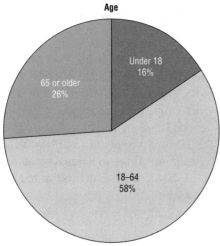

SOURCE: "Basis for Eligibility and Age of Recipients, December 2009," in *Fast Facts and Figures about Social Security, 2010*, Social Security Administration, Office of Retirement and Disability Policy, Office of Research, Evaluation, and Statistics, August 2010, http://www.ssa.gov/policy/docs/chartbooks/fast_facts/2010/fast_facts10.pdf (accessed February 18, 2011)

TABLE 4.8

Number and percentage distribution of federally administered SSI awards, by sex, age, and eligibility category, 2008

Sex and age	Total	Adults			Blind and disabled children[a]
		Aged	Blind	Disabled	
All persons					
Number	919,146	106,513	3,383	621,152	188,098
Percent	100.0	100.0	100.0	100.0	100.0
Percentage distribution by sex					
Male	52.6	39.7	54.1	51.2	64.6
Female	47.4	60.3	45.9	48.8	35.4
Percentage distribution by age					
Under 5	8.6	—	—	—	42.1
5–9	5.5	—	—	—	27.0
10–14	3.8	—	—	—	18.5
15–17	1.8	—	—	—	8.8
18–21	5.5	—	14.0	7.0	3.6
22–29	6.2	—	9.6	9.2	—
30–39	9.4	—	12.4	13.8	—
40–49	17.2	—	21.1	25.4	—
50–59	24.1	—	31.2	35.5	—
60–64	6.1	—	9.2	8.9	—
65–69	6.6	55.8	0.9	0.2	—
70–74	2.4	20.4	0.4	b	—
75–79	1.4	12.1	0.5	b	—
80 or older	1.4	11.7	0.7	b	—
Male					
Number	483,379	42,306	1,829	317,734	121,510
Percent	100.0	100.0	100.0	100.0	100.0
Under 5	9.9	—	—	—	39.5
5–9	7.6	—	—	—	30.2
10–14	4.8	—	—	—	19.1
15–17	2.0	—	—	—	7.9
18–21	6.2	—	13.0	8.0	3.3
22–29	6.3	—	9.6	9.6	—
30–39	8.7	—	14.5	13.1	—
40–49	16.3	—	22.7	24.7	—
50–59	23.6	—	29.6	35.7	—
60–64	5.7	—	9.0	8.7	—
65–69	5.2	57.6	0.6	0.2	—
70–74	1.9	21.7	0.2	b	—
75–79	1.0	11.8	0.5	b	—
80 or older	0.8	8.9	0.3	b	—
Female					
Number	435,767	64,207	1,554	303,418	66,588
Percent	100.0	100.0	100.0	100.0	100.0
Under 5	7.2	—	—	—	46.8
5–9	3.2	—	—	—	21.2
10–14	2.7	—	—	—	17.4
15–17	1.6	—	—	—	10.3
18–21	4.9	—	15.2	6.0	4.3
22–29	6.1	—	9.6	8.7	—
30–39	10.1	—	10.0	14.5	—
40–49	18.2	—	19.2	26.1	—
50–59	24.7	—	33.1	35.2	—
60–64	6.5	—	9.4	9.2	—
65–69	8.3	54.7	1.3	0.3	—
70–74	2.9	19.5	0.6	b	—
75–79	1.8	12.3	0.5	b	—
80 or older	2.0	13.5	1.1	b	—

Notes: Totals do not necessarily equal the sum of rounded components.
— = not applicable.
[a]Includes students aged 18–21.
[b]Less than 0.05 percent.

SOURCE: "Table 7.E2. Percentage Distribution of Federally Administered Awards, by Sex, Age, and Eligibility Category, 2008," in *Annual Statistical Supplement to the Social Security Bulletin, 2009*, Social Security Administration, February 2010, http://www.ssa.gov/policy/docs/statcomps/supplement/2009/7e.pdf (accessed February 17, 2011)

FIGURE 4.11

Percentage of the total population receiving SSI by age, 1975–2006

[In percent]

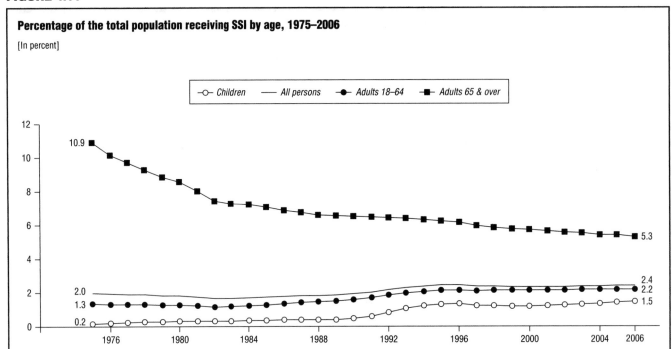

Note: December population figures used as the denominators are obtained by averaging the U.S. Census Bureau's July 1 population estimates for the current and the following year.

SOURCE: Gil Grouse, Susan Hauan, and Annette Waters Rogers, "Figure IND 3c. Percentage of the Total Population Receiving SSI by Age: 1975–2006," in *Indicators of Welfare Dependence: Annual Report to Congress, 2008*, U.S. Department of Health and Human Services, December 2008, http://aspe.hhs .gov/hsp/indicators08/ch2.pdf (accessed February 18, 2011)

FIGURE 4.12

Percentage of recipients receiving assistance from multiple programs, 2005

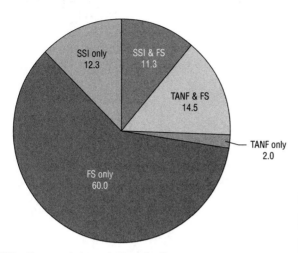

TANF = Temporary Assistance for Needy Families.
SSI = Supplemental Security Income.
FS = food stamps.
Note: Categories are mutually exclusive. SSI receipt is based on individual receipt; AFDC/TANF and food stamp receipt are based on the full recipient unit. In practice, individuals do not tend to receive both AFDC/TANF and SSI; hence, no individual receives benefits from all three programs. The percentage of individuals receiving assistance from any one program in an average month (shown here) is lower than the percentage residing in families receiving assistance at some point over the course of a year. Spouses are not present in the female-headed and male-headed family categories.

SOURCE: Gil Grouse, Susan Hauan, and Annette Waters Rogers, "Figure IND 5. Percentage of Recipients Receiving Assistance from Multiple Programs—TANF, Food Stamps, and SSI: 2005," in *Indicators of Welfare Dependence: Annual Report to Congress, 2008*, U.S. Department of Health and Human Services, December 2008, http://aspe.hhs.gov/hsp/indicators08/ch2.pdf (accessed February 18, 2011)

TABLE 4.9

Percentage of population receiving assistance from multiple means-tested assistance programs by selected characteristics, 2005

| | Any receipt | One program only | | | Two programs | |
		TANF	FS	SSI	TANF & FS	FS & SSI
All persons	**10.2**	**0.2**	**6.2**	**1.3**	**1.5**	**1.2**
Racial/ethnic categories						
Non-Hispanic white	6.7	0.1	4.1	0.9	0.7	0.8
Non-Hispanic black	24.9	0.5	15.1	2.0	4.4	2.9
Hispanic	14.6	0.4	8.5	1.7	2.7	1.3
Age categories						
Children ages 0–5	20.7	0.6	13.4	0.7	5.3	0.7
Children ages 6–10	17.6	0.5	11.6	0.7	4.2	0.6
Children ages 11–15	15.9	0.7	10.2	0.9	3.3	0.8
Women ages 16–64	9.6	0.1	6.1	0.9	1.2	1.3
Men ages 16–64	6.3	0.1	3.8	1.2	0.4	0.9
Adults ages 65 and over	8.0	0.0	2.4	3.1	0.0	2.4
Family categories						
Persons in married-couple families	4.8	0.1	3.0	0.7	0.5	0.4
Persons in female-headed families	33.4	0.7	20.1	2.5	7.4	2.7
Persons in male-headed families	13.9	0.3	8.2	2.2	1.9	1.3
Unrelated persons	9.4	0.0	4.9	1.8	0.0	2.7

TANF = Temporary Assistance for Needy Families.
SSI = Supplemental Security Income.
FS = food stamps.
Note: Categories are mutually exclusive. SSI receipt is based on individual receipt; AFDC/TANF and food stamp receipt are based on the full recipient unit. In practice, individuals do not tend to receive both AFDC/TANF and SSI; hence, no individual receives benefits from all three programs. The percentage of individuals receiving assistance from any one program in an average month (shown here) is lower than the percentage residing in families receiving assistance at some point over the course of a year. Spouses are not present in the female-headed and male-headed family categories. Persons of Hispanic ethnicity may be of any race. Beginning in 2002, estimates for whites and blacks are for persons reporting a single race only. Persons who reported more than one race are included in the total for all persons but are not shown under any race category. Due to small sample size, American Indians/Alaska Natives, Asians and Native Hawaiians/other Pacific Islanders are included in the total for all persons but are not shown separately.

SOURCE: Gil Grouse, Susan Hauan, and Annette Waters Rogers, "Table IND 5a. Percentage of Population Receiving Assistance from Multiple Means-Tested Assistance Programs by Selected Characteristics: 2005," in *Indicators of Welfare Dependence: Annual Report to Congress, 2008*, U.S. Department of Health and Human Services, December 2008, http://aspe.hhs.gov/hsp/indicators08/ch2.pdf (accessed February 18, 2011)

FIGURE 4.13

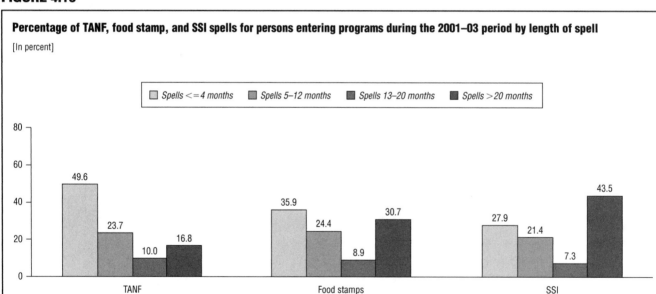

Percentage of TANF, food stamp, and SSI spells for persons entering programs during the 2001–03 period by length of spell

TANF = Temporary Assistance for Needy Families. SSI = Supplemental Security Income. FS = food stamps.
Note: Spell length categories are mutually exclusive. Spells separated by only 1 month are not considered separate spells. Due to the length of the observation period, actual spell lengths for spells that lasted more than 20 months cannot be observed. Program spells are defined as those starting during the 2001 Survey of Income and Program Participation (SIPP) panel. For certain age categories, data are not available (NA) because of insufficient sample size.

SOURCE: Gil Grouse, Susan Hauan, and Annette Waters Rogers, "Figure IND 7. Percentage of TANF, Food Stamp and SSI Spells for Persons Entering Programs during the 2001–2003 Period by Length of Spell," in *Indicators of Welfare Dependence: Annual Report to Congress, 2008*, U.S. Department of Health and Human Services, December 2008, http://aspe.hhs.gov/hsp/indicators08/ch2.pdf (accessed February 18, 2011)

FIGURE 4.14

Percentage of AFDC/TANF recipients by years of receipt during the 1995–2004 period

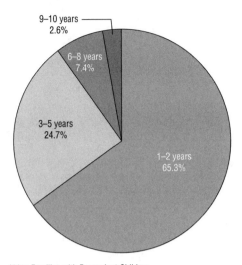

AFDC = Aid to Families with Dependent Children.
TANF = Temporary Assistance for Needy Families.

The base for the percentages consists of mothers who received at least $1 of AFDC/TANF in any year in the ten-year period. Child recipients are defined by age in the first year of the 10-year period. This indicator measures years of recipiency over the specified ten-year time periods and does not take into account years of recipiency that may have occurred before or after each ten-year period.

SOURCE: Gil Grouse, Susan Hauan, and Annette Waters Rogers, "Figure IND 9. Percentage of AFDC/TANF Recipients by Years of Receipt during the 1995–2004 Period," in *Indicators of Welfare Dependence: Annual Report to Congress, 2008*, U.S. Department of Health and Human Services, December 2008, http://aspe.hhs.gov/hsp/indicators08/ch2.pdf (accessed February 18, 2011)

CHAPTER 5

CHARACTERISTICS OF THE HOMELESS

AUTHORITATIVE ESTIMATES OF HOMELESSNESS

The Facts Are Hard to Determine

Broad national assessments of homelessness were undertaken by several agencies and organizations during the 1980s and mid-1990s, including *A Report to the Secretary on the Homeless and Emergency Shelters* (1984) by the U.S. Department of Housing and Urban Development (HUD), Martha R. Burt and Barbara E. Cohen's *America's Homeless: Numbers, Characteristics, and Programs that Serve Them* (1989), and Martha R. Burt et al.'s *Homelessness: Programs and the People They Serve* (December 1999, http://www.urban.org/UploadedPDF/homelessness .pdf). In 2002 Burt et al. summarized in *Evaluation of Continuums of Care for Homeless People* (May 2002, http://www.huduser.org/publications/pdf/continuums_of _care.pdf) the difficulty of addressing homelessness without a continuing census or other governmental program to track the homeless population.

In 2001 Congress directed HUD to begin collecting nationwide data on homelessness. In June 2010 HUD released *The 2009 Annual Homeless Assessment Report to Congress* (http://www.hudhre.info/documents/5thHomeless AssessmentReport.pdf). The report includes both a point-in-time count of the homeless and data on sheltered homeless people over a 12-month period. Both of these counts are nationally representative samples, rather than full counts. Regardless, they were the most accurate counts of the homeless population available as of April 2011.

Several other organizations periodically collect data on the homeless population. The National Alliance to End Homelessness has collected information that can be used to measure homelessness over time. In 2007 the organization compiled data from 461 local Continuum of Care point-in-time counts from across the nation and published an estimate of the national homeless population in *Homelessness Counts: Changes in Homelessness from 2005 to 2007* (January 12, 2009, http://www.endhomelessness.org/ content/article/detail/2158). In 2011 M. William Sermons and Peter Witte of the National Alliance to End Homelessness published *State of Homelessness in America* (January 2011, http://www.endhomelessness.org/content/article/ detail/3668). In this report, Sermons and Witte use HUD data to build on the earlier analysis and examine how the economic recession that lasted from December 2007 to June 2009 affected homelessness.

According to Sermons and Witte, HUD data indicate that in 2009, 656,129 people experienced homelessness. (See Figure 5.1.) Of these, 403,308 (61.5%) were sheltered and 252,821 (38.5%) were unsheltered. Nearly two-thirds (412,973, or 62.9%) were homeless individuals and 243,156 (37.1%) were members of homeless families. An estimated 112,076 (17.1%) homeless people were chronically homeless—in other words, they had been homeless repeatedly or for a long period of time. The National Alliance to End Homelessness notes in *Homelessness Counts* that the number of homeless people had dropped 10% between 2005 and 2007, although in some groups there were more dramatic drops. The number of chronically homeless people dropped 28%, and the number of people in homeless families dropped 18%. However, the alliance cautions that point-in-time estimates tell only how many people are homeless at a given time and that, in reality, many more people experience homelessness at some point in a given year.

How Numbers Are Used

When hearing reports about the homeless, the ordinary citizen envisions people, including children, who live on the street permanently and sleep in cars or in cardboard boxes under bridges. There are, of course, people in this category, but they are the minority among the homeless. The National Alliance to End Homelessness labels such people the chronically homeless and estimates that in 2009

FIGURE 5.1

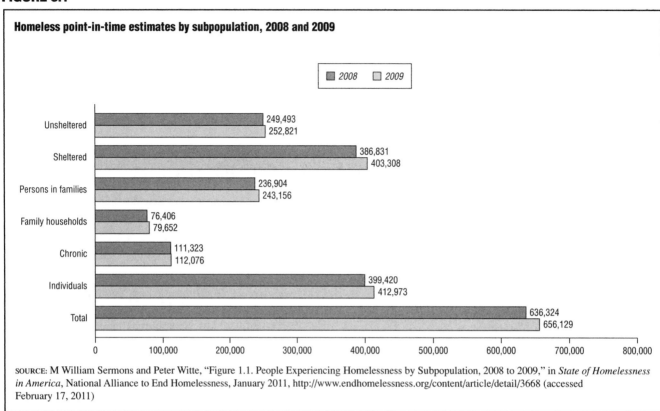

Homeless point-in-time estimates by subpopulation, 2008 and 2009

Legend: ■ 2008　□ 2009

Subpopulation	2008	2009
Unsheltered	249,493	252,821
Sheltered	386,831	403,308
Persons in families	236,904	243,156
Family households	76,406	79,652
Chronic	111,323	112,076
Individuals	399,420	412,973
Total	636,324	656,129

SOURCE: M William Sermons and Peter Witte, "Figure 1.1. People Experiencing Homelessness by Subpopulation, 2008 to 2009," in *State of Homelessness in America*, National Alliance to End Homelessness, January 2011, http://www.endhomelessness.org/content/article/detail/3668 (accessed February 17, 2011)

their number was 112,076. (See Figure 5.1.) Most of the homeless are not chronically homeless but are temporarily without a residence. After some period of homelessness, they find permanent shelter or move in with relatives; however, people who have moved in with family as well as people who are doubled up are also counted as homeless by some programs and homeless advocates, although not by HUD.

A more accurate definition of the homeless population is the group of people who are, on any day, without proper shelter. When agencies or the media cite numbers in the 600,000 to 800,000 range, they mean the size of the homeless population at any one point in time. Individuals are continuously joining this population, and others are leaving it. If all people who are homeless at some point during a given year were counted, the number would reach between 2.5 million and 3.5 million individuals, as indicated by Burt et al. in *Evaluation of Continuums of Care for Homeless People*. The researchers estimated this number by using counts of the number of people who sought homeless services during one week in October 1996. During that week an estimated 36,900 individuals began spells of homelessness, whereas the total number of people in the homeless population in any one week in 1996 was estimated to be 444,000. The annual projection assumed that each week 36,900 people became homeless and an equal number phased out of the homeless status. Thus, multiplying 36,900 by 52 weeks in the year, and then adding

that amount to 444,000 produced the count of 2.3 million people who were homeless at least once in 1996. This number does not mean that there were 2.3 million homeless people during the entire span of 1996.

In *2009 Annual Homeless Assessment Report to Congress*, HUD notes that it conducted a count of all homeless individuals who used a shelter during 2009. Approximately 1.6 million individuals, or one out of every 200 U.S. residents, used an emergency shelter or transitional housing. This count underrepresents the number of women, because the residents of domestic violence shelters are not reported. It also does not include the unsheltered homeless population.

Counting Homeless Children

In *Education for Homeless Children and Youths Program* (April 2009, http://www2.ed.gov/programs/homeless/data-comp-04-07.pdf), the National Center for Homeless Education of the U.S. Department of Education states that 794,617 children who experienced homelessness at some point during the year were enrolled during the 2007–08 school year. (See Table 5.1.) This number was almost certainly much lower than the number of children who actually experienced homelessness during that period, as the homeless status of children does not always come to the attention of school officials and many homeless children are not enrolled in school. Regardless, the number was up 16.9% from the 2006–07 school year, most likely due to the economic recession.

TABLE 5.1

Total homeless children enrolled in school by state, 2006–07 and 2007–08

State	2006–07	2007–08	+/−
Alabama	10,907	11,687	1,719
Alaska	3,216	2,963	−253
Arizona	19,628	21,380	1,752
Arkansas	7,080	5,917	−1,163
Bureau of Indian Education	290	626	336
California	178,014	224,249	46,235
Colorado	11,978	12,302	324
Connecticut	1,980	2,017	37
Delaware	1,842	1,982	140
District of Columbia	824	1,005	181
Florida	30,554	33,993	3,439
Georgia	14,017	15,700	1,683
Hawaii	1,132	925	−207
Idaho	1,875	2,125	250
Illinois	19,821	26,238	6,417
Indiana	8,249	8,480	231
Iowa	2,886	5,918	3,032
Kansas	3,569	4,890	1,321
Kentucky	18,337	17,735	−602
Louisiana	34,102	29,234	−4,868
Maine	1,055	1,379	324
Maryland	8,456	8,813	357
Massachusetts	11,863	12,449	586
Michigan	24,066	18,435	−5,631
Minnesota	6,008	8,163	2,155
Mississippi	12,856	9,926	−2,930
Missouri	13,620	11,977	−1,643
Montana	2,202	887	−1,315
Nebraska	1,633	1,530	−103
Nevada	5,374	6,647	1,273
New Hampshire	1,983	2,087	104
New Jersey	4,279	6,033	1,754
New Mexico	4,383	6,152	1,769
New York	44,018	71,218	27,200
North Carolina	12,659	16,937	4,278
North Dakota	1,209	686	−523
Ohio	13,578	14,483	905
Oklahoma	8,284	9,179	895
Oregon	15,517	15,839	322
Pennsylvania	12,935	11,756	−1,179
Puerto Rico	5,976	4,336	−1,640
Rhode Island	667	746	79
South Carolina	6,033	7,413	1,380
South Dakota	1,038	1,430	392
Tennessee	6,567	8,031	1,464
Texas	33,896	53,242	19,346
Utah	9,991	11,270	1,279
Vermont	764	789	25
Virginia	9,898	11,776	1,878
Washington	16,853	18,670	1,817
West Virginia	2,984	2,909	−75
Wisconsin	8,103	9,331	1,228
Wyoming	675	732	57
Total enrolled all states	**679,724**	**794,617**	**114,893**

SOURCE: "Total Enrolled by State, Two-Year Comparison," in *Education for Homeless Children and Youths Program*, National Center for Homeless Education, April 2009, http://www2.ed.gov/programs/homeless/data-comp-04-07.pdf (accessed February 18, 2011)

In 2009 the National Center on Family Homelessness published *America's Youngest Outcasts: State Report Card on Child Homelessness* (February 2009, http://www.homelesschildrenamerica.org/pdf/rc_full_report.pdf). The organization uses data collected by 12,550 local education agencies as mandated by the McKinney-Vento Homeless Assistance Act to estimate that 1.5 million children experience homelessness each year. It further notes that one

out of 50 American children was homeless at some point during the 2005–06 school year. In Louisiana 18.7% of all children were homeless, which was by far the worst state in the nation. The center indicates that nationwide, few homeless children lived without shelter—56% of homeless children lived doubled-up, 24% lived in shelters, 7% lived in hotels/motels, and 3% were unsheltered.

PROFILES OF THE HOMELESS
Gender and Race

Studies of homeless people and surveys of officials knowledgeable about homeless clients conducted since the 1990s show similar patterns of gender and racial data for the homeless, although the percentages vary from study to study.

HUD reports in *2009 Annual Homeless Assessment Report to Congress* that in 2009, 36.3% of the sheltered homeless population was female and 63.7% was male. HUD states that the overrepresentation of males in the sheltered homeless population was probably due to several factors, including unemployment, the inability to qualify for Temporary Assistance for Needy Families, higher rates of substance abuse than among women, and the greater likelihood that men have been incarcerated.

African-Americans are overrepresented among the homeless population as well. HUD indicates that in 2009, 38.7% of the sheltered homeless population was African-American and 38.1% was non-Hispanic white. About 19.5% of the homeless population was Hispanic. HUD states that African-Americans are overrepresented among the homeless population because homelessness is concentrated in urban areas. About 46% of African-Americans live in principal cities, compared with 16% of non-Hispanic whites and 35% of Hispanics.

The Association of Gospel Rescue Missions (AGRM) regularly surveys the homeless population at more than a hundred missions serving inner cities. AGRM surveys are based on large numbers of homeless served. For example, in "Many American Families Are Living on the Edge" (November 2010, http://www.agrm.org/i4a/pages/index.cfm?pageID=3609), the AGRM finds that men made up 75% of the homeless population in 2010. The AGRM also notes that 57% of those seeking services were women with children, which was down from 66% in 2008, whereas 22% were intact families (families with married parents), up from 14% in 2008.

The AGRM indicates that the race and ethnic makeup of the homeless population seeking services had stayed relatively stable between 2008 and 2010. In 2010, 47% were white, 36% were African-American, 11% were Hispanic, 2% were Native American, and 1% were Asian-American.

The surveys thus exhibit similar patterns. More of the homeless are male than female, but these proportions are gradually changing. In all surveys, African-Americans are greatly overrepresented among the homeless—most surveys state that African-Americans make up about 38% of the homeless population, whereas Karen R. Humes, Nicholas A. Jones, and Roberto R. Ramirez of the U.S. Census Bureau report in *Overview of Race and Hispanic Origin: 2010* (March 2011, http://www.census.gov/prod/cen2010/briefs/c2010br-02.pdf) that they made up only 12.6% of the U.S. population in 2010. Hispanics' representation among the homeless was near their share of the total U.S. population, at 16.3%.

Family Structure

In *2009 Annual Homeless Assessment Report to Congress*, HUD finds that among the sheltered homeless population staying alone, 71% were adult men and 25% were adult women. However, among homeless families, 79.6% of adults were women. According to the U.S. Conference of Mayors, in *Hunger and Homelessness Survey: A Status Report on Hunger and Homelessness in America's Cities, a 27-City Survey* (December 2010, http://www.usmayors.org/pressreleases/uploads/2010HungerHomelessness ReportfinalDec212010.pdf), on an average night in 2010, 27,102 single adults were homeless on the streets, 20,643 stayed in emergency shelters, and 12,088 were in transitional housing, for a total of 59,833 homeless individuals in the 26 cities that were surveyed. (See Table 5.2.) By contrast, most homeless people in families stayed in transitional housing (15,255) or emergency shelters (10,926), while only 1,105 stayed on the streets, for a total of 27,286 homeless people in families. Thus, only 30.9% of the homeless counted were members of families.

In *Homelessness Counts*, the National Alliance to End Homelessness does not specify gender in its count of the 2009 homeless population, but it does break the count down into individuals (412,973, or 62.9%) and people in families (243,156, or 37.1%). (See Figure 5.1.) The AGRM presents in "Many American Families Are Living on the Edge" 2010 data about the structure of homeless families. The organization speculates that the recession

affected single women with children harder than any other group, at least at first, as demonstrated by the fact that women with children made up 66% of homeless families counted in 2008, a jump from 55% the year before. However, that proportion declined as the proportion of married couples with children increased by 2010. The National Center on Family Homelessness suggests in "What Is Family Homelessness? (The Problem)" (2011, http://www.familyhomelessness.org/facts.php?p=sm) that "as the gap between housing costs and income continues to widen and housing foreclosures increase, more and more families are at risk of homelessness."

Age

Burt et al. find in *Homelessness* that in 1996, 25% of the homeless were between 25 and 34 years of age, 38% were between 35 and 44, and 17% were between 45 and 54. The AGRM notes that in 2010, 15% of the homeless were between 26 and 35 years of age, 22% were between 36 and 45, and 40% were between 46 and 65.

CHILDREN AND YOUTHS. Homeless children and youths have always received special attention from both the public and welfare agencies. In the terminology of the 19th century, children are considered "worthy" poor, because if they are homeless, they did nothing to deserve this status.

Estimates provided by the Conference of Mayors give some indication of the proportion of children and runaway teens (unaccompanied youth) among the homeless population. (See Table 5.2.) On an average night in 2010, the vast majority (94.8% or 27,102) of people living on the streets in the survey cities were single adults and only 3.9% (1,105) were people in families and 1.3% (382) were unaccompanied youth. Homeless families were much more likely to be living in permanent supportive housing or transitional housing. In 2010, 10,926 people in families were living in emergency shelters on an average night, 34.2% of the total people in emergency shelters, and 15,255 were living in transitional housing, 55% of the total people in transitional shelters.

The National Center for Homeless Education collects estimates of homeless children from selected school district records. The data exclude infants but include some children of preschool age. In *Education for Homeless Children and Youths Program*, the center indicates that a total of 773,832 children and youth had been served during the 2007–08 school year, a 12.4% increase from the previous year. The center finds that 65% of these children were living "doubled up," 21% were living in shelters, 7% were living in hotels or motels, and 7% were unsheltered. (See Figure 5.2.)

Much of the increase in homelessness among children was due to the economic recession that began in December 2007. Michelle D. Anderson reports in "Schools Facing Rise in Homeless Students" (*Christian Science Monitor*,

TABLE 5.2

Homeless persons on an average night in 26 survey cities, 2010

Household type	On the streets	In emergency shelter	In transitional housing
Single adults	27,102	20,643	12,088
Persons in families	1,105	10,926	15,255
Unaccompanied youths	382	361	379

SOURCE: "Homeless Persons on Average Night in 26 Survey Cities," in *Hunger and Homelessness Survey: A Status Report on Hunger and Homelessness in America's Cities, a 27-City Survey*, U.S. Conference of Mayors, December 2010, http://www.usmayors.org/pressreleases/uploads/2010_Hunger-Homelessness_Report-final%20Dec%2021%202010.pdf (accessed February 18, 2011)

FIGURE 5.2

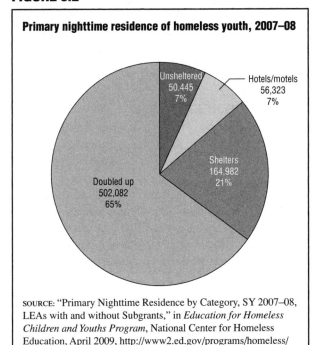

Primary nighttime residence of homeless youth, 2007–08

Unsheltered
50,445
7%

Hotels/motels
56,323
7%

Shelters
164,982
21%

Doubled up
502,082
65%

SOURCE: "Primary Nighttime Residence by Category, SY 2007–08, LEAs with and without Subgrants," in *Education for Homeless Children and Youths Program*, National Center for Homeless Education, April 2009, http://www2.ed.gov/programs/homeless/data-comp-04-07.pdf (accessed February 18, 2011)

April 12, 2011) that the handful of schools around the nation that serve exclusively homeless children were facing a growing enrollment due to the rise in foreclosures and unstable housing conditions in 2011. For example, Anderson notes that the Monarch School in San Diego, California, saw a 74% increase in enrollments between 2008 and 2011, and the Children First Academy in Phoenix, Arizona, saw the number of children on its waitlist quadruple, from 12 percent to 18 percent.

Even though the National Center for Homeless Education's 2009 report omits estimates of the total number of homeless children in the population, *Education for Homeless Children and Youth Program, Report to Congress, Fiscal Year 2000* (2001, http://www.ed.gov/programs/homeless/rpt2000.doc) does include this information. The department finds that of total children estimated by school districts to be homeless in 2000, only a portion were enrolled and even a smaller number attended school regularly. Among the estimated 343,340 homeless elementary students, 305,920 (89.1%) were enrolled and 271,906 (79.2%) attended regularly. However, Arun Venugopal indicates in "Advocates Say City Undercounts Homeless Kids" (September 14, 2006, http://www.wnyc.org/news/articles/64264) that the Department of Education undercounts the number of homeless kids, which would place the number of homeless kids not enrolled in or attending school even higher. For example, in *2007 Greater Los Angeles Homeless Count* (2007, http://www.lahsa.org/docs/homelesscount/2007/LAHSA.pdf), a survey of homeless respondents in Los Angeles, California, the Los Angeles Homeless Services Authority finds that 11% of

homeless families with school-age children stated their children were not attending school in 2007. When homeless children do attend school, they have less than optimal conditions for educational achievement.

The National Center on Family Homelessness indicates in *America's Youngest Outcasts: State Report Card on Child Homelessness* that during the 2005–06 school year homeless children had lower proficiency scores when compared with all students. At the elementary school level, the math and reading proficiency scores for all students were 39.6% and 33.8%, respectively; for homeless children, their scores were 21.5% and 24.4%, respectively. At the high school level, the math proficiency scores for all students were 32.2% and for homeless children, 11.4%; and the reading proficiency scores for all students were 30.9% and for homeless children, 14.6%.

The poor educational achievement of homeless youth puts them at an increased risk for homelessness in their adulthood. The National Center on Family Homelessness explains that "poverty traps poor students who need a good education to better their living standards. But in a classic Catch 22, poor children are more likely to do worse than nonpoor children on measures of school achievement. They are twice as likely as their nonpoor counterparts to have repeated a grade, to have been expelled or suspended from school, or to have dropped out of high school." The result is that fewer than a quarter of homeless children graduate from high school. Furthermore, the center notes that "82% of children whose parents have less than a high school diploma live in poverty."

Military Background

The U.S. Department of Veterans Affairs reports in *Veteran Homelessness: A Supplemental Report to the 2009 Annual Homeless Assessment Report to Congress* (January 2011, http://www.va.gov/HOMELESS/docs/Center/2009_AHAR-Vet_Report_Final_2011.pdf) that on a single night in January 2009, 75,609 veterans were homeless, making up 16% of all adults experiencing homelessness. Over the course of a year, an estimated 136,334 veterans spent at least one night at a shelter or transitional housing program. This is similar to the proportion of homeless veterans found by the Conference of Mayors. According to its survey, 14% of the homeless in the surveyed cities were veterans. (See Table 5.3.)

The Department of Veterans Affairs finds that in 2009, 92.5% of all sheltered homeless veterans were male, whereas only 7.5% were female. However, 58.7% of all veterans who experienced homelessness as part of a family group were female. African-American veterans are overrepresented among the homeless. Even though 10.5% of all veterans were African-American in 2009, 34% of all sheltered homeless veterans were African-American. White veterans are underrepresented among the homeless. In

TABLE 5.3

Demographic characteristics of adult homeless persons as reported by cities, 2010

QUESTION 26: COMPLETE THE FOLLOWING TABLE ON THE PERCENTAGE OF HOMELESS ADULTS IN THE FOLLOWING CATEGORIES, NOTE THAT THE SAME PERSONS COULD BELONG IN MULTIPLE CATEGORIES.

Categories	Overall percentage
Employed	19%
Veterans	14%
Physically disabled	20%
HIV positive	3%
Severely mentally ill	24%
Domestic violence victims	14%

SOURCE: "Question 26. Complete the following table on the percentage of homeless adults in the following categories, note that the same persons could belong in multiple categories," in *Hunger and Homelessness Survey: A Status Report on Hunger and Homelessness in America's Cities, a 27-City Survey*, U.S. Conference of Mayors, December 2010, http://www.usmayors.org/pressreleases/uploads/2010_Hunger-Homelessness_Report-final%20Dec%2021%202010.pdf (accessed February 18, 2011)

2009 they made up 81.2% of all veterans but just 49.2% of sheltered homeless veterans.

President Barack Obama (1961–) responded to the crisis of homelessness among veterans by allocating $1.5 billion to the Homelessness Prevention Fund in the American Recovery and Reinvestment Act, with was signed into law in February 2009. According to HUD, in "Homelessness Prevention Fund Overview" (February 25, 2009, http://www.ncceh.org/attachments/contentmanagers/685/HUD HomelessnessPreventionFundOverview.pdf), "this program will provide financial and other assistance to prevent individuals and families from becoming homeless and help those who are experiencing homelessness to be quickly re-housed and stabilized." According to HUD, in *FY 2012 Budget Summary* (February 2011, http://portal.hud.gov/hudportal/documents/huddoc?id=fy2012budget.pdf), Obama's proposed fiscal year (FY) 2012 budget included $2.3 billion for Homeless Assistance Grants, $145 million in new housing vouchers, and $50 million to test new incentives to encourage landlords to serve more homeless people.

DURATION AND RECURRENCE OF HOMELESSNESS

Most homeless people will become homeless again. In *Homelessness*, Burt et al. note that 51% of all homeless people surveyed in 1996 had been homeless before. The AGRM finds in "Many American Families Are Living on the Edge" that in 2010, 63% of the homeless had been homeless before—25% had been homeless only once before. Thirty-nine percent of the homeless studied by Burt et al. had been homeless less than six months and 61% had been homeless for more than half a year. Six out of 10 (59%) of those surveyed by the AGRM in 2010 had been homeless for less than a year.

These studies confirm that homelessness is usually a recurring experience and lasts for months at a time, suggesting that programs that help the homeless do not uniformly help clients solve the fundamental problems that can lead to life on the streets.

WHERE THE HOMELESS LIVE

Homelessness varies, in both the numbers of homeless people and the numbers of sheltered homeless people. Figure 5.3 shows the state breakdowns of the homeless rate as well as each state's number of risk factors, including high rates of unemployment, foreclosures, cost-burdened households, uninsured, and doubling-up. States with the highest homeless rates also tended to have the highest national indicator rates, whereas states with the lowest homeless rates tended to have the lowest national indicator rates.

Rural Homelessness

Most studies on the homeless have been focused on urban areas, leaving the impression that this problem exists only on city sidewalks. Homelessness is more common in the cities, where the bulk of the population resides, but many areas of rural America also experience the phenomenon. In "Fact Sheet: Rural Homelessness" (January 17, 2010, http://www.endhomelessness.org/content/general/detail/1613), the National Alliance to End Homelessness reports that rural communities have higher poverty rates than do urban areas. Furthermore, rural communities have fewer official shelters and fewer public places (e.g., heating grates, subways, or train stations) where the homeless can find temporary shelter. Therefore, they are more likely to live in a car or camper, or with relatives in overcrowded or rundown housing. Also, finding the rural homeless is more difficult for investigators of the problem.

The National Coalition for the Homeless (NCH) reports in the fact sheet "Rural Homelessness" (August 2007, http://www.nationalhomeless.org/publications/facts/Rural.pdf) that the rural homeless are more likely to be white, female, married, and currently working than are the urban homeless. They are also more likely to be homeless for the first time and generally experience homelessness for a shorter period of time than the urban homeless. Furthermore, the NCH notes that domestic violence is more likely to be a cause of homelessness in rural areas and that alcohol and substance abuse is less likely to be a cause. The odds of being poor are higher in rural areas than in urban areas, which sometimes results in homelessness. In addition, those living in rural areas have fewer employment opportunities, typically earn lower wages, and remain unemployed for longer periods of time than do people living in metropolitan areas.

Burt et al. determine in *Homelessness* that in 1996, 21% of all homeless people in their study lived in suburban

FIGURE 5.3

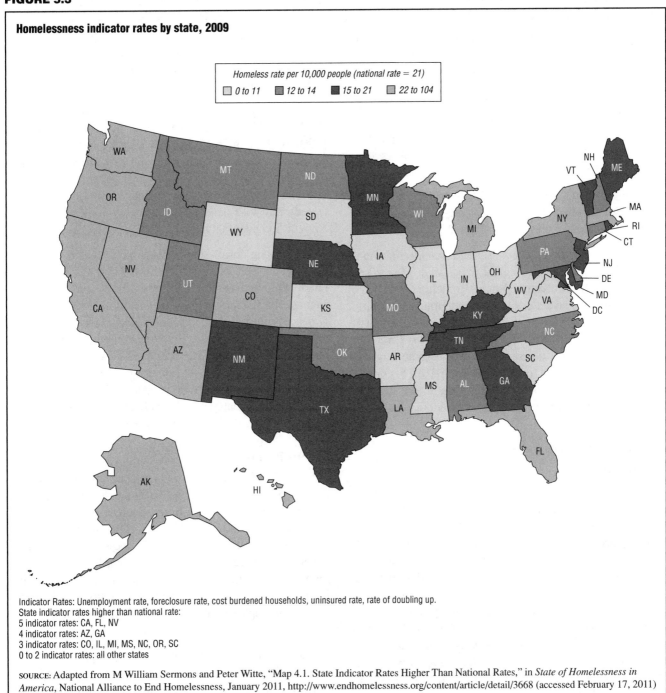

Homelessness indicator rates by state, 2009

Homeless rate per 10,000 people (national rate = 21)
☐ 0 to 11   ▨ 12 to 14   ■ 15 to 21   ▨ 22 to 104

Indicator Rates: Unemployment rate, foreclosure rate, cost burdened households, uninsured rate, rate of doubling up.
State indicator rates higher than national rate:
5 indicator rates: CA, FL, NV
4 indicator rates: AZ, GA
3 indicator rates: CO, IL, MI, MS, NC, OR, SC
0 to 2 indicator rates: all other states

SOURCE: Adapted from M William Sermons and Peter Witte, "Map 4.1. State Indicator Rates Higher Than National Rates," in *State of Homelessness in America*, National Alliance to End Homelessness, January 2011, http://www.endhomelessness.org/content/article/detail/3668 (accessed February 17, 2011)

areas and 9% lived in rural communities. The rural homeless surveyed were more likely to be working, or to have worked recently, than the urban homeless—65% of the rural homeless had worked for pay in the last month. Homeless people living in rural areas were also more likely to be experiencing their first spell of homelessness (60%). In 55% of the cases the homeless period lasted three months or less.

In *Hard to Reach: Rural Homelessness and Health Care* (January 2002, http://www.nhchc.org/Publications/RuralHomeless.pdf), Patricia A. Post of the National Health

Care for the Homeless Council argues that rural residents typically deal with a lack of permanent housing not by sleeping on the streets, like their urban counterparts, but by first moving in with a series of friends; second, by moving into abandoned shacks, cars, or campgrounds; and finally, by moving to cities in search of employment. They also differ from urban homeless people in other ways: Rural homeless people have less education, typically hold temporary jobs with no benefits, are less likely to receive government assistance or have health insurance, and are more likely to have been incarcerated.

Several types of rural areas generate higher-than-average levels of homelessness, including regions that:

- Are primarily agricultural—residents often lose their livelihood because of either a reduced demand for farm labor or a shrinking service sector

- Depend on declining extractive industries, such as mining or timber

- Are experiencing economic growth—new or expanding industrial plants often attract more job seekers than what can be absorbed

- Have persistent poverty, such as Appalachia and the rural South, where the young and able-bodied may have to relocate before they can find work

The Homeless Emergency Assistance and Rapid Transition to Housing Act was signed into law in May 2009, reauthorizing the McKinney-Vento Homeless Assistance Grants Program. The act created a Rural Housing Stability Program, which, when fully implemented, will allow rural communities greater flexibility to respond to the particular needs of rural homeless people and permit some funds to be used for construction to house those at risk of becoming homeless. Obama requested $126 million in FY 2012 to fund new competitive projects in this program.

TRENDS IN HOMELESSNESS

Poverty Estimates

There is an undeniable connection between homelessness and poverty. People in poverty live from day to day, with little or no financial safety net for times when unforeseen expenses arise. If a family's resources are small, expenditures on necessities such as food, shelter, and health care have to be carefully decided and sometimes sacrifices have to be made. Should one spend money on food, a visit to the doctor, buying necessary medicines, or paying the rent? In 2011 a full-time job paying minimum wage for 40 hours per week provided an income under the poverty line for a family of three. (See Chapter 3.) Being poor often means that an illness, an accident, or a missed paycheck could be enough to cause homelessness.

Housing costs for such a family may be out of reach. According to the Joint Center for Housing Studies of Harvard University, in "America's Rental Housing—The Key to a Balanced National Policy" (May 2008, http://www.jchs.harvard.edu/publications/rental/rh08_americas_rental_housing/rh08_intro.pdf), the foreclosure crisis in 2007 and 2008 pushed previous homeowners into the rental market, who then competed for the limited number of affordable housing units. The organization points out that "no single minimum-wage earner working 40 hours a week, 52 weeks a year, earns enough to cover the cost of a modest rental anywhere in the country." Low income and high-rent payments often result in substandard housing

accommodation, doubled-up living, or living on the street or in a public shelter. The necessity of basic sustenance and medical care usually leaves little money to meet housing needs. People in poverty have further difficulties finding housing if they have previously defaulted on their rent or mortgage, resulting in homelessness.

After large decreases in the poverty rate during the 1960s and 1970s, the poverty rate increased during the 1990s to a high of 15.1% in 1993. (See Table 1.2 in Chapter 1.) Steady gains in decreasing the proportion of people living below the poverty threshold were made between 1994 and 2001. However, between 2001 and 2009 the poverty rate rose once again, to a high of 14.3% in 2009; 43.6 million people lived below the poverty level that year.

No strong correlation between poverty and homelessness can be seen in these data; however, there is a definite relationship between homelessness and poverty. The NCH suggests in *Foreclosure to Homelessness 2009: The Forgotten Victims of the Subprime Crisis* (June 2009, http://www.nationalhomeless.org/advocacy/ForeclosuretoHomelessness0609.pdf) that the economic downturn that began in 2007 and the rise in foreclosures led to increasing numbers of homeless people. When service providers were asked what percentage of their clients had become homeless due to foreclosure, the average response was 19%.

Trends Profiled in Cities

The Conference of Mayors reports in *Hunger and Homelessness Survey* that in 2010 homelessness increased in 52% of the responding cities, decreased in 36% of the cities, and stayed the same in three cities. On average, cities reported a 2% increase in homelessness, but some cities experienced increases of up to 26%. Fourteen cities (58%) reported that family homelessness in particular was on the increase. Mayors attributed the rise in family homelessness to high unemployment, a lack of affordable housing, and poverty.

Sermons and Witte indicate that changes in key economic indicators in 2008 and 2009 accounted for the rise in overall homelessness as well as for increases in family homelessness. Table 5.4 shows that in 2009 nearly 5.9 million households were experiencing a severe housing cost burden, up 9% from 2008. Unemployment had skyrocketed; in 2009, 14.3 million people experienced unemployment, up 59.9% from 2008. The average annual income of working poor people had declined to just $9,151. Furthermore, the total number of housing units in foreclosure had risen 21.2% from the year before, to 2.8 million units. As Table 5.5 shows, all but 10 states saw an increase in foreclosures in 2009. In some states, the proportion of foreclosures was staggering. For example, in Nevada one out of every 10 housing units was in foreclosure in 2009. All of these indicators had worsened since 2008. Sermons and Witte suggest that these statistics show

TABLE 5.4

National changes among economic conditions that contribute to homelessness, 2008 and 2009

Measure	2008	2009	2009
Poor households experiencing severe housing cost burden	5,398,379	5,886,293	+9.00%
Unemployed persons	8,924,000	14,265,000	+59.90%
Average annual income of working poor people	$9,353	$9,151	−2.16%
Housing units in foreclosure	2,330,483	2,824,674	+21.20%

SOURCE: M William Sermons and Peter Witte, "Figure 2.4. National Changes among Economic Indicators," in *State of Homelessness in America*, National Alliance to End Homelessness, January 2011, http://www.endhomelessness .org/content/article/detail/3668 (accessed February 17, 2011).

"the reasons why homelessness, after decreasing considerably between 2005 and 2008, increased from 2008 to 2009."

EMPLOYMENT AND THE HOMELESS

It is extremely difficult for people to escape homelessness without a job. Yet, it is equally difficult for homeless people to find and keep good jobs. The NCH lists in the fact sheet "Employment and Homelessness" (July 2009, http://www.nationalhomeless.org/factsheets/ employment.html) the following barriers to employment for homeless people:

- Lack of education
- Lack of competitive work skills
- Lack of transportation
- Lack of day care
- Disabling conditions

In addition, the homeless, like other workers, are subject to the state of the labor market. The availability of jobs and the wages and benefits paid for those available jobs often determine whether or not people can remove themselves from homelessness. Many homeless are underemployed—that is, they would like to work full time but have been unsuccessful at finding full-time work.

Burt et al. indicate in *Homelessness* that in 1996, 44% of homeless respondents reported working in the previous month. Two percent earned income as self-employed entrepreneurs—by peddling or selling belongings. Forty-two percent of the homeless respondents worked for, and were paid by, an employer. The Conference of Mayors finds in *Hunger and Homelessness Survey* that in 2010, 19% of homeless adults were employed at the time of the survey.

According to the NCH, advocates for the homeless are concerned that this dependency on wages, combined with the unfavorable labor market conditions, actually supports continued homelessness. The wage of a single adult working year round, full time is insufficient to support a family of three. The recession placed an additional downward pressure on wages. The NCH notes that "in today's economy, one of the hardest burdens for workers is the continued dramatic decline in wage growth." In addition, because most homeless people do not have more than a high school education and because a majority of the low-paying jobs go to those with at least a high school education, advocates worry that the available job opportunities for homeless people provide an insufficient base for exiting homelessness.

It costs money to live. Even homeless people have needs that can only be met with money. From needing something as simple as a toothbrush or a meal, to money for a newspaper or a phone call to a job prospect, homeless people need money to begin to improve their lives. Out of the need to survive, homeless people have come up with a number of ways to earn money.

Day Labor

Regular work, which is characterized by a permanent and ongoing relationship between employer and employee, does not figure significantly in the lives and routines of most homeless, as it is usually unavailable or inaccessible. Homelessness makes getting and keeping regular work difficult because of the lack of a fixed address, communication, and, in many cases, the inability to get a good night's sleep, clean up, and dress appropriately. Studies find that the longer a person is homeless, the less likely he or she is to pursue wage labor and the more likely he or she is to engage in some other form of work. For those who do participate in regular jobs, in most cases, the wages received are not sufficient to escape living on the street.

Day labor (wage labor secured on a day-to-day basis, typically at lower wages and changing locations) is somewhat easier for the homeless to secure. Tim Bartley and Wade T. Roberts state in "Relational Exploitation: The Informal Organization of Day Labor Agencies" (*WorkingUSA: The Journal of Labor and Society*, vol. 9, March 2006) that "popular and scholarly depictions of homelessness have often portrayed homeless individuals as disconnected from the world of work—implicitly or explicitly equating homelessness with joblessness.... Yet ... homeless persons engage in far more paid work than usually assumed." In fact, the Center for Urban Economic Development at the University of Illinois, Chicago, reports in "A Fair Day's Pay? Homeless Day Laborers in Chicago" (2000, http://www.urbaneconomy.org/node/35) that the majority of adults living in shelters work at temporary, contingent, or day-labor jobs. In "In the Shadows, Day Laborers Left Homeless as Work Vanishes" (*New York Times*, January 1, 2010), Fernanda Santos reports that

TABLE 5.5

Foreclosed housing units by state, 2008 and 2009

State	2009 # of foreclosed units	2008 # of foreclosed units	2008 to 2009 change in %	2009 rate of foreclosure (1/every × housing units)
AK	2,442	1,946	25.49%	116
AL	19,896	7,764	156.26%	107
AR	16,547	14,277	15.90%	78
AZ	163,210	116,911	39.60%	16
CA	632,573	523,624	20.81%	21
CO	50,514	50,396	0.23%	42
CT	19,679	21,925	−10.24%	73
DC	3,235	4,182	−22.64%	88
DE	3,034	2,516	20.59%	128
FL	516,711	385,309	34.10%	17
GA	106,110	85,254	24.46%	37
HI	9,002	3,185	182.64%	56
IA	5,681	5,385	5.50%	234
ID	17,161	8,512	101.61%	37
IL	131,132	99,488	31.81%	40
IN	41,405	45,937	−9.87%	67
KS	9,056	6,218	45.64%	135
KY	9,682	7,244	33.66%	197
LA	11,750	7,129	64.82%	158
MA	36,119	44,342	−18.54%	75
MD	43,248	32,338	33.74%	54
ME	3,178	2,851	11.47%	219
MI	118,302	106,058	11.54%	38
MN	31,697	20,282	56.28%	73
MO	28,519	31,254	−8.75%	93
MS	5,402	2,293	135.59%	232
MT	1,373	1,246	10.19%	317
NC	28,384	33,819	−16.07%	145
ND	390	371	5.12%	796
NE	1,845	3,190	−42.16%	423
NH	7,210	6,636	8.65%	82
NJ	63,208	62,514	1.11%	55
NM	7,212	3,727	93.51%	120
NV	112,097	77,693	44.28%	10
NY	50,369	50,032	0.67%	158
OH	101,614	113,570	−10.53%	50
OK	12,937	12,465	3.79%	125
OR	34,121	18,001	89.55%	47
PA	44,732	37,210	20.21%	122
RI	5,065	6,583	−23.06%	89
SC	25,163	14,995	67.81%	80
SD	765	402	90.30%	467
TN	40,733	44,153	−7.75%	67
TX	100,045	96,157	4.04%	94
UT	27,140	14,836	82.93%	34
VA	52,127	49,011	6.36%	63
VT	143	137	4.38%	2,178
WA	35,268	26,058	35.34%	78
WI	35,252	19,695	78.99%	73
WV	1,479	685	115.91%	597
WY	717	677	5.91%	338

SOURCE: M William Sermons and Peter Witte, "Table 2.8. Foreclosed Housing Units by State," in *State of Homelessness in America*, National Alliance to End Homelessness, January 2011, http://www.endhomelessness.org/content/article/detail/3668 (accessed February 17, 2011)

during the recession even day labor dried up, leaving people who had depended on that work even more likely to become homeless.

Day labor may involve unloading trucks, cleaning up warehouses, cutting grass, or washing windows. Day labor often fits the abilities of the homeless because transportation may be provided to the worksite, and appearance, work history, and references are less important than in regular employment. Day labor usually pays cash at quitting time, thus providing immediate pocket money. Day labor jobs are, however, by definition, without a future, and Bartley and Roberts point out the exploitation that many day laborers face. Because of the growth of day labor, agencies have sprung up to profit from making these informal arrangements more formal. Many of these agencies do not pay workers for the time they wait until being assigned or charge fees for equipment or check-cashing. Such jobs might provide for daily survival on the street but are not generally sufficient to get a person off the street. Consequently, many homeless turn to shadow work.

Shadow Work

Shadow work refers to methods of getting money that are outside the normal economy, some of them illegal. David Levinson, the editor of *Encyclopedia of Homelessness* (2004), explains that these methods include panhandling, scavenging, selling possessions, picking up aluminum cans and selling them, selling one's blood or plasma, theft, or peddling illegal goods, drugs, or services. A homeless person seldom engages in all these activities consistently but may turn to some of them as needed. Researchers estimate that 60% of homeless people engage in some shadow work. Shadow work is more common for homeless men than for homeless women. Theft is more common for younger homeless people.

In "Buddy, Can You Spare a Dime?: Homelessness, Panhandling, and the Public" (*Urban Affairs Review*, vol. 38, no. 3, 2003), Barrett A. Lee and Chad R. Farrell of Pennsylvania State University note that a mixture of institutionalized assistance, wage labor, and shadow work is typical of those who live on the streets. For example, Laura Christine Hein indicates in "Survival Strategies among Male Homeless Adolescents" (May 2006, http://etd.library.vanderbilt.edu/available/etd-03082006-112327/unrestricted/HeinDissertation.pdf) that homeless adolescents use a combination of strategies to survive, including accessing homeless services, robbing or stealing, prostitution, panhandling, dumpster diving, and working. Studies find that many homeless people are resourceful in surviving the rigors of street life and recommend that this resourcefulness be somehow channeled into training that can lead to jobs paying a living wage. However, the NCH reports in "Employment and Homelessness" that some observers suggest that homeless people who have adapted to street life may likely need transitional socialization programs as much as programs that teach them a marketable skill.

Institutionalized Assistance

A certain proportion of homeless people receive some form of institutionalized assistance. This would include institutionalized labor, such as that provided by soup kitchens, shelters, and rehabilitation programs that sometimes pay the homeless for work related to facility operation. The number of people employed by these agencies is a small percentage of the homeless population. In addition, the pay—room, board, and a small stipend—tends to tie the homeless to the organization rather than providing the means to get off the street.

Institutionalized assistance also includes income supplements that are provided by the government, family, and friends. Researchers indicate, however, that even though a considerable number of the homeless may receive some financial help from family or friends, it is usually small. Women seem to receive more help from family and friends and to remain on the streets for shorter periods

than men. Cash from family and friends seems to decline with the amount of time spent on the street and with age.

Street Newspapers: Bootstrap Initiatives

In the United States, as well as overseas, homeless people are writing, publishing, and selling their own newspapers. Many street newspaper publishers belong to the North American Street Newspaper Association (NASNA), which was organized in Chicago in 1996. The NASNA holds an annual conference, offers business advice and services, and supports street newspaper publishers in the same way that any professional organization supports its membership. It also lobbies the government on homeless issues. The NASNA (http://www.nasna.org/) indicates that in March 2011 it had 31 members, up from 27 members just two years before.

Generally, the street newspapers are loaned on credit to homeless vendors who then sell them for $1 each. At the end of the workday, the vendor pays the publisher the agreed-on price and pockets the remainder as profit. For example, Boston's *Spare Change* newspaper publishes 9,000 copies every two weeks. Vendors purchase newspapers for $0.25 each and resell them for $1.00, pocketing $0.75 for each paper sold. Some street newspapers charge vendors nothing at all. California's *Street Sheet* makes its papers free to vendors.

This cooperative arrangement among publishers, vendors, and consumers has many benefits:

- Creation of jobs
- Supports the work ethic
- Accommodates the mobility of homeless people
- Provides reliable employment despite crisis living conditions
- Informs the public about homelessness
- Erases stereotypes of the drunken, illiterate, and "unworthy" homeless person
- Gives the writers and vendors a sense of accomplishment
- Provides immediate cash to people who desperately need it

Most of the homeless newspaper vendors do not earn enough just from selling newspapers to move themselves from homelessness, but as the quality and availability of these publications grow, homeless people envision the street newspaper industry becoming a means of moving tens of thousands from homelessness.

EXITING HOMELESSNESS

According to Burt et al., in *Homelessness*, homeless people said in 1996 that the primary reason they could not exit homelessness is insufficient income. Of those clients surveyed, 54% mentioned employment-related reasons for why they remained homeless—30% cited insufficient income and 24% cited lack of a job.

Data used by Burt et al. show how little income the homeless earned in 1996. Eighty-one percent of the "currently" homeless had incomes of less than $700 in the 30 days before the study; the average monthly income was $367. Most of the homeless in the study were receiving their income from Aid to Families with Dependent Children (now Temporary Assistance for Needy Families). Of the formerly homeless people surveyed, the median (the middle value—half are higher and half are lower) monthly income of $470 would amount to an annual income of $5,640, an amount well below the poverty level for a single person ($7,740 in 1996).

In *2007 Greater Los Angeles Homeless Count*, the Los Angeles Homeless Services Authority reports that homeless people mentioned a variety of reasons for their continued homelessness. Among the top five reasons for being homelessness, 37% cited health issues (such as having an illness, mental health issues, or problems with alcohol or drugs), 19% cited social issues (such as experiencing domestic violence, familial conflict, or divorce), 17% cited economic issues (such as losing a job, being evicted, or failing to pay rent), 15% cited youth-related issues (such as aging out of foster care or running away from home), and 13% cited external issues (such as losing a home to a fire, flood, or other type of natural disaster). The *2009 Greater Los Angeles Homeless Count* (December 2009, http://www.lahsa.org/docs/HC09/Homeless-Count-2009-Report.pdf) did not contain this information.

These findings clearly demonstrate the financial difficulty a homeless person encounters when trying to permanently exit homelessness or poverty. However, exiting homelessness—especially by the chronically homeless—requires more than income. Persistent medical assistance, sometimes for an entire lifetime, has to be available for the mentally ill or for people with addiction and substance abuse problems. Furthermore, without programs such as job training, assistance with general education, help with socialization skills, and counseling, the maintenance of a degree of independent life for the long term can be difficult for the chronically homeless.

CHAPTER 6
THE HOUSING PROBLEM

At one time a home was defined as a place where a family resided, but as American society changed, so did the definition of the term *home*. A home is now considered a place where one or more people live together, a private place to which they have legal right and where strangers may be excluded. It is the place where people keep their belongings and where they feel safe from the outside world. For housing to be considered a home, it should be permanent with an address. Furthermore, in the best of circumstances a home should not be substandard but should still be affordable. Many people would agree that a place to call home is a basic human right.

Those people who have no fixed address and no private space of their own are the homeless. The obvious solution to homelessness would be to find a home for everyone who needs one. There is enough housing available in the United States; as such, the problem lies in the affordability of that housing. Most of the housing in the United States costs far more than poor people can afford to rent or buy.

HIGH HOUSING COSTS AND HOMELESSNESS

According to Mary Cunningham and Sharon McDonald, in *Promising Strategies to End Family Homelessness* (June 2006, http://www.hoopsforthehomeless.org/docs/hoops paperfinal.pdf), research indicates that the primary cause of most homelessness is the inability to pay for housing, which is caused by some combination of low income and high housing costs. Even though many other factors may contribute to homelessness, such as a low level of educational achievement or mental illness, addressing these problems will seldom bring someone out of homelessness by itself. The underlying issue of not being able to afford housing will still need to be addressed.

Furthermore, the National Alliance to End Homelessness notes in "Snapshot of Homelessness" (2011, http://www.endhomelessness.org/section/about_homelessness/snapshot_of_homelessness) that homeless people and homeless families are similar to other poor people. The main reason people become homeless is that they cannot acquire or maintain affordable housing. The alliance indicates that 20% of homeless people can be characterized as chronically homeless and that the chronically homeless do differ substantially from the general population of poor people. According to the National Alliance to End Homelessness, the chronically homeless have higher rates of chronic disabilities, substance abuse disorders, physical disabilities, the human immunodeficiency virus (HIV), and the acquired immunodeficiency syndrome (AIDS). Because of these disabilities and diseases, the alliance suggests that the chronically homeless need housing that is linked to other supportive services to help them move out of homelessness.

Veterans make up a disproportionate number of homeless people. A main cause of homelessness among this population is the high cost of housing. In *Vital Mission: Ending Homelessness among Veterans* (November 2007, http://www.endhomelessness.org/content/article/detail/1837), Mary Cunningham, Meghan Henry, and Webb Lyons explain that a "lack of affordable housing is the primary driver of homelessness [among veterans]. . . . There is a subset of veterans who have severe housing cost burden." The researchers explain that there is a pressing need to target veterans in homelessness prevention programs.

HOUSING THE POOR

When 30% or more of a meager income is spent on housing, hardship is the result. For this reason the federal government establishes the official standard for low-income housing at 30% of a family's annual income. If the rent and utilities cost more than 30% of a family's annual income, the family is said to be in poverty. Low-income housing is housing that is affordable to those in poverty based on this formula. In 2011 a family of two with an annual income of less than $14,710 was in poverty; a family of four was in poverty if its income was less than $22,350. (See Table 1.1 in Chapter 1.) Thus, in 2011 a family of two qualified for low-income housing if its housing costs were more than 30% of $14,710 annually, or more than $368 per month; a family of four qualified if its housing costs were more than 30% of $22,350 annually, or more than $559 per month.

However, the price of rental units has been on the rise since 1980, at the same time that the real income of renters has been declining. The Joint Center for Housing Studies (JCHS) of Harvard University finds in *The State of the Nation's Housing, 2010* (June 2010, http://www.jchs.har vard.edu/publications/markets/son2010/son2010.pdf) that in 2009 dollars renters in 1980 had a median (the middle value—half are higher and half are lower) income of $2,640 per month and a median gross rent (including rent and utilities) of $678. (See Table 6.1.) By 2009 gross rent had risen while income had remained about the same. In that year renters had a median income of $2,664 per month and a median gross rent of $807.

According to the U.S. Census Bureau, the median monthly gross rent for renter-occupied housing units was $842 in 2009. (See Table 6.2.) As a result of such high rents, across the nation 47.7% of households in rental property spent 30% or more of their household income on rent. (See Table 6.3.) Renters in California faced partic-ularly difficult circumstances. The median monthly rent there was the highest in the continental United States ($1,155) and more than half (52.8%) of renters spent 30% or more of their household income on housing.

TABLE 6.1

Income and housing costs for owners and renters, 1980–2009

| | Monthly income | | | | Owner costs | | Renter costs | | Cost as percent of income | | | |
| | | | | | | | | | Owners | | Renters | |
Year	Owner	Renter	Home price	Mortgage rate (%)	Before-tax mortgage payment	After-tax mortgage payment	Contract rent	Gross rent	Before-tax mortgage payment	After-tax mortgage payment	Contract rent	Gross rent
1980	4,599	2,640	131,891	13.7	1,382	1,173	602	678	30.1	25.5	22.8	25.7
1981	4,467	2,605	122,558	16.6	1,539	1,284	595	673	34.5	28.7	22.8	25.8
1982	4,474	2,631	116,819	16.0	1,417	1,203	605	689	31.7	26.9	23.0	26.2
1983	4,575	2,624	121,270	13.2	1,228	1,047	622	710	26.8	22.9	23.7	27.1
1984	4,694	2,705	119,805	13.9	1,267	1,083	629	717	27.0	23.1	23.3	26.5
1985	4,819	2,745	121,077	12.4	1,157	993	647	734	24.0	20.6	23.6	26.7
1986	4,989	2,777	127,855	10.2	1,026	888	674	759	20.6	17.8	24.3	27.3
1987	5,021	2,750	132,809	10.2	1,068	950	677	758	21.3	18.9	24.6	27.6
1988	5,048	2,832	134,887	10.3	1,096	998	675	754	21.7	19.8	23.8	26.6
1989	5,116	2,927	136,228	10.3	1,105	1,005	669	746	21.6	19.6	22.9	25.5
1990	4,965	2,835	133,057	10.1	1,062	969	662	736	21.4	19.5	23.3	26.0
1991	4,891	2,717	129,705	9.3	960	885	657	731	19.6	18.1	24.2	26.9
1992	4,853	2,642	128,980	8.4	884	825	654	727	18.2	17.0	24.8	27.5
1993	4,813	2,614	128,482	7.3	794	751	650	723	16.5	15.6	24.9	27.7
1994	4,861	2,580	129,826	8.4	889	834	649	721	18.3	17.2	25.2	28.0
1995	4,907	2,647	129,959	7.9	853	805	647	717	17.4	16.4	24.4	27.1
1996	4,990	2,670	130,991	7.8	849	801	645	715	17.0	16.1	24.2	26.8
1997	5,104	2,731	132,542	7.6	842	796	649	719	16.5	15.6	23.8	26.3
1998	5,256	2,785	137,335	6.9	817	777	660	727	15.6	14.8	23.7	26.1
1999	5,372	2,885	142,903	7.4	894	839	666	732	16.6	15.6	23.1	25.4
2000	5,317	2,903	148,213	8.1	983	912	667	735	18.5	17.1	23.0	25.3
2001	5,209	2,878	154,659	7.0	923	865	678	750	17.7	16.6	23.5	26.0
2002	5,179	2,771	163,955	6.5	937	879	693	762	18.1	17.0	25.0	27.5
2003	5,206	2,678	173,551	5.8	919	889	698	769	17.7	17.1	26.1	28.7
2004	5,169	2,640	185,141	5.8	982	941	698	770	19.0	18.2	26.4	29.2
2005	5,217	2,658	197,763	5.9	1,052	999	695	772	20.2	19.2	26.2	29.0
2006	5,293	2,731	204,156	6.4	1,151	1,079	698	778	21.7	20.4	25.5	28.5
2007	5,310	2,743	201,318	6.3	1,126	1,060	707	788	21.2	20.0	25.8	28.7
2008	5,155	2,643	180,467	6.0	977	934	706	790	19.0	18.1	26.7	29.9
2009	5,172	2,664	172,100	5.0	835	825	725	807	16.2	16.0	27.2	30.3

Notes: All dollar amounts are expressed in 2009 constant dollars using the Consumer Price Index for All Urban Consumers (CPI-U) for all items. Renters exclude those paying no cash rent. Home price is the 2009 median sales price of existing single-family homes determined by the National Association of Realtors, indexed by the Freddie Mac Conventional Mortgage Home Price Index. Mortgage rates are contract rates from the Freddie Mac Primary Mortgage Market Survey. Mortgage payments assume a 20-year mortgage with 10% down. After-tax mortgage payment equals mortgage payment less tax savings of homeownership. Tax savings are based on the excess of housing (mortgage interest and real-estate taxes) plus non-housing deductions over the standard deduction. Contract rent equals median 2007 contract rent from the American Housing Survey, indexed by the Consumer Price Index (CPI) residential rent index with adjustments for depreciation in the stock before 1987. Gross rent equals median 207 gross rent from the American Housing Survey, indexed by a weighted combination of the CPI residential rent index, the CPI gas and electricity index, and the CPI water and sewer index.

SOURCE: "Table A-1. Income and Housing Costs, U.S. Totals: 1980–2009," in *The State of the Nation's Housing, 2010*, Joint Center for Housing Studies of Harvard University, June 2010, http://www.jchs.harvard.edu/publications/markets/son2010/son2010.pdf (accessed February 19, 2011). Reprinted from *The State of the Nation's Housing, 2010* with permission from the Joint Center for Housing Studies of Harvard University. All rights reserved.

TABLE 6.2

Median monthly housing costs for renter-occupied housing units by state, 2009

Geographic area	Median
United States	$842
Alabama	657
Alaska	1,007
Arizona	859
Arkansas	606
California	1,155
Colorado	851
Connecticut	1,006
Delaware	949
District of Columbia	1,059
Florida	952
Georgia	800
Hawaii	1,293
Idaho	694
Illinois	828
Indiana	687
Iowa	611
Kansas	671
Kentucky	613
Louisiana	715
Maine	722
Maryland	1,108
Massachusetts	988
Michigan	716
Minnesota	757
Mississippi	644
Missouri	668
Montana	627
Nebraska	644
Nevada	993
New Hampshire	918
New Jersey	1,108
New Mexico	680
New York	984
North Carolina	720
North Dakota	564
Ohio	670
Oklahoma	636
Oregon	819
Pennsylvania	738
Rhode Island	890
South Carolina	706
South Dakota	562
Tennessee	682
Texas	788
Utah	793
Vermont	829
Virginia	989
Washington	911
West Virginia	552
Wisconsin	708
Wyoming	700
Puerto Rico	419

Notes: While the 2009 American Community Survey (ACS) data generally reflect the November 2008 Office of Management and Budget (OMB) definitions of metropolitan and micropolitan statistical areas; in certain instances the names, codes, and boundaries of the principal cities shown in ACS tables may differ from the OMB definitions due to differences in the effective dates of the geographic entities.

Estimates of urban and rural population, housing units, and characteristics reflect boundaries of urban areas defined based on Census 2000 data. Boundaries for urban areas have not been updated since Census 2000. As a result, data for urban and rural areas from the ACS do not necessarily reflect the results of ongoing urbanization.

SOURCE: Adapted from "GCT2514. Median Monthly Housing Costs for Renter-Occupied Housing Units," in *2009 American Community Survey 1-Year Estimates*, U.S. Census Bureau, 2010, http://factfinder.census.gov/servlet/GCTTable?_bm=y&-geo_id=D&-ds_name=D&-_lang=en&-redoLog=false&-format=ST-13F&-mt_name=ACS_2009_1YR_G00_GCT2514_US9 (accessed February 18, 2011)

TABLE 6.3

Percent of renter-occupied units spending 30% or more of household income on rent and utilities by state, 2009

Geographic area	Percent
United States	47.7
Alabama	44.2
Alaska	36.6
Arizona	48.0
Arkansas	42.8
California	52.8
Colorado	49.3
Connecticut	49.4
Delaware	49.9
District of Columbia	46.7
Florida	55.9
Georgia	47.6
Hawaii	52.3
Idaho	44.0
Illinois	47.4
Indiana	45.3
Iowa	40.2
Kansas	41.9
Kentucky	41.7
Louisiana	44.3
Maine	46.5
Maryland	49.2
Massachusetts	46.3
Michigan	51.6
Minnesota	46.8
Mississippi	44.1
Missouri	43.1
Montana	38.2
Nebraska	39.1
Nevada	49.9
New Hampshire	45.8
New Jersey	49.9
New Mexico	42.2
New York	48.8
North Carolina	45.6
North Dakota	36.7
Ohio	46.0
Oklahoma	41.4
Oregon	48.5
Pennsylvania	44.2
Rhode Island	46.9
South Carolina	44.9
South Dakota	36.2
Tennessee	45.5
Texas	45.5
Utah	45.8
Vermont	47.2
Virginia	45.6
Washington	47.3
West Virginia	40.5
Wisconsin	45.3
Wyoming	32.8
Puerto Rico	31.9

Notes: While the 2009 American Community Survey (ACS) data generally reflect the November 2008 Office of Management and Budget (OMB) definitions of metropolitan and micropolitan statistical areas; in certain instances the names, codes, and boundaries of the principal cities shown in ACS tables may differ from the OMB definitions due to differences in the effective dates of the geographic entities.

Estimates of urban and rural population, housing units, and characteristics reflect boundaries of urban areas defined based on Census 2000 data. Boundaries for urban areas have not been updated since Census 2000. As a result, data for urban and rural areas from the ACS do not necessarily reflect the results of ongoing urbanization.

SOURCE: Adapted from "GCT2515. Percent of Renter-Occupied Units Spending 30 Percent or More of Household Income on Rent and Utilities: 2009," in *2009 American Community Survey 1-Year Estimates*, U.S. Census Bureau, 2011, http://factfinder.census.gov/servlet/GCTTable?_bm=y&-geo_id=D&-ds_name=D&-_lang=en&-redoLog=false&-format=US-36&-mt_name=ACS_2009_1YR_G00_GCT2515_US9 (accessed February 18, 2011)

Homeownership is also well beyond the reach of most low-income families. The National Association of Realtors reports in the press release "Home Price Stabilization Seen in Most Metro Areas during Fourth Quarter, Sales Up" (February 10, 2011, http://www.realtor.org/press_room/news_releases/2011/02/metro_areas) that the median price for existing single-family homes was $170,600 during the fourth quarter of 2010, up slightly from a year earlier, reflecting the high percentage of distressed sales (sales of foreclosed houses and sales of homes below market value). A third (34%) of all home sales during the fourth quarter were distressed sales. Even though the median price of homes fell, they were still out of reach of low-income families because of the uncertain economy and the credit crunch that began in 2008.

Not Enough Affordable Units Available

In December 2000 Congress established the bipartisan Millennial Housing Commission to examine the role of the federal government in meeting the nation's housing needs. In *Meeting Our Nation's Housing Challenges* (May 30, 2002, http://permanent.access.gpo.gov/lps19766/www.mhc.gov/mhcfinal.pdf), the commission states that "there is simply not enough affordable housing. The inadequacy of supply increases dramatically as one moves down the ladder of family earnings. The challenge is most acute for rental housing in high-cost areas, and the most egregious problem is for the very poor."

Researchers agree that the number of housing units that are affordable to the poor is insufficient to meet needs. The JCHS finds in *State of the Nation's Housing, 2008* (June 2008, http://www.jchs.harvard.edu/publications/markets/son2008/son2008.pdf) that in 2008 there were 3 million more lowest-income renter households than there were affordable units available. Higher-income renters occupied approximately half of the affordable rental units; as a result, 6 million of the lower-income renter households did not have affordable housing.

The limited availability of affordable housing is a problem across the nation. According to Christiana McFarland, Casey Dawkins, and C. Theodore Koebel, in *The State of America's Cities 2007, Local Housing Conditions and Contexts: A Framework for Policy Making* (2007), 32% of city officials believed general housing affordability was a major problem in their area and another 49% believed it was a moderate problem. The JCHS notes that between 1997 and 2007, 13.4% of rental units that cost less than $400 had been demolished or otherwise permanently removed from the low-cost housing market. (See Figure 6.1.) In contrast, only 10% of units with rents between $400 and $599 were lost, 5.6% of units with rents between $600 and $799 were lost, and 4.2% of units with rents of $800 or more were lost.

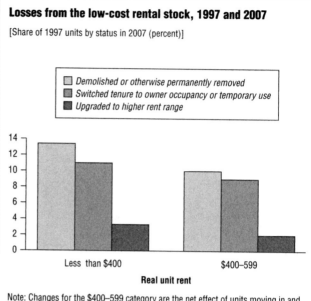
At Risk of Becoming Homeless

The severe shortage of affordable housing means that many low-income people and families constantly face the threat of homelessness, and the problem is not getting better. In February 2011 the U.S. Department of Housing and Urban Development (HUD) released the results of the in-depth study *Worst Case Housing Needs 2009: A Report to Congress* (http://www.huduser.org/portal/publications/affhsg/wc_HsgNeeds09.html). HUD finds that the proportion of households paying more than 30% of their income in rent rose from 28.7% in 2001 to 36.9% in 2009. (See Table 6.4). Among renter households, the proportion with rent burdens of higher than 30% of income rose from 39.5% in 2001 to 48.7% in 2009. However, other problems, such as severely or moderately inadequate housing and crowded housing, decreased between 2001 and 2009.

HUD takes a close look at housing problems among very-low-income renters by race and ethnicity and concludes that severe problems occur across all races and ethnicities. Among non-Hispanic white very-low-income renters, 47.6% paid half or more of their income for rent in 2009, whereas 50.3% of African-Americans and 51.2% of Hispanics did. (See Table 6.5.) Another 2.9% of non-Hispanic whites, 4.1% of African-Americans, and 3.9%

TABLE 6.4

Percent of renters and owners with severe housing problems, selected years 2001–09

	2001	2003	2005	2007	2009
Total households	**100.0%**	**100.0%**	**100.0%**	**100.0%**	**100.0%**
Unassisted with severe problems	12.8%	12.7%	14.8%	15.3%	17.2%
Unassisted with non-severe problems only	18.2%	18.7%	19.1%	20.5%	20.8%
Unassisted with no problems	63.0%	62.8%	60.0%	59.5%	57.7%
Assisted	6.0%	5.9%	6.0%	4.7%	4.4%
Cost burden >50% of income	12.6%	12.5%	15.1%	15.5%	17.4%
Cost burden 30–50% of income	16.1%	16.9%	17.8%	19.1%	19.5%
Severely inadequate housing	2.0%	1.9%	1.9%	1.6%	1.7%
Moderately inadequate housing	4.3%	4.1%	3.8%	3.6%	3.5%
Crowded housing	2.5%	2.4%	2.4%	2.3%	2.2%
Renter households	**100.0%**	**100.0%**	**100.0%**	**100.0%**	**100.0%**
Unassisted with severe problems	17.1%	17.5%	20.2%	19.9%	22.8%
Unassisted with non-severe problems only	21.6%	22.5%	21.5%	24.1%	23.2%
Unassisted with no problems	42.7%	41.5%	39.0%	41.2%	40.1%
Assisted	18.6%	18.5%	19.3%	14.7%	13.8%
Rent burden >50% of income	19.0%	19.3%	23.2%	22.2%	25.4%
Rent burden 30–50% of income	20.5%	22.2%	22.1%	23.8%	23.3%
Severely inadequate housing	3.5%	3.1%	3.2%	3.1%	2.8%
Moderately inadequate housing	7.4%	7.5%	7.5%	6.8%	6.4%
Crowded housing	4.9%	4.8%	4.8%	4.3%	4.2%
Owner households	**100.0%**	**100.0%**	**100.0%**	**100.0%**	**100.0%**
Unassisted with severe problems	10.8%	10.4%	12.4%	13.2%	14.6%
Unassisted with non-severe problems only	16.6%	16.9%	18.1%	18.9%	19.6%
Unassisted with no problems	72.6%	72.7%	69.5%	67.9%	65.8%
Cost burden >50% of income	9.6%	9.3%	11.4%	12.4%	13.7%
Cost burden 30–50% of income	14.0%	14.4%	15.9%	16.9%	17.8%
Severely inadequate housing	1.3%	1.3%	1.2%	1.0%	1.1%
Moderately inadequate housing	2.8%	2.5%	2.2%	2.1%	2.1%
Crowded housing	1.4%	1.3%	1.3%	1.3%	1.3%

SOURCE: Adapted from Barry L. Steffen et al., "Table A-2B. Housing Conditions of Renters and Owners, 1998–2009—Percentage of Households," in *Worst Case Housing Needs 2009: A Report to Congress*, U.S. Department of Housing and Urban Development, February 2011, http://www.huduser.org/portal/publications/affhsg/wc_HsgNeeds09.html (accessed February 17, 2011)

of Hispanics had severely inadequate housing. In other words, these are extremely impoverished people who do not own their housing and can barely afford to pay their housing costs or can only afford to stay in the worst housing. Of all housed people, they are the ones closest to being forced into homelessness. The number of renters who experienced these worst-case housing needs jumped from 5.9 million in 2007 to 7.1 million in 2009. HUD explains that "this rise in hardship is due to shrinking incomes and upward pressure on rents caused by growing competition for already-scarce affordable units."

HUD also indicates that in 2009 only 32 units of adequate and affordable rental housing were available for every 100 very-low-income renters. This scarcity was worst in central cities and suburbs. HUD notes that the major causes of the increases in worst-case needs among very-low-income renters were shrinking incomes due to unemployment, a growing lack of federal rental assistance, and competition for affordable units. The JCHS explains in "America's Rental Housing—The Key to a Balanced National Policy" (May 2008, http://www.jchs.harvard.edu/publications/rental/rh08_americas_rental_housing/rh08_intro.pdf) that the soaring foreclosure rates in 2007 and

2008 only increased pressure on the affordable housing stock, as previous homeowners began looking for rental housing.

For as long as worst-case needs have been reported by HUD, affordability rather than housing quality has been the main problem facing renters. A household that spends more than 50% of its income on housing is considered severely cost burdened. According to the JCHS, in *State of the Nation's Housing, 2010*, the number of households with severe cost burdens increased by 4.7 million between 2001 and 2008 to a record 18.6 million households. (See Table 6.6.) Almost half (13.8 million households, or 48.7%) of households in the bottom income quartile were severely cost burdened in 2008.

Working Families Struggle to Keep Up

In *Out of Reach 2010: Renters in the Great Recession, the Crisis Continues* (June 2010, http://www.nlihc.org/oor/oor2010/), the National Low Income Housing Coalition (NLIHC) compares the fair market rent (FMR; HUD's estimate of what a household seeking modest rental housing must expect to pay for rent and utilities) for a two-bedroom rental unit against the median hourly wage. In

TABLE 6.5

Incidence of housing problems among very-low-income renters, by race and Hispanic origin, 2007 and 2009

	2007	2009	2007	2009
Non-Hispanic white (1,000)	**7,477**	**8,051**	**100.0%**	**100.0%**
Unassisted with severe problems	2,919	3,436	39.0%	42.7%
Unassisted with non-severe problems only	1,696	1,905	22.7%	23.7%
Unassisted with no problems	1,099	1,105	14.7%	13.7%
Assisted	1,763	1,606	23.6%	19.9%
Any with severe problems	**3,469**	**3,938**	**46.4%**	**48.9%**
Rent burden >50%of income	3,374	3,832	45.1%	47.6%
Severely inadequate housing	197	232	2.6%	2.9%
[Rent burden only]	3,007	3,453	40.2%	42.9%
Any with non-severe problems only	**2,271**	**2,404**	**30.4%**	**29.9%**
Rent burden 30–50% of income	2,101	2,223	28.1%	27.6%
Moderately inadequate housing	289	320	3.9%	4.0%
Crowded housing	87	104	1.2%	1.3%
[Rent burden only]	1,917	2,001	25.6%	24.9%
Any with no problems	**1,737**	**1,708**	**23.2%**	**21.2%**
Non-Hispanic black (1,000)	**4,040**	**4,493**	**100.0%**	**100.0%**
Unassisted with severe problems	1,345	1,640	33.3%	36.5%
Unassisted with non-severe problems only	752	806	18.6%	17.9%
Unassisted with no problems	362	338	9.0%	7.5%
Assisted	1,581	1,710	39.1%	38.1%
Any with severe problems	**1,960**	**2,359**	**48.5%**	**52.5%**
Rent burden >50% of income	1,853	2,258	45.9%	50.3%
Severely inadequate housing	177	183	4.4%	4.1%
[Rent burden only]	1,644	2,020	40.7%	45.0%
Any with non-severe problems only	**1,253**	**1,322**	**31.0%**	**29.4%**
Rent burden 30–50% of income	1,082	1,202	26.8%	26.8%
Moderately inadequate housing	203	204	5.0%	4.5%
Crowded housing	114	77	2.8%	1.7%
[Rent burden only]	945	1,051	23.4%	23.4%
Any with no problems	**827**	**812**	**20.5%**	**18.1%**
Hispanic (1,000)	**3,297**	**3,493**	**100.0%**	**100.0%**
Unassisted with severe problems	1,234	1,582	37.4%	45.3%
Unassisted with non-severe problems only	1,049	932	31.8%	26.7%
Unassisted with no problems	301	308	9.1%	8.8%
Assisted	713	672	21.6%	19.2%
Any with severe problems	**1,504**	**1,841**	**45.6%**	**52.7%**
Rent burden >50% of income	1,446	1,787	43.9%	51.2%
Severely inadequate housing	145	135	4.4%	3.9%
[Rent burden only]	1,249	1,578	37.9%	45.2%
Any with non-severe problems only	**1,279**	**1,151**	**38.8%**	**33.0%**
Rent burden 30–50% of income	1,130	1,016	34.3%	29.1%
Moderately inadequate housing	152	148	4.6%	4.2%
Crowded housing	313	256	9.5%	7.3%
[Rent burden only]	857	776	26.0%	22.2%
Any with no problems	**513**	**501**	**15.6%**	**14.3%**

SOURCE: Barry L. Steffen et al., "Table A-9. Incidence of Housing Problems among Very-Low-Income Renters by Race and Ethnicity, 2007 and 2009, Number and Percentage," in *Worst Case Housing Needs 2009: A Report to Congress*, U.S. Department of Housing and Urban Development, February 2011, http://www.huduser.org/portal/publications/affhsg/wc_HsgNeeds09.html (accessed February 17, 2011).

2010 the hourly wage needed to pay the FMR for a two-bedroom apartment spending no more than 30% of one's income on rent was $18.44. However, the estimated average hourly wage of renters in the United States was $14.44, and the federal minimum wage was $7.25. The NLIHC states that besides minimum-wage workers not being able to find affordable two-bedroom apartments, "there is no county in the U.S. where even a one-bedroom unit at the FMR is affordable to someone working full-time at the minimum wage." In most cities in the nation, the housing wage was at least twice the federal minimum wage. In other words, to afford the FMR for a two-bedroom apartment, a household must have two or three minimum-wage workers working full time. As Figure 6.2 shows, 40% of renters with one or two minimum wage earners in the household were severely cost burdened in 2008.

FEDERALLY SUBSIDIZED HOUSING

The national effort to provide housing for those in need is far more massive than would be indicated by the fiscal year (FY) 2012 proposed budget of $2.3 billion on assis-

TABLE 6.6

Housing cost-burdened households by tenure and income, 2001 and 2008

[Thousands]

Tenure and income	2001				2008				Percent change 2001–08			
	No burden	Moderate burden	Severe burden	Total	No burden	Moderate burden	Severe burden	Total	No burden	Moderate burden	Severe burden	Total
Owners												
Bottom decile	771	709	2,506	3,986	570	647	2,758	3,975	−26.1	−8.8	10.1	−0.3
Bottom quintile	3,381	1,906	3,921	9,208	2,721	1,974	4,616	9,312	−19.5	3.6	17.7	1.1
Bottom quartile	5,065	2,549	4,428	12,042	4,206	2,694	5,385	12,286	−16.9	5.7	21.6	2.0
Lower-middle quartile	10,695	3,630	1,456	15,781	10,202	4,345	2,550	17,097	−4.6	19.7	75.1	8.3
Upper-middle quartile	16,015	2,882	465	19,362	15,979	4,136	1,113	21,228	−0.2	43.5	139.5	9.6
Top quartile	21,457	1,208	137	22,802	22,080	2,321	330	24,731	2.9	92.1	141.2	8.5
Total	**53,231**	**10,270**	**6,485**	**69,986**	**52,467**	**13,496**	**9,378**	**75 342**	**−1.4**	**31.4**	**44.6**	**7.7**
Renters												
Bottom decile	1,309	789	4,559	6,657	1,293	812	5,229	7,335	−1.2	3.0	14.7	10.2
Bottom quintile	2,731	2,798	6,550	12,079	2,618	2,873	7,817	13,308	−4.1	2.7	19.3	10.2
Bottom quartile	3,705	3,962	6,901	14,567	3,514	4,087	8,389	15,989	−5.2	3.1	21.6	9.8
Lower-middle quartile	7,698	2,710	419	10,828	7,100	3,325	753	11,178	−7.8	22.7	79.6	3.2
Upper-middle quartile	6,771	437	39	7,247	6,299	681	68	7,048	−7.0	55.8	72.1	−2.7
Top quartile	3,735	71	2	3,807	3,464	80	0	3,544	−7.3	12.4	−74.3	−6.9
Total	**21,908**	**7,180**	**7,361**	**36,449**	**20,376**	**8,172**	**9,210**	**37,759**	**−7.0**	**13.8**	**25.1**	**3.6**
All households												
Bottom decile	2,080	1,498	7,065	10,643	1,863	1,459	7,987	11,309	−10.5	−2.6	13.1	6.3
Bottom quintile	6,112	4,704	10,472	21,287	5,340	4,847	12,433	22,619	−12.6	3.0	18.7	6.3
Bottom quartile	8,769	6,511	11,328	26,609	7,720	6,780	13,774	28,275	−12.0	4.1	21.6	6.3
Lower-middle quartile	18,393	6,340	1,876	26,609	17,302	7,670	3,304	28,275	−5.9	21.0	76.1	6.3
Upper-middle quartile	22,786	3,319	504	26,609	22,278	4,817	1,180	28,275	−2.2	45.1	134.2	6.3
Top quartile	25,191	1,280	138	26,609	25,544	2,401	330	28,275	1.4	87.6	138.7	6.3
Total	**75,140**	**17,450**	**13,846**	**106,436**	**72,844**	**21,668**	**18,588**	**113,101**	**−3.1**	**24.2**	**34.2**	**6.3**

Notes: Income deciles/quintiles/quartiles are equal tenths/fifths/fourths of all households sorted by pre-tax income. Moderate (severe) burdens are defined as housing costs of 30–50% (more than 50%) of household income.

SOURCE: "Table A-5. Housing Cost-Burdened Households by Tenure and Income: 2001 and 2008," in *The State of the Nation's Housing, 2010*, Joint Center for Housing Studies of Harvard University, June 2010, http://www.jchs.harvard.edu/publications/markets/son2010/son2010.pdf (accessed February 19, 2011). Reprinted from *The State of the Nation's Housing, 2010* with permission from the Joint Center for Housing Studies of Harvard University. All rights reserved.

tance grants to the homeless. HUD notes in *FY 2012 Budget Summary* (February 2011, http://portal.hud.gov/hudportal/documents/huddoc?id=fy2012budget.pdf) that its proposed expenditures on public and Native American housing were estimated to be $26.7 billion in FY 2012. If these funds are added to the projected expenditures on homeless grant programs, the total spending on subsidized housing in FY 2012 would be $29 billion. Of this total, 7.9% would be allocated to helping the homeless and 92.1% to ensuring that people do not become homeless. To help people stay housed, the government has housing programs that help poor and low-income people.

Most government housing programs are targeted to poor and low-income households. For this reason subsidized housing is means-tested, meaning that the income of those receiving help must be below a certain threshold. The qualifying income level—much like the definition of poverty—changes over time. Beneficiaries of housing assistance never receive cash outright. The benefits are therefore labeled "means-tested noncash benefits." In 2008, 10.8 million people, or 3.6% of the population, lived in subsidized housing. (See Table 6.7.)

HUD operates many different kinds of housing programs, but these can be classified under three headings: public housing owned by the government, tenant-based programs that provide people vouchers to subsidize rent, and project-based programs that underwrite the costs of private owners who pledge to house low-income people.

Public housing and voucher programs account for roughly equal proportions of subsidized units. Project-based programs, also known as private subsidized projects, account for the most units, but these private subsidies take many forms, some that are quite complicated. A look at the major programs follows.

Public Housing

HUD's FY 2011 budget appropriated $26.4 billion for public and Native American housing. (See Table 6.8). In FY 2011, $2.5 billion was allocated to the capital fund to finance major repairs and modernize units. An additional $200 million was allocated to the HOPE VI grant program to help public housing authorities replace and revitalize the most severely distressed public housing and implement community service and supportive service

FIGURE 6.2

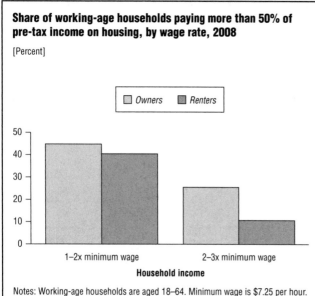

Share of working-age households paying more than 50% of pre-tax income on housing, by wage rate, 2008

[Percent]

Notes: Working-age households are aged 18–64. Minimum wage is $7.25 per hour. Full-time minimum wage job equivalent income is based on working 35 hours per week for 50 weeks. Households with severe cost burdens spend more than 50% of pre-tax income on housing.

SOURCE: "Figure 5. Even Households Earning Multiples of the Minimum Wage Cannot Afford Housing," in *The State of the Nation's Housing, 2010*, Joint Center for Housing Studies of Harvard University, June 2010, http://www.jchs.harvard.edu/publications/markets/son2010/son2010.pdf (accessed February 19, 2011). Reprinted from *The State of the Nation's Housing, 2010* with permission from the Joint Center for Housing Studies of Harvard University. All rights reserved.

improvements in those projects. HUD reports in *Annual Performance Report* (March 2011, http://portal.hud.gov/hudportal/documents/huddoc?id=fy2010apr.pdf) that one of the department's goals in FYs 2010 and 2011 was to provide 207,000 new families with affordable rental housing.

The management of public housing is handled by housing agencies (sometimes called authorities) that have been established by local governments to administer HUD housing programs. The U.S. Housing Act of 1937 required that public housing agencies (PHAs) submit annual plans to HUD and declared that it was the policy of the United States "to vest in public housing agencies that perform well, the maximum amount of responsibility and flexibility in program administration, with appropriate accountability to public housing residents, localities, and the general public."

Thus, PHAs operate under plans that are approved by HUD and under HUD supervision. However, they are also expected to operate with some independence and to be accountable to their residents, local (or state) governments, and the public. Regardless, not all PHAs have performed well, and HUD has been accused of lax supervision. PHAs and public housing generally reflect the distressed economic conditions of the population living in government-owned

housing. Many PHAs have been charged with neglecting maintenance, tolerating unsafe living conditions for tenants, and conducting fraudulent or careless financial practices.

Troubled housing refers to low-income projects that are badly deteriorated, are located in unsafe neighborhoods, or are in danger of being lost to market-rate housing conversion or foreclosure. In an effort to improve its accountability for the conditions of low-income housing, HUD implemented the Public Housing Assessment System (PHAS) in January 2000. The PHAS is used to measure the performance of PHAs. The assessment system consists of four primary components:

- Ensure, through physical inspection, that PHAs meet the minimum standard of being decent, safe, sanitary, and in good repair

- Oversee the finances of PHAs

- Evaluate the effectiveness of the management of PHAs

- Receive feedback from PHA residents on housing conditions

The U.S. Government Accountability Office (GAO) finds in "Major Management Challenges at the Department of Housing and Urban Development" (February 8, 2005, http://www.gao.gov/pas/2005/hud.htm) that in 2005 HUD continued to have major problems addressing the effective management of PHAs. It had made progress since implementing the PHAS; however, because "some of HUD's corrective actions are still in the early stages of implementation and additional steps are needed to resolve ongoing problems," its rental housing assistance programs remained "high risk." Nevertheless, David G. Wood of the GAO's Financial Markets and Community Investments notes in *Public Housing: Information on the Roles of HUD, Public Housing Agencies, Capital Markets, and Service Organizations* (February 15, 2006, http://www.gao.gov/new.items/d06419t.pdf) that in many cases HUD's enforcement actions against troubled PHAs (e.g., technical assistance and training or sanctions such as withholding of funding) resulted in some improvements in 2006.

In *Public Housing: HUD's Oversight of Housing Agencies Should Focus More on Inappropriate Use of Program Funds* (June 2009, http://www.gao.gov/new.items/d0933.pdf), the GAO determines that HUD's reliance on single audits and the PHAS to identify inappropriate use and mismanagement of public housing funds limits HUD's ability to identify at-risk PHAs. For example, the GAO notes that between 2002 and 2006, 200 PHAs had written checks exceeding the amounts in their checking accounts by $25,000 or more. However, 75% of these agencies had received passing PHAS scores, raising questions about not only serious management issues by PHAs but also HUD's ability to adequately oversee them.

TABLE 6.7

Persons living in households receiving selected noncash benefits, 2008

[In thousands (301,041 represents 301,041,000), except percent]

Age, sex, and race	Total	In household that received means-tested assistance[a]		In household that received means-tested cash assistance		In household that received food stamps		In household in which one or more persons were covered by Medicaid		Lived in public or authorized housing	
		Number	Percent	Number	Percent	Number	Percent	Number	Percent	Number	Percent
Total	301,041	83,906	27.9	19,484	6.5	27,644	9.2	66,729	22.2	10,838	3.6
Under 18 years	74,068	30,934	41.8	5,591	7.5	11,582	15.6	25,019	33.8	3,896	5.3
18 to 24 years	28,688	8,640	30.1	1,952	6.8	2,882	10.0	7,117	24.8	1,120	3.9
25 to 34 years	40,520	11,688	28.8	2,268	5.6	4,023	9.9	9,596	23.7	1,307	3.2
35 to 44 years	41,322	10,496	25.4	2,139	5.2	2,984	7.2	8,137	19.7	993	2.4
45 to 54 years	44,366	9,293	20.9	2,914	6.6	2,806	6.3	7,301	16.5	1,048	2.4
55 to 59 years	18,755	3,370	18.0	1,337	7.1	974	5.2	2,591	13.8	463	2.5
60 to 64 years	15,534	2,642	17.0	1,064	6.9	693	4.5	2,028	13.1	376	2.4
65 years and over	37,788	6,843	18.1	2,218	5.9	1,700	4.5	4,940	13.1	1,635	4.3
65 to 74 years	20,404	3,612	17.7	1,170	5.7	978	4.8	2,730	13.4	777	3.8
75 years and over	17,384	3,231	18.6	1,048	6.0	722	4.2	2,210	12.7	858	4.9
Male	147,862	39,075	26.4	9,000	6.1	12,051	8.2	31,082	21.0	4,279	2.9
Female	153,179	44,832	29.3	10,484	6.8	15,593	10.2	35,647	23.3	6,559	4.3
White alone[b]	240,548	58,393	24.3	12,463	5.2	17,410	7.2	46,872	19.5	5,416	2.3
Black alone[b]	37,966	18,394	48.4	5,306	14.0	8,165	21.5	14,093	37.1	4,372	11.5
Asian alone[b]	13,310	3,194	24.0	659	5.0	590	4.4	2,636	19.8	481	3.6
Hispanic[c]	47,398	23,814	50.2	3,962	8.4	7,163	15.1	18,751	39.6	2,292	4.8
White alone, Non-Hispanic[b]	196,940	36,562	18.6	8,937	4.5	10,960	5.6	29,689	15.1	3,451	1.8

[a]Means-tested assistance includes means-tested cash assistance, food stamps, Medicaid, and public or authorized housing.
[b]Refers to people who reported specific race and did not report any other race category.
[c]People of Hispanic origin may be of any race.
Notes: Persons, as of March 2009, who lived with someone (a nonrelative or a relative) who received aid. Not every person tallied here received the aid themselves. Persons living in households receiving more than one type of aid are counted only once. Excludes members of the Armed Forces except those living off post or with their families on post. Population controls for 2008 based on Census 2000 and an expanded sample of households. Based on Current Population Survey.

SOURCE: "Table 541. Persons Living in Households Receiving Selected Noncash Benefits: 2008," in *Statistical Abstract of the United States: 2011*, 130th ed., U.S. Census Bureau, January 2011, http://www.census.gov/compendia/statab/2011/tables/11s0541.pdf (accessed February 18, 2011)

Vouchers

Voucher programs pay a portion of the rent for qualifying families. Only low-income families are eligible, specifically those with incomes lower than half of an area's median income. Under some circumstances, families with up to 80% of the local median income may also qualify; such cases may involve, for instance, families that have been displaced by public housing demolition. The family pays 30% of its income toward the rent and the voucher covers the remaining balance. Vouchers are issued by the local PHA, which executes assistance contracts with the landlord, who must also qualify.

Two major voucher programs are available: tenant based and project based. In tenant-based programs the voucher follows the tenant when the tenant moves to another qualifying unit. In project-based programs the voucher is attached to a project. Families are directed to participating projects after they qualify. Tenants cannot automatically transfer their voucher from one project-based dwelling to another, but they may qualify for another tenant-based voucher after they move.

Besides these two basic programs, HUD also has five other voucher programs. Conversion vouchers are used to help tenants relocate when public housing is demolished. Family unification vouchers are used to help families stay together. Homeownership vouchers assist families in purchasing a first home or another home if the family has not lived in a house in the past three years. Participants must be employed and have an income of at least minimum wage. Vouchers for people with disabilities and welfare-to-work vouchers assist the elderly or nonelderly disabled and families transitioning from welfare to work.

In all these programs the housing supplied is privately owned and operated and the rents paid are at or below the FMR. HUD determines the FMR in every locality of the nation by an annual survey of new rental contracts that have been signed during the past 15 months. In most cities the FMR is set at the 40th percentile of rents paid, meaning that 40% of renters paid a lower rent and 60% paid a higher rent; in certain cities the FMR is calculated at the 50th percentile. HUD has chosen the 40th percentile to increase housing choices while keeping budgets at reasonable levels. Table 6.9 presents the FMRs that were used by HUD in a sample of cities around the country in 2011.

TABLE 6.8

Housing and Urban Development (HUD) budget authority for public housing programs, 2010–12

[Dollars in millions]

Public and Indian Housing	2010 Actual	2011 Estimate	2012 Estimate
Transforming Rental Assistance (TRA)			
Rental assistance and administrative fees			
Public housing	—	—	117
Multifamily	—	—	50
Resident mobility	—	—	33
Total, TRA	**—**	**—**	**200**
Tenant-Based Rental Assistance (TBRA)			
Section 8 contract renewals	16,339	16,339	17,194
Renewal set-aside	[150]	[150]	[135]
Administrative fees	1,575	1,575	1,648
Family self-sufficiency coordinators	60	60	60
Section 8 rental assistance (Tenant protection vouchers)	120	120	75
Family unification program	15	15	—
Advanced appropriation for fiscal year 2010	[4,000]	[—]	[—]
Advanced appropriation for fiscal year 2011	[(4,000)]	[4,000]	[—]
Advanced appropriation for fiscal year 2012	[—]	[(4,000)]	[4,000]
Advanced appropriation for fiscal year 2013	[—]	[—]	[(4,000)]
Mainstream voucher renewals	—	—	114
Housing and services initiative—vouchers	—	—	57
Veterans affairs supportive housing	75	75	75
Disaster displacement assistance	—	—	[50]
Transfer to transformation initiative fund	[100]	[—]	[—]
Total, TBRA	**18,184**	**18,184**	**19,223**
Public housing capital fund			
Formula grants	$2,371	$2,371	$2,365
ROSS	50	50	—
Emergency capitalization needs	20	20	20
Administrative receivership	9	9	5
Early childhood education, job training facilities	35	35	—
Financial and physical assessment support	15	15	15
Transfer to transformation initiative fund	[25]	[—]	[—]
Total, public housing capital fund	**2,500**	**2,500**	**2,405**
Revitalization of severely distressed public housing (HOPE VI)			
Revitalization grants	125	125	—
Choice neighborhoods initiative demonstration	65	65	—
Technical assistance	10	10	—
Transfer to transformation initiative fund	[2]	[—]	[—]
Total, HOPE VI	**200**	**200**	**—**
Choice neighborhoods			
Choice neighborhoods grants	—	—	240
Technical assistance	—	—	10
Total, choice neighborhoods	**—**	**—**	**250**
Public housing operating fund			
Operating subsidy	4,775	4,775	4,962
Transfer to transformation initiative fund	[15]	[—]	[—]
Subtotal, public housing operating fund	4,775	4,775	4,962
Offset of excess operating reserves	—	—	(1,000)
Total, public housing operating fund	**4,775**	**4,775**	**3,962**
Native American housing block grants			
Formula grants	690	690	698
Technical assistance	4	4	—
Native American housing interest TA and capacity building	4	4	—
Title VI federal guarantees for tribal housing activities			
Program account	2	2	2
Loan guarantee limitation	[18]	[18]	[20]
Total, Native American housing block grants	**700**	**700**	**700**

Of the cities shown in Table 6.9, the highest FMR for a two-bedroom unit in the continental United States was in San Francisco, California ($1,833 per month). The lowest FMR was in Bismarck, North Dakota ($592 per month).

According to HUD, in *Resident Characteristics Report* (2011, https://pic.hud.gov/pic/RCRPublic/rcrmain .asp), the amount of subsidized housing and the number of Section 8 housing vouchers declined across all cate-

TABLE 6.8

Housing and Urban Development (HUD) budget authority for public housing programs, 2010–12 [CONTINUED]

[Dollars in millions]

Public and Indian Housing	2010 Actual	2011 Estimate	2012 Estimate
Indian housing loan guarantee fund			
Program account	6	6	6
Loan guarantee contracts	1	1	1
Limitation level	[919]	[919]	[428]
Total, Indian housing loan guarantee	**7**	**7**	**7**
Native Hawaiian loan guarantee fund			
Program account	1	1	—
Limitation level	[42]	[42]	[—]
Total, section Native Hawaiian loan guarantee	**1**	**1**	**—**
Native Hawaiian housing block grants			
Formula grants	13	13	10
Technical assistance	[0.3]	[0.3]	[0.3]
Total, Native Hawaiian housing block grants	**13**	**13**	**10**
Subtotal, public and Indian housing	**26,380**	**26,380**	**26,747**

SOURCE: Adapted from "Budget Authority by Program, Comparative Summary, Fiscal Years 2010–2012," in *FY 2012 Budget Summary*, U.S. Department of Housing and Urban Development, February 2011, http://portal.hud.gov/hudportal/documents/huddoc?id=fy2012budget.pdf (accessed February 18, 2011)

TABLE 6.9

Fair market rental rates for selected metropolitan areas, fiscal year 2011

Area definition	Fair market rental rate				
	0 bedroom	1 bedroom	2 bedroom	3 bedroom	4 bedroom
Bismarck, ND	$455	$477	$592	$859	$883
San Juan-Guaynabo, PR	$463	$502	$558	$739	$874
Lexington-Fayette, KY	$477	$573	$707	$950	$980
Cincinnati-Middletown, OH-KY-IN	$490	$581	$752	$1,007	$1,045
Albuquerque, NM	$546	$642	$811	$1,181	$1,416
Kansas City, MO-KS	$610	$733	$842	$1,139	$1,198
Memphis, TN-MS-AR	$628	$682	$758	$1,010	$1,041
Salt Lake City, UT	$630	$685	$826	$1,162	$1,353
Minneapolis-St.Paul-Bloomington, MN-WI	$646	$761	$924	$1,210	$1,359
Ann Arbor, MI	$647	$725	$882	$1,110	$1,142
Dallas, TX	$666	$738	$891	$1,160	$1,372
Charlotte-Gastonia-Rock Hill NC-SC	$681	$738	$819	$1,032	$1,201
Anchorage, AK	$726	$826	$1,036	$1,492	$1,817
Portland, ME	$729	$865	$1,121	$1,412	$1,513
Atlanta-Sandy Springs-Marietta, BA	$731	$792	$881	$1,072	$1,170
Gulfport-Biloxi, MS	$732	$776	$906	$1,181	$1,213
New Orleans-Metairie-Kenner, LA	$767	$850	$994	$1,276	$1,319
Las Vegas-Paradise, NV	$770	$907	$1,067	$1,483	$1,785
Philadelphia-Camden-Wilmington, PA-NJ-DE-MD	$789	$900	$1,077	$1,317	$1,589
Chicago-Naperville-Joliet, IL	$790	$904	$1,016	$1,242	$1,403
Orlando-Kissimmee-Sanford, FL	$795	$865	$988	$1,237	$1,456
Flagstaff, AZ	$845	$1,005	$1,136	$1,461	$1,843
Seattle-Bellevue, WA	$857	$977	$1,176	$1,662	$2,030
Baltimore-Towson, MD	$931	$1,052	$1,263	$1,622	$2,003
Los Angeles-Long Beach, CA	$973	$1,173	$1,465	$1,967	$2,367
Boston-Cambridge-Quincy, MA-NH	$1,083	$1,149	$1,349	$1,613	$1,773
Washington-Arlington-Alexandria, DC-VA-MD	$1,131	$1,289	$1,461	$1,885	$2,466
New York, NY	$1,166	$1,261	$1,403	$1,726	$1,941
Honolulu, HI	$1,190	$1,396	$1,702	$2,470	$2,764
San Francisco, CA	$1,191	$1,465	$1,833	$2,447	$2,586

SOURCE: Adapted from "Schedule B. FY 2011 Final Fair Market Rents for Existing Housing," in *Fair Market Rents*, U.S. Department of Housing and Urban Development, September 2010, http://www.huduser.org/datasets/fmr/fmr2011f/FY2011F_ScheduleB_rev2.pdf (accessed February 18, 2011)

gories between 2003 and 2011. Project-based Section 8 housing has declined dramatically because funding for new construction stopped in 1983 with some minor exceptions (including construction/rehabilitation aimed at supporting homeless programs). Support of housing in such units continues, but the housing stock is going out of use through demolitions and conversions. Only 37,178 project-based vouchers were available in March 2011. As a result, the vast majority of Section 8 housing vouchers were tenant based; 1.9 million were available in March 2011.

According to HUD, tenant-voucher residents had an average household income of $12,540 and an average household of 2.5 people in March 2011. Sixty-five percent of voucher users had an extremely low income of under 30% of the median income in their area. In contrast, 19% of public housing residents had an extremely low income. Therefore, voucher users were more impoverished than public housing residents. The shift of the subsidized population from public housing toward voucher housing represents a change in policy, whereby the provision of housing in the future appears to be headed for privatization. Tenant-based voucher programs give low-income people choices in housing, which can help poor families be more flexible and move to areas with better job opportunities and transportation options, as well as help reverse the trend of the concentration of poverty in certain urban areas.

Other Housing Assistance Programs

The two biggest low-income housing programs in the United States are public housing and the Section 8 voucher programs. Section 8 funds are distributed under HUD's Housing Certificate Fund. Other HUD programs fund housing for people living with AIDS, elderly people, Native Americans and Native Hawaiians, and people with disabilities. The Prisoner Reentry Initiative, begun in 2005, helps former prisoners find housing and receive job training and other services.

Other federal programs aim to increase privately owned low-income housing stock. HUD explains in *Annual Performance Report* that the Federal Housing Administration (FHA) offers mortgage insurance for multifamily projects, tax credits to housing developers who provide a portion of their projects at low rents, and a Community Development Block Grant program that is used to rehabilitate housing within urban communities that have people with low and moderate income.

HUD maintains demographic and income data only on participants in its major programs. For that reason, information on the characteristics of participants in many other HUD subsidy programs aimed at low-income people is unavailable. The previously cited programs do not include mortgage insurance and other FHA programs that are aimed to assist the more affluent general population to own a home.

Rural Housing Programs

The U.S. Department of Agriculture's Rural Housing Service (RHS) administers a variety of rural housing programs. (See Table 6.10.) These programs make federal

TABLE 6.10

Funding for selected rural housing programs in millions of dollars, fiscal years 1990–2010

Rural housing program	Total dollars spent, fiscal year 1990	Total dollars spent, fiscal year 2000	Total dollars requested, fiscal year 2010	Type of assistance
Single-family housing direct loans (sec. 502)	1,311	1,141	2,417	Loans subsidized as low as 1% Interest
Single-family housing guaranteed loans (sec. 502)	n/a	2,151	13,618	No money down, no monthly mortgage insurance loans
Single-family home repair grants and loans (sec. 504)	24.2	57.8	66.4	Grants for elderly and loans subsidized as low as 1% interest
Single-family housing mutual self-help grants (sec. 523)	5.3	28	56.4	Grants to nonprofit and public entities to provide technical assistance
Multifamily direct rural rental housing loans (sec. 515)	571	113.8	69.5	Loans to developers subsidized as low as 1% interest
Multifamily housing guaranteed loans (sec. 538)	n/a	99.7	141.5	Guaranteed loans for developing moderate-income apartments
Multifamily housing farm labor grants and loans (secs. 516/514)	22.1	48.1	39.1	Grants and loans subsidized at 1% interest
Multifamily housing preservation grans (sec. 533)	19.1	5.5	10.1	Grants to nonprofit organizations, local governments, and Native American tribes, usually leveraged with outside funding
Multifamily housing rental assistance (sec. 521)	296.4	639.6	980.3	Rental assistance to about one-half the residents in RHS rental and farm labor units
Totals	**2,249.1**	**4,284.5**	**17,398.3**	

SOURCE: Adapted from Bruce E. Foote, "Table 1. Funding for Selected Rural Housing Programs, FY1980–FY2010," and "Table 2. Funding for Selected Rural Housing Programs, FY1980–FY2010," in *USDA Rural Housing Programs: An Overview*, Congressional Research Service, October 2010, http://www.nationalaglawcenter.org/assets/crs/RL33421.pdf (accessed February 19, 2011)

money available for housing in rural areas, which are considered places with populations of 50,000 or less. Eligibility for rural housing programs is similar to that of subsidized urban programs. The requirements vary from region to region, and applicants must meet minimum and maximum income guidelines. The subsidies come in the form of grants or low-interest loans to repair substandard housing, subsidized mortgages for low-income home ownership, and grants to cover down payment and purchasing costs of low-income homes.

Table 6.10 shows the various programs that were available under RHS funding in millions of dollars. In 2010, $17.4 billion was appropriated for rural housing programs; of that, $16.2 billion subsidized single-family home loans (sections 502, 504, and 523) and $980.3 million provided rental assistance to families (section 521).

Much of the rural low-income housing where renters, migrant workers, and a large proportion of minorities live is substandard. Substandard housing may have a leaking roof, broken windows, exposed electrical wiring, major plumbing problems, holes in the floor, or other major problems. There are four major areas that are affected by housing inadequacies: the Mississippi Delta, Native American trust lands, the colonias (poor neighborhoods) bordering Mexico, and Appalachia. Table 6.11 shows that the majority of Americans were living in adequate housing in 2005. However, 4.9% of people were living in housing with a leaky roof, 3% were living with broken windows, 1.9% were living with plumbing problems, 0.6% were living with holes in the floor big enough to trip, and 0.6% were living with exposed electrical wiring.

The RHS, like HUD, has been plagued by accusations of mismanagement. William B. Shear of the GAO suggests in *Rural Housing Service: Opportunities to Improve Management* (June 19, 2003, http://www.gao.gov/new.items/ d03911t.pdf) that the RHS can be improved if it reduces costs and centralizes its administration. The GAO indicates in *Rural Housing Service: Agency Has Overestimated Its Rental Assistance Budget Needs over the Life of the Program* (May 2004, http://www.gao.gov/new.items/d04752 .pdf) that the RHS consistently overestimates its budget needs. In "Rural Housing Service: Overview of Program Issues" (March 10, 2005, http://www.gao.gov/highlights/ d05382thigh.pdf), the GAO states that "several issues prevent the agency from making the best use of resources," including the policy of grandfathering communities, which inhibits an accurate determination of metropolitan versus rural areas; the consistent overestimation of the RHS's rental assistance budget needs and insufficiently monitoring the use of the agency's funds; and the implementation of inaccurate data collection methods.

In *Rural Housing Service: Opportunities Exist to Strengthen Farm Labor Housing Program Management and Oversight* (March 2011, http://www.gao.gov/new

.items/d11329.pdf), the GAO looks specifically at the Farm Labor Housing Loan and Grant Program, which supports the development of affordable housing for farm workers. The GAO finds the same type of management problems in this program that it has found in other RHS programs. The GAO states that the "RHS management processes have hindered the agency's ability to assure farmworkers access to decent and safe housing and compliance with program requirements." Specifically, the GAO notes that the RHS has difficulty determining whether farm labor housing borrowers are in compliance and that enforcement measures to

TABLE 6.11

Percent of households with selected measures of material well-being, 1992, 1998, 2003, 2005

	1992	1998	2003	2005
Appliances and electronic goods				
Washing machine	84.7	90.9	92.2	84.0
Clothes dryer	77.6	86.8	89.1	81.2
Dishwasher	49.3	56.0	62.3	64.0
Refrigerator	99.1	99.3	99.3	99.3
Freezer	37.2	34.9	36.9	36.6
Television[a]	96.5	98.4	98.8	98.9
Gas or electric stove	99.0	98.7	98.9	98.8
Microwave	82.2	90.7	95.9	96.4
Videocassette recorder[b]	73.9	85.2	90.0	92.2
Air conditioner	69.2	77.7	84.6	85.7
Computer	20.7	42.0	63.1	67.1
Landline telephone	94.9	96.2	94.1	90.6
Cellular phone[c]	(NA)	36.3	62.8	71.3
Housing conditions				
General conditions				
No leaking roof	91.5	93.1	94.6	95.1
No problem with pests	85.3	87.3	90.5	90.2
No broken windows	92.5	95.9	97.0	97.0
No exposed electrical wiring	98.6	99.2	99.4	99.4
No holes or cracks in the wall	95.4	96.0	97.1	97.2
No plumbing problems	95.1	97.4	97.9	98.1
No holes in floor large enough to trip	98.9	99.1	99.4	99.4
Satisfaction				
Satisfied with warmth of home in winter	(NA)	91.2	93.4	93.1
Satisfied with coolness of home in summer	(NA)	89.7	92.5	92.2
Satisfied with state of repair of home	(NA)	92.2	93.4	93.3
Generally satisfied with home	(NA)	95.7	96.1	96.2
Neighborhood conditions and community services				
Safety				
Did not stay home for safety	89.2	87.1	90.4	89.2
Did not carry anything to protect self	88.4	92.5	94.3	94.4
Did not travel with someone for safety	(NA)	88.5	91.9	90.7
Not afraid to walk alone at night	(NA)	71.3	78.0	77.5
Home is considered safe	94.2	95.9	96.7	97.0
Neighborhood considered safe	91.0	91.4	92.8	92.3
General conditions				
No trash or litter on streets	88.8	91.8	92.6	92.7
Streets not in need of repair	80.2	83.6	86.0	87.1
No abandoned buildings	89.8	92.1	93.0	93.0
No street noise or heavy traffic	75.9	78.6	81.8	81.9
No smoke or odors in neighborhood	92.9	95.1	96.3	96.6
No problem industry or business	90.6	92.7	94.5	94.4
Satisfaction				
Satisfied with neighborhood conditions	(NA)	95.0	95.3	95.3
Satisfied with relationship with neighbors	(NA)	95.1	95.4	95.2
Satisfied with hospitals	(NA)	89.2	90.8	91.0
Satisfied with police services	(NA)	91.9	93.0	92.9
Satisfied with fire department services	(NA)	95.8	96.5	96.6

TABLE 6.11

Percent of households with selected measures of material well-being, 1992, 1998, 2003, 2005 [CONTINUED]

	1992	1998	2003	2005
Meeting basic needs				
No unmet essential expenses	85.5	86.0	87.1	85.6
No unpaid rent or mortgage	92.2	94.6	94.5	93.9
No unpaid utilities	89.9	90.9	91.3	90.2
No disconnected utilities	98.0	98.7	98.5	98.3
Phone was not disconnected	96.4	96.2	95.9	95.8
Saw a doctor when needed or had no need to see a doctor	92.0	93.9	93.7	93.2
Saw a dentist when needed or had no need to see a dentist	89.6	92.1	92.4	91.5
Help expected if need arose				
Expect help from family if needed	41.2	43.8	47.6	47.5
Expect help from friends if needed	25.7	31.4	35.9	37.4
Expect help from social agency or church	12.5	16.7	21.1	22.7

ªIn 2005 the wording was changed from "television" to "color television"
ᵇIn 2005 the wording was changed from "videocassette recorder (VCR)" to "VCR or DVD (or other video recorder-player such as TiVo)"
ᶜIn 2005 the wording was changed from "cellular phone or car phone" to "cellular phone or mobile phone"

SOURCE: "Table 10. Percent of Households with Selected Measures of Material Well-Being: 1992, 1998, 2003, 2005," in *Extended Measures of Well-Being: Living Conditions in the United States, 2005*, U.S. Census Bureau, November 2009, http://www.census.gov/hhes/well-being/publications/extended-05.html (accessed February 18, 2011)

bring borrowers back in compliance are insufficient. Also, because the RHS routinely overestimates its costs, it does not make available the full amount of low-interest financing to potential borrowers.

FORECLOSURE PREVENTION PROGRAMS

HUD notes in *Annual Performance Report* that one of its goals for FYs 2010 and 2011 was to assist 3.1 million homeowners who were at risk of losing their homes to foreclosure. With the collapse of the housing market during the economic recession, which lasted from late 2007 to mid-2009, millions of Americans saw the values of their homes drop below what they owed on their mortgages, leaving it difficult or impossible to refinance or sell their homes. Even though the recession ended in mid-2009, many U.S. homeowners continued to struggle making their mortgage payments, and as a result, foreclosures continued. Janna Herron reports in "Highest Number of Foreclosures in Forecast" (Associated Press, January 14, 2011) that more people were expected to lose their homes in 2011 than in any year since the crisis began. Several new federal programs were established to respond to the foreclosure crisis.

The FHA put in place an early delinquency intervention program to assist up to 400,000 homeowners avoid foreclosure. Through the FHA, lenders could offer formal forbearance agreements (agreements that lending institutions will delay foreclosing on a loan provided the bor-

rowers perform certain agreed on terms and conditions) to borrowers who were under 90 days in default of their loans. Loss mitigation (the process of attempting to collect past-due mortgage payments) programs were also put in place by the FHA to assist an additional 300,000 homeowners. Mortgage modifications, pre-foreclosure sales, and special forbearance agreements were also offered by the early delinquency intervention program.

A joint program offered by HUD and the U.S. Department of the Treasury, the Making Home Affordable program, aimed to assist homeowners refinance or modify mortgages to make them more affordable. Part of the program was designed to specifically assist borrowers who owed more on their mortgage than their home was worth. In addition, HUD reoriented its free counseling programs that had previously helped consumers make well-informed decisions about taking on mortgages. By FY 2010 most counseling services were geared toward helping homeowners avoid foreclosure.

HUD indicates in *Annual Performance Report* that it, along with the Department of the Treasury, helped 1.2 million homeowners avoid foreclosure in FY 2010. The early delinquency intervention program and the loss mitigation programs helped over 400,000 homeowners, and the Making Home Affordable program helped over 800,000 homeowners.

REASONS FOR THE LACK OF LOW-INCOME HOUSING

The JCHS notes in *State of the Nation's Housing, 2010* that President Barack Obama's (1961–) FY 2011 budget cut HUD funding by 5%, although $2.2 billion was shifted into rental assistance programs, which helped boost the number of needy households that were being served. Nevertheless, only a quarter of eligible households received federal assistance in FY 2011. This highlights one of the major reasons for the lack of low-income housing: declining federal support. Other reasons that low-income housing is diminishing are bureaucratic red tape, fraud and waste, and a variety of local factors that affect new construction.

Declining Federal Support

The poor essentially have two rental options: low-income housing units that are operated by local PHAs and privately owned housing, whose owners accept Section 8 rental assistance vouchers (also called Housing Choice vouchers). The vouchers pay the difference between 30% of the renter's income and the fair market value of the rental. However, there are concerns that HUD is not committed to keeping private owners in the Section 8 program. The GAO indicates in *Project-Based Rental Assistance: HUD Should Update Its Policies and Procedures to Keep Pace with the Changing Housing Market* (April 2007, http://www.gao.gov/new.items/d07290.pdf) that between 2001 and 2005 only 92% of Section 8 rental assistance contracts were renewed, and even among those contracts that were renewed, there were 5% fewer units covered. Owners who left Section 8 did so to "seek higher rents in the private market or to convert their units into condominiums." According to the GAO, rents permitted under the voucher program have not kept pace with actual rents in many markets. The GAO suggests that some HUD policies, such as the one-for-one replacement policy that does not allow owners to reduce the total number of units in a property when a contract is renewed and therefore does not allow them to reconfigure a property and offer larger units, may compel private owners to leave the program. In addition, adjustments to rent are slow, administrative costs are high, and subsidy payments are often late, forcing some owners to leave the program. The GAO recommends that HUD modify some of its policies and address other concerns of private owners in the program to preserve Section 8 rental stock.

Low-income people hoping for housing assistance from the federal government face formidable obstacles. In *Federal Programs for Addressing Low-Income Housing Needs: A Policy Primer* (December 2008, http://www.urban.org/UploadedPDF/411798_low-income_housing.pdf), Margery Austin Turner and G. Thomas Kingsley of the Urban Institute report that only about one out of four eligible households receive federal housing assistance. Section 8 waiting lists and conventional public housing waiting lists are long and often closed in surveyed cities. For example, in the fact sheet "About NYCHA" (March 18, 2011, http://www.nyc.gov/html/nycha/downloads/pdf/factsheet.pdf), the New York City Housing Authority indicates that it had not processed applicants for Section 8 housing since the wait list was reopened for two months in early 2007. As of March 2011, 124,617 families were on the Section 8 wait list, and another 143,960 families were on the wait list for conventional public housing units. In another example, the Chicago Housing Authority reopened its waiting list for public housing between June 14 and July 9, 2010; it was the first time families could put themselves on the waiting list since 1999. However, the article "Public Housing Wait List to Reopen after 10 Years" (*Chicago Breaking News*, May 10, 2010) notes that there was little hope any new applicants would get housing soon—some people on the current waiting list had already waited 12 years.

NEGLECT OF HOUSING STOCK. The contracts that HUD establishes with private owners limit profits and often limit the monies that are put back into the property for repairs. As a result, the existing housing that is available to renters at the lowest income levels often suffers from a lack of upkeep. Neglected maintenance results in deterioration and sometimes removal from the housing inventory altogether.

In addition, the National Alliance to End Homelessness reports in the fact sheet "Affordable Housing Shortage" (June 19, 2007, http://www.endhomelessness.org/content/article/detail/1658) that funding for upkeep of existing public housing units decreased 25% between 1999 and 2006. As a result, the number of public housing units that are available is dwindling.

Factors That Inhibit Construction

Construction of low-income units has been hampered by community resistance, by regulations that increase the cost of construction, and by limits on federal tax credits that make new construction unprofitable.

In "Dissenting Statement to the Report of the Millennial Housing Commission" (May 31, 2002, http://www.heritage.org/Research/Welfare/WM102.cfm), Robert Rector of the Heritage Foundation complains, "It is a simple fact that those cities that have the greatest 'affordability' problem are those that have 'smart growth' or other regulatory policies that severely limit new housing growth. Policies such as restrictive zoning, antiquated building codes, and high impact fees for new construction reduce housing supply and greatly increase costs for everyone in a community."

These regulatory policies are put in place in part because, to many people, the prospect of low-income subsidized housing is synonymous with rising crime, falling property values, and overcrowded classrooms, and it is cause for protest. Resistance to the construction of low-income housing is said to be evidence of a not in my backyard (NIMBY) way of thinking. However, in *From NIMBY to Good Neighbors: Recent Studies Reinforce That Apartments Are Good for a Community* (May 1, 2006, http://www.nmhc.org/Content/ServeFile.cfm?FileID=5408), the National Multi Housing Council summarizes research showing that smart growth (long-term goals for managing the growth of a community) may depend on the development of more high-density housing, such as apartments. The council states, "The good news is that there is an ever-increasing body of research that indicates that apartments (including affordable apartments) are not a threat to local property values and are a net plus to communities."

However, developers complain that there is no profit to be made from building and operating low-income housing. To provide incentives to developers, the 1986 Low-Income Housing Tax Credit program gave the states $1.25 per capita (per person) in tax credits toward the private development of low-income housing. In "A New Era for Affordable Housing" (March 1, 2003, http://nreionline.com/news/developer/real_estate_new_era_affordable/), H. Lee Murphy reports on the National Council of State Housing Agencies' data indicating that construction hit a high in 1994, when 117,100 apartment units were built with the credits. Skyrocketing construction costs brought a decline in new construction, which reached a low of 66,900 units in 2000. In 2001 Congress raised the per capita allotment to $1.75 and provided that the formula would rise each year with inflation. The tax credits financed the construction of 75,000 new units in 2001. HUD reports in "Low-Income Housing Tax Credits" (February 16, 2010, http://www.huduser.org/portal/datasets/lihtc.html) that between 1995 and 2007 an average of 108,000 housing units per year were built because of the tax credit. However, this rate of construction still did not keep pace with the number of affordable housing units that are demolished each year.

WHERE THE HOMELESS LIVE

When faced with high rents and low housing availability, many poor people become homeless. What happens to them? Where do they live? Research shows that after becoming homeless, many people move around, staying in one place for a while, then moving on to another place. Many homeless people take advantage of homeless shelters at some point. Such shelters may be funded by the federal government, by religious organizations, or by other private homeless advocates.

Emergency Housing: Shelters and Transitional Housing

Typically, a homeless shelter provides dormitory-style sleeping accommodations and bathing facilities, with varying services for laundry, telephone calls, and other needs. Residents are often limited in the length of their stay and must leave the shelter during the day under most circumstances. By contrast, transitional housing is intended to bridge the gap between the shelter or street and permanent housing, with appropriate services to move the homeless into independent living. It may be a room in a hotel or motel, or it may be a subsidized apartment. According to M. William Sermons and Peter Witte of the National Alliance to End Homelessness, in *State of Homelessness in America* (January 2011, http://www.endhomelessness.org/content/article/detail/3668), in 2009 there were 176,855 beds in emergency shelters and 185,763 beds in transitional housing available. (See Figure 6.3.) The number of permanent supportive housing beds had increased by 11.5% from 2008, to 215,208 beds.

Illegal Occupancy

Poor neighborhoods are often full of abandoned buildings. Even the best-intentioned landlords cannot afford to maintain their properties in these areas. Many have let their buildings deteriorate or have simply walked away, leaving the fate of the building and its residents in the hands of the government. Despite overcrowding and unsafe conditions, many homeless people move into these dilapidated buildings illegally, glad for what shelter they can find. Municipal governments, which are overwhelmed by long waiting lists for public housing, by a lack of funds and personnel, and by an inadequate supply of emergency shelter beds, are often unable or unwilling to strictly enforce housing laws, allowing the homeless to become squatters rather than forcing them into the streets. Some deliberately turn a blind eye to the problem, knowing they have no better solution for the homeless.

The result is a multitude of housing units with deplorable living conditions—tenants bedding down in illegal boiler basements, sharing beds with children or in-laws, or sharing bathrooms with strangers. The buildings may have leaks and rot, rusted fire escapes, and rat and roach infestations. Given the alternative, many homeless people feel lucky to be sheltered at all.

As a result of the housing crisis that began in 2008, some homeless people began turning to foreclosed homes in their search for shelter. According to the article "Some Homeless Turn to Foreclosed Homes" (Associated Press,

FIGURE 6.3

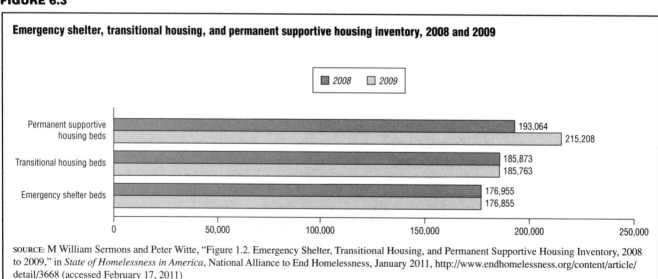

Emergency shelter, transitional housing, and permanent supportive housing inventory, 2008 and 2009

SOURCE: M William Sermons and Peter Witte, "Figure 1.2. Emergency Shelter, Transitional Housing, and Permanent Supportive Housing Inventory, 2008 to 2009," in *State of Homelessness in America*, National Alliance to End Homelessness, January 2011, http://www.endhomelessness.org/content/article/detail/3668 (accessed February 17, 2011)

February 17, 2008), many homeless began moving into these vacant homes and became squatters. The article notes that "foreclosed homes often have an advantage over boarded-up and dilapidated houses that have been abandoned because of rundown conditions: Sometimes the heat, lights and water are still working." The article "Activist Moves Homeless into Foreclosures" (Associated Press, December 1, 2008) explains that in 2008 homeless people were squatting in foreclosed homes in southern Florida with the help of the national organization Take Back the Land. This group finds empty foreclosed properties, arranges to have the utilities turned on, and becomes a pseudo landlord. Taryn Wobbema reports in "City Foreclosures Open Space for Squatters" (MNDaily.com, March 4, 2009) that in Minneapolis, Minnesota, the Poor People's Economic Human Rights Campaign places homeless people in empty homes illegally.

In "Homeless Squatting in Foreclosed City Homes" (13wham.com, December 20, 2010), Rachel Barnhart indicates that in 2010 homeless squatters were moving into some of the 3,000 empty houses in Rochester, New York. The squatters were helped by Take Back the Land. Similar actions were taking place around the country. Take Back the Land explains in "US Senators Contact Take Back the Land–Rochester to Address the Housing Crisis" (http://www.takebacktheland.org/) that in March 2011 it staged a two-week-long community eviction defense by physically blocking authorities from evicting Catherine Lennon and 10 extended family members from her Rochester home, which had been foreclosed. A SWAT team was eventually brought in to forcibly evict Lennon. In all, seven defenders were arrested. Intense media scrutiny led Representative Louis McIntosh Slaughter (1929–; D-NY) to intervene and ask the federal authorities to negotiate with Lennon.

CHAPTER 7
DEALING WITH THE PROBLEM OF HOMELESSNESS

FEDERAL GOVERNMENT AID FOR THE HOMELESS

What should the role of the government be in combating homelessness? Some people believe it is the duty of the government to take care of all citizens in times of need. Others point out that government help has often been misdirected or inadequate; in some instances, it has even added to the problem. Some people assert that people in trouble should solve their problems themselves. Federal programs for the homeless reflect a consensus that limited government help is important and necessary, but that homeless people also need to help themselves.

Since 1860 the federal government has been actively involved with the housing industry, specifically the low-income housing industry. In 1860 the government conducted the first partial census of housing—by counting slave dwellings. Twenty years later the U.S. census focused on the living quarters of the rest of the population by conducting a full housing census. Since then the federal government has played an increasingly larger role in combating housing problems in the United States:

- 1937—the U.S. Housing Act established the Public Housing Administration (which was later merged into the Federal Housing Administration [FHA] and the U.S. Department of Housing and Urban Development [HUD]) to create low-rent housing programs across the country through the establishment of local public housing agencies.

- 1949—the Housing Act set the goals of "a decent home and a suitable environment" for every family and authorized an 810,000-unit public housing program over the next six years. Title I of the act created the Urban Renewal Program, and Title V created the basic rural housing program under the FHA, which put the federal government directly into the mortgage business.

- 1965—Congress established HUD. Its goal was to create a new rent supplement program for low-income households in private housing.

- 1974—the Housing and Community Development Act created a new leased-housing program that included a certificate (voucher) program, expanding housing choices for low-income tenants. The voucher program soon became known as Section 8, after the section of the act that established it.

THE MCKINNEY-VENTO HOMELESS ASSISTANCE ACT

Widespread public outcry over the plight of the homeless during the early 1980s prompted Congress to pass the Stewart B. McKinney Homeless Assistance Act of 1987. Congress renamed the act the McKinney-Vento Homeless Assistance Act in 2000 to honor Representative Bruce F. Vento's (1940–2000; D-MN) service to the homeless. The range and reach of the act has broadened over the years. Most of the money authorized by the act went, initially, toward the funding of homeless shelters. The program also funded a Supportive Housing Program, a Shelter Plus Care Program, and the Single Room Occupancy Program besides the Emergency Shelter Grants Program. Amendments to the act later enabled funding and other services to support permanent housing and other programs to help the homeless. HUD administers most McKinney-Vento funds.

In 2011 programs administered under the McKinney-Vento Homeless Assistance Act fell into three distinct categories. A cluster of activities known as the Continuum of Care programs provided competitive grants intended to help communities and organizations offer comprehensive services to the homeless. The Emergency Shelter Grants Program, a noncompetitive formula grant program, provided funds for emergency shelters to states, large cities, urban counties, and U.S. territories. The Title V program freed properties for use to house the homeless.

Continuum of Care

According to HUD, in "Homeless Assistance Programs" (2011, http://www.hud.gov/offices/cpd/homeless/programs/index.cfm), the concept behind Continuum of Care programs is as follows: "A continuum of care system is designed to address the critical problem of homelessness through a coordinated community-based process of identifying needs and building a system to address those needs. The approach is predicated on the understanding that homelessness is not caused merely by a lack of shelter, but involves a variety of underlying, unmet needs—physical, economic, and social."

Nonprofit groups and local government entities applying for funds under these programs are expected to survey and assess local needs and to write a comprehensive plan for combating homelessness and meeting needs. Grant recipients are required to assess their clients' progress and make changes in the program in response to ongoing evaluation. Three major programs—the Supportive Housing Program, the Shelter Plus Care Program, and the Single Room Occupancy Program—as well as some additional demonstration and rural efforts have developed over the years.

SUPPORTIVE HOUSING PROGRAM. The aim of the Supportive Housing Program (SHP) is to provide housing and services that will enable homeless clients to achieve economic independence and control over their life. In *Supportive Housing Program Desk Guide* (2008, http://hudhre.info/documents/SHPDeskguide.pdf), HUD explains that the SHP provides matching funds for the construction of new buildings for housing homeless people; it also provides funding for the acquisition or refurbishing of existing buildings. The program underwrites 75% of the operating cost, including administration, and up to 80% of the cost of support programs. These programs must help clients achieve independence by providing skills training, child care, education, transportation assistance, counseling, and job referrals. Elements of the program include transitional housing for 24 months, permanent housing for the disabled, supportive services without housing, havens for the hard-to-reach and the mentally ill, and other innovative programs to solve problems of homelessness.

SHELTER PLUS CARE PROGRAM. HUD notes in "Shelter Plus Care Program (S+C)" (2011, http://www.hud.gov/offices/cpd/homeless/programs/splusc/) that the Shelter Plus Care Program helps agencies that specifically target the hardest-to-serve homeless: those with mental and physical disabilities living on the street or in shelters, including drug addicts and people who are suffering from the acquired immunodeficiency syndrome (AIDS). The program provides rental assistance and other support. Housing in this program can be in the form of group homes or individual units with supportive services. Grant funds must be matched with local dollars. Subsidies for projects are available for 10 years; assistance to sponsors and tenants is available for five years. A range of supportive services for tenants must be funded through other sources. Rental assistance includes four types of contracts:

- Tenant-Based Rental Assistance—direct contract with a low-income tenant
- Project-Based Rental Assistance—building owner contracts
- Sponsor-Based Rental Assistance—contracts with nonprofit organizations
- Single-Room Occupancy–Based Rental Assistance—single-room occupancy contracts provided by public housing authorities

SINGLE ROOM OCCUPANCY PROGRAM. According to HUD, in "Single Room Occupancy Program (SRO)" (2011, http://www.hud.gov/offices/cpd/homeless/programs/sro/), single-room occupancy housing is housing in a dormitory-style building where each person has his or her own private room but shares kitchens, bathrooms, and lounges. Single Room Occupancy Program housing is generally the cheapest type of housing available. Funding is intended to encourage the establishment and operation of such housing. Subsidy payments fund a project for a period of 10 years in the form of rental assistance in amounts equal to the rent, including utilities, minus the portion of rent payable by the tenants.

OTHER PROGRAM COMPONENTS. Other programs folded under the Continuum of Care designation by HUD include demonstration programs for safe havens for the homeless, innovative homeless programs, and rural homeless housing programs.

Emergency Shelter Grants Program

The Emergency Shelter Grants Program is HUD's formula grant program administered as a part of its community planning and development grant program. In "Emergency Shelter Grants (ESG) Program" (2011, http://www.hud.gov/offices/cpd/homeless/programs/esg/), HUD explains that this "program provides homeless persons with basic shelter and essential supportive services. It can assist with the operational costs of the shelter facility, and for the administration of the grant. ESG also provides short-term homeless prevention assistance to persons at imminent risk of losing their own housing due to eviction, foreclosure, or utility shutoffs." Recipients of funding are states, large cities, urban counties, and U.S. territories that have filed consolidated community development plans with HUD. The program is called a formula program because the amounts allocated are based in part on population and poverty levels within the planning entities that participate. Grant funds flow from governmental entities to organizations that actually operate shelters and provide services to homeless people or people at risk of becoming homeless. Money may be used to help individuals avoid homelessness by providing them with emergency funds. All grantees except for state governments must match grant funds dollar for dollar.

Title V

HUD notes in "Title V" (2011, http://www.hud.gov/offices/cpd/homeless/programs/t5/) that it maintains information about and publishes listings of federal properties categorized as unutilized, underutilized, in excess, or in surplus. States, local governments, and nonprofit organizations can apply to use such properties to house the homeless. Title V does not provide funding; it provides properties to agencies for housing use. Groups may apply for funding under the Continuum of Care program to modify, refurbish, or adapt such structures for residential uses.

Consolidations, New Initiatives, and Reorganizations

HUD's programs, particularly those under Continuum of Care, have overlapping objectives yet operate under separate rules and requirements. The U.S. General Accounting Office (GAO; now the U.S. Government Accountability Office) studied the McKinney programs in 1999 and concluded in *Homelessness: Coordination and Evaluation of Programs Are Essential* (February 1999, http://www.gao.gov/archive/1999/rc99049.pdf) that the number of programs and the differences between them create barriers to their efficient use. Stanley J. Czerwinski states in *Homelessness: Improving Program Coordination and Client Access to Programs* (March 6, 2002, http://www.gao.gov/new.items/d02485t.pdf) that even though "HUD has taken actions that have improved the coordination of homeless assistance programs within communities and have helped reduce some of the administrative burdens that separate programs cause," consolidating the McKinney-Vento programs could harm homeless people if a system was not first devised to hold mainstream programs accountable for serving the homeless.

In fiscal year (FY) 2011 HUD's proposed budget for programs to help the homeless was a record $2.3 billion. HUD reports in *FY 2012 Budget Summary* (February 2011, http://portal.hud.gov/hudportal/documents/huddoc?id=fy2012budget.pdf) that the increased funding would enable the department to assist approximately 78,000 additional homeless people and families.

In February 2007 the Homeless Emergency Assistance and Rapid Transition to Housing (HEARTH) Act was introduced in the U.S. House of Representatives to reauthorize the McKinney-Vento Homeless Assistance Programs; it was reintroduced in September 2008. The bill was passed in the House in October 2008 and was introduced in the U.S. Senate in April 2009. Senator Jack Reed (1949–; D-RI) explains in the press release "Reed Unveils New Approach to Preventing and Reducing Homelessness" (April 7, 2009, http://reed.senate.gov/newsroom/details.cfm?id=311261) that the HEARTH Act provided $2.2 billion for targeted homelessness assistance programs as well as expanded the definition of homelessness. The Senate passed the bill and President Barack Obama (1961–) signed it into law in May 2009.

The HEARTH Act requires the federal government to submit an annual plan to eliminate homelessness. In 2010 the U.S. Interagency Council on Homelessness released *Opening Doors: The Federal Strategic Plan to Prevent and End Homelessness* (June 2010, http://www.usich.gov/PDF/OpeningDoors_2010_FSPPreventEndHomeless.pdf), the first comprehensive federal plan on ending homelessness. In the introduction to the report, President Obama states that "veterans should never find themselves on the streets, living without care and without hope. It is simply unacceptable for a child in this country to be without a home." The plan outlines four goals: ending chronic homelessness within five years, preventing and ending homelessness among veterans within five years, preventing and ending homelessness for families and children within 10 years, and eventually eliminating homelessness altogether. The federal government aims to increase collaborative efforts among government and organizations, increase access to affordable housing, increase economic security, improve health, and revamp homeless services to better respond to crises.

Education for Homeless Children and Youth

In response to reports that over 50% of homeless children were not attending school regularly, Congress enacted the McKinney-Vento Homeless Assistance Act's Education for Homeless Children and Youth program in 1987. The program ensures that homeless children and youth have equal access to the same free, appropriate education, including preschool education, that is provided to other children. Education for Homeless Children and Youth also provides funding for state and local school districts to implement the law. States are required to report estimated numbers of homeless children and the problems encountered in serving them. The act includes the following guidelines:

- Homeless children cannot be segregated.

- Transportation has to be provided to and from schools of origin if requested (a school of origin is the school the student attended when permanently housed, or the school in which the student was last enrolled).

- In case of a placement dispute, immediate enrollment is required pending the outcome.

- Local education agencies must put the "best interest of the child" first in determining the feasibility of keeping children in their school of origin.

- Local education agencies must designate a local liaison for homeless children and youth.

- States have to subgrant 50% to 75% of their allotments under Education for Homeless Children and Youth competitively to local education agencies.

At the time the McKinney-Vento Homeless Assistance Act was passed, only an estimated 57% of homeless children were enrolled in school. By 2000 the percentage had increased to 88%. The National Center on Family Homelessness estimates in "Homeless Children: America's New Outcasts" (March 2004, http://www.ucdenver.edu/academics/colleges/ArchitecturePlanning/discover/centers/CYE/Publications/Documents/outcasts.pdf) that in 2004 only about 80% of homeless children actually attended school. In *Education for Homeless Children and Youths Program* (April 2009, http://www2.ed.gov/programs/homeless/data-comp-04-07.pdf), the National Center for Homeless Education notes that during the 2007–08 school year 794,617 children were enrolled in school across the nation, up 114,893 from the year before, possibly due to the worsening housing crisis and rising unemployment.

In implementing the legislation, school districts found that barriers arose in areas such as residency, guardian requirements, incomplete or missing documentation (including immunization records and birth certificates), and transportation. Consequently, some school districts established separate schools for homeless children. According to Kristen Kreisher, in "Educating Homeless Children" (*Children's Voice*, September–October 2002), in 2001 there were an estimated 40 separate schools for the homeless in 19 states, and even though separate schools were outlawed with the 2002 reauthorization of the McKinney-Vento Homeless Assistance Act, those schools that already existed were allowed to remain.

Transportation became an issue for school districts providing education to homeless students. Nicole Brode reports in "New York's School Choice Leaves More Homeless Children with Hour-Plus Commutes" (*Knight-Ridder/Tribune Business News*, February 10, 2003) that 34% of the 226 students in one New York homeless shelter faced commutes of longer than an hour because their parents had opted to keep the children in the same schools they had attended before they became homeless, a right guaranteed by the new law. In "Homeless Kids Lack School to Call Home" (*Chicago Tribune*, February 13, 2009), Carlos Sadovi notes that homeless children must either change schools often or face commutes of up to several hours. According to Kathleen Kingsbury, in "Keeping Homeless Kids in School" (*Time*, March 12, 2009), in March 2009, when nearly one out of 10 children in Minneapolis, Minnesota, was homeless, children faced commutes of an hour or more.

In the fact sheet "Education of Homeless Children and Youth" (August 2007, http://www.nationalhomeless.org/publications/facts/education.html), the National Coalition for the Homeless (NCH) indicates that funding for the Education for Homeless Children and Youth program has been insufficient to meet the needs of homeless children. The National Association for the Education of Homeless Children and Youth notes in "Legislative Update" (April 11, 2011, http://www.naehcy.org/update.html) that in FY 2011 the program received $65 million. The association notes that the number of homeless children nationwide had risen markedly during the 2008–09 school year to 956,914 children due to foreclosures and the economic recession, which lasted from late 2007 to mid-2009. It also states that the current level of funding left 300,000 identified homeless children without services during the 2008–09 school year.

RESTRICTIVE ORDINANCES

According to the Centers for Disease Control and Prevention, in "Health Effects of Gentrification" (November 16, 2009, http://www.cdc.gov/healthyplaces/healthtopics/gentrification.htm), gentrification is the transformation of low-value neighborhoods to high-value neighborhoods. It typically displaces earlier—and usually poorer—residents and often destroys ethnic communities. Even though gentrification has positive aspects—reduced crime, new investment in the community, and increased economic activity—these benefits are typically enjoyed by the newcomers while the existing residents are marginalized. When a neighborhood is gentrified, the long-term population can suffer due to the lack of affordable housing. Furthermore, the visible homeless are often viewed as a blight on the quality of life of the new residents. The presence of homeless people can drive away tourists and frustrate the proprietors of local businesses. The widening gap between the haves and the have-nots in American society is evident in the plight of homeless people. As more and more privately owned, federally subsidized apartment buildings and former "skid rows" were gentrified during the economic boom of the 1990s, more of the poorest people were forced into homelessness.

In recent years there has been an increase in the enactment of laws and ordinances intended to regulate the activities of homeless people. Advocates for the homeless contend that such practices deny the homeless their most basic human, legal, and political rights.

Some local ordinances prevent homeless people from sleeping on the streets or in parks, even though there may not be enough shelter beds to accommodate every homeless person every night. The homeless may be turned out of shelters to fend for themselves during the day, yet local ordinances prevent them from loitering in public places or resting in bus stations, libraries, or public buildings. Begging or picking up cans for recycling may help the homeless to support themselves, yet often there are restrictions against panhandling (begging) or limits on the number of cans they can redeem. To see the homeless bathe or use the toilet in public makes people uncomfortable; consequently, laws are passed to prohibit such activities.

Are homeless people targeted by these laws and consequently denied their civil rights? Do such ordinances criminalize homelessness by singling out the minority (the unhoused) but not the majority (the housed)? For example, drinking alcoholic beverages in public is illegal, but the police may selectively enforce the law against street people while ignoring other drinkers, such as tourists. Ordinances disallowing life-sustaining activities performed by homeless individuals may be said to exclude the homeless from equal protection under the law.

Most measures regulating the behavior of homeless people are enacted at the community level. Sometimes the most restrictive of these laws have been challenged in federal court on the grounds that they violate the rights of the homeless people they seek to regulate. For example, a federal court may be asked to determine whether begging or panhandling is considered protected conduct under the First Amendment (freedom of speech).

Criminalizing Homelessness

Homeless people live in and move about public spaces, and many Americans believe society has a right to control or regulate what homeless people can do in these shared spaces. A city or town may introduce local ordinances or policies that are designed to restrict homeless people's activities, remove their belongings, or destroy their nontraditional living places. In many cities municipal use of criminal sanctions to protect public spaces has come into conflict with efforts by civil rights and homeless advocates to prevent the criminalization of the necessary activities of the homeless population.

There have been other approaches. Several cities have proposed or created community courts that specifically handle so-called public nuisance crimes. Other cities have implemented plans to privatize public property as a way of restricting the access of homeless people to certain areas.

Other localities pass ordinances that target homeless people in the hopes of driving them from the community. According to the National Law Center on Homelessness and Poverty and the NCH, in *Homes Not Handcuffs: The Criminalization of Homelessness in U.S. Cities* (July 2009, http://www.nationalhomeless.org/publications/crimreport/CrimzReport_2009.pdf), of 235 cities surveyed in 2009, 30% prohibited sitting or lying in some public places; 33% prohibited camping in some places and 17% prohibited it citywide; 47% prohibited loitering in some places and 19% prohibited it citywide; and 47% prohibited begging in some places, 49% prohibited aggressive panhandling, and 23% had citywide prohibitions. The number of

laws prohibiting sitting or lying, begging, and aggressive panhandling in some public places had all increased from the previous survey in 2006 by 5% or more.

Violating Human Rights

Homes Not Handcuffs states that as successful lawsuits have shown, "many of the practices and policies that punish homeless people for the public performance of life-sustaining activities violate homeless persons' constitutional rights." The report notes that nearly all the communities surveyed lacked sufficient shelter space to accommodate the homeless and suggests that the effort and money spent on bringing the homeless into the courthouse might be better directed toward addressing the nation's lack of affordable housing.

Table 7.1 illustrates the antihomeless laws that existed in some of the cities surveyed for the 2009 report. Prohibited or restricted behaviors fell under the categories of begging, panhandling, sleeping, sitting/lying, loitering/loafing/vagrancy, and obstruction of sidewalks or other public places.

Homes Not Handcuffs names Los Angeles, California; St. Petersburg, Florida; Orlando, Florida; Atlanta, Georgia; and Gainesville, Florida, as the five "meanest cities" in 2009 based on the number of antihomeless laws passed or pending, the enforcement and severity of their laws, the local support for the "meanest" designation, and the "general political climate" with regard to the homeless, among other criteria. Two examples of the practices of these cities follow.

Los Angeles spends $6 million per year to assign 50 extra police officers to the Skid Row area in downtown, which is home to the country's largest stable population of homeless people, while spending only $5.7 million per year for homeless services. Citations issued to homeless people include the crimes of jaywalking and loitering. Homeless advocates found that during an 11-month period, 24 people were arrested 201 times, at a cost of $3.6 million—an amount that could have provided housing for 225 homeless people. Based on these findings, homeless advocates and civil rights groups brought several lawsuits against the city. In October 2007 the city agreed, in *Jones v. City of Los Angeles* (505 F.3d 1006 [9th Cir.]), not to enforce a law making it illegal to sit or lay on sidewalks between the hours of 9 p.m. and 6 a.m. until it builds 1,250 units of permanent supportive housing. The city and the American Civil Liberties Union settled *Fitzgerald v. City of Los Angeles* (No. CV 03-1876 NM [C.D. Cal. 2003], 485 F. Supp. 2d 1137 [C.D. Cal.]) in December 2008. Per the settlement, police are no longer allowed to search people for jaywalking or sleeping on the street and are not allowed to place handcuffs on anyone unless the detainee is thought to be harmful or a flight risk.

TABLE 7.1

Prohibited conduct in selected cities, 2009

Column1	Begging in public places city-wide	Begging in particular public places	"Aggressive" panhandling	Sleeping in public city-side	Sleeping in particular public places	Sitting/Lying in particular public places	Loitering, loafing, vagrancy city-wide	Obstruction of sidewalks or other public places
Atlanta, GA		X	X		X	X		X
Baltimore, MD		X	X				X	X
Boston, MA		X	X		X	X		X
Chicago, IL		X	X					
Cincinnati, OH		X	X			X		X
Dallas, TX		X	X	X				X
Detroit, MI	X						X	X
Las Vegas, NV		X	X		X			X
Los Angeles, CA		X	X		X	X		X
Miami, FL		X	X	X				X
New York, NY	X		X					
Philadelphia, PA		X	X			X		X
Phoenix, AZ		X	X	X		X		X
Portland, OR		X				X		X
San Francisco, CA		X	X		X			X
Seattle, WA			X			X		X
Trenton, NJ		X	X	X		X		X
Washington, D.C.		X	X		X	X	X	X

SOURCE: Adapted from "Prohibited Conduct Chart," in *Homes Not Handcuffs: The Criminalization of Homelessness in U.S. Cities*, The National Law Center on Homelessness and Poverty and The National Coalition for the Homeless, July 2009, http://www.nationalhomeless.org/publications/crimreport/CrimzReport_2009.pdf (accessed February 18, 2011).

In January 2007 St. Petersburg police raided two homeless encampments and destroyed nearly 20 tents with scissors and knives that the owners would not take down. The raid resulted in such negative press that the city authorized a temporary tent city on a vacant lot next to a homeless service provider. That same month the St. Petersburg public defender announced that he would no longer represent homeless people charged with violating city ordinances to protest what he believed were excessive arrests of homeless people in the city. Several new ordinances targeting homeless people were passed during the same period, including prohibitions on panhandling, storage of personal belongings on public property, and sleeping outside at various locations.

The Rationale for Restrictive Ordinances

Local officials often restrict homeless people's use of public space to protect public health and safety—either of the general public, the homeless themselves, or both. Dangers to the public have included tripping over people and objects on sidewalks, intimidation of passersby caused by aggressive begging, and the spreading of diseases. Many people believe the very presence of the homeless is unsightly and their removal improves the appearance of public spaces. Other laws are based on the need to prevent crime. New York's campaign is based on the broken windows theory of the criminologists James Q. Wilson (1931–1997) and George L. Kelling (1935–), who discuss this theory in "Broken Windows" (*Atlantic Monthly*, March 1982). They argue that allowing indications of disorder, such as a broken window or street people, to remain unaddressed shows a loss of public order and control, as well as apathy in a neighborhood, which breeds more serious criminal activity. Therefore, keeping a city neat and orderly should help prevent crime.

All these are legitimate concerns to some degree. The problem, critics say, is that rather than trying to eliminate or reduce homelessness by helping the homeless find housing and jobs, most local laws try to change the behavior of the homeless by punishing them. They target the homeless with legal action, ignoring the fact that many would gladly stop living on the streets and panhandling if they had any feasible alternatives. Even though these laws may be effective in the sense that the shanties are gone and homeless people are not allowed to bed down in subway tunnels or doorways, the fact remains that homelessness has not been eradicated. Homeless people have simply been forced to move to a different part of town, have hidden themselves, or have been imprisoned. Furthermore, many of these laws have been challenged in court as violating the legal rights of the homeless people they target.

Alternative Strategies

Homes Not Handcuffs emphasizes that criminalization does nothing to address the problem and that local government, police officials, and business groups should work with advocates and providers for the homeless to come up with solutions that prevent and end homelessness. For example, more resources should be made available for affordable housing projects, homeless shelters, and other services. Business groups could put resources toward solutions to end homelessness rather than toward lobbying for criminalization methods. *Homes Not Handcuffs* states that "practices that criminalize homelessness do nothing to address the underlying causes of homelessness. Instead, they drastically exacerbate the problem. They frequently move people away from services. When homeless persons are arrested and charged under these ordinances, they may develop a criminal record, making it more difficult to obtain the employment and/or housing that could help them become self-sufficient."

Alternatives to criminalizing homeless behavior can be implemented with help from community leaders and homeless advocates, who have intimate knowledge from close contact with the homeless. *Homes Not Handcuffs* details the innovative programs that some cities have put in place to better deal with the problem of homelessness.

A key element in the most successful programs is the partnering of the local government with advocacy organizations. For example, in Cleveland, Ohio, the city contracted with the Northeast Ohio Coalition for the Homeless to bring groups who serve food to the homeless together to talk about how to improve services. Because the city was concerned about food being served in the public square in the city center, the city provided a parking lot with access to bathrooms and an indoor location 18 blocks to the east. The city also provided an overnight indoor location where churches can bring food and clothing for distribution to the homeless.

Portland, Oregon, provides another successful example. The city funds a program called "A Key Not a Card" that enables workers from homeless service organizations to offer housing to homeless people. Between 2005 and 2009, 936 people in 451 households had been housed; after one year, three-quarters of the households remained housed, demonstrating the success of the initiative.

CONSTITUTIONAL RIGHTS OF THE HOMELESS

The U.S. Constitution and its amendments, especially the Bill of Rights, guarantee certain freedoms and rights to all U.S. citizens, including the homeless. As more and more cities move to deal with homelessness by aggressively enforcing public place restrictions, the restrictions are increasingly being challenged in court as unconstitutional. Sometimes a city ordinance is declared unconstitutional; at other times a court finds that there are special circumstances that allow the ordinance to stand.

There are many ways in which ordinances affecting the homeless can violate their rights. Many court challenges claim that the law in question is unconstitutionally broad or vague. Others claim that a particular law denies the homeless equal protection under the law or violates their right to due process, as guaranteed by the Fifth and 14th Amendments. There are also cases based on a person's right to travel, and others that claim restrictions on

the homeless constitute "cruel and unusual punishment," which is prohibited by the Eighth Amendment. Many cities have ordinances against panhandling, but charitable organizations freely solicit in public places. As a result, according to those challenging the ordinances, the right to free expression under the First Amendment is available to organizations but denied to the homeless.

The appearance of poverty should not deny an individual's right against unreasonable search and seizure, as guaranteed by the Fourth Amendment. Often, homeless people's property has been confiscated or destroyed (such as camping gear or personal possessions) without warning because it was found on public property. The state of homelessness is such that even the most personal living activities have to be performed in public. Denying activities that are necessary for survival may infringe on an individual's rights under the Eighth Amendment.

The 14th Amendment's right to equal protection under the law may be at issue when the homeless are cited for sleeping in the park, but others lying on the grass sunning themselves or taking a nap during a picnic, for instance, are not.

Testing the Constitutionality of Laws in Court

Some court cases test the law through civil suits, and others challenge the law by appealing convictions in criminal cases. Many advocates for the homeless, or the homeless themselves, challenge laws that they believe infringe on the rights of homeless people.

NO BED, NO ARREST. The concept of "no bed, no arrest" first arose out of a 1988 class action suit filed by the Miami Chapter of the American Civil Liberties Union on behalf of about 6,000 homeless people living in Miami, Florida. The city had a practice of sweeping the homeless from the areas where the Orange Bowl Parade and other related activities were held. The complaint in *Pottinger v. City of Miami* (S.D.Fla. 810 F. Supp. 1551 [1992]) alleged that the city had "a custom, practice and policy of arresting, harassing and otherwise interfering with homeless people for engaging in basic activities of daily life— including sleeping and eating—in the public places where they are forced to live. Plaintiffs further claim that the City has arrested thousands of homeless people for such life-sustaining conduct under various City of Miami ordinances and Florida Statutes. In addition, plaintiffs assert that the city routinely seizes and destroys their property and has failed to follow its own inventory procedures regarding the seized personal property of homeless arrestees and homeless persons in general."

The U.S. District Court for the Southern District of Florida ruled in *Pottinger* that the city's practices were cruel and unusual, in violation of the Eighth Amendment's ban against punishment based on status (only the homeless were being arrested). Furthermore, the court found the police practices of taking or destroying the property of the homeless to be in violation of the Fourth and Fifth Amendments' rights of freedom from unreasonable seizure and confiscation of property.

The city appealed the district court's judgment. Ultimately, a settlement was reached in which Miami agreed that a homeless person who is observed committing a "life-sustaining conduct" misdemeanor may be warned to stop, but if there is no available shelter, no warning is to be given. If there is an available shelter, the homeless person is to be told of its availability. If the homeless person accepts assistance, no arrest is to take place.

In *In re Eichorn* (81 Cal. Rptr. 2d 535 [Cal. App. Dep't. Super. Ct. 2000]), James Eichorn challenged his arrest for sleeping outside a county office building in Santa Ana, California. He attempted to prove, per the "no bed, no arrest" policy, that on the night he was arrested there were no shelter beds available. However, the court would not allow a jury to consider his necessity defense, and Eichorn was subsequently convicted and lost his appeal. Eichorn's lawyer then filed a writ of habeas corpus. The appeals court found that Eichorn should have been allowed to present his necessity defense, and the conviction was set aside and remanded back to the municipal court. Subsequently, the district attorney decided not to retry him. In essence, the case reaffirmed the "no bed, no arrest" policy.

In *Sipprelle v. City of Laguna Beach* (No. 8:2008-cv01447 [2008]), a group of homeless people challenged a city ordinance in Laguna Beach, California, that prohibits sleeping in public places. The complaint states that the police prohibit the homeless from carrying out life-sustaining activities, including sleeping in public places, when there are no shelter beds available. The lawsuit was successful when the city council repealed the ordinance in June 2009.

SLEEPING OUTDOORS. Sarasota, Florida, passed a series of ordinances after 2000 that were designed to criminalize sleeping outdoors; two were overturned by state courts. A third ordinance made it illegal to sleep outdoors on either private or public property without permission of the property owner or the city manager if one of the following conditions existed: many personal objects were present (indicating the person is homeless), the person is cooking or maintaining a fire, the person is digging, or the person states he or she is homeless. This law survived the constitutionality test in *City of Sarasota v. McGinnis* (No. 2005 MO 16411 NC [Fla. Cir. Ct. 2005]). However, Sarasota's ordinance against sleeping outdoors was found unconstitutional in *City of Sarasota v. Nipper* (No. 2005 MO 4369 NC [Fla. Cir. Ct. 2005]), in which the court found that the law punished innocent conduct and left too much discretion in the hands of the police.

LOITERING OR WANDERING. In 2000 homeless street dwellers and shelter residents of the Skid Row area (the plaintiffs) sought a temporary restraining order (TRO) against the Los Angeles Police Department (the defendant), claiming that their First and Fourth Amendment rights were being violated. The plaintiffs alleged that they were being stopped without cause and their identification demanded on threat of arrest; that they were being ordered to "move along" even though they were not in anyone's way; that their belongings were being confiscated; and that they were being ticketed for loitering. In *Justin v. City of Los Angeles* (No. CV-00-12352 LGB, 2000 U.S. Dist. Lexis 17881 [C.D. Cal. December 5, 2000]), Judge Lourdes G. Baird (1935–) denied a TRO that would have prevented the defendant from asking the plaintiffs to "move along." The TRO was granted with reference to the following actions when in the Skid Row area:

- Detention without reasonable suspicion
- Demand of identification on threat of arrest
- Searches without probable cause
- Removal from sidewalks unless free passage of pedestrians was obstructed
- Confiscation of personal property that was not abandoned
- Citation of those who may "annoy or molest" if interference was reasonable and free passage of pedestrians was not impeded

LIVING IN AN ENCAMPMENT. In 1996 advocates for the homeless sought an injunction against a Tucson, Arizona, resolution barring homeless encampments from city-owned property on Eighth Amendment and equal protection grounds. In *Davidson v. City of Tucson* (924 F. Supp. 989), the court held that the plaintiffs did not have standing to raise a cruel and unusual punishment claim, as they had not been convicted of a crime and no one had been arrested under the ordinance. The equal protection claim failed because the court did not consider homeless people a suspect class and the right to travel did not include the right to ignore trespass laws or remain on property without regard to ownership.

A Sarasota law prohibited camping on public and private property between sunset and sunrise. Five homeless people challenged the law, arguing that it punished innocent conduct and was unconstitutionally vague. The circuit court found in *City of Sarasota v. Tillman* (No. 2003 CA 15645 NC [Fla. Cir. Ct. 2004]) that the law was unconstitutional for criminalizing the noncriminal act of sleeping.

PANHANDLING. One of the notable court cases addressing panhandling involved Jennifer Loper, who moved from her parents' suburban New York home to beg on the streets of New York City. From time to time she and her friend William Kaye were ordered by police to move on, in accordance with the city ordinance, which stated: "A person is guilty of loitering when he: '(1) Loiters, remains or wanders about in a public place for the purpose of begging.'" In 1992 Loper and Kaye sued the city, claiming that their free speech rights had been violated and that the ordinance was unconstitutional. A district court declared the ordinance unconstitutional on First Amendment grounds. On appeal, the police department argued that begging has no expressive element that is protected by the First Amendment. In *Loper v. New York City Police Department* (999 F.2d 699 [2d Cir. 1993]), the U.S. Court of Appeals for the Second Circuit declared the city's ban on begging invalid, noting that the regulations applied to sidewalks, which have historically been acknowledged to be a public forum. The court agreed that the ban deprived beggars of all means to express their message. Even if a panhandler does not speak, "the presence of an unkempt and disheveled person holding out his or her hand or a cup to receive a donation itself conveys a message of need for support and assistance."

In *Chase v. City of Gainesville* (2006 WL 2620260 [N.D. Fla. Sept. 11, 2006]), a group of homeless people challenged the constitutionality of three antisolicitation laws in Gainesville. Two of the laws prohibited holding signs on sidewalks or by the side of the road soliciting donations, while the third law required anyone seeking charitable contributions on sidewalks or roadways to obtain a permit. The homeless people argued that soliciting donations should be protected under the First Amendment. The court granted a preliminary injunction and in September 2006 the lawsuit was settled, which included a permanent injunction against enforcement of the three laws.

ZONING THE HOMELESS OUT OF DOWNTOWN. In 1998 Alan Mason, a homeless man, sought an injunction, damages, and relief against the city of Tucson and the city police for zoning homeless people. The suit alleged that homeless people were arrested without cause, were charged with misdemeanors, and were then released only if they agreed to stay away from the area where they had been arrested. Mason himself had been restricted from certain downtown areas, such as federal, state, and local courts (including the court in which his case was tried); voter registration facilities; a soup kitchen; places of worship; and many social and transportation agencies.

The plaintiff argued that such restrictions violated his constitutional right to travel, deprived him of liberty without due process in violation of the Fifth Amendment, and implicated the equal protection clause of the 14th Amendment. In *Mason v. Tucson* (D. Arizona, 1998), the district court granted a temporary injunction against enforcing the law, saying the zone restrictions were overbroad. The case was subsequently settled out of court.

SLEEPING ON SIDEWALKS. In 2006 a federal appeals court in Pasadena, California, ruled that ordinances against homeless people "sitting, lying, or sleeping" on sidewalks are unconstitutional. In *Jones v. City of Los Angeles* (444 F.3d 1118 [9th Cir.]), the court ruled that Los Angeles enforced the law only against homeless people, therefore criminalizing "the status of homelessness," which violated the Eighth Amendment. It was the first time in more than a decade that a law criminalizing homelessness had been struck down in court.

CHAPTER 8
HEALTH AND HUNGER

HEALTH OF POOR PEOPLE

Connection between Poor Health and Poverty

The National Center for Health Statistics (NCHS) points out in *Health, United States, 2010* (February 2011, http://www.cdc.gov/nchs/data/hus/hus10.pdf) that poverty causes poor health due to its connection with a nutritionally poor diet, substandard housing, exposure to the elements and environmental hazards, unhealthy lifestyle, and decreased access to and use of health care services. Testifying before the U.S. House of Representatives' Committee on Ways and Means on January 24, 2007, Jane Knitzer (http://www.nccp.org/publications/pdf/text_705.pdf), the director of the National Center for Children in Poverty, stated that economic hardship in childhood is linked to poor health and that poor health adversely affects educational attainment and future productivity, leading to a cycle of poverty.

Poor people are more likely to suffer from chronic (long-term) conditions that limit their activities. According to the NCHS, 14.8% of the population had difficulty with basic actions or limitations on complex activity in 2009. Nearly three out of 10 (29.3%) people living below the poverty line suffered from these issues, compared with 22.6% of those whose household incomes were 100% to 199% of the poverty level, 15% of those whose household incomes were 200% to 399% of the poverty level, and 7.3% of those whose incomes were 400% or more of the poverty level. In addition, 14.3% of adults with incomes below the poverty line had difficulty seeing even with corrective lenses, compared with 11.1% of people with incomes 100% to 199% of the poverty line, 8% of people with incomes 200% to 399% of the poverty line, and 5.7% of people with incomes 400% of the poverty line or higher.

The NCHS also reports that poor respondents were much more likely to rate their health as only fair or poor, compared with their more affluent peers. In 2009 more than one out of five (21.8%) people with incomes below the poverty level rated their health as fair or poor, compared with 14.9% of people with incomes 100% to 199% of the poverty level, 8.6% of people with incomes 200% to 399% of the poverty level, and only 4.3% of people with incomes 400% of the poverty level or higher.

According to the NCHS, poor people also have more mental health problems. In 2008–09 only 1.1% of people with incomes 400% of the poverty level or higher reported that they suffered from serious psychological distress within the past 30 days. However, 4.9% of people with incomes 100% to 199% of the poverty line and 9% of people with incomes below the poverty level reported such psychological distress.

Poverty and Access to Health Care

The NCHS notes in *Health, United States, 2010* that poor and near-poor people have reduced access to medical care. In 2009, 24.8% of those living below the poverty level and 24% of those with incomes of 100% to 199% of the poverty level reported either not receiving care or delaying care because of cost. In contrast, 16.8% of those with incomes of 200% to 399% of the poverty level and 7.2% of people with incomes of 400% of the poverty level or higher reported not receiving or delaying health care due to cost. In addition, 20.5% of people with incomes below the poverty level and 18.8% of people with incomes 100% to 199% of the poverty level did not get prescription drugs because of the cost, compared with 12.2% of people with incomes 200% to 399% of the poverty level and only 4.1% of those with incomes 400% of the poverty level or higher. The percentage of people unable to access prescription drugs because of their cost has risen markedly in all socioeconomic groups since 1997. Nearly all Americans are affected by skyrocketing health care costs. The Kaiser Family Foundation explains in *Public Opinion on Health Care Issues* (March 2011, http://www.kff.org/kaiserpolls/upload/8166-F.pdf) that more than half of

American families postponed or did without medical treatments in 2010 due to the lack of affordable health care.

A higher percentage of poor and low-income children in 2008–09 had not visited the doctor in the previous 12 months than children in higher income families; this was particularly true among Hispanic children. According to the NCHS, 15.4% of Hispanic children living in households with incomes below the poverty level and 17.7% of Hispanic children with incomes 100% to 199% of the poverty level had not visited a doctor in the previous year, whereas 12.4% of Hispanic children living in households with incomes 200% to 399% of the poverty level and 9.7% of Hispanic children living in households with incomes at 400% of the poverty level or higher had not visited a doctor in the past year. Among non-Hispanic white children, 13.4% of those living below the poverty level, 12.8% of those living at 100% to 199% of the poverty level, 8.7% of those living at 200% to 399% of the poverty level, and 4.8% of those living at 400% or more of the poverty level had not seen a doctor in the previous year. Among African-American children, 11.8% of those living below the poverty level, 13.4% of those living at 100% to 199% of the poverty level, 10.5% of those living at 200% to 399% of the poverty level, and 7.7% of those living at 400% or more

of the poverty level had failed to see a doctor within the past year.

HEALTH INSURANCE

The scope of health issues regarding the impoverished and homeless in the United States is related in part to the number of uninsured Americans. People without insurance are less likely to seek medical care. When they do seek medical care, they are more likely to go to an emergency department, which leads to skyrocketing health care costs. Figure 8.1 shows that the number of uninsured people rose sharply during the so-called Great Recession, which lasted from late 2007 to mid-2009. The uninsured rate in 2009, at 16.7%, was the highest it had been in decades. The number of uninsured nonelderly adults rose sharply between 2008 and 2009, from 38.4 million to 42.5 million. (See Figure 8.2.) Even though the number of uninsured children had been dropping since 2006, it rose slightly again to 7.5 million in 2009.

In 2009 Hispanic people were the most likely to be uninsured. A third (34%) of Hispanics were uninsured, followed by Native Americans (28%) and non-Hispanic African-Americans (23%). (See Figure 8.3.) In contrast,

FIGURE 8.1

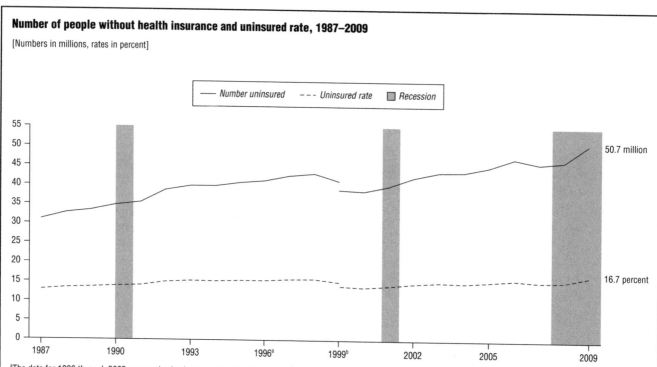

Number of people without health insurance and uninsured rate, 1987–2009

[Numbers in millions, rates in percent]

— Number uninsured   - - - Uninsured rate   ▨ Recession

50.7 million

16.7 percent

aThe data for 1996 through 2003 were revised using an approximation method for consistency with the revision to the 2004 and 2005 estimates.
bImplementation of Census 2000-based population controls occurred for the 2000 Annual Social and Economic Supplement (ASEC), which collected data for 1999. The estimates also reflect the results of follow-up verification questions, which were asked of people who responded "no" to all questions about specific types of health insurance coverage in order to verify whether they were actually uninsured. This change increased the number of percentage of people covered by health insurance, bringing the Current Population Survey (CPS) more in line with estimates from other national surveys.
Notes: Respondents were not asked detailed health insurance questions before the 1988 CPS. The data points are placed at the midpoints of the respective years.

SOURCE: Carmen DeNavas-Walt, Bernadette D. Proctor, and Jessica C. Smith, "Figure 7. Number Uninsured and Uninsured Rate: 1987 to 2009," in *Income, Poverty, and Health Insurance Coverage in the United States: 2009*, Current Population Reports, U.S. Census Bureau, September 2010, http://www.census.gov/prod/2010pubs/p60-238.pdf (accessed February 17, 2011)

FIGURE 8.2

Number of children and nonelderly adults without health insurance, 2004–09

[In millions]

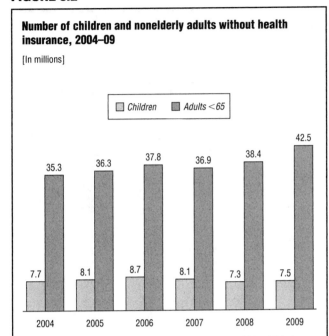

SOURCE: "Figure 8. Number of Uninsured Children and Non-Elderly Adults, 2004–2009," in "The Uninsured: A Primer" (#7296), The Henry J. Kaiser Family, December 2010, http://www.kff.org/uninsured/upload/7451-06.pdf (accessed February 18, 2011). This information was reprinted with permission from the Henry J. Kaiser Family Foundation. The Kaiser Family Foundation is a non-profit private operating foundation, based in Menlo Park, California, dedicated to producing and communicating the best possible analysis and information on health issues.

FIGURE 8.3

Health insurance coverage of nonelderly persons by race and Hispanic origin, 2009

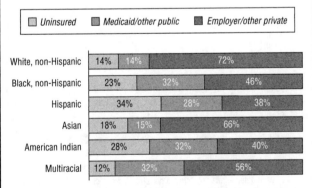

Notes: Asian group includes Pacific Islanders. American Indian Group includes Aleutian Eskimos. Data may not total 100% due to rounding.

SOURCE: "Figure 5. Insurance Coverage of Nonelderly by Race/Ethnicity, 2009," in "The Uninsured: A Primer" (#7296), The Henry J. Kaiser Family, December 2010, http://www.kff.org/uninsured/upload/7451-06.pdf (accessed February 18, 2011). This information was reprinted with permission from the Henry J. Kaiser Family Foundation. The Kaiser Family Foundation is a non-profit private operating foundation, based in Menlo Park, California, dedicated to producing and communicating the best possible analysis and information on health issues.

18% of Asian-Americans and 14% of non-Hispanic whites were uninsured.

Certain demographic factors make it more likely that a family will not have health insurance. The lower a household's income, the more likely a family does not carry health insurance. In 2009, 26.6% of households earning less than $25,000 per year had no health insurance. (See Table 8.1.) In contrast, only 9.1% of households with incomes of $75,000 or more per year were uninsured. In addition, young adults aged 18 to 24 years were the most likely group to not have health insurance coverage—three out of 10 (30.4%) were uninsured. Foreign-born residents were more likely to be uninsured than were native-born residents (34.5% and 14.1%, respectively).

Table 8.2 lists the uninsured rate by state in 2008. In that year the national uninsured rate was 15.4%. In some states the uninsured rate was much higher. For example, more than one out of five people in Louisiana (20.1%) and New Mexico (23.7%) and a quarter of people in Texas (25.1%) lacked health insurance. Other states had much lower rates, especially Massachusetts (5.5%), where a state law requires most individuals to carry health insurance. Figure 8.4 shows that the states with the highest uninsured rates in 2008–09 were concentrated in the South and West, whereas states with the lowest uninsured rates were concentrated in the Midwest and Northeast.

Children in poverty were much more likely than children in general to be uninsured in 2009 (15.1% and 10%, respectively). (See Figure 8.5.) However, this rate varied greatly by race. Hispanic children (16.8%) were far more likely to be uninsured than African-American children (11.5%), Asian-American children (10%), or non-Hispanic white children (7%).

Barack Obama (1961–) campaigned for the presidency in 2008 with a pledge to reform the health care system in order to provide accessible health care for all Americans. Once President Obama took office in January 2009, he signed into law the reauthorization of the Children's Health Insurance Program (CHIP), which will provide coverage for an additional 4 million children by 2013. The American Recovery and Reinvestment Act of 2009, which was signed into law in February 2009, included $1 billion to digitize medical records and provide information on treatments to doctors, measures that the administration believes will reduce health care costs.

Health Care Reform

However, Obama's biggest achievement during his first two years in office was shepherding through Congress a comprehensive health care reform law. The fight over the proposed reform began soon after Obama's inauguration and was divided along partisan lines. In the end, no Republicans voted for the final version because they believed the

TABLE 8.1

People without health insurance coverage by selected characteristics, 2008 and 2009

[Numbers in thousands]

Characteristic	2008			2009			Change in uninsured[a]	
	Total	Uninsured		Total	Uninsured		Number	Percent
		Number	Percent		Number	Percent		
Total	**301,483**	**46,340**	**15.4**	**304,280**	**50,674**	**16.7**	**4,335**	**1.3**
Family status								
In families	248,301	35,248	14.2	249,384	38,228	15.3	2,981	1.1
Householder	78,874	10,535	13.4	78,867	11,586	14.7	1,050	1.3
Related children under 18	72,980	7,025	9.6	73,410	7,202	9.8	177	0.2
Related children under 6	24,884	2,142	8.6	25,104	2,275	9.1	134	0.5
In unrelated subfamilies	1,207	300	24.9	1,357	364	26.8	64	1.9
Unrelated individuals	51,975	10,791	20.8	53,539	12,082	22.6	1,290	1.8
Race[b] and Hispanic origin								
White	240,852	34,890	14.5	242,403	38,399	15.8	3,509	1.4
White, not Hispanic	197,159	21,322	10.8	197,436	23,658	12.0	2,336	1.2
Black	38,076	7,284	19.1	38,624	8,102	21.0	818	1.8
Asian	13,315	2,344	17.6	14,011	2,409	17.2	65	−0.4
Hispanic (any race)	47,485	14,558	30.7	48,901	15,820	32.4	1,263	1.7
Age								
Under 65 years	263,695	45,693	17.3	265,667	49,998	18.8	4,305	1.5
Under 18 years	74,510	7,348	9.9	75,040	7,513	10.0	165	0.1
18 to 24 years	28,688	8,200	28.6	29,313	8,923	30.4	723	1.9
25 to 34 years	40,520	10,754	26.5	41,085	11,963	29.1	1,209	2.6
35 to 44 years	41,322	8,035	19.4	40,447	8,759	21.7	723	2.2
45 to 64 years	78,655	11,355	14.4	79,782	12,840	16.1	1,485	1.7
65 years and older	37,788	646	1.7	38,613	676	1.8	30	—
Nativity								
Native born	264,733	34,036	12.9	266,674	37,694	14.1	3,658	1.3
Foreign born	36,750	12,304	33.5	37,606	12,980	34.5	677	1.0
Naturalized citizen	15,475	2,792	18.0	16,024	3,044	19.0	252	1.0
Not a citizen	21,274	9,511	44.7	21,581	9,936	46.0	425	1.3
Region								
Northeast	54,191	6,277	11.6	54,654	6,789	12.4	512	0.8
Midwest	65,672	7,588	11.6	66,096	8,770	13.3	1,181	1.7
South	110,845	20,154	18.2	112,312	22,105	19.7	1,951	1.5
West	70,775	12,321	17.4	71,218	13,011	18.3	690	0.9
Residence								
Inside metropolitan statistical areas	253,399	39,023	15.4	256,383	43,028	16.8	4,006	1.4
Inside principal cities	97,364	17,963	18.4	97,856	19,270	19.7	1,307	1.2
Outside principal cities	156,036	21,060	13.5	158,527	23,758	15.0	2,699	1.5
Outside metropolitan statistical areas[c]	48,083	7,317	15.2	47,897	7,646	16.0	329	0.7
Household income								
Less than $25,000	55,814	13,673	24.5	58,159	15,483	26.6	1,811	2.1
$25,000 to $49,999	69,621	14,908	21.4	71,340	15,278	21.4	369	—
$50,000 to $74,999	57,525	8,034	14.0	58,381	9,352	16.0	1,318	2.1
$75,000 or more	118,523	9,725	8.2	116,400	10,561	9.1	836	0.9
Work experience								
Total, 18 to 64 years old	**189,185**	**38,345**	**20.3**	**190,627**	**42,485**	**22.3**	**4,140**	**2.0**
All workers	148,463	27,772	18.7	145,184	29,263	20.2	1,491	1.4
Worked full-time, year-round	100,626	14,723	14.6	95,808	14,589	15.2	−134	0.6
Less than full-time, year-round	47,837	13,049	27.3	49,376	14,674	29.7	1,625	2.4
Did not work	40,723	10,573	26.0	45,443	13,222	29.1	2,649	3.1

—Represents or rounds to zero.

[a]Details may not sum to totals because of rounding.

[b]Federal surveys now give respondents the option of reporting more than one race. Therefore, two basic ways of defining a race group are possible. A group such as Asian may be defined as those who reported Asian and no other race (the race-alone or single-race concept) or as those who reported Asian regardless of whether they also reported another race (the race-alone-or-in-combination concept). This table shows data using the first approach (race alone). The use of the single-race population does not imply that it is the preferred method of presenting or analyzing data. The Census Bureau uses a variety of approaches. Information on people who reported more than one race, such as white and American Indian and Alaska Native or Asian and black or African American, is available from Census 2000 through American FactFinder. About 2.6 percent of people reported more than one race in Census 2000. Data for American Indians and Alaska Natives, Native Hawaiians and other Pacific Islanders, and those reporting two or more races are not shown separately.

[c]The "Outside metropolitan statistical areas" category includes both micropolitan statistical areas and territory outside of metropolitan and micropolitan statistical areas.

SOURCE: Carmen DeNavas-Walt, Bernadette D. Proctor, and Jessica C. Smith, "Table 8. People without Health Insurance Coverage by Selected Characteristics: 2008 and 2009," in *Income, Poverty, and Health Insurance Coverage in the United States: 2009*, Current Population Reports, U.S. Census Bureau, September 2010, http://www.census.gov/prod/2010pubs/p60-238.pdf (accessed February 17, 2011).

TABLE 8.2

Persons with and without health insurance coverage by state, 2008

[255,143 represents 255,143,000]

State	Total persons covered (1,000)	Total persons not covered		Children not covered	
		Number (1,000)	Percent of total	Number (1,000)	Percent of total
U.S.*	255,143	46,340	15.4	7,348	9.9
AL	4,159	561	11.9	41	3.6
AK	539	133	19.8	26	14.5
AZ	5,264	1,273	19.5	278	16.0
AR	2,322	505	17.8	65	9.2
CA	29,868	6,822	18.6	998	10.5
CO	4,136	780	15.9	150	12.3
CT	3,094	343	10.0	44	5.4
DE	769	94	10.8	19	9.1
DC	533	59	10.0	7	6.3
FL	14,430	3,619	20.0	676	16.7
GA	7,850	1,703	17.8	266	10.5
HI	1,159	98	7.8	15	5.4
ID	1,282	236	15.6	37	8.9
IL	11,065	1,638	12.9	205	6.4
IN	5,522	772	12.3	96	6.0
IA	2,707	283	9.5	38	5.3
KS	2,394	330	12.1	78	11.0
KY	3,574	682	16.0	102	10.0
LA	3,465	869	20.1	127	11.3
ME	1,182	137	10.4	16	5.7
MD	4,870	669	12.1	81	6.0
MA	6,069	352	5.5	49	3.4
MI	8,665	1,151	11.7	113	4.7
MN	4,676	444	8.7	81	6.6
MS	2,388	519	17.9	105	13.4
MO	5,132	739	12.6	96	6.8
MT	819	158	16.1	23	10.5
NE	1,565	211	11.9	46	10.1
NV	2,097	487	18.8	129	19.1
NH	1,168	133	10.2	11	3.6
NJ	7,323	1,201	14.1	231	11.3
NM	1,510	468	23.7	82	16.1
NY	16,617	2,720	14.1	310	7.1
NC	7,832	1,421	15.4	216	9.3
ND	552	74	11.8	12	7.9
OH	10,088	1,309	11.5	161	5.8
OK	3,060	498	14.0	65	7.2
OR	3,194	621	16.3	102	11.6
PA	10,984	1,211	9.9	185	6.7
RI	921	123	11.8	19	7.9
SC	3,762	707	15.8	137	12.8
SD	698	100	12.5	20	9.9
TN	5,252	931	15.1	139	9.4
TX	18,110	6,084	25.1	1,217	17.9
UT	2,396	364	13.2	83	9.5
VT	555	57	9.2	5	3.8
VA	6,786	962	12.4	129	6.9
WA	5,732	808	12.4	107	6.8
WV	1,528	271	15.0	24	6.3
WI	5,020	535	9.6	77	5.8
WY	458	72	13.6	12	8.8

*The estimates are revised from the originally published data.

SOURCE: "Table 152. Persons with and without Health Insurance Coverage by State: 2008," in *Statistical Abstract of the United States: 2011*, 130th ed., U.S. Census Bureau, January 2011, http://www.census.gov/compendia/statab/2011/tables/11s0152.pdf (accessed February 18, 2011)

law gave the government too much control over the health care system.

The Affordable Care Act was signed into law in March 2010. The law provided tax credits for small businesses offering health insurance to their employees and expanded the coverage offered by Medicaid. By the end of 2010 several important provisions of the law had taken effect, including providing people with preexisting conditions access to a Preexisting Condition Insurance Plan, extending coverage for children under parents' health care plans until the children are 26 years old, mandating free preventive care, eliminating lifetime limits on insurance coverage, prohibiting insurance companies from denying coverage of children based on preexisting conditions, assisting states to implement measures to stop insurance companies from hiking premium rates, and funding expanded health care services. In 2011 seniors received prescription drug discounts and free preventive care, and a provision of the law took effect that required insurers to spend 80% to 85% of all premiums collected on health care services.

Several measures to increase efficiency in the health care system are slated to take effect in 2012. In 2013 Medicaid payments to primary care doctors are projected to increase and CHIP will receive additional funding.

The major provisions of the law will take effect by the end of 2014. Discrimination based on preexisting conditions or gender will be illegal, annual limits on health insurance coverage will be eliminated, tax credits for the purchase of health insurance will take effect, and the small business tax credit on providing health care coverage to employees will increase. Medicaid coverage will be expanded and Health Insurance Exchanges will be established that will allow individuals to purchase health insurance in a competitive marketplace. At that time, most people will be required to buy insurance or pay a fee.

Challenges to the Affordable Care Act were ongoing as of April 2011. When the Republicans took control of the House following the 2010 congressional elections, the House voted to repeal the law in a largely symbolic vote, as the Democratic-controlled U.S. Senate quickly voted down the bill. The article "Health Care Reform" (*New York Times*, March 4, 2011) reports that by March 2011 over 20 challenges to the law had been filed in courts around the nation. Most of the challenges centered on the requirement that nearly all Americans buy insurance or pay a penalty. The article surmises that "the issue is considered almost certain to be determined by the Supreme Court."

Medicaid

Medicaid, which is authorized under Title XIX of the Social Security Act, is a federal-state program that provides medical insurance for low-income people who are aged, blind, disabled, or members of families with dependent children and for certain other pregnant women and children. Within federal guidelines, each state designs and administers its own program. For this reason, there may be considerable differences from state to state as to who is covered, what type of coverage is provided, and how much is paid for medical services. States receive federal matching payments

FIGURE 8.4

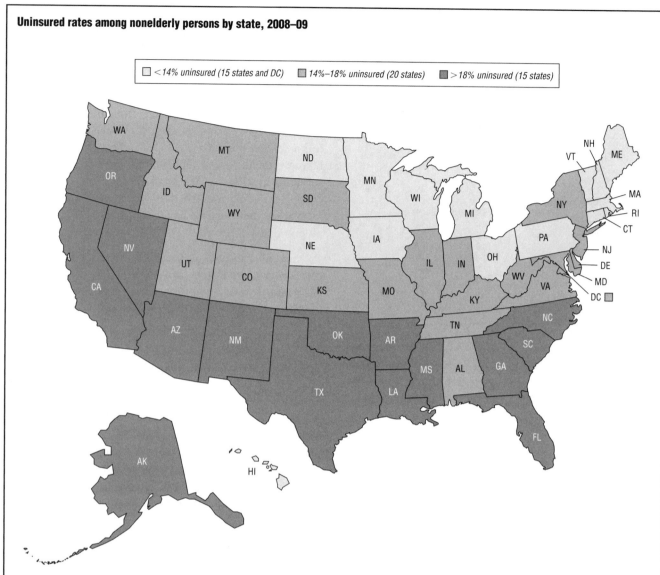

Uninsured rates among nonelderly persons by state, 2008–09

☐ <14% uninsured (15 states and DC)   ▨ 14%–18% uninsured (20 states)   ▧ >18% uninsured (15 states)

SOURCE: "Figure 7. Uninsured Rates among Nonelderly by State, 2008–2009," in "The Uninsured: A Primer" (#7296), The Henry J. Kaiser Family, December 2010, http://www.kff.org/uninsured/upload/7451-06.pdf (accessed February 18, 2011). This information was reprinted with permission from the Henry J. Kaiser Family Foundation. The Kaiser Family Foundation is a non-profit private operating foundation, based in Menlo Park, California, dedicated to producing and communicating the best possible analysis and information on health issues.

based on their Medicaid expenditures and the state's per capita (per person) income. The federal match ranges from 50% to 80% of Medicaid expenditures. Figure 8.6 illustrates the importance of Medicaid; in 2009, 15.7% of Americans were covered by Medicaid. Carmen DeNavas-Walt, Bernadette D. Proctor, and Jessica C. Smith of the U.S. Census Bureau report in *Income, Poverty, and Health Insurance Coverage in the United States: 2009* (September 2010, http://www.census.gov/prod/2010pubs/p60-238.pdf) that this was the highest rate of Medicaid coverage since 1987.

Even though Medicaid eligibility had been linked to receipt of, or eligibility to receive, benefits under Aid to Families with Dependent Children or Supplemental Security Income, legislation gradually extended coverage during

the 1980s and 1990s. In 1986 benefits were extended to low-income children and pregnant women not on welfare. States must cover children less than six years of age and pregnant women with family incomes below 133% of the federal poverty level. Pregnant women are only covered for medical services that are related to their pregnancies, and children receive full Medicaid coverage. The states may cover children under one year old and pregnant women with incomes more than 133%, but not more than 185%, of the poverty level. Medicaid also covers aged and disabled people receiving Medicare whose incomes are below 100% of the poverty level.

States may deny Medicaid benefits to adults who lose Temporary Assistance for Needy Families (TANF) benefits because they refuse to work. However, the law

FIGURE 8.5

Uninsured children by poverty status, household income, age, race and Hispanic origin, and nativity, 2009

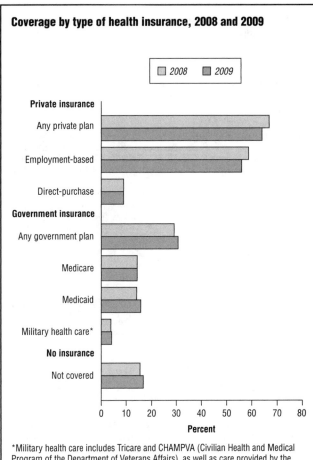

(Bar chart showing percent uninsured, 0 to 35)

- All children
- Children in poverty

Household income
- Less than $25,000
- $25,000 to $49,999
- $50,000 to $74,999
- $75,000 or more

Age
- Under 6 years
- 6 to 11 years
- 12 to 17 years

Race* and Hispanic origin
- White, not Hispanic
- Black
- Asian
- Hispanic (any race)

Nativity
- Native born
- Naturalized citizen
- Not a citizen

Percent

*Federal surveys now give respondents the option of reporting more than one race. This figure shows data using the race-alone concept. For example, Asian refers to people who reported Asian and no other race.

SOURCE: Carmen DeNavas-Walt, Bernadette D. Proctor, and Jessica C. Smith, "Figure 9. Uninsured Children by Poverty Status, Household Income, Age, Race and Hispanic Origin, and Nativity: 2009," in *Income, Poverty, and Health Insurance Coverage in the United States: 2009*, Current Population Reports, U.S. Census Bureau, September 2010, http://www.census.gov/prod/2010pubs/p60-238.pdf (accessed February 17, 2011)

FIGURE 8.6

Coverage by type of health insurance, 2008 and 2009

(Bar chart, legend: 2008, 2009; percent 0 to 80)

Private insurance
- Any private plan
- Employment-based
- Direct-purchase

Government insurance
- Any government plan
- Medicare
- Medicaid
- Military health care*

No insurance
- Not covered

Percent

*Military health care includes Tricare and CHAMPVA (Civilian Health and Medical Program of the Department of Veterans Affairs), as well as care provided by the Department of Veterans Affairs and the military.
Note: The estimates by type of coverage are not mutually exclusive; people can be covered by more than one type of health insurance during the year.

SOURCE: Carmen DeNavas-Walt, Bernadette D. Proctor, and Jessica C. Smith, "Figure 8. Coverage by Type of Health Insurance: 2008 and 2009," in *Income, Poverty, and Health Insurance Coverage in the United States: 2009*, Current Population Reports, U.S. Census Bureau, September 2010, http://www.census.gov/prod/2010pubs/p60-238.pdf (accessed February 17, 2011)

exempts poor pregnant women and children from this provision, requiring their continued Medicaid eligibility. In addition, the welfare law requires state plans to ensure Medicaid for children receiving foster care or adoption assistance.

DeNavas-Walt, Proctor, and Smith report that in 2009, 7.5 million (10%) children were uninsured. In an effort to reach these uninsured children, many states are simplifying the Medicaid application process. In addition, the 1996 welfare law gives states the option to use Medicaid to provide health care coverage to low-income working parents. About half (49%) of poor adults without children, 44% of poor parents, and 17% of poor children were uninsured in 2009. (See Figure 8.7.) Even though the income of these households was below the federal poverty line, working poor parents were ineligible for publicly funded health insurance. In addition, low-wage jobs often do not offer affordable employer-sponsored coverage.

Over 56.8 million people were enrolled in Medicaid in 2007; on average, each Medicaid recipient received benefits totaling $4,867. (See Table 8.3.) The majority of Medicaid recipients were dependent children under 21 years of age (26.6 million) and adults in families with dependent children (12.4 million). (See Table 8.4.) The remainder of Medicaid recipients were disabled (8.4 million) or elderly (4 million). The number receiving Medicaid coverage had more than doubled since 1985, when 21.8 million people were enrolled.

The rapid growth in spending for Medicaid has contributed to the concern over the rising cost of health care. Not accounting for inflation, spending skyrocketed from $37.5 billion in 1985 to $276.5 billion in 2007. (See Table 8.4.) The largest proportion of the money went for the disabled ($119.6 billion, or 43.3%) and the elderly ($57.4 billion, or 20.7%). In addition, considerable amounts were

FIGURE 8.7

Health insurance coverage of low-income adults and children, 2009

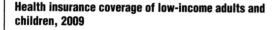

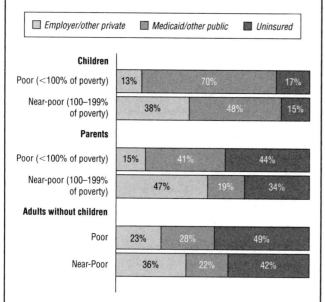

Note: Data may not total 100% due to rounding.

SOURCE: "Figure 19. Health Insurance Coverage of Low-Income Adults and Children, 2009," in "The Uninsured: A Primer" (#7296), The Henry J. Kaiser Family, December 2010, http://www.kff.org/uninsured/upload/7451-06.pdf (accessed February 18, 2011). This information was reprinted with permission from the Henry J. Kaiser Family Foundation. The Kaiser Family Foundation is a non-profit private operating foundation, based in Menlo Park, California, dedicated to producing and communicating the best possible analysis and information on health issues.

spent on dependent children under the age of 21 years ($47.8 billion, or 17.3%) and adults in families with dependent children ($33.8 billion, or 12.2%). On average, in 2007 Medicaid spent $14,200 on each disabled person in the program, $14,187 on every elderly recipient, and $1,797 on each dependent child under the age of 21 years.

State Child Health Insurance Program

The Balanced Budget Act of 1997 set aside $24 billion over five years to fund CHIP in an effort to reach children who were uninsured. This was the nation's largest children's health care investment since the creation of Medicaid in 1965. The Children's Health Insurance Program Reauthorization Act was signed into law by President Obama in February 2009, extending and expanding the existing CHIP. CHIP requires states to use the funding to cover uninsured children whose families earn too much for Medicaid but too little to afford private coverage. States may use this money to expand their Medicaid programs, design new child health insurance programs, or create a combination of the two. The expanding legislation is expected to provide coverage to an additional 4 million children by 2013.

TABLE 8.3

Number of Medicaid recipients, amount of payments, and average payment, by state, fiscal year 2007

State	Number of recipients	Total payments (millions of dollars)	Average payment (dollars)
United States[a]	56,824,770	276,539	4,867
Alabama	829,714	3,902	4,703
Alaska	120,314	937	7,789
Arizona	1,020,773	3,434	3,364
Arkansas	922,904	3,106	3,365
California	10,386,032	30,100	2,898
Colorado	616,378	2,720	4,412
Connecticut	518,675	3,976	7,665
Delaware	172,666	1,000	5,792
District of Columbia	159,984	1,453	9,080
Florida	2,905,180	13,158	4,529
Georgia	1,702,785	6,393	3,754
Hawaii[b]	227,043	989	4,354
Idaho	218,137	1,135	5,204
Illinois	2,178,494	10,380	4,765
Indiana	986,229	4,605	4,669
Iowa	443,105	2,413	5,447
Kansas	340,483	2,057	6,041
Kentucky	867,563	4,291	4,946
Louisiana	1,151,767	4,342	3,770
Maine[c]	301,540	1,649	5,467
Maryland	745,883	5,335	7,153
Massachusetts	1,193,015	8,384	7,028
Michigan	1,906,764	7,872	4,128
Minnesota	741,193	5,871	7,922
Mississippi	683,100	3,263	4,776
Missouri	1,043,506	4,843	4,641
Montana	111,995	620	5,537
Nebraska	246,653	1,466	5,942
Nevada	253,466	1,079	4,259
New Hampshire	126,074	1,042	8,262
New Jersey	1,019,936	7,319	7,176
New Mexico	491,758	2,639	5,366
New York	4,769,657	40,026	8,392
North Carolina	1,618,599	8,713	5,383
North Dakota	71,464	493	6,894
Ohio	2,061,230	12,119	5,879
Oklahoma	746,202	3,121	4,182
Oregon	476,196	2,208	4,636
Pennsylvania	2,181,821	12,094	5,543
Rhode Island	208,429	1,632	7,830
South Carolina	848,527	4,049	4,772
South Dakota	132,986	626	4,710
Tennessee	1,444,519	5,919	4,098
Texas	3,859,693	14,593	3,781
Utah	242,650	1,395	5,748
Vermont	157,240	812	5,166
Virginia	814,790	4,459	5,473
Washington	1,152,686	5,363	4,653
West Virginia	368,906	2,256	6,114
Wisconsin	966,685	4,441	4,594
Wyoming	69,381	449	6,472

Note: Totals do not necessarily equal the sum of rounded components.
[a]Excludes recipients in Puerto Rico and the U.S. Virgin Islands. Data are not available.
[b]Fiscal year 2007 data are not available for Hawaii. Fiscal year 2006 data have been substituted.
[c]Fiscal year 2007 data are not available for Maine. Fiscal year 2005 data have been substituted.

SOURCE: "Table 8.H1. Number of Recipients, Total Payments, and Average Payment, by State, Fiscal Year 2007," in *Annual Statistical Supplement to the Social Security Bulletin, 2009*, Social Security Administration, February 2010, http://www.ssa.gov/policy/docs/statcomps/supplement/2009/8h.pdf (accessed February 17, 2011)

States must enroll all children who meet Medicaid's eligibility requirements in the Medicaid program rather than in CHIP. They are not allowed to use CHIP to replace

TABLE 8.4

Number of total Medicaid recipients, total vendor payments, and average amounts, by type of eligibility category, fiscal years 1985–2007

Year	Total[a]	Aged 65 or older	Blind	Permanent and total disability	Dependent children under age 21	Adults in families with dependent children	Other
				Number of recipients (thousands)			
1985	21,814	3,061	80	2,937	9,757	5,518	1,214
1986	22,515	3,140	82	3,100	10,029	5,647	1,362
1987	23,109	3,224	85	3,296	10,168	5,599	1,418
1988	22,907	3,159	86	3,401	10,037	5,503	1,343
1989	23,511	3,132	95	3,496	10,318	5,717	1,175
1990	25,255	3,202	83	3,635	11,220	6,010	1,105
1991	28,280	3,359	85	3,983	13,415	6,778	658
1992	30,926	3,742	84	4,378	15,104	6,954	664
1993	33,432	3,863	84	4,932	16,285	7,505	763
1994	35,053	4,035	87	5,372	17,194	7,586	779
1995	36,282	4,119	92	5,767	17,164	7,604	1,537
1996	36,118	4,285	95	6,126	16,739	7,127	1,746
1997	34,872	3,955	—	6,129	15,791	6,803	2,195
1998	40,649	3,964	—	6,638	18,964	7,908	3,176
1999	40,300	4,241	—	7,303	20,119	8,552	846
2000	42,886	4,289	—	7,479	21,086	10,543	862
2001	46,163	4,420	—	7,703	22,533	11,639	869
2002	49,329	3,890	—	7,411	22,421	11,253	4,354
2003	51,971	4,041	—	7,669	23,992	11,679	4,591
2004	55,002	4,318	—	7,933	25,613	12,225	4,913
2005[b]	57,643	4,396	—	8,210	26,337	12,529	6,171
2006[c]	57,732	4,375	—	8,332	26,771	12,598	5,656
2007[d]	56,825	4,043	—	8,424	26,584	12,371	5,402
				Total vendor payments (millions of dollars)			
1985	37,508	14,096	249	13,203	4,414	4,746	798
1986	41,005	15,097	277	14,635	5,135	4,880	980
1987	45,050	16,037	309	16,507	5,508	5,592	1,078
1988	48,710	17,135	344	18,250	5,848	5,883	1,198
1989	54,500	18,558	409	20,476	6,892	6,897	1,268
1990	64,859	21,508	434	23,969	9,100	8,590	1,257
1991	77,048	25,453	475	27,798	11,690	10,439	1,193
1992	90,814	29,078	530	33,326	14,491	12,185	1,204
1993	101,709	31,554	589	38,065	16,504	13,605	1,391
1994	108,270	33,618	644	41,654	17,302	13,585	1,467
1995	120,141	36,527	848	48,570	17,976	13,511	2,708
1996	121,685	36,947	869	51,196	17,544	12,275	2,853
1997	124,430	37,721	—	54,130	17,544	12,307	2,727
1998	142,318	40,602	—	60,375	22,806	14,833	3,702
1999	147,372	40,470	—	63,028	20,765	15,141	7,966
2000	168,442	44,560	—	72,772	23,490	17,671	9,948
2001	186,913	48,431	—	80,493	26,770	20,096	11,121
2002	213,497	52,012	—	92,414	31,595	23,525	13,950
2003	233,206	55,271	—	102,014	35,079	26,689	14,153
2004	257,748	59,541	—	111,614	39,194	30,522	16,877
2005[b]	275,569	63,358	—	119,647	42,012	32,385	18,167
2006[c]	268,505	58,109	—	116,209	44,645	32,871	16,670
2007[d]	276,539	57,362	—	119,621	47,763	33,764	18,029
				Average payment (dollars)			
1985	1,719	4,605	3,104	4,496	452	860	658
1986	1,821	4,808	3,401	4,721	512	864	719
1987	1,949	4,975	3,644	5,008	542	999	761
1988	2,126	5,425	4,005	5,366	583	1,069	891
1989	2,318	5,926	4,317	5,858	668	1,206	1,079
1990	2,568	6,717	5,212	6,595	811	1,429	1,138
1991	2,725	7,577	5,572	6,979	871	1,540	1,813
1992	2,936	7,770	6,298	7,612	959	1,752	1,813
1993	3,042	8,168	7,036	7,717	1,013	1,813	1,824
1994	3,089	8,331	7,412	7,755	1,006	1,791	1,884

existing health coverage. In addition, states must decide on what kind of cost-sharing, if any, to require of low-income families without keeping them from accessing the program. The only federal requirement is that cost-sharing cannot exceed 5% of family income. In August 2008 the administration of George W. Bush (1946–) limited the ability of states to expand coverage under CHIP to children living in families that had incomes above 250% of the poverty level. President Obama withdrew this directive in February 2009.

Health Care for the Homeless

In 1987 Congress passed the Stewart B. McKinney Homeless Assistance Act to provide services to the homeless, including job training, emergency shelter, education,

TABLE 8.4

Number of total Medicaid recipients, total vendor payments, and average amounts, by type of eligibility category, fiscal years 1985–2007 [CONTINUED]

Year	Total[a]	Aged 65 or older	Blind	Permanent and total disability	Dependent children under age 21	Adults in families with dependent children	Other
				Average payment (dollars)			
1995	3,311	8,868	9,256	8,422	1,047	1,777	1,762
1996	3,369	8,622	9,143	8,357	1,048	1,722	1,635
1997	3,568	9,538	—	8,832	1,111	1,809	3,597
1998	3,501	10,242	—	9,095	1,203	1,876	1,166
1999	3,657	9,541	—	8,630	1,032	1,770	9,407
2000	3,928	10,388	—	9,729	1,114	1,676	11,536
2001	4,049	10,957	—	10,449	1,188	1,727	12,792
2002	4,328	13,370	—	12,470	1,409	2,091	3,204
2003	4,487	13,677	—	13,303	1,462	2,285	3,083
2004	4,686	13,790	—	14,070	1,530	2,497	3,435
2005[b]	4,781	14,413	—	14,574	1,595	2,585	2,944
2006[c]	4,651	13,283	—	13,947	1,668	2,609	2,947
2007[d]	4,867	14,187	—	14,200	1,797	2,729	3,337

Notes: Totals do not necessarily equal the sum of rounded components.
Beginning in 1997, "Disability" includes blindness. "Children" includes foster care children, and "Other" are "Unknowns." In 1999 and 2000, "Other" includes foster care children and "Unknowns." In 2001 and 2002, "Other" includes foster care children, "Unknowns," and individuals covered under the Breast and Cervical Cancer Prevention and Treatment Act of 2000. Beginning with 1999, excludes recipients in Puerto Rico and the U.S. Virgin Islands. Data are not available.
— = not applicable.
[a]Total represents the unduplicated number of recipients receiving any type of medical service during the year.
[b]Fiscal year 2005 data are not available for Maine. Fiscal year 2004 data have been substituted.
[c]Fiscal year 2006 data are not available for Maine and Nevada. Fiscal year 2004 data have been substituted for Maine, and fiscal year 2005 data have been substituted for Nevada.
[d]Fiscal year 2007 data are not available for Hawaii and Maine. Fiscal year 2006 data have been substituted for Hawaii, and fiscal year 2005 data have been substituted for Maine.

SOURCE: "Table 8.E2. Unduplicated Number of Recipients, Total Vendor Payments, and Average Payment, by Type of Eligibility Category, Fiscal Years, 1985–2007," in *Annual Statistical Supplement to the Social Security Bulletin, 2009*, Social Security Administration, February 2010, http://www.ssa.gov/policy/docs/statcomps/supplement/2009/8e.pdf (accessed February 17, 2011)

and health care. Title VI of the act funds Health Care for the Homeless (HCH) programs. The U.S. Interagency Council on Homelessness reports in *Fiscal Year 2012 Federal Government Homelessness Budget Fact Sheet* (February 14, 2011, http://library.constantcontact.com/download/get/file/1011269667270-77/FY+12+Budget+Fact+Sheet_02_14_11.pdf) that President Obama's proposed fiscal year (FY) 2011 budget asked for $252 million for HCH programs, which was substantially higher than the FY 2010 budget of $171 million. His FY 2012 budget asked for $258 million for these programs.

Nonprofit private organizations and public entities, including state and local government agencies, may apply for grants from the program. The grants may be used to continue to provide services for up to one year to individuals who have obtained permanent housing if services were provided to them when they were homeless.

The goal of the HCH programs is to improve the health of homeless individuals and families by improving access to primary health care and substance abuse services. The HCH programs provide outreach, counseling to clients explaining available services, case management, and linkages to services such as mental health treatment, housing, benefits, and other critical supports. Access to around-the-clock emergency services is available, as is help in establishing eligibility for assistance and obtaining services under entitlement programs.

LIVING IN PUBLIC: INCREASED HEALTH PROBLEMS

Poor people can be catapulted into homelessness because of the expenses and missed work caused by poor health. Homelessness itself causes a person's health to deteriorate further. Thus, health problems can both cause and result from homelessness. For example, a health problem that prevents an impoverished person from working can result in a loss of income that leads to homelessness. For those living on the streets, lack of adequate shelter and proper facilities for maintaining personal hygiene can exacerbate illness. Alcoholism, mental illnesses, diabetes, and depression become visible and more pronounced in homeless people. Other serious illnesses (e.g., tuberculosis [TB]) are almost exclusively associated with the unhealthy living conditions brought on by poverty. In general, experts agree that homeless people suffer from more types of illnesses, for longer periods of time, and with more harmful consequences than housed people. In addition, the National Coalition for the Homeless (NCH) explains in "Health Care and Homelessness" (July 2009, http://www.nationalhomeless.org/factsheets/health.html) that health care delivery is complicated by a patient's homeless status, making management of chronic diseases such as diabetes, human immunodeficiency virus (HIV), and hypertension more difficult. Most Americans suffer illness and disease at some point during their life, but for people experiencing homelessness and poverty, illness often leads to serious health concerns or premature death.

The rates of both chronic and acute (short-term) health problems are disproportionately high among the homeless population. Except for obesity, strokes, and cancer, homeless people are far more likely than housed people to suffer from every category of chronic health problems. Conditions that require regular, uninterrupted treatment, such as TB, HIV, acquired immunodeficiency syndrome (AIDS), diabetes, hypertension, malnutrition, severe dental problems, addictive disorders, and mental disorders, are extremely difficult to treat or control among those without adequate housing.

Street living comes with a set of health conditions that living in a home does not. Homeless people fall prey to parasites, frostbite, leg ulcers, and infections. They are also at greater risk of physical and psychological trauma resulting from muggings, beatings, and rape. With no safe place to store belongings, the proper storage or administration of medications becomes difficult. In addition, some homeless people with mental disorders may use drugs or alcohol to self-medicate, and those with addictive disorders are more susceptible to HIV and other communicable diseases.

Homeless people may also lack the ability to access some of the basic rituals of self-care: bed rest, good nutrition, and good personal hygiene. For example, the luxury of taking it easy for a day or two is almost impossible for homeless people; they must often keep walking or remain standing all day to avoid criminal charges.

Unwell homeless people also remain untreated longer than their sheltered counterparts because obtaining food and shelter takes priority over health care. As a result, relatively minor illnesses go untreated until they develop into major emergencies, requiring expensive acute care treatment and long-term recovery.

Mortality Rates

Studies find that homelessness increases the risk of death. James J. O'Connell of the Boston Health Care for the Homeless program reviews in *Premature Mortality in Homeless Populations: A Review of the Literature* (December 2005, http://www.nhchc.org/PrematureMortalityFinal .pdf) the literature concerning the connection between homelessness and mortality. He finds that "a remarkable consistency ... transcends borders, cultures and oceans: homeless persons are 3–4 times more likely to die than the general population." In addition, he notes that the average age of death of homeless people in the studies reviewed was between 42 and 52 years, despite a life expectancy of around 80 years in the United States. These premature deaths were highly associated with the coexistence of acute and chronic medical conditions with either mental illness or substance abuse. In "Homelessness as an Independent Risk Factor for Mortality: Results from a Retrospective Cohort Study" (*International Journal of Epidemiology*, March 21, 2009), David S. Morrison of the

University of Glasgow concludes that homelessness itself is an independent risk factor for deaths; it appears to substantially increase mortality risk from specific causes.

Access to Care

Martha R. Burt et al. analyze in *Homelessness: Programs and the People They Serve* (December 1999, http://www.urban.org/UploadedPDF/homelessness.pdf) the results of the 1996 National Survey of Homeless Assistance Providers and Clients, the only survey of its kind (studies of the homeless tend to focus on local populations). The researchers note that in the year preceding the survey 25% of the clients studied had needed medical attention but were not able to see a doctor or a nurse. They also reveal that newly housed people were even less likely to receive medical help when needed.

Burt et al. attribute the higher rate of health problems among newly housed people to several factors, including:

- The loss of convenient health care in centers or shelters

- The habit of enduring untreated ailments

- A lack of health care benefits (which is common among people below the poverty level)

In "The Behavioral Model for Vulnerable Populations: Application to Medical Care Use and Outcomes for Homeless People" (*Health Services Research*, vol. 34, no. 6, February 2000), Lillian Gelberg, Ronald M. Andersen, and Barbara D. Leake report the results of a study on the prevalence of certain disease conditions among homeless adults, which revealed that 37% suffered from functional vision impairment; 36% experienced skin, leg, and foot problems; and 31% tested positive for TB. The researchers indicate that homeless people who had a community clinic or a private physician as a regular source of care exhibited better health outcomes. Gelberg, Andersen, and Leake also suggest that clinical treatment of the homeless be accompanied by efforts to help them find permanent housing.

Ailments of Homeless People

Local studies offer a glimpse into common health conditions that are suffered by homeless people. For example, *Connecticut Counts 2009: Point-in-Time Homeless Count* (August 18, 2009, http://www.cceh.org/pdf/count/ 2009_pit_report.pdf), a 2009 Connecticut count of homeless people, finds that health issues were prevalent among the homeless population. A fair number of people had been hospitalized for mental health, including 36% of sheltered single adults, 35% of unsheltered single adults, and 17% of sheltered adults in families. Seventy-two percent of unsheltered single adults, 54% of sheltered single adults, and 17% of sheltered adults in families had been in detox or rehab for substance abuse. Four out of 10 (39%) sheltered single adults, 30% of unsheltered single adults, and 17% of sheltered adults living in families had a chronic, limiting health condition. Seven percent of sheltered single adults, 5% of sheltered adults living in families, and 2% of unsheltered single adults had HIV or AIDS.

In "2007 San Mateo County Homeless Census and Survey" (May 2007, http://www.redwoodcityhousing.org/pdf/2007_SMCO_Homeless_Census_and_Survey.pdf), a 2007 survey of homeless people in San Mateo County, California, Housing Our People Effectively finds that both psychological and physical problems were prevalent among the homeless population. Over half (57%) of respondents reported being depressed, 35% reported having a mental illness, 33% reported they abused drugs, 31% reported they abused alcohol, and 26% reported experiencing post-traumatic stress disorder. A third (35%) reported having a physical disability, 28% reported chronic physical health problems, and 2% reported having HIV/AIDS.

Gillian Silver and Rea Pañares summarize in *The Health of Homeless Women: Information for State Mental and Child Health Programs* (March 2000, http://www.jhsph.edu/WCHPC/Publications/homeless.PDF) one study's findings regarding the health problems faced by

homeless women, who made up about one-third (32%) of the homeless population in 2000. This group was prone to the same physical ailments that affect the general homeless population but also reported high rates of gastrointestinal problems, neurological disorders, chronic obstructive pulmonary disease, and peripheral vascular disease. (See Table 8.5.)

Physical Disorders and Diseases

The following is a description of a few of the chronic problems that are suffered by homeless people.

TUBERCULOSIS. Several kinds of acute, nonspecific respiratory diseases are common among homeless people. These diseases are easily spread through group living in overcrowded shelters without adequate nutrition. TB, a disease at one time almost eliminated from the general American population, has become a major health problem among the homeless. This disease is associated with exposure, poor diet, alcoholism, injection drug use, HIV, and other illnesses that lower the body's resistance to infection. TB is spread by long personal contact, making it a potential

TABLE 8.5

Health problems faced by homeless women

Health issue	Key findings
Chronic disease	• The most common chronic physical conditions (excluding substance abuse) are hypertension, gastrointestinal problems, neurological disorders, arthritis and other musculoskeletal disorders, chronic obstructive pulmonary disease, and peripheral vascular disease.
Infectious disease	• The most common infectious diseases reported were chest infection, cold, cough, and bronchitis; reporting was the same for those formerly homeless, currently homeless, and other service users. • Homeless patients with tuberculosis (TB) were more likely to present with a more progressed form than nonhomeless. • Widespread screening for TB in shelters may miss most homeless persons because many do not live in the shelter, and instead present in emergency departments.
STDs/HIV/AIDS	• A mobile women's health unit in Chicago reported that of 104 female homeless clients, 30 percent had abnormal Pap smears—14 percent with atypia and 10 percent with inflammation; the incidence of chlamydia was 3 percent, gonorrhea 6 percent, and trichomoniasis 26 percent. • HIV infection was found to be 2.35 times more prevalent in homeless, drug-abusing women than homeless, drug-abusing men.
Stress	• Homeless mothers reported higher levels of stress, depression, and avoidant and anti-cognitive coping strategies than low-income, housed mothers.
Nutrition	• Currently and formerly homeless clients are more likely to report not getting enough to eat (28 and 25 percent respectively) than among all U.S. households (4 percent) and among poor households (12 percent). • Contrary to their opinions, homeless women and their dependents were consuming less than 50 percent of the 1989 recommended daily allowance for iron, magnesium, zinc, folic acid, and calcium. • Subjects of all ages consumed higher than desirable quantities of fats. • The health risk factors of iron deficiency anemia, obesity, and hypercholesterolemia were prevalent.
Smoking	• More than half of both homeless mothers and low-income housed mothers were current smokers, compared with 22.6 percent of female adults 18 years and over.
Violence	• Poor women are at higher risk for violence than women overall; poverty increases stress and lowers the ability to cope with the environment and live safely. • In a study of 436 sheltered homeless and poor housed women: 84 percent of these women had been severely assaulted at some point in their lives; 63 percent had been severely assaulted by parental caretakers while growing up; 40 percent had been sexually molested at least once before reaching adulthood; 60 percent had experienced severe physical attacks by a male intimate partner, and 33 percent had been assaulted by their current or most recent partner. • A study of 53 women homeless for at least three months in the past year demonstrated that this group is at a very high risk of battery and rape, with 91 percent exposed to battery and 56 percent exposed to rape.
Substance abuse	• Homeless women comprise a subpopulation at high risk for substance abuse; rates of substance use disorder range from 16 percent to 67 percent. There exists an imbalance between treatment need and treatment access. • Some homeless people with mental disorders may use drugs or alcohol to self-medicate.
Mental health/depression	• A case-control study of 100 homeless women with schizophrenia and 100 nonhomeless women with schizophrenia found that homeless women had higher rates of a concurrent diagnosis of alcohol abuse, drug abuse, antisocial personality disorder, and also had less adequate family support. • Many homeless women with serious mental illness are not receiving care; this is due to lack of perception of a mental health problem and lack of services designed to meet the needs of homeless women.

SOURCE: Gillian Silver and Rea Pañares, "Table 2. Summary of Study Findings Related to Health Problems Faced by Homeless Women," in *The Health of Homeless Women: Information for State Mental and Child Health Programs*, Women's and Children's Health Policy Center, Johns Hopkins Bloomberg School for Public Health, 2000, http://www.jhsph.edu/WCHPC/Publications/homeless.PDF (accessed February 18, 2011)

hazard not only to shelter residents but also to the general public.

According to the Centers for Disease Control and Prevention (CDC), in *Reported Tuberculosis in the United States, 2009* (October 2010, http://www.cdc.gov/tb/statistics/reports/2009/pdf/report2009.pdf), between 1953 and 1985 the United States experienced a decrease of 74% in the number of reported TB cases. However, in 1986 the number of TB cases began to rise, reaching 26,673 cases in 1992. The CDC notes that rising homelessness and poverty account, in part, for the resurgence of TB. Poor ventilation systems in shelters and impoverished homes, as well as the inability to quarantine poor or transient victims, contribute to the rise. The CDC finds that by 2009 the number of TB cases had dropped to 10,893; 5.3% of those infected with TB were homeless, which was a much higher rate of infection than among the general population. (See Table 8.6.) State-by-state breakdowns showing high rates of infection among the homeless populations of some states give one indication of the contagious nature of the disease. In 2009, for example, Mississippi reported that 20.7% of those

TABLE 8.6

Tuberculosis (TB) cases by homeless status, 2009

Reporting area	Total cases	Cases with information on homeless status[a]		Cases reported as being homeless	
		No.	(%)	No.	(%)
United States	**10,893**	**10,729**	**(98.5)**	**567**	**(5.3)**
Alabama	159	159	(100.0)	9	(5.7)
Alaska	35	35	(100.0)	4	(11.4)
Arizona	216	194	(89.8)	8	(4.1)
Arkansas	73	73	(100.0)	4	(5.5)
California	2,347	2,326	(99.1)	103	(4.4)
Colorado	74	74	(100.0)	5	(6.8)
Connecticut	91	91	(100.0)	1	(1.1)
Delaware	18	18	(100.0)	1	(5.6)
District of Columbia	40	40	(100.0)	1	(2.5)
Florida	793	747	(94.2)	61	(8.2)
Georgia	391	389	(99.5)	47	(12.1)
Hawaii	115	104	(90.4)	6	(5.8)
Idaho	15	15	(100.0)	0	(0.0)
Illinois	402	393	(97.8)	25	(6.4)
Indiana	112	111	(99.1)	16	(14.4)
Iowa	40	40	(100.0)	0	(0.0)
Kansas	59	58	(98.3)	6	(10.3)
Kentucky	75	75	(100.0)	5	(6.7)
Louisiana	186	186	(100.0)	13	(7.0)
Maine	7	7	(100.0)	1	(14.3)
Maryland	206	204	(99.0)	6	(2.9)
Massachusetts	231	231	(100.0)	16	(6.9)
Michigan	141	136	(96.5)	12	(8.8)
Minnesota	142	142	(100.0)	4	(2.8)
Mississippi	116	116	(100.0)	24	(20.7)
Missouri	74	69	(93.2)	3	(4.3)
Montana	7	7	(100.0)	1	(14.3)
Nebraska	29	29	(100.0)	1	(3.4)
Nevada	90	90	(100.0)	5	(5.6)
New Hampshire	16	16	(100.0)	0	(0.0)
New Jersey	391	391	(100.0)	8	(2.0)
New Mexico	48	48	(100.0)	2	(4.2)
New York State[b]	223	212	(95.1)	4	(1.9)
New York City	734	719	(98.0)	28	(3.9)
North Carolina	233	232	(99.6)	16	(6.9)
North Dakota	5	5	(100.0)	0	(0.0)
Ohio	173	169	(97.7)	10	(5.9)
Oklahoma	85	78	(91.8)	6	(7.7)
Oregon	88	88	(100.0)	9	(10.2)
Pennsylvania	225	225	(100.0)	10	(4.4)
Rhode Island	23	23	(100.0)	0	(0.0)
South Carolina	147	147	(100.0)	4	(2.7)
South Dakota	18	18	(100.0)	1	(5.6)
Tennessee	191	191	(100.0)	15	(7.9)
Texas	1,395	1,395	(100.0)	39	(2.8)
Utah	33	33	(100.0)	1	(3.0)
Vermont	6	6	(100.0)	0	(0.0)
Virginia	250	250	(100.0)	9	(3.6)
Washington	239	239	(100.0)	11	(4.6)
West Virginia	18	18	(100.0)	1	(5.6)
Wisconsin	66	65	(98.5)	5	(7.7)
Wyoming	2	2	(100.0)	0	(0.0)

TABLE 8.6

Reporting area	Total cases	Cases with information on homeless status[a]		Cases reported as being homeless	
		No.	(%)	No.	(%)
American Samoa[c]	4	4	(100.0)	0	(0.0)
Fed. States of Micronesia[c]	86	86	(100.0)	0	(0.0)
Guam[c]	74	74	(100.0)	0	(0.0)
Marshall Islands[c]	113	111	(98.2)	1	(0.9)
N. Mariana Islands[c]	32	32	(100.0)	0	(0.0)
Puerto Rico[c]	61	61	(100.0)	0	(0.0)
Republic of Palau[c]	18	18	(100.0)	0	(0.0)
U.S. Virgin Islands[c]	—	—	—	—	—

[a]Homeless within past 12 months of TB diagnosis. Percentage based on 52 reporting areas (50 states, New York City, and the District of Columbia). Counts and percentages shown only for reporting areas with information reported for ≥75% of cases.
[b]Excludes New York City.
[c]Not included in U.S. totals.
Note: Dashes indicate data not available.

SOURCE: "Table 30. Tuberculosis Cases and Percentages by Homeless Status, Age > or = 15: Reporting Areas, 2009," in *Reported Tuberculosis in the United States, 2009*, U.S. Department of Health and Human Services, Centers for Disease Control and Prevention, October 2010, http://www.cdc.gov/tb/statistics/reports/2009/pdf/report2009.pdf (accessed February 18, 2011)

testing positive for TB were homeless, whereas Idaho, Iowa, New Hampshire, North Dakota, Rhode Island, Vermont, and Wyoming had no cases of TB among their homeless populations.

Clinical data from the federally funded HCH programs find prevalence rates for TB to be much higher among the homeless population than among the overall general population. For example, Bonnie D. Kerker et al. find in "A Population-Based Assessment of the Health of Homeless Families in New York City" (*American Journal of Public Health*, vol. 101, no. 3, March 2011) that rates of TB infection among homeless families were three times higher than among low-income families. Maryam B. Haddad et al. report in "Tuberculosis and Homelessness in the United States, 1994–2003" (*Journal of the American Medical Association*, vol. 293, no. 22, June 8, 2005) that many of the risk factors for TB in the United States overlap with the risk factors associated with homelessness, including having a history of incarceration or substance abuse. An additional contributing factor was the emergence of drug-resistant strains of TB. Experts report that to control the spread of TB, the homeless population must receive frequent screenings for TB and the infected must get long-term care and rest.

A campaign for increased public awareness, particularly among members of the medical community, was launched in 1990 to identify and screen those at the greatest risk for TB. Some researchers, such as Mary Lashley of Towson University, in "A Targeted Testing Program for Tuberculosis Control and Prevention among Baltimore City's Homeless Population" (*Public Health Nursing*, vol. 24, no. 1, January– February 2007), and Maryann Duchene of Backus Home Health Care in Norwich, Connecticut, in "Infection Control in Soup Kitchens and Shelters" (*Home Healthcare Nurse*, vol. 28, no. 8, September 2010), tested pilot programs to better identify and treat homeless people infected with TB. Other studies, such as Jacqueline Peterson Tulsky et al., in "Can the Poor Adhere? Incentives for Adherence to TB Prevention in Homeless Adults" (*International Journal of Tuberculosis and Lung Disease*, vol. 8, no. 1, January 2004), and Adeline Nyamathi et al., in "Efficacy of Nurse Case-Managed Intervention for Latent Tuberculosis among Homeless Subsamples" (*Nursing Research*, vol. 57, no. 1, January–February 2008), investigated how best to help homeless adults adhere to treatment for latent TB infection. The CDC notes in *Reported Tuberculosis in the United States, 2009* that the number of reported TB cases in the United States declined from 12,906 in 2008 to 11,545 in 2009, a decrease of 10.5%.

SKIN AND BLOOD VESSEL DISORDERS. Frequent exposure to severe weather, insect bites, and other infestations make skin lesions fairly common among the homeless. Being forced to sit or stand for extended periods results in many homeless people being plagued with edema (swelling of the feet and legs), varicose veins, and skin ulcerations. This population is more prone to conditions that can lead to chronic phlebitis (inflammation of the veins). A homeless person with circulatory problems who sleeps sitting up in a doorway or a bus station can develop open lacerations that may become infected or maggot-infested if left untreated.

Regular baths and showers are luxuries to most homeless people, so many suffer from various forms of dermatitis (inflammation of the skin), often due to infestations of lice or scabies (a contagious skin disease caused by a parasitic mite that burrows under the skin to deposit eggs, causing intense itching). The lack of bathing increases the opportunity for infection to develop in cuts and other lacerations.

HIV/AIDS. The CDC notes in *Diagnoses of HIV Infection and AIDS in the United States and Dependent Areas, 2009: HIV Surveillance Report* (February 2011, http://www.cdc.gov/hiv/surveillance/resources/reports/2009report/index.htm) that in 2009 there were an estimated 42,011 new cases of HIV infection. It also notes that an estimated 16,088 people with AIDS died in 2008. In addition, at the end of 2008 an estimated 663,084 people were living with HIV infection and 479,868 people were living with AIDS in the United States.

In "Rapid HIV Testing" (July 24, 2009, http://www.cdc.gov/hiv/topics/testing/rapid/), the CDC estimates that up to one-fifth of people infected with HIV are not aware of their condition. The CDC is working with health officials to make rapid HIV tests widely available, particularly in places where likely victims reside, such as homeless shelters, drug treatment centers, and jails.

According to "Study: Disparity between Rich and Poor Mortality: Poor, Disadvantaged People Develop AIDS Faster" (*AIDS Alert*, vol. 18, no. 8, August 2003), a study of AIDS patients in San Francisco, California, poor people die sooner from AIDS. Within five years of diagnosis, fewer than 70% of people living in the city's poorest neighborhoods were still alive, compared with more than 85% of people who lived in the richest neighborhoods. Poor people with HIV usually have a number of co-occurring disorders, such as drug dependence, mental illness, and unstable housing arrangements. The lack of affordable and appropriate housing can be an acute crisis for these individuals, who need a safe shelter that provides protection and comfort, as well as a base from which to receive services, care, and support.

The National Alliance to End Homelessness points out in the fact sheet "Homelessness and HIV/AIDS" (August 10, 2006, http://www.endhomelessness.org/content/general/detail/1073) that HIV/AIDS is more prevalent in homeless populations. As many as 3.4% of homeless people are HIV positive, a rate that is three times higher than that of the general population. The high costs of medical care may even put individuals with HIV/AIDS at a greater risk of homelessness. Furthermore, the homeless life poses a grave threat to the health of those with HIV/AIDS, whose immune systems are compromised by the disease. Shelter conditions expose people to dangerous infections, and exposure to the elements and malnutrition exacerbate chronic illness. In addition, homeless people have difficulty obtaining and using common HIV/AIDS medications.

Mental Health and Substance Abuse

Before the 1960s people with chronic mental illness were often committed involuntarily to state psychiatric hospitals. The development of medications that could control the symptoms of mental illness coincided with a growing belief that involuntary hospitalization was warranted only when a mentally ill person posed a threat to him- or herself or to others. Gradually, large numbers of mentally ill people were discharged from hospitals and other treatment facilities. Because the community-based treatment centers that were supposed to take the place of state hospitals were often either inadequate or nonexistent, many of these people ended up living on the streets.

In "Prevalence and Risk Factors for Homelessness and Utilization of Mental Health Services among 10,340 Patients with Serious Mental Illness in a Large Public Mental Health System" (*American Journal of Psychiatry*, vol. 162, no. 2, February 2005), David P. Folsom et al. find that 15% of patients treated for serious mental illness were homeless at some point during a one-year period. Twenty percent of patients with schizophrenia, 17% of patients with bipolar disorder, and 9% of patients with depression were homeless. Folsom et al. find that mentally ill people are at a much higher risk of homelessness than the general population. The researchers emphasize that homelessness among the mentally ill was associated with two other factors: substance use disorders and a lack of Medicaid insurance. Folsom et al. state, "Although it would be naive to assume that treatment for substance use disorders and provision of Medicaid insurance could solve the problem of homelessness among persons with serious mental illness, further research is warranted to test the effect of interventions designed to treat patients with dual diagnoses and to assist homeless persons with serious mental illness in obtaining and maintaining entitlement benefits."

Table 8.5 shows the results of a study of 100 homeless women with schizophrenia and 100 nonhomeless women with schizophrenia. The study, which is summarized by Silver and Pañares, finds that homeless schizophrenic women had higher rates of co-occurring disorders, including alcohol and/or drug abuse and antisocial personality disorder.

Silver and Pañares note that families with children make up about 40% of the total homeless population and that the vast majority (about 90%) are female-headed. They also report on a study of 436 sheltered homeless and low-income housed mothers. The study found that 84% of these women had a history of having been severely assaulted at some point during their life. Research shows that mothers with a history of abuse are more likely to have children with mental health problems.

PREVALENCE AND TREATMENT. Experts debate the rate of mental disorders among homeless populations, but they generally agree that it is greater among the homeless than the general population. In "The Prevalence of Mental Disorders among the Homeless in Western Countries: Systematic Review and Meta-regression Analysis" (*PLoS Medline*, vol. 5, no. 12, December 2, 2008), Seena Fazel et al.

analyze data from 29 surveys of the homeless in Western countries to find the prevalence of mental disorders in this population. The researchers find that the most common mental disorders were alcohol and drug dependence. The prevalence rates of psychosis and depression ranged from 2.8% to 42.3%. Fazel et al. conclude that the prevalence of substance abuse disorder, psychotic disorders, and depression are higher among the homeless population than among the general population.

Mentally ill homeless people present special problems for health care workers. They may not be as cooperative and motivated as other patients. Because of their limited resources, they may have difficulty getting transportation to treatment centers. They frequently forget to show up for appointments or to take medications. The addition of drug abuse can make them unruly or unresponsive. Among people with severe mental disorders, those at greatest risk of homelessness are both the most severely ill and the most difficult to help.

The National Alliance on Mental Illness states in "Dual Diagnosis and Integrated Treatment of Mental Illness and Substance Abuse Disorder" (2011, http://www.nami.org/Template.cfm?Section=By_Illness&Template=/Tagged Page/TaggedPageDisplay.cfm&TPLID=54&ContentID=23049) that mental illness and substance abuse frequently occur together; clinicians call this dual diagnosis. Experts explain that in the absence of appropriate treatment, people with mental illness often resort to self-medication—that is, using alcohol or drugs to silence the voices in their head or to calm the fears that torment them. Approximately 50% of individuals with severe mental disorders also abuse drugs or alcohol. Homeless people with dual diagnoses are frequently excluded from mental health programs because of treatment problems created by their substance abuse and are excluded from substance abuse programs due to problems in treating their mental illness. Experts note that the lack of an integrated system of care plays a major role in these people's recurrent homelessness and stress that transitional or assisted housing initiatives for homeless substance abusers must realistically address the issue of abstinence and design measures for handling relapses that do not place people back on the streets.

THE HEALTH OF HOMELESS CHILDREN

The National Center on Family Homelessness reports in "Children" (2010, http://www.familyhomelessness.org/children.php?p=ts) that one out of every 50 American children experiences homelessness each year. The organization points out that homeless children tend to have both acute and chronic health problems and that the stress and trauma in their lives has profound developmental effects. They are sick four times more often than housed children, have three times more emotional and behavioral problems than housed children, and go hungry twice as often as housed children.

The American Academy of Pediatrics reviews in "Policy Statement: Providing Care for Immigrant, Homeless, and Migrant Children" (*Pediatrics*, vol. 115, no. 4, April 2005) the literature on the health of homeless children. The policy statement enumerates many health effects of homelessness, including that homeless children are more likely to experience poor health or fair health than are other children. In particular, they have more trauma-related injuries, a greater incidence of sinus infections, anemia, asthma, eczema, visual and neurologic deficits, and digestive disorders. In addition, obesity and hunger are common. Unaccompanied youth as well as children in families living on the streets are at a higher risk of experiencing violence or victimization.

John C. Buckner of the Harvard Medical School summarizes the results of several studies of homeless children's mental and physical health in "Understanding the Impact of Homelessness on Children: Challenges and Future Research Directions" (*American Behavioral Scientist*, vol. 51, no. 6, February 2008). He finds that both homeless and low-income housed children have higher rates of physical and mental health problems than do other children. He also notes that most studies find that homeless children evidence greater health problems than do low-income housed children. However, he calls for more research to investigate these probable differences.

VICTIMS OF VIOLENCE
Violence toward Homeless Women

Homeless women are at a high risk of interpersonal violence. According to Ellen Bassuk, Ree Dawson, and Nicholas Huntington, in "Intimate Violence in Extremely Poor Women: Longitudinal Patterns and Risk Markers" (*Journal of Family Violence*, vol. 21, no. 6, August 2006), almost two-thirds of 280 homeless and extremely poor housed women had experienced intimate partner violence during their lifetime. Women who had been molested during childhood, who had inadequate emotional support from professionals, or who had poor self-esteem were the most likely to have experienced intimate partner violence in the past 12 months. In "Relative Contributions of Parent Substance Use and Childhood Maltreatment to Chronic Homelessness, Depression, and Substance Abuse Problems among Homeless Women: Mediating Roles of Self-Esteem and Abuse in Adulthood" (*Child Abuse and Neglect*, vol. 26, no. 10, October 2002), Judith A. Stein, Michelle Burden Leslie, and Adeline Nyamathi note that recent intimate partner violence actually contributes to a greater likelihood of chronic homelessness among women.

Suzanne L. Wenzel et al. find in "Sexual Risk among Impoverished Women: Understanding the Role of Housing

Status" (*AIDS and Behavior*, vol. 11, supplement 6, November 2007) that impoverished women who are homeless or who have been recently victimized are also more likely to engage in risky sexual behavior that can lead to HIV infection. The researchers indicate that homeless African-American and Hispanic women had from two to five times greater odds of engaging in risky sexual behavior than women who were housed.

In "Correlates of Adult Assault among Homeless Women" (*Journal of Health Care for the Poor and Underserved*, vol. 21, no. 4, November 2010), Angela L. Hudson et al. find that some homeless women are more likely than others to experience violence. Noting that "homeless women are highly susceptible to victimization," the researchers cite research that finds that a third of homeless women reported experiencing sexual assault within the past year and another third reported being physically assaulted within the past year. Hudson et al. studied homeless women in Los Angeles, California, to uncover relationships among homeless women's psychological functioning, past victimization, and the likelihood of adult victimization. They determine that mental illness and low self-esteem were important risk factors for physical and sexual victimization among the homeless women in their study. Physical victimization was also associated with a history of physical abuse as a child, and sexual victimization was associated with a history of sexual abuse as a child. Current and previous substance abuse as well as involvement in the sex trade placed homeless women at great risk for physical and sexual victimization.

Hate Crimes

The NCH reports in *Hate Crimes against the Homeless: America's Growing Tide of Violence* (August 2010, http://www.nationalhomeless.org/publications/hatecrimes/hatecrimes2009.pdf) that "this year's report draws an especially gruesome and disturbing trend in the frequency and manner of the offenses. Violent, often fatal, attacks on homeless Americans now outnumber all other categories of hate crimes combined." The NCH identifies 291 deaths and 1,074 nonlethal attacks on homeless people between 1999 and 2009—117 attacks in 2009 alone, resulting in 43 deaths. The crimes occurred in 47 states, the District of Columbia, and Puerto Rico.

The NCH recommends the following actions to address the problem of violence against homeless individuals:

- Federal and state recognition of attacks on homeless people as hate crimes

- Issuing of a public statement by the U.S. Department of Justice acknowledging that violence against homeless people is a serious national problem

- Training for local police in investigating crimes and working with people experiencing homelessness

HUNGER

The Extent of the Problem

During the 1980s a number of studies found that some Americans, especially children, were suffering from hunger. Many observers did not believe these reports or thought they had been exaggerated. In 1984 a Task Force on Food Assistance appointed by President Ronald Reagan (1911–2004) found that it could not find evidence on the extent of hunger because there was no agreed-on way to measure hunger.

In response, the Food Research and Action Center (FRAC), an advocacy group for the poor, launched the Community Childhood Hunger Identification Project (CCHIP) to determine the extent of hunger in the United States. The first FRAC survey conducted interviews in 2,335 households with incomes at or below 185% of the poverty level and with at least one child under the age of 12 years. The results of this survey, as reported by Cheryl A. Wehler et al. in *Community Childhood Hunger Identification Project: A Survey of Childhood Hunger in the United States* (1991), indicated that 32% of U.S. households with incomes at or below 185% of the poverty level experienced hunger. At least one child out of every eight under the age of 12 years suffered from hunger. Another 40% of low-income children were at risk for hunger.

Between 1992 and 1994 FRAC sponsored a second round of CCHIP surveys in nine states and the District of Columbia (5,282 low-income families with at least one child aged 12 years and younger). For the purposes of its report, FRAC defined hunger as food insufficiency (skipping meals, eating less, or running out of food) that occurred because of limited household resources. The results were reported by Wehler et al. in *Community Childhood Hunger Identification Project: A Survey of Childhood Hunger in the United States* (1995). FRAC concluded in the 1995 CCHIP survey that about 4 million children aged 12 years and younger experienced hunger for one or more months during the previous year. Another 9.6 million children were at risk of becoming hungry.

The 1995 CCHIP survey studied one child in each household (the child with the most recent birthday) and found that, in comparison with nonhungry children, hungry children were:

- More than three times as likely to suffer from unwanted weight loss

- More than four times as likely to suffer from fatigue

- Almost three times as likely to suffer from irritability

- More than three times as likely to have frequent headaches

- Almost one and a half times as likely to have frequent ear infections

- Four times as likely to suffer from concentration problems

- Almost twice as likely to have frequent colds

Based on the findings from the 1991 and 1995 CCHIP surveys, FRAC concluded that even though federal food programs are targeted to households most in need, a common barrier to program participation is a lack of information, particularly about eligibility guidelines. FRAC contended that if federal, state, and local governments made a greater effort to ensure that possible recipients were aware of their eligibility for food programs, such as the Special Supplemental Food Program for Women, Infants, and Children and the School Breakfast Program, there would be a large drop in hunger in the United States.

In 1997 the Urban Institute conducted the National Survey of American Families (NSAF; 2006, http://www.urban.org/center/anf/snapshots.cfm). Nearly half of low-income families (those with family incomes up to 200% of the federal poverty line) who were interviewed in 1997 reported that the food they purchased ran out before they got money to buy more or they worried they would run out of food. Four out of five of these families with food problems reported suffering actual food shortages, and one out of five worried about food shortages. More children than adults lived in families that worried about or had trouble affording food—54% of low-income children experienced this problem. The NSAF was repeated in 1999, and families reported fewer problems affording food than in 1997. Four out of 10 low-income families were either concerned about or had difficulty affording food, down 10% from 1997. However, approximately half of all low-income children still lived in families with difficulties affording food or families that had concern about the lack of food.

A third NSAF was conducted in 2002, and the results were released in 2004. According to Sandi Nelson of the Urban Institute, in "Trends in Parents' Economic Hardship" (March 2004, http://www.urban.org/UploadedPDF/310970_snapshots3_no21.pdf), the 2002 report showed that 51.3% of low-income parents and 59.4% of single parents experienced food hardship. The report also indicated that the gains made between 1997 and 1999 had been erased.

Since 1995 the U.S. Department of Agriculture's (USDA) Food and Nutrition Service and the Census Bureau have conducted annual surveys of food security, low food security (or food insecurity), and very low food insecurity (previously called hunger). (Food-secure households are those that have access at all times to enough food for an active, healthy life. Low-food-security households are uncertain of having, or unable to acquire, enough food to meet basic needs at all times during the year.) According to Mark Nord et al. of the Economic Research Service, in *Household Food Security in the United States, 2009*

(November 2010, http://www.ers.usda.gov/Publications/ERR108/ERR108.pdf), the survey is based on an 18-item scale:

1. Worried food would run out before (I/we) got money to buy more

2. Food bought didn't last and (I/we) didn't have money to get more

3. Couldn't afford to eat balanced meals

4. Adult(s) cut size of meals or skipped meals

5. Respondent ate less than felt he/she should

6. Adult(s) cut size or skipped meals in 3 or more months

7. Respondent hungry but didn't eat because couldn't afford

8. Respondent lost weight

9. Adult(s) did not eat for whole day

10. Adult(s) did not eat for whole day in 3 or more months

11. Relied on few kinds of low-cost food to feed child(ren)

12. Couldn't feed child(ren) balanced meals

13. Child(ren) were not eating enough

14. Cut size of child(ren)'s meals

15. Child(ren) were hungry

16. Child(ren) skipped meals

17. Child(ren) skipped meals in 3 or more months

18. Child(ren) did not eat for whole day

Figure 8.8 shows that levels of food insecurity steadily rose from 1999 to 2004, but dropped in 2005 before rising again. It rose precipitously, however, between 2007 and 2009, probably as a result of the worsening economic conditions. The prevalence rate of very low food security rose between 1999 and 2009. (Households with very low food security often worry that their food will run out, report that their food does run out before they have money to get more, cannot afford to eat balanced meals, often have adults who skip meals because there is not enough money for food, and report that they eat less than they should because of a lack of money.) In 2009, 9% of households reported low food security at some time during the year and an additional 5.7% reported having very low food security. (See Figure 8.9.)

Poor and low-income households were more likely to experience food insecurity and very low food security during the year than were households with higher incomes. Nord et al. indicate that in 2009, 24.4% of households with an income below the poverty line reported low food security and an additional 18.5% of these households reported very low food security. In comparison, 20.4% of households with

FIGURE 8.8

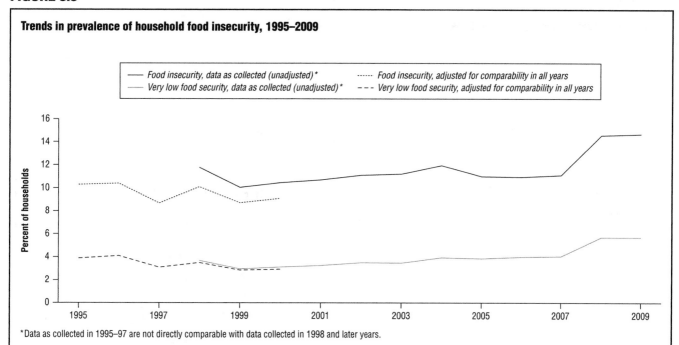

Trends in prevalence of household food insecurity, 1995–2009

— Food insecurity, data as collected (unadjusted)*
— Very low food security, data as collected (unadjusted)*
······ Food insecurity, adjusted for comparability in all years
--- Very low food security, adjusted for comparability in all years

*Data as collected in 1995–97 are not directly comparable with data collected in 1998 and later years.

SOURCE: Mark Nord et al., "Figure 3. Trends in the Prevalence of Food Insecurity in U.S. Households, 1995–2009," in *Household Food Security in the United States, 2009*, U.S. Department of Agriculture, Economic Research Service, November 2010, http://www.ers.usda.gov/Publications/ERR108/ERR108.pdf (accessed February 20, 2011).

FIGURE 8.9

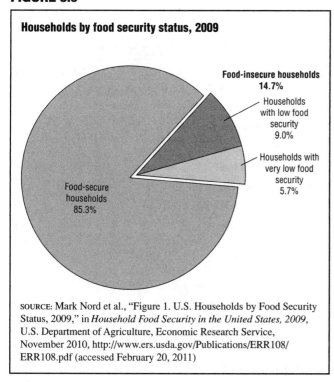

Households by food security status, 2009

Food-insecure households 14.7%

Households with low food security 9.0%

Households with very low food security 5.7%

Food-secure households 85.3%

SOURCE: Mark Nord et al., "Figure 1. U.S. Households by Food Security Status, 2009," in *Household Food Security in the United States, 2009*, U.S. Department of Agriculture, Economic Research Service, November 2010, http://www.ers.usda.gov/Publications/ERR108/ERR108.pdf (accessed February 20, 2011).

very low food security had either risen or stayed the same in nearly all the categories between 2008 and 2009. (See Figure 8.10 and Figure 8.11.)

Among the children, 12.1% experienced low food security and 1.3% experienced very low food security in 2009. (See Table 8.7.) The poorest families experienced low food security the most often; only 48.8% of households with an income-to-poverty ratio under 1.00 were food secure, compared with 52.5% of families with income-to-poverty ratios under 1.30, 56.3% of families with income-to-poverty ratios under 1.85, and 90% of families with income-to-poverty ratios of 1.85 and over. Families headed by married couples are much less likely to experience low food security than are families headed by single females. In 2009, 17.1% of married-couple households reported low food security, compared with 38.4% of female-headed households. Low food security was also more prevalent among non-Hispanic African-American families, 34.6% of whom experienced low food security, and Hispanic families, 34.9% of whom experienced low food security, than among non-Hispanic whites, 16.7% of whom experienced low food security.

Emergency Food Assistance

Feeding America is the nation's largest charitable hunger-relief organization, serving over 37 million people per year. In *Hunger Study 2010* (February 2010, http://feedingamerica.issuelab.org/research/listing/hunger_in_america

an income-to-poverty ratio under 1.85 experienced low food security and 14.4% experienced very low food security. Only 4.9% of households with higher incomes experienced low food security. The prevalence of food insecurity and

FIGURE 8.10

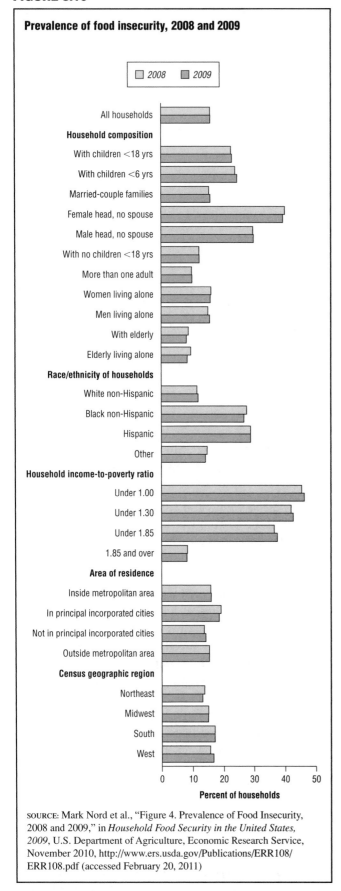

Prevalence of food insecurity, 2008 and 2009

□ 2008   ■ 2009

SOURCE: Mark Nord et al., "Figure 4. Prevalence of Food Insecurity, 2008 and 2009," in *Household Food Security in the United States, 2009*, U.S. Department of Agriculture, Economic Research Service, November 2010, http://www.ers.usda.gov/Publications/ERR108/ERR108.pdf (accessed February 20, 2011)

FIGURE 8.11

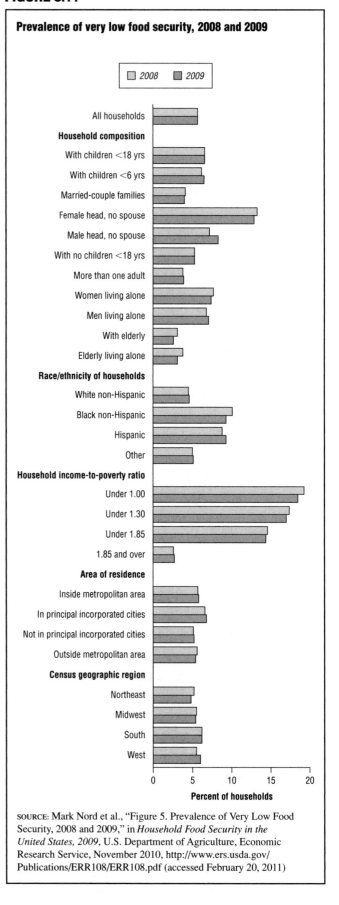

Prevalence of very low food security, 2008 and 2009

□ 2008   ■ 2009

SOURCE: Mark Nord et al., "Figure 5. Prevalence of Very Low Food Security, 2008 and 2009," in *Household Food Security in the United States, 2009*, U.S. Department of Agriculture, Economic Research Service, November 2010, http://www.ers.usda.gov/Publications/ERR108/ERR108.pdf (accessed February 20, 2011)

TABLE 8.7

Number of children by food security status of households and selected household characteristics, 2009

Category	Total[a] 1,000	In food-secure households 1,000	In food-secure households Percent	In food-insecure households[b] 1,000	In food-insecure households[b] Percent	In households with food-insecure children[c] 1,000	In households with food-insecure children[c] Percent	In households with very low food security among children 1,000	In households with very low food security among children Percent
All children	74,207	57,010	76.8	17,197	23.2	8,957	12.1	988	1.3
Household composition									
With children <6 yrs	38,020	28,373	74.6	9,647	25.4	4,824	12.7	463	1.2
Married-couple families	50,884	42,203	82.9	8,681	17.1	4,286	8.4	451	0.9
Female head, no spouse	18,089	11,142	61.6	6,947	38.4	3,881	21.5	480	2.7
Male head, no spouse	4,303	3,072	71.4	1,231	28.6	631	14.7	44	1.0
Other household with child[d]	931	593	63.7	338	36.3	160	17.2	NA	NA
Race/ethnicity of households									
White non-Hispanic	43,582	36,299	83.3	7,283	16.7	3,444	7.9	294	0.7
Black non-Hispanic	10,840	7,088	65.4	3,752	34.6	2,020	18.6	251	2.3
Hispanic[e]	15,139	9,861	65.1	5,278	34.9	3,049	20.1	377	2.5
Other	4,646	3,762	81.0	884	19.0	444	9.6	66	1.4
Household income-to-poverty ratio									
Under 1.00	14,097	6,874	48.8	7,223	51.2	4,184	29.7	593	4.2
Under 1.30	19,673	10,338	52.5	9,335	47.5	5,198	26.4	727	3.7
Under 1.85	26,796	15,093	56.3	11,703	43.7	6,409	23.9	818	3.1
1.85 and over	34,511	31,074	90.0	3,437	10.0	1,559	4.5	109	0.3
Income unknown	12,900	10,843	84.1	2,057	15.9	989	7.7	NA	NA
Area of residence[f]									
Inside metropolitan area	62,491	47,949	76.7	14,542	23.3	7,552	12.1	893	1.4
In principal cities[g]	19,532	13,838	70.8	5,694	29.2	3,162	16.2	383	2.0
Not in principal cities	32,578	26,203	80.4	6,375	19.6	3,132	9.6	367	1.1
Outside metropolitan area	11,715	9,060	77.3	2,655	22.7	1,405	12.0	95	0.8
Census geographic region									
Northeast	12,342	9,932	80.5	2,410	19.5	1,388	11.2	217	1.8
Midwest	16,042	12,555	78.3	3,487	21.7	1,514	9.4	102	0.6
South	27,810	20,819	74.9	6,991	25.1	3,667	13.2	333	1.2
West	18,012	13,702	76.1	4,310	23.9	2,388	13.3	335	1.9

NA = Not reported; fewer than 10 households in the survey with this characteristic had very low food security among children.
[a]Totals exclude households whose food security status is unknown because they did not give a valid response to any of the questions in the food security scale. In 2009, these represented 202,000 children (0.3 percent).
[b]Food-insecure households are those with low or very low food security among adults or children or both.
[c]Households with food-insecure children are those with low or very low food security among children.
[d]Households with children in complex living arrangements, e.g., children of other relatives or unrelated roommate or boarder.
[e]Hispanics may be of any race.
[f]Metropolitan area residence is based on 2003 Office of Management and Budget delineation. Prevalence rates by area of residence are comparable with those for 2004 and later years but are not precisely comparable with those of earlier years.
[g]Households within incorporated areas of the largest cities in each metropolitan area. Residence inside or outside of principal cities is not identified for about 17 percent of children living in metropolitan statistical areas.

SOURCE: Mark Nord et al., "Table 6. Number of Children by Food Security Status of Households and Selected Household Characteristics, 2009," in *Household Food Security in the United States, 2009*, U.S. Department of Agriculture, Economic Research Service, November 2010, http://www.ers.usda.gov/Publications/ERR108/ERR108.pdf (accessed February 20, 2011)

_2010_national_report), a study based on more than 61,000 interviews with clients and 37,000 questionnaires from Feeding America agencies, the organization finds the following characteristics of recipients of emergency food assistance:

- Nearly 14 million children were served.

- More than a third (36%) of all emergency client households had at least one member working.

- Seven out of 10 (70%) of the households had incomes below the poverty level.

- One out of 10 (10%) clients were homeless.

- Over a third (36%) of households served sometimes went hungry.

- A significant proportion of clients had to choose between food and other necessities; 46% reported having to choose between paying for food and paying for utilities, 39% had to choose between paying for food and paying their rent or mortgage, and 34% had to choose between paying for food and paying for medical care.

Malnutrition among the Homeless

Homeless people face a daily challenge to fulfill their basic need for food. They often go hungry. This is borne out by Burt et al. Clients of homeless assistance programs were found to have higher levels of food problems than poor people in general; 28% reported not getting enough to eat sometimes or often, compared with 12% of poor

American adults. Close to four out of 10 (39%) of the homeless clients had been hungry in the past 30 days but did not eat because they had no money for food, and 40% reported going at least one whole day without eating. Undernourishment and vitamin deficiency can cause or aggravate other physical conditions.

Meg Wilson of the University of Saint Francis finds in "Health-Promoting Behaviors of Sheltered Homeless Women" (*Family and Community Health*, vol. 28, no. 1, January–March 2005) that despite being homeless, many homeless women practiced "health-promoting behaviors." However, because of their homelessness, they had difficulty getting adequate nutrition.

The diet of homeless people, even those who live in shelters or in cheap motels, is generally not balanced or of good quality. Homeless people often rely on ready-cooked meals, fast-food restaurants, garbage cans, and the sometimes infrequent meal schedules of free food sources, such as soup kitchens, shelters, and drop-in centers. However, many soup kitchens serve only one meal per day, and many shelters that serve meals—and not all of them do—serve only two meals per day.

In *Hunger and Homelessness Survey: A Status Report on Hunger and Homelessness in America' s Cities, a 27-City Survey* (December 2010, http://www.usmayors.org/pressreleases/uploads/2010HungerHomelessnessReportfinal Dec212010.pdf), the U.S. Conference of Mayors indicates that 100% of cities surveyed in 2010 reported an increase in requests for emergency food assistance over the course of the year by an average of 24%. The majority (56%) of people requesting emergency food assistance were in families and 19% were senior citizens. (See Table 8.8.) Three out of 10 individuals requesting assistance were employed and 17% were homeless. Eighty percent of the cities reported that the demand for food assistance was larger than the supply. Officials cited unemployment (88.5%), high housing costs (50%), and low wages and poverty (46%) as the major causes of hunger in their cities.

GOVERNMENT PROGRAMS TO COMBAT HUNGER

Supplemental Nutrition Assistance Program

The Supplemental Nutrition Assistance Program (SNAP; previously called the Food Stamp Program), administered by the USDA, is the largest food assistance program in the United States. SNAP is designed to help low-income families purchase a nutritionally adequate, low-cost diet. Generally, SNAP may only be used to buy food to be prepared at home. It cannot be used for alcohol, tobacco, or hot foods that are intended to be consumed immediately, such as restaurant or delicatessen food.

TABLE 8.8

Requests for emergency food assistance as reported by cities by category, 2010

QUESTION 9: WHAT PERCENT OF REQUESTS FOR EMERGENCY FOOD ASSISTANCE REQUESTS COME FROM PERSONS IN THE FOLLOWING CATEGORIES (PLEASE NOTE THAT THESE CATEGORIES ARE NOT MUTUALLY EXCLUSIVE, THE SAME PERSON CAN BELONG TO MORE THAN ONE GROUP).

A) PERSONS IN FAMILIES
B) THE ELDERLY
C) PERSONS WHO ARE EMPLOYED
D) PERSONS WHO ARE HOMELESS

Type of persons	Average percentage for each
Persons in families	56%
The elderly	19%
Persons who are employed	30%
Persons who are homeless	17%

Note: For question 9, 11 cities provided responses for persons in families, 12 cities provided responses for the elderly, eight cities provided responses for persons who are employed, and nine cities provided responses for persons who are homeless.

SOURCE: "Question 9. What percent of requests for emergency food assistance requests come from persons in the following categories," in *Hunger and Homelessness Survey: A Status Report on Hunger and Homelessness in America's Cities, a 27-City Survey*, U.S. Conference of Mayors, December 2010, http://www.usmayors.org/pressreleases/uploads/2010_Hunger-Homelessness_Report-final%20Dec%2021%202010.pdf (accessed February 18, 2011)

The typical U.S. household spends 30% of its monthly income on food purchases. The program calculates 30% of the family's earnings and then issues enough food stamps to make up the difference between that amount and the amount that is needed to buy an adequate diet. These monthly allotments are usually provided electronically through an electronic benefit transfer, a debit card that is similar to a bank card.

The cash value of these benefits is based on the size of the household and how much the family earns. Households without an elderly or disabled member generally must have a monthly total (gross) cash income at or below 130% of the poverty level and may not have liquid assets (cash, savings, or other assets that can be easily sold) of more than $2,000. (If the household has a member aged 60 years and older, the asset limit is $3,000.) The net monthly income limit (gross income minus any approved deductions for child care, some housing costs, and other expenses) must be 100% or less of the poverty level, or $1,838 per month for a family of four between October 2010 and September 2011. (See Table 8.9.)

With some exceptions, SNAP is automatically available to Supplemental Security Income and TANF recipients. SNAP benefits are higher in states with lower TANF benefits because those benefits are considered a part of a family's countable income. To receive SNAP, certain household members must register for work, accept suitable job offers, or fulfill work or training requirements (such as looking or training for a job).

TABLE 8.9

Income chart for eligibility to receive SNAP, 2010–11

Household size	Gross monthly income (130 percent of poverty)	Net monthly income (100 percent of poverty)
1	$1,174	$903
2	1,579	1,215
3	1,984	1,526
4	2,389	1,838
5	2,794	2,150
6	3,200	2,461
7	3,605	2,773
8	4,010	3,085
Each additional member	+406	+312

Notes: SNAP = Supplemental Nutrition Assistance Program. Gross income means a household's total, non-excluded income, before any deductions have been made. Net income means gross income minus allowable deductions. SNAP gross and net income limits are higher in Alaska and Hawaii.

SOURCE: "Income," in *Supplemental Nutrition Assistance Program: Eligibility Requirements*, U.S. Department of Agriculture, Food and Nutrition Service, September 2010, http://www.fns.usda.gov/snap/applicant_recipients/eligibility.htm (accessed February 20, 2011)

Even though the federal government sets guidelines and provides funding, SNAP is actually administered by the states. State agencies certify eligibility as well as calculate and issue benefit allotments. Most often, the welfare agency and staff that administer the TANF and Medicaid programs also run SNAP. The program operates in all 50 states, the District of Columbia, Guam, and the Virgin Islands. (Puerto Rico is covered under a separate nutrition-assistance program.)

Except for some small differences in Alaska, Hawaii, and the territories, the program is run the same way throughout the United States. The states pay 50% of the administrative costs, and the federal government pays 100% of SNAP benefits and the other 50% of the administrative costs. In 2001 the federal government paid only $15.5 billion in SNAP benefits, but by 2010 it paid $64.7 billion in SNAP benefits, or an estimated average monthly benefit of $133.79 per recipient. (See Table 8.10.) The amount spent on SNAP had nearly doubled since 2008 as a result of the American Recovery and Reinvestment Act, which was signed into law as a response to the severe economic recession that began in late 2007. The legislation provided an additional $500 million to support participation in the program. The act also authorized an increase in benefits of up to 113.6% of the value of the Thrifty Food Plan (a plan that serves as the basis for maximum food stamp allotments).

SNAP participation decreased significantly after the Personal Responsibility and Work Opportunity Reconciliation Act of 1996 went into force, from a high of 27.5 million program participants in 1994 to a low of 17.2 million in 2000. (See Table 8.10.) However, with the worsening economy at the start of the 21st century, participation rates steadily increased, surpassing 1994 levels in 2008. In that year 28.2 million people participated in the program. By 2010, 40.3 million people participated in the program.

SNAP is the nation's largest source of food assistance, helping approximately 33.7 million Americans in an average month in 2009. The Food and Nutrition Service notes in "Characteristics of Supplemental Nutrition Assistance Program Households: Fiscal Year 2009 Summary" (October 2010, http://www.fns.usda.gov/ora/MENU/Published/snap/FILES/Participation/2009CharacteristicsSummary.pdf) that in 2009, 48% of the participants were children and 8% were aged 60 years and older. Three out of 10 (29%) SNAP recipients lived in a household with earnings as the primary source of income, and most SNAP households did not receive cash welfare benefits—only 10% received TANF. Most SNAP households were poor; only 14% of households had incomes above the poverty level and more than 41% had incomes at or below half the poverty level.

The average household receiving SNAP benefits received a monthly benefit of $272 in 2009. Table 8.11 shows the maximum monthly SNAP allotments between 2010 and 2011 for households of varying sizes within the continental United States. During this period the maximum monthly benefit for a four-person household was $668.

National School Lunch and School Breakfast Programs

The National School Lunch Program (NSLP) and the School Breakfast Program (SBP) provide federal cash and commodity support to participating public and private schools and to nonprofit residential institutions that serve meals to children. Children from households with incomes at or below 130% of the poverty line receive free meals. Children from households with incomes between 130% and 185% of the poverty level receive meals at a reduced price (no more than $0.40). Table 8.12 shows the income eligibility guidelines, based on the poverty guidelines, effective from July 1, 2009, to June 30, 2010. The levels were higher in Alaska and Hawaii than in the 48 contiguous states, the District of Columbia, Guam, and other U.S. territories. Children in TANF families are automatically eligible to receive free breakfasts and lunches. Almost 90% of federal funding for the NSLP is used to subsidize free and reduced-price lunches for low-income children.

The NSLP, which was created in 1946 under the National School Lunch Act, supplies subsidized lunches to children in almost all schools and in 6,000 residential and day care institutions. During the 1996–97 school year the USDA changed certain policies so that school meals would meet the recommendations of the Dietary Guidelines for America, the federal standards for what constitutes a healthy diet. Approximately 20.5 million children, or 65.3% of all children served lunch, received free or reduced-price lunches in FY 2010. (See Table 8.13.)

TABLE 8.10

Supplemental Nutrition Assistance Program participation and costs, 1969–2010

Fiscal year	Average participation (thousands)	Average benefit per person[a] (dollars)	Total benefits (millions of dollars)	All other costs[b]	Total costs
1969	2,878	6.63	228.80	21.70	250.50
1970	4,340	10.55	549.70	27.20	576.90
1971	9,368	13.55	1,522.70	53.20	1,575.90
1972	11,109	13.48	1,797.30	69.40	1,866.70
1973	12,166	14.60	2,131.40	76.00	2,207.40
1974	12,862	17.61	2,718.30	119.20	2,837.50
1975	17,064	21.40	4,385.50	233.20	4,618.70
1976	18,549	23.93	5,326.50	359.00	5,685.50
1977	17,077	24.71	5,067.00	394.00	5,461.00
1978	16,001	26.77	5,139.20	380.50	5,519.70
1979	17,653	30.59	6,480.20	459.60	6,939.80
1980	21,082	34.47	8,720.90	485.60	9,206.50
1981	22,430	39.49	10,629.90	595.40	11,225.20
1982[c]	21,717	39.17	10,208.30	628.40	10,836.70
1983	21,625	42.98	11,152.30	694.80	11,847.10
1984	20,854	42.74	10,696.10	882.60	11,578.80
1985	19,899	44.99	10,743.60	959.60	11,703.20
1986	19,429	45.49	10,605.20	1,033.20	11,638.40
1987	19,113	45.78	10,500.30	1,103.90	11,604.20
1988	18,645	49.83	11,149.10	1,167.70	12,316.80
1989	18,806	51.71	11,669.78	1,231.81	12,901.59
1990	20,049	58.78	14,142.79	1,304.47	15,447.26
1991	22,625	63.78	17,315.77	1,431.50	18,747.27
1992	25,407	68.57	20,905.68	1,556.66	22,462.34
1993	26,987	67.95	22,006.03	1,646.94	23,652.97
1994	27,474	69.00	22,748.58	1,744.87	24,493.45
1995	26,619	71.27	22,764.07	1,856.30	24,620.37
1996	25,543	73.21	22,440.11	1,890.88	24,330.99
1997	22,858	71.27	19,548.86	1,958.68	21,507.55
1998	19,791	71.12	16,890.49	2,097.84	18,988.32
1999	18,183	72.27	15,769.40	2,051.52	17,820.92
2000	17,194	72.62	14,983.32	2,070.70	17,054.02
2001	17,318	74.81	15,547.39	2,242.00	17,789.39
2002	19,096	79.67	18,256.20	2,380.82	20,637.02
2003	21,250	83.94	21,404.28	2,412.01	23,816.28
2004	23,811	86.16	24,618.89	2,480.14	27,099.03
2005	25,628	92.89	28,567.88	2,504.25	31,072.13
2006	26,549	94.75	30,187.35	2,716.56	32,903.90
2007	26,316	96.18	30,373.27	2,817.19	33,190.46
2008	28,223	102.19	34,608.40	3,034.06	37,642.46
2009	33,490	125.31	50,359.92	3,270.03	53,629.95
2010	40,302	133.79	64,704.47	3,596.42	68,300.89

Notes: Fiscal year 2010 data are preliminary; all data are subject to revision.
[a]Represents average monthly benefits per person.
[b]Includes the Federal share of State administrative expenses and Employment and Training programs. Also includes other Federal costs (e.g., printing and processing of stamps; anti-fraud funding; program evaluation).
[c]Puerto Rico initiated food stamp operations during fiscal year 1975 and participated through June of fiscal year 1982. A separate Nutrition Assistance Grant began in July 1982.

SOURCE: "Supplemental Nutrition Assistance Program Participation and Costs," in *Program Data: Supplemental Nutrition Assistance Program*, U.S. Department of Agriculture, Food and Nutrition Service, January 2011, http://www.fns.usda.gov/pd/SNAPsummary.htm (accessed February 20, 2011)

The SBP, which was created under the Child Nutrition Act of 1966, serves far fewer students than does the NSLP. The SBP also differs from the NSLP in that most schools offering the program are in low-income areas, and the children who participate in the program are mainly from low- and moderate-income families. In FY 2010 over 9.7 million students, or about 83.5% of all children served breakfast, participated. (See Table 8.14.)

In December 2010 President Obama signed the Healthy, Hunger-Free Kids Act into law. This act upgraded nutritional standards for school meal programs and required schools to make information on the nutritional quality of meals available to parents. The act provided several ways to certify additional children for the free and reduced meal programs, including using Medicaid data to directly certify children rather than relying on paper applications or using census data in high-poverty communities to certify school-wide income eligibility. In addition, the act expanded the school meal program to afterschool meals through the existing Child and Adult Care Food Program providers across the nation.

Special Supplemental Food Program for Women, Infants, and Children

The Special Supplemental Food Program for Women, Infants, and Children (WIC) provides food assistance as well as nutrition counseling and health services to low-income pregnant women, to women who have just given birth and their babies, and to low-income children up to five years old. Participants in the program must have incomes at or below 185% of the poverty level (all but five states use this cutoff level) and must be nutritionally at risk.

As explained by the Child Nutrition Act of 1966, nutritional risk includes abnormal nutritional conditions, medical conditions related to nutrition, health-impairing dietary deficiencies, or conditions that might predispose a person to these conditions. Pregnant women may receive benefits throughout their pregnancies and for up to six months after childbirth or up to one year for nursing mothers.

Those receiving WIC benefits get supplemental food each month in the form of actual food items or, more commonly, vouchers (coupons) for the purchase of specific items at the store. Permitted foods contain high amounts of protein, iron, calcium, vitamin A, and vitamin C. Items that may be purchased include milk, cheese, eggs, infant for-

TABLE 8.11

Maximum SNAP allotments, 2010–11

Household size	48 states and DC
1	$200
2	$367
3	$526
4	$668
5	$793
6	$952
7	$1,052
8	$1,202
Each additional person	$150

SOURCE: "Maximum SNAP Allotments," in *Supplemental Nutrition Assistance Program (SNAP): FY 2011 SNAP Cost-of-Living Adjustments*, U.S. Department of Agriculture, Food and Nutrition Service, August 2, 2010, http://www.fns.usda.gov/snap/rules/Memo/2010/080210.pdf (accessed February 20, 2011)

TABLE 8.12

Income eligibility guidelines for free or reduced-price meals, 2009–10

Income eligibility guidelines

Household size	Federal poverty guidelines Annual	Effective from July 1, 2009 to June 30, 2010									
		Reduced price meals—185%					Free meals—130%				
		Annual	Monthly	Twice per month	Every two weeks	Weekly	Annual	Monthly	Twice per month	Every two weeks	Weekly
48 contiguous states, District of Columbia, Guam, and territories											
1	10,830	20,036	1,670	835	771	386	14,079	1,174	587	542	271
2	14,570	26,955	2,247	1,124	1,037	519	18,941	1,579	790	729	365
3	18,310	33,874	2,823	1,412	1,303	652	23,803	1,984	992	916	458
4	22,050	40,793	3,400	1,700	1,569	785	28,665	2,389	1,195	1,103	552
5	25,790	47,712	3,976	1,988	1,836	918	33,527	2,794	1,397	1,290	645
6	29,530	54,631	4,553	2,277	2,102	1,051	38,389	3,200	1,600	1,477	739
7	33,270	61,550	5,130	2,565	2,368	1,184	43,251	3,605	1,803	1,664	832
8	37,010	68,469	5,706	2,853	2,634	1,317	48,113	4,010	2,005	1,851	926
For each add'l family member, add	3,740	6,919	577	289	267	134	4,862	406	203	187	94
Alaska											
1	13,530	25,031	2,086	1,043	963	482	17,589	1,466	733	677	339
2	18,210	33,689	2,808	1,404	1,296	648	23,673	1,973	987	911	456
3	22,890	42,347	3,529	1,765	1,629	815	29,757	2,480	1,240	1,145	573
4	27,570	51,005	4,251	2,126	1,962	981	36,841	2,987	1,494	1,379	690
5	32,250	59,663	4,972	2,486	2,295	1,148	41,925	3,494	1,747	1,613	807
6	36,930	68,321	5,694	2,847	2,628	1,314	48,009	4,001	2,001	1,847	924
7	41,610	76,979	6,415	3,208	2,961	1,481	54,093	4,508	2,254	2,081	1,041
8	46,290	85,637	7,137	3,569	3,294	1,647	60,177	5,015	2,508	2,315	1,158
For each add'l family member, add	4,680	8,658	722	361	333	167	6,084	507	254	234	117
Hawaii											
1	12,460	23,051	1,921	961	887	444	16,198	1,350	675	623	312
2	16,760	31,006	2,584	1,292	1,193	597	21,788	1,816	908	838	419
3	21,060	38,961	3,247	1,624	1,499	750	27,378	2,282	1,141	1,053	527
4	25,360	46,916	3,910	1,955	1,805	903	32,968	2,748	1,374	1,268	634
5	29,660	54,871	4,573	2,287	2,111	1,056	38,558	3,214	1,607	1,483	742
6	33,260	62,826	5,236	2,618	2,417	1,209	44,148	3,679	1,840	1,698	849
7	38,260	70,781	5,899	2,950	2,723	1,362	49,738	4,145	2,073	1,913	957
8	42,560	78,736	6,562	3,281	3,029	1,615	55,328	4,611	2,306	2,128	1,064
For each add'l family member, add	4,300	7,955	663	332	306	153	5,590	466	233	215	108

SOURCE: "Income Eligibility Guidelines," in "Child Nutrition Programs—Income Eligibility Guidelines," *Federal Register*, vol. 74, no. 58, March 27, 2009, http://www.fns.usda.gov/cnd/governance/notices/iegs/IEGs09-10.pdf (accessed February 20, 2011)

TABLE 8.13

National school lunch program participation and lunches served, fiscal years 1969–2010

Fiscal year	Free	Reduced price	Full price	Total	Total lunches served	Percent free/reduced price of total
			Millions			%
1969	2.9	*	16.5	19.4	3,368.2	15.1
1970	4.6	*	17.8	22.4	3,565.1	20.7
1971	5.8	0.5	17.8	24.1	3,848.3	26.1
1972	7.3	0.5	16.6	24.4	3,972.1	32.4
1973	8.1	0.5	16.1	24.7	4,008.8	35.0
1974	8.6	0.5	15.5	24.6	3,981.6	37.1
1975	9.4	0.6	14.9	24.9	4,063.0	40.3
1976	10.2	0.8	14.6	25.6	4,147.9	43.1
1977	10.5	1.3	14.5	26.2	4,250.0	44.8
1978	10.3	1.5	14.9	26.7	4,294.1	44.4
1979	10.0	1.7	15.3	27.0	4,357.4	43.6
1980	10.0	1.9	14.7	26.6	4,387.0	45.1
1981	10.6	1.9	13.3	25.8	4,210.6	48.6
1982	9.8	1.6	11.5	22.9	3,755.0	50.2
1983	10.3	1.5	11.2	23.0	3,803.3	51.7
1984	10.3	1.5	11.5	23.4	3,826.2	51.0
1985	9.9	1.6	12.1	23.6	3,890.1	49.1
1986	10.0	1.6	12.2	23.7	3,942.5	49.1
1987	10.0	1.6	12.4	23.9	3,939.9	48.6
1988	9.8	1.6	12.8	24.2	4,032.9	47.4
1989	9.7	1.6	12.9	24.2	4,004.9	47.2
1990	9.8	1.7	12.6	24.1	4,009.0	48.3
1991	10.3	1.8	12.2	24.2	4,050.7	50.4
1992	11.2	1.7	11.7	24.6	4,101.4	53.1
1993	11.7	1.7	11.4	24.9	4,137.7	54.8
1994	12.2	1.8	11.3	25.3	4,201.6	55.9
1995	12.4	1.9	11.4	25.7	4,253.3	56.4
1996	12.6	2.0	11.3	25.9	4,313.2	56.9
1997	12.9	2.1	11.3	26.3	4,409.0	57.6
1998	13.0	2.2	11.4	26.6	4,425.0	57.8
1999	13.0	2.4	11.6	27.0	4,513.6	57.6
2000	13.0	2.5	11.9	27.3	4,575.0	57.1
2001	12.9	2.6	12.0	27.5	4,585.2	56.8
2002	13.3	2.6	12.0	28.0	4,716.6	57.6
2003	13.7	2.7	11.9	28.4	4,762.9	58.5
2004	14.1	2.8	12.0	29.0	4,842.4	59.1
2005	14.6	2.9	12.2	29.6	4,976.5	59.4
2006	14.8	2.9	12.4	30.1	5,027.9	59.3
2007	15.0	3.1	12.6	30.6	5,071.3	59.3
2008	15.4	3.1	12.5	31.0	5,208.9	60.1
2009	16.3	3.2	11.9	31.3	5,186.2	62.5
2010	17.5	3.0	11.1	31.6	5,275.5	65.3

Notes: Fiscal year 2010 data are preliminary; all data are subject to revision. Participation data are 9-month averages (summer months are excluded).
*Included with free meals.

SOURCE: "National School Lunch Program: Participation and Lunches Served," U.S. Department of Agriculture, Food and Nutrition Service, January 2011, http://www.fns.usda.gov/pd/slsummar.htm (accessed February 20, 2011)

TABLE 8.14

National school breakfast program participation and meals served, fiscal years 1969–2010

Fiscal years	Free	Reduced price	Paid	Total	Meals served	Free/reduced price of total meals
			Millions			Percent
1969	—	—	—	0.22	39.70	71.0
1970	—	—	—	0.45	71.80	71.5
1971	0.60	*	0.20	0.80	125.50	76.3
1972	0.81	*	0.23	1.04	169.30	78.5
1973	0.99	*	0.20	1.19	194.10	83.4
1974	1.14	*	0.24	1.37	226.70	82.8
1975	1.45	0.04	0.33	1.82	294.70	82.1
1976	1.76	0.06	0.37	2.20	353.60	84.2
1977	2.02	0.11	0.36	2.49	434.30	85.7
1978	2.23	0.16	0.42	2.80	478.80	85.3
1979	2.56	0.21	0.54	3.32	565.60	84.1
1980	2.79	0.25	0.56	3.60	619.90	85.2
1981	3.05	0.25	0.51	3.81	644.20	86.9
1982	2.80	0.16	0.36	3.32	567.40	89.3
1983	2.87	0.15	0.34	3.36	580.70	90.3
1984	2.91	0.15	0.37	3.43	589.20	89.7
1985	2.88	0.16	0.40	3.44	594.90	88.6
1986	2.93	0.16	0.41	3.50	610.60	88.7
1987	3.01	0.17	0.43	3.61	621.50	88.4
1988	3.03	0.18	0.47	3.68	642.50	87.5
1989	3.11	0.19	0.51	3.81	658.45	86.8
1990	3.30	0.22	0.55	4.07	707.49	86.7
1991	3.61	0.25	0.58	4.44	771.86	87.3
1992	4.05	0.26	0.61	4.92	852.43	88.0
1993	4.41	0.28	0.66	5.36	923.56	87.9
1994	4.76	0.32	0.75	5.83	1,001.52	87.4
1995	5.10	0.37	0.85	6.32	1,078.92	86.8
1996	5.27	0.41	0.90	6.58	1,125.74	86.5
1997	5.52	0.45	0.95	6.92	1,191.21	86.5
1998	5.64	0.50	1.01	7.14	1,220.90	86.1
1999	5.72	0.56	1.09	7.37	1,267.62	85.4
2000	5.73	0.61	1.21	7.55	1,303.35	84.2
2001	5.80	0.67	1.32	7.79	1,334.51	83.2
2002	6.03	0.70	1.41	8.15	1,404.76	82.9
2003	6.22	0.74	1.47	8.43	1,447.90	82.8
2004	6.52	0.80	1.58	8.90	1,524.91	82.4
2005	6.80	0.86	1.70	9.36	1,603.95	82.1
2006	6.99	0.92	1.86	9.76	1,663.07	81.2
2007	7.15	0.98	1.99	10.12	1,713.96	80.6
2008	7.48	1.04	2.08	10.61	1,812.93	80.6
2009	7.99	1.07	2.01	11.08	1,866.67	82.1
2010	8.68	1.05	1.94	11.67	1,966.78	83.5

*Included with free participation
Notes: Fiscal year 2010 data are preliminary; all data are subject to revision. Participation data are 9-month averages (summer months are excluded).

SOURCE: "School Breakfast Program Participation and Meals Served," U.S. Department of Agriculture, Food and Nutrition Service, January 2011, http://www.fns.usda.gov/pd/sbsummar.htm (accessed February 20, 2011)

mula, cereals, and fruit or vegetable juices. Mothers participating in WIC are encouraged to breastfeed their infants if possible, but state WIC agencies will provide formula for mothers who choose to use it.

The USDA estimates that the national average monthly cost of a WIC food package in FY 2010 was $41.45 per participant, including food and administrative costs. (See Table 8.15.) The federal government spent an estimated $6.7 billion to operate WIC in FY 2010, and the

program served approximately 9.2 million women, infants, and children. WIC works in conjunction with the Farmers' Market Nutrition Program, which was established in 1992, to provide WIC recipients with increased access, in the form of vouchers, to fresh fruits and vegetables.

WIC is not an entitlement program. That is, the number of participants is limited by the amount of funds that are available rather than by eligibility. Patty Connor et al. indicate in *WIC Participant and Program Characteristics 2008* (January 2010, http://www.fns.usda.gov/ora/menu/published/wic/FILES/pc2008.pdf) that of the

TABLE 8.15

Special Supplemental Food Program for Women, Infants, and Children (WIC) program participation and costs, fiscal years 1974–2010

[Data as of March 2, 2011]

Fiscal year	Total participation[a]	Program costs			Average monthly food cost per person
		Food	NSA	Total[b]	
	Thousands	Millions of dollars			Dollars
1974	88	8.2	2.2	10.4	15.68
1975	344	76.7	12.6	89.3	18.58
1976	520	122.3	20.3	142.6	19.60
1977	848	211.7	44.2	255.9	20.80
1978	1,181	311.5	68.1	379.6	21.99
1979	1,483	428.6	96.8	525.4	24.09
1980	1,914	584.1	140.5	727.7	25.43
1981	2,119	708.0	160.6	871.6	27.84
1982	2,189	757.6	190.5	948.8	28.83
1983	2,537	901.8	221.3	1,126.0	29.62
1984	3,045	1,117.3	268.8	1,388.1	30.58
1985	3,138	1,193.2	294.4	1,489.3	31.69
1986	3,312	1,264.4	316.4	1,582.9	31.82
1987	3,429	1,344.7	333.1	1,679.6	32.68
1988	3,593	1,434.8	360.6	1,797.5	33.28
1989	4,119	1,489.4	416.5	1,910.9	30.14
1990	4,517	1,636.8	478.7	2,122.4	30.20
1991	4,893	1,751.9	544.0	2,301.0	29.84
1992	5,403	1,960.5	632.7	2,600.6	30.24
1993	5,921	2,115.1	705.6	2,828.6	29.77
1994	6,477	2,325.2	834.4	3,169.3	29.92
1995	6,894	2,511.6	904.6	3,436.2	30.36
1996	7,186	2,689.9	985.1	3,695.4	31.20
1997	7,407	2,815.5	1,008.2	3,843.8	31.68
1998	7,367	2,808.1	1,061.4	3,890.4	31.76
1999	7,311	2,851.6	1,063.9	3,938.1	32.50
2000	7,192	2,853.1	1,102.6	3,982.1	33.06
2001	7,306	3,007.9	1,110.6	4,153.3	34.31
2002	7,491	3,129.7	1,182.3	4,339.8	34.82
2003	7,631	3,230.3	1,260.0	4,524.4	35.28
2004	7,904	3,562.0	1,272.4	4,887.3	37.55
2005	8,023	3,603.0	1,335.5	4,993.0	37.42
2006	8,088	3,598.0	1,403.0	5,073.0	37.07
2007	8,285	3,880.7	1,479.0	5,409.2	39.03
2008	8,705	4,534.5	1,607.5	6,190.4	43.41
2009	9,122	4,641.0	1,788.0	6,471.0	42.40
2010	9,175	4,564.1	1,912.3	6,703.1	41.45

Notes: NSA = Nutrition Services and Administrative costs. Nutrition Services includes nutrition education, preventative and coordination services (such as health care), and promotion of breastfeeding and immunization. Fiscal year 2010 data are preliminary; all data are subject to revision.
[a]Participation data are annual averages (6 months in fiscal year 1974; 12 months all subsequent years).
[b]In addition to food and NSA costs, total expenditures includes funds for program evaluation, Farmers' Market Nutrition Program (fiscal year 1989 onward), special projects and infrastructure.

SOURCE: "WIC Program Participation and Costs," U.S. Department of Agriculture, Food and Nutrition Service, January 2011, http://www.fns.usda.gov/pd/wisummary.htm (accessed February 20, 2011)

FIGURE 8.12

Distribution of individuals enrolled in the WIC program, 2008

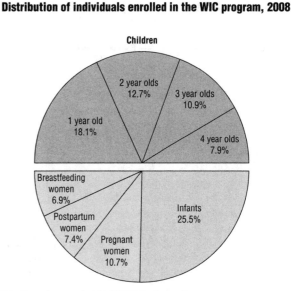

Note: Percents may not add to 100.0% due to rounding.
WIC = Women, Infants, and Children (public health program).

SOURCE: Patty Connor et al., "Exhibit E.2. Distribution of Individuals Enrolled in the WIC Program," in *WIC Participant and Program Characteristics 2008*, U.S. Department of Agriculture, Food and Nutrition Service, Office of Research and Analysis, January 2010, http://www.fns.usda.gov/ora/menu/published/wic/FILES/pc2008.pdf (accessed February 20, 2011)

FIGURE 8.13

Poverty levels of WIC participants compared to the U.S. population, 2008

Notes: WIC = Women, Infants, and Children (public health program). Percents may not add to 100.0% due to rounding.

SOURCE: Patty Connor et al., "Exhibit E.3. Comparison of Poverty Levels of WIC Participants Reporting Income to Persons in the U.S. Population," in *WIC Participant and Program Characteristics 2008*, U.S. Department of Agriculture, Food and Nutrition Service, Office of Research and Analysis, January 2010, http://www.fns.usda.gov/ora/menu/published/wic/FILES/pc2008.pdf (accessed February 20, 2011)

approximately 9.5 million participants in 2008, 49.6% were children and 25.5% were infants. (See Figure 8.12.) In that year, 25% of WIC participants were women—10.7% were pregnant, 6.9% were breastfeeding, and 7.4% were in the postpartum period, recovering from giving birth.

Connor et al. find that in 2008, 68.3% of WIC participants had household incomes at or below the poverty level, compared with 12.5% of the general population. (See Figure 8.13.) Nearly two-thirds (64.4%) of WIC participants received ben-

FIGURE 8.14

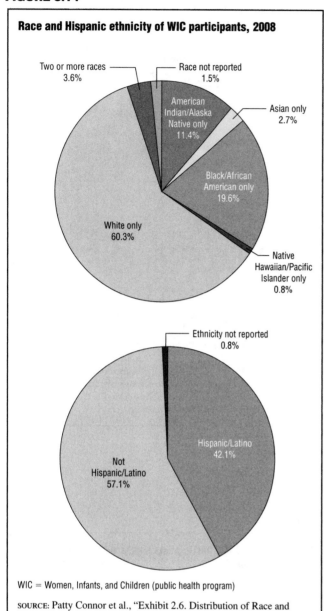

Race and Hispanic ethnicity of WIC participants, 2008

Two or more races
3.6%

Race not reported
1.5%

American
Indian/Alaska
Native only
11.4%

Asian only
2.7%

Black/African
American only
19.6%

White only
60.3%

Native
Hawaiian/Pacific
Islander only
0.8%

Ethnicity not reported
0.8%

Hispanic/Latino
42.1%

Not
Hispanic/Latino
57.1%

WIC = Women, Infants, and Children (public health program)

SOURCE: Patty Connor et al., "Exhibit 2.6. Distribution of Race and Ethnicity of WIC Participants," in *WIC Participant and Program Characteristics 2008*, U.S. Department of Agriculture, Food and Nutrition Service, Office of Research and Analysis, January 2010, http://www.fns.usda.gov/ora/menu/published/wic/FILES/pc2008.pdf (accessed February 20, 2011)

efits from at least one other public assistance program. Of the WIC participants who received additional benefits, 6.5% received TANF, 22.6% received SNAP, and 62% were covered by Medicaid.

Connor et al. also note that the racial and ethnic composition of WIC participants has been changing since 1992 as the percentage of Hispanic enrollees has risen and the percentage of non-Hispanic white and African-American enrollees has declined. In 2008, 42.1% of all WIC participants were Hispanic, 60.3% were white (Hispanic or non-Hispanic), and 19.6% were African-American. (See Figure 8.14.)

IMPORTANT NAMES AND ADDRESSES

American Public Human Services Association
1133 19th St. NW, Ste. 400
Washington, DC 20036
(202) 682-0100
FAX: (202) 289-6555
URL: http://www.aphsa.org/

Association of Gospel Rescue Missions
7222 Commerce Center Dr., Ste. 120
Colorado Springs, CO 80919
(719) 266-8300
1-800-473-7283
FAX: (719) 266-8600
E-mail: info@agrm.org
URL: http://www.agrm.org/

Center for Law and Social Policy
1200 18th St. NW, Ste. 200
Washington, DC 20036
(202) 906-8000
FAX: (202) 842-2885
URL: http://www.clasp.org/

Center for the Study of Social Policy
1575 Eye St. NW, Ste. 500
Washington, DC 20005
(202) 371-1565
FAX: (202) 371-1472
E-mail: info@cssp.org
URL: http://www.cssp.org/

Center on Budget and Policy Priorities
820 First St. NE, Ste. 510
Washington, DC 20002
(202) 408-1080
FAX: (202) 408-1056
E-mail: center@cbpp.org
URL: http://www.cbpp.org/

Children's Defense Fund
25 E St. NW
Washington, DC 20001
1-800-233-1200
E-mail: cdfinfo@childrensdefense.org
URL: http://www.childrensdefense.org/

Child Welfare League of America
1726 M St. NW, Ste. 500
Washington, DC 20036
(202) 688-4200
FAX: (202) 833-1689
URL: http://www.cwla.org/

Feeding America
35 E. Wacker Dr., Ste. 2000
Chicago, IL 60601
1-800-771-2303
FAX: (312) 263-5626
URL: http://www.feedingamerica.org/

Food Research and Action Center
1875 Connecticut Ave. NW, Ste. 540
Washington, DC 20009
(202) 986-2200
FAX: (202) 986-2525
URL: http://www.frac.org/

Habitat for Humanity International
121 Habitat St.
Americus, GA 31709-3498
1-800-422-4828
URL: http://www.habitat.org/

Homes for the Homeless
50 Cooper Square, Fourth Floor
New York, NY 10003
(212) 529-5252
FAX: (212) 529-7698
E-mail: info@hfhnyc.org
URL: http://www.homes
forthehomeless.com/

Housing Assistance Council
1025 Vermont Ave. NW, Ste. 606
Washington, DC 20005
(202) 842-8600
FAX: (202) 347-3441
E-mail: hac@ruralhome.org
URL: http://www.ruralhome.org/

Institute for Research on Poverty University of Wisconsin, Madison
1180 Observatory Dr.
3412 Social Science Bldg.
Madison, WI 53706-1393
(608) 262-6358
FAX: (608) 265-3119
E-mail: djohnson@ssc.wisc.edu
URL: http://www.irp.wisc.edu/

Joint Center for Housing Studies Harvard University
1033 Massachusetts Ave., Fifth Floor
Cambridge, MA 02138
(617) 495-7908
FAX: (617) 496-9957
URL: http://www.jchs.harvard.edu/
index.htm

Kaiser Family Foundation
2400 Sand Hill Rd.
Menlo Park, CA 94025
(650) 854-9400
FAX: (650) 854-4800
URL: http://www.kff.org/

National Alliance to End Homelessness
1518 K St. NW, Ste. 410
Washington, DC 20005
(202) 638-1526
FAX: (202) 638-4664
E-mail: naeh@naeh.org
URL: http://www.endhomelessness.org/

National Alliance of HUD Tenants
42 Seaverns Ave.
Boston, MA 02130
(617) 267-9564
FAX: (617) 522-4857
E-mail: naht@saveourhomes.org
URL: http://www.saveourhomes.org/

National Alliance on Mental Illness
3803 N. Fairfax Dr., Ste. 100
Arlington, VA 22203
(703) 524-7600
FAX: (703) 524-9094
URL: http://www.nami.org/

National Association for the Education of Homeless Children and Youth
PO Box 26274
Minneapolis, MN 55426
(866) 862-2562
FAX: (763) 545-9499
E-mail: info@naehcy.org
URL: http://www.naehcy.org/

National Center for Children in Poverty
215 W. 125th St., Third Floor
New York, NY 10027
(646) 284-9600
FAX: (646) 284-9623
E-mail: info@nccp.org
URL: http://www.nccp.org/

National Coalition for the Homeless
2201 P St. NW
Washington, DC 20037
(202) 462-4822
FAX: (202) 462-4823
E-mail: info@nationalhomeless.org
URL: http://www.nationalhomeless.org/

National Coalition for Homeless Veterans
333 ½ Pennsylvania Ave. SE
Washington, DC 20003-1148
(202) 546-1969
1-800-VET-HELP
FAX: (202) 546-2063
E-mail: info@nchv.org
URL: http://www.nchv.org/

National Health Care for the Homeless Council
PO Box 60427
Nashville, TN 37206-0427
(615) 226-2292
FAX: (615) 226-1656
URL: http://www.nhchc.org/

National Housing Conference
1900 M St. NW, Ste. 200
Washington, DC 20036
(202) 466-2121
FAX: (202) 466-2122
URL: http://www.nhc.org/

National Housing Law Project
703 Market St., Ste. 2000
San Francisco, CA 94103
(415) 546-7000
FAX: (415) 546-7007
URL: http://www.nhlp.org/

National Law Center for Children and Families
211 N. Union St., Ste. 100
Alexandria, VA 22314
(703) 548-5522
FAX: (703) 548-5544
URL: http://www.nationallawcenter.org/

National Law Center on Homelessness and Poverty
1411 K St. NW, Ste. 1400
Washington, DC 20005
(202) 638-2535
FAX: (202) 628-2737
URL: http://www.nlchp.org/

National League of Cities
1301 Pennsylvania Ave. NW, Ste. 559
Washington, DC 20004
(202) 626-3100
FAX: (202) 628-3043
URL: http://www.nlc.org/

National Low Income Housing Coalition
727 15th St. NW, Sixth Floor
Washington, DC 20005
(202) 662-1530
FAX: (202) 393-1973
URL: http://www.nlihc.org/

National Rural Housing Coalition
1331 G St. NW, 10th Floor
Washington, DC 20005
(202) 393-5229
E-mail: nrhc@ruralhousingcoalition.org
URL: http://www.nrhcweb.org/

National Women's Law Center
11 Dupont Circle NW, Ste. 800
Washington, DC 20036
(202) 588-5180
FAX: (202) 588-5185
E-mail: info@nwlc.org
URL: http://www.nwlc.org/

Rural Policy Research Institute
University of Missouri, Columbia
214 Middlebush Hall
Columbia, MO 65211
(573) 882-0316
FAX: (573) 884-5310
URL: http://www.rupri.org/

Urban Institute
2100 M St. NW
Washington, DC 20037
(202) 833-7200
URL: http://www.urban.org/

U.S. Conference of Mayors
1620 Eye St. NW
Washington, DC 20006
(202) 293-7330
FAX: (202) 293-2352
E-mail: info@usmayors.org
URL: http://www.usmayors.org/

U.S. Interagency Council on Homelessness
Federal Center SW
409 Third St. SW, Ste. 310
Washington, DC 20024
(202) 708-4663
FAX: (202) 708-1216
E-mail: usich@usich.gov
URL: http://www.ich.gov/

RESOURCES

The federal government remains the premier source of facts on many issues, including poverty, employment, welfare, and housing. Some particularly excellent sources of information from the U.S. Census Bureau are *Dynamics of Economic Well-Being: Poverty, 2004–2006* (Robin J. Anderson, March 2011), *2009 American Community Survey 1-Year Estimates* (2011), *America's Families and Living Arrangements: 2010* (November 2010), *Tables of NAS-Based Poverty Estimates: 2009* (October 2010), *Income, Poverty, and Health Insurance Coverage in the United States: 2009* (Carmen DeNavas-Walt, Bernadette D. Proctor, and Jessica C. Smith, September 2010), *Statistical Abstract of the United States: 2011* (2010), *Custodial Mothers and Fathers and Their Child Support: 2007* (Timothy S. Grall, November 2009), *Extended Measures of Well-Being: Living Conditions in the United States, 2005* (November 2009), *Participation of Mothers in Government Assistance Programs: 2004* (Jane Lawler Dye, May 2008), and *Dynamics of Economic Well-Being: Participation in Government Programs, 2001 through 2003: Who Gets Assistance?* (Tracy A. Loveless and Jan Tin, October 2006).

The monthly *Employment and Earnings* of the U.S. Bureau of Labor Statistics (BLS) provides data on wages and work patterns, and *A Profile of the Working Poor, 2008* (March 2010) details labor information about low-income workers. Many of the BLS data are published in the *Monthly Labor Review*. Other material used in preparing this book comes from the BLS's *Characteristics of Minimum Wage Workers: 2009* (March 2010) and *Current Population Survey (CPS) Tables: Household Data Annual Averages* (2011).

Other publications of the federal government used in this book include the U.S. Department of Housing and Urban Development's *The 2009 Annual Homeless Assessment Report to Congress* (June 2010), *FY 2012 Budget Summary* (February 2011), and *Worst Case Housing Needs 2009: A Report to Congress* (February 2011). The U.S. Department of Education's National Center for Homeless Education published *Education for Homeless Children and Youths Program* (April 2009). The Federal Interagency Forum on Child and Family Statistics published *America's Children in Brief: Key National Indicators of Well-Being, 2010* (July 2010), which has provided information for this publication. The Social Security Administration published *Annual Statistical Supplement to the Social Security Bulletin, 2009* (February 2010), which provides a statistical overview of major welfare programs. The Administration for Children and Families published *Indicators of Welfare Dependence: Annual Report to Congress, 2008* (Gil Grouse, Susan Hauan, and Annette Waters Rogers, December 2008), which describes the Temporary Assistance for Needy Families program.

The National Center for Health Statistics, which issues periodic reports such as *Health, United States, 2010* (February 2011), as well as vital statistics on birth rates, marital status, and health status, is a part of the Centers for Disease Control and Prevention (CDC). Reports from the CDC used in this book include "Births: Preliminary Data for 2009" (Brady E. Hamilton, Joyce A. Martin, and Stephanie J. Ventura, December 2010), *Reported Tuberculosis in the United States, 2009* (October 2010), and *Diagnoses of HIV Infection and AIDS in the United States and Dependent Areas, 2009: HIV Surveillance Report* (February 2011).

The U.S. Department of Agriculture's Food and Nutrition Service provides detailed tables about the National School Lunch Program, the School Breakfast Program, the Supplemental Nutrition Assistance Program, and the Special Supplemental Food Program for Women, Infants, and Children, as well as data from *Household Food Security in the United States, 2009* (Mark Nord et al., November 2010) and *WIC Participant and Program Characteristics 2008* (Patty Connor et al., January 2010).

The periodically published *The Green Book: Background Material and Data on the Programs within the Jurisdiction of the Committee on Ways and Means* by the U.S. House of Representatives provides the most complete information on the U.S. welfare system in a single source.

Many different organizations study the poor and homeless. Notable among them for its many large studies on homelessness is the Urban Institute. This organization's ongoing studies of the homeless are among the largest and most comprehensive in the United States. Its publications were a major source of information for this volume, especially "The Great Recession, Unemployment Insurance, and Poverty" (Wayne Vroman, April 2010), "Jobs in an Uncertain Economy: A Research Focus of the Urban Institute" (2010), *Federal Programs for Addressing Low-Income Housing Needs: A Policy Primer* (Margery Austin Turner and G. Thomas Kingsley, December 2008), "Government Work Supports and Low-Income Families: Facts and Figures" (July 2006), "A Decade of Welfare Reform: Facts and Figures—Assessing the New Federalism" (June 2006), *Child Care Subsidies and TANF: A Synthesis of Three Studies on Systems, Policies, and Parents* (Pamela A. Holcomb et al., 2006), *America's Homeless II: Populations and Services* (February 2000), and *Homelessness: Programs and the People They Serve—Findings of the National Survey of Homeless Assistance Providers and Clients* (Martha R. Burt et al., December 1999).

The Center on Budget and Policy Priorities is an advocacy organization that releases reports, papers, updates, and studies on welfare. Its publications include "Income Gaps between Very Rich and Everyone Else More Than Tripled in Last Three Decades, New Data Show" (Arloc Sherman and Chad Stone, June 2010), "Policy Basics: An Introduction to TANF" (Liz Schott, March 2009), and *State Earned Income Tax Credits: 2010 Legislative Update* (Erica Williams, Nicholas Johnson, and Jon Shure, December 2010).

Excellent sources of information on the national homeless population are the U.S. Conference of Mayors, the National Alliance to End Homelessness, and the Association of Gospel Rescue Missions. *State of Homelessness in America* (M. William Sermons and Peter Witte, January 2011) analyzes national and state level homeless counts from the Department of Housing and Urban Development and explores economic and demographic drivers of homelessness. *Hunger and Homelessness Survey: A Status Report on Hunger and Homelessness in America' s Cities, a 27-City Survey* (December 2010) by the Conference of Mayors and "Many American Families are Living on the Edge" (November 2010) by the Association of Gospel Rescue Missions also provide a great deal of information on the homeless population.

The many organizations that advocate for the homeless and their issues are also crucial sources for this book. The National Coalition for the Homeless is certainly one of the most important of these organizations. Its publication *Homes Not Handcuffs: The Criminalization of Homelessness in U.S. Cities* (July 2009) is particularly recommended. The Applied Survey Research, the Economic Policy Institute, the Joint Center for Housing Studies of Harvard University, Health Care for the Homeless, the National Coalition for Homeless Veterans, the Millennial Housing Commission, the National Multi Housing Council, the Kaiser Family Foundation, and the National Law Center on Homelessness and Poverty all provide extensive coverage of important aspects of the housing and homelessness issues.

INDEX

McKinney-Vento Homeless Assistance Act, 121–124
Tax Reform Act, 1986, 67
Liabilities and assets, 6
Local ordinances, 15–16, 124–129, 126*t*
Loitering, 128
Loper v. New York City Police Department, 129
Los Angeles, California, 16, 102, 125, 128
Low-income housing, 103–104, 109–110, 116–118

M

Making Home Affordable program, 116
Marital status
child support, 30*t*
family groups, 34*t*–36*t*
households, 27*t*
living arrangements, 37*t*–38*t*
unemployment, 79*t*
Mason v. Tucson, 129
McGinnis, City of Sarasota v., 128
McKinney-Vento Homeless Assistance Act, 9–11, 16, 121–124, 139–140
Measurement
homelessness, 12–14, 91–93
income, 6–7
poverty levels, 2–3, 5–6
Medicaid, 6, 58, 135–138, 138*t*, 139*t*–140*t*
Medicare, 6
Mental health problems, 131, 145–146
Miami, Florida, 15, 127–128
Millennial Housing Commission, 106
Minimum wage, 65–66, 65*t*, 66*t*
Mortality rates of homeless persons, 141
Mortgage crisis, 100*t*, 116
Mothers
government assistance recipients, by program and fertility status, 73(*f*4.4)
overlapping services, 77, 79
poverty status, 39*f*
program participation, 74*f*, 75*t*
TANF, 69–70, 72, 74

N

National Academy of Sciences, 6–7, 7*t*, 8*t*
National Alliance to End Homelessness, 91, 94
National Center for Health Statistics (NCHS), 131
National Center on Family Homelessness, 93, 95
National Law Center on Homelessness, 13–14
National School Lunch Program. *See* School lunch and breakfast programs
NCHS (National Center for Health Statistics), 131
New York City, 128–129
New York City Police Department, Loper v., 129

Newspapers, street, 101
Nighttime residences of homeless persons, 94*t*, 95*f*
Nipper, City of Sarasota v., 128
Noncitizens, 58
Nonfamily living situations, 7–8
Northeast Ohio Coalition for the Homeless, 127

O

Obama, Barack
American Recovery and Reinvestment Act, 39, 56
health care reform, 133, 135
Healthy, Hunger-Free Kids Act, 154
homeless assistance funding, 16
homeless veterans, 96
Supplemental Nutrition Assistance Program, 59
Olympia, Washington, 15–16
Oprah Winfrey Show, 12
Orlando, Florida, 15
Orshansky, Mollie, 1

P

Panhandling, 128–129
Personal Responsibility and Work Opportunity Reconciliation Act (PRWORA)
block grants, 57–58
child care, 58–59
child protection funds, 58
criticism of, 55–56
noncitizens, 58
nutrition programs, 59
reauthorization, 60
Supplemental Security Income, 58
PHAs (public housing agencies), 110, 111, 116
Portland, Oregon, 127
Pottinger v. City of Miami, 127–128
Poverty
children, 22*t*–25*t*
custodial parents, 39*f*
definition, 1
demographic characteristics, 5*t*, 20*t*–21*t*, 49*f*
duration, 47–49, 48*f*
education, 30, 33, 50*t*, 51*t*
elderly, 22–23
employment status, 39*t*
episodic, annual, and chronic rates, 47*f*
families, 52*t*
food expenditures as measurement of, 2–3, 5–6
guidelines, 1, 2*t*
health, 131
health care, 131–132
health insurance coverage, 138*f*

homelessness, 98
income sources, 70*f*, 71*t*
mothers, 75*t*
National Academy of Sciences, 7*t*, 8*t*
race/ethnicity, 19–20, 29
reduction efforts, 1–2
Special Supplemental Food Program for Women, Infants, and Children, 157(*f*8.13)
trends, 3*t*, 4*f*
uninsured children, 137(*f*8.5)
uninsured persons, 133
urban areas, 23–24
work experience, 29–30
workers, 49, 52, 53*t*
Prescription drugs, 131
PRWORA. *See* Personal Responsibility and Work Opportunity Reconciliation Act
Public housing, 109–110, 112*t*–113*t*
Public housing agencies (PHAs), 110, 111, 116
Public Housing Assessment System, 110
Public opinion, 16

R

Race/ethnicity
child support, 30*t*
children in poverty, 22*t*–25*t*
family status and poverty, 26–28
food insecurity, 149, 150*f*, 151*t*
government assistance recipients, 40
health care, 132
health insurance coverage, 133(*f*8.3)
homeless veterans, 95–96
homelessness, 13*t*, 16, 17(*t*1.11), 93–94
households, 27*t*
housing affordability problems, 106–107, 108*t*
income, 10*t*, 25(*t*2.3), 71*t*
living arrangements of children, 37*t*–38*t*
marital status, 28*t*–29*t*
minimum wage workers, 66*t*
mothers, 70, 75*t*
poverty, 19–20, 20*t*–21*t*, 29, 49*f*
poverty duration, 48*f*
poverty rates, 5*t*, 47
poverty status, by educational attainment, 51*t*
poverty status of working people, 50*t*
program participation duration, 82
single parent family groups, 34*t*–36*t*
Special Supplemental Food Program for Women, Infants, and Children, 158, 158*f*
unemployment, 79*t*
unemployment compensation, 74–75
uninsured children, 137(*f*8.5)
uninsured persons, 132–133, 134*t*
unmarried couples with children, 31*t*–33*t*